The media student's book

The Media Student's Book provides a comprehensive introduction for
students of Media Studies on A-Level, BTEC, GNVQ and undergraduate
courses. It relates very intimately to the sharpest contemporary cultural
pleasures and draws on a range of difficult theories to understand these
experiences. It covers all the key topics encountered in Media Studies,
including:

- Images and languages
- Narratives
- Genres
- Representations
- Advertising, marketing and fashion
- Realisms
- Modernism and postmodernism
- Technologies
- Industries
- Institutions
- Independents and alternatives
- Audiences
- Producing

This introductory textbook has been written by two experienced teachers
of Media Studies, and it is specially designed to be easy to use and
understand. It includes in-depth case studies, notes on key terms and
references, follow-up activities and suggestions for further reading.
Throughout the book, examples are provided from a rich range of media
forms, including advertising, films, television, radio, newspapers,
magazines and photography.

Gill Branston is Lecturer in Film and Television Studies at the Centre for
Journalism Studies, University College, Cardiff. **Roy Stafford** is a
freelance media educator based in West Yorkshire.

The media student's book

GILL BRANSTON
and
ROY STAFFORD

London and New York

First published 1996
by Routledge
11 New Fetter Lane, London EC4P 4EE

Simultaneously published in the USA and Canada
by Routledge
29 West 35th Street, New York, NY 10001

Routledge is an International Thomson Publishing Company I(T)P

Typeset by 𝍏\ Tek-Art, Croydon, Surrey
Printed and bound in Great Britain by
Butler & Tanner Ltd, Frome and London

British Library Cataloguing in Publication Data

A catalogue record for this book is available from the British Library

Library of Congress Cataloguing in Publication Data

Branston, Gill.
    The media student's book/Gill Branston and Roy Stafford.
        p.   cm.
    Includes bibliographical references and index.
    1. Mass media.   I. Stafford, Roy.   II. Title.
P90.B6764   1996   95–47309
302.23–dc20   CIP

ISBN 0–415–11405–5
        0–415–11406–3 (pbk)

Contents

Acknowledgements

Thanks to assorted helpers and challengers: Lauren Branston, Lucy Branston, Marion Pencavel, Jack Carter, Nick Lacey, Alan Lovell, Rob Seago, Granville Williams; and to Rod Brookes, Cindy Carter, Alison Charles, David Dawson and Brian Winston at Cardiff; Jo Brown, Val Hill, Jason Toynbee at Coventry; Peter Kennard, Tana Wollen in London; Malcolm Hoddy, Editor of the *Keighley News*; the staff of BFI Stills and to all of the long-suffering editorial team at Routledge.

Finally, none of this would have been possible without the help of all the students and teachers with whom we have worked over many years.

Figure acknowledgements

The following figures were reproduced with the kind permission of their rights holders and sources:

1.2   Courtesy Perrier UK Ltd
1.3   Courtesy Perrier UK Ltd
1.6   Courtesy Camelot
1.7, 3.6 Courtesy Paul Chedlow, photographer
1.8a–d   Courtesy Whitbread PLC, BBH and Tiff Hunter, photographer
3.3   Photo from *Daily Mail*, courtesy Solo Syndication Ltd
3.5   Source: *The Classic Fairy Tales*, Iona and Peter Opie, Oxford, Oxford University Press, 1974. Courtesy Oxford University Press. Originally published in *Fairy Tales Told Again*, illustrated by Gustave Doré, London, Paris and New York, Cassell, Petter & Galpin, 1872
4.2   *Psycho* poster, courtesy British Film Institute
4.3   Courtesy Anna Holmes
5.1   Source: Paul Kagan Associates, published in *Screen International*, 21 October 1994
5.2   Source: 'Entertainment and Utopia', *Movie* no. 24, Spring 1977, pp. 2–13
5.3   Courtesy Fleetway Publications
5.4   Courtesy British Film Institute
5.5   © 1995 Cinergi Productions N.V. Inc.
6.1   Courtesy British Film Institute
7.1   Illustration Dick Bruna copyright © Mercis b.v. 1978
7.2   Published in the *Guardian*, Spring 1995, and reproduced with the permission of BBC Monitoring
7.3   SCOPE/Spastics ad, courtesy SCOPE
7.4   NUJ code on race reporting, courtesy NUJ Equality Council
8.1   Cartoon by Posy Simmonds, reprinted by permission of Peters Fraser & Dunlop Group Ltd
8.2   Courtesy British Film Institute
8.3   Courtesy Leeds Postcards
9.2   *Now, Voyager* © 1942 Turner Entertainment Co. All rights reserved
10.1   Courtesy of *Keighley News*

11.1   Christian Aid ad, courtesy Christian Aid
11.2   Courtesy of BBC News and Current Affairs Publicity Department
11.3   Vauxhall ad, courtesy Vauxhall Motors
11.4   Courtesy Leeds Postcards
11.5   Courtesy Chase Creative Consultants Ltd
12.1   Reuters page on video news releases, courtesy Reuters Television Ltd
12.2   By kind permission of *UK Press Gazette*
12.3   Courtesy Rex Features Ltd
14.1   Courtesy Red Ferns Picture Library
15.1   By kind permission of the Syndics of Cambridge University Library
15.2   Courtesy Kramsie Ltd, Gibraltar
15.3   Photomontage by Peter Kennard
16.1   Courtesy of Paul Chedlow, photographer
17.1   Courtesy Whitbread PLC, BBH and Tiff Hunter, photographer
18.2   Photo by Roy Stafford, taken with permission at NMPFT, Bradford, in 1992
19.2   Courtesy the Kobal Collection
20.1   Source: David Pirie (ed.), *Anatomy of the Movies*, London, Windward, p. 178
20.2a, b   Charts compiled by Roy Stafford from a variety of sources, but primarily Screen Finance/CAVIAR and BFI Yearbook
22.1   *The Story of Louis Pasteur* © 1936 Turner Entertainment Co. All rights reserved
22.2   *The White Angel* © 1936 Turner Entertainment Co. all rights reserved
23.1   *Now, Voyager* © 1942 Turner Entertainment Co. All rights reserved
23.2   Courtesy the Kobal Collection
24.1   Charts compiled by Roy Stafford. Data from JICTARS (1977) and RAJAR (1993/5), published in *Broadcast*, 15 September 1995
27.1   By kind permission of LWT
27.2   *Lust for Life* © 1956 Turner Entertainment Co. All rights reserved
27.3   Still from film *A Bout de Souffle*, courtesy Oasis Films
28.1   Courtesy BFI Distribution
29.1   Courtesy Turner Publishing Inc.
29.2   Source: David Morley, *The Nationwide Audience*, London, BFI, 1980
29.3   Courtesy of *Clothes Show* magazine
29.4   Source: C. Geraghty, *Women and Soap Opera*, London, Polity Press, 1992
30.1   Courtesy Herald of Wales
30.2   Courtesy TSMS
30.3   Courtesy of HTV
30.4   Courtesy of *Clothes Show* magazine
30.5a–c   Magazine advertising information, courtesy National Readership Surveys Ltd

Introduction

Media Studies is now an established area of work in many schools and colleges. Yet there are very few books designed to help students through a subject which both relates very intimately to the sharpest contemporary cultural pleasures, and has to draw on a range of difficult theories to understand these experiences. Added to these challenges is the fact that many of you have a range of non-school educational experiences upon which to draw. TV, from children's programmes, through schools and educational programmes, to '**infotainment**' forms, has probably taught you a great deal, in ways that books cannot hope to emulate. You may also have quite sophisticated experience of computers, at home, school or college, and may even have played with interactive material like music CD-ROMs, on which you can remix tracks.

Such ways of learning have major implications for anyone setting out to write a textbook. Sometimes we have tried to keep the print media's ability to sustain quite complicated arguments, where this needs to be done, in longish chapters. Often, you'll come across a history of a key term or debate which you may not want or need to go into straight away. To follow these you may need some of the patience more traditionally associated with books than with computers (but hopefully not *too* much patience).

Terms in Media Studies

Some students have problems in Media Studies because of its terminology. Words that have fairly straightforward meanings in everyday life outside the subject (like '**sign**' or '**closed**') take on rather different ones within it. This can be confusing. We've tried, wherever possible, to warn you of potential misunderstandings.

The development of Media Studies has often been 'driven' by developments in higher education. From the 1960s onwards, many academics, trying to get modern media taken seriously as objects for study, had to present arguments couched in very specialised language.

Along with an excitement with theoretical developments, such as **structuralism** and **semiotics**, which seemed to promise radical political possibilities, this produced a very difficult set of theoretical terms – especially for those who had not been involved in the years of struggling through, applying and familiarising themselves with these terms. Now the dust has settled, the real gains of some of these approaches can be brought into study of the media.

We've adopted the computer's engaging ability to offer information in different-sized chunks and formats. We hope you'll like and use the jokes and quotes in the margins, the case studies, the activities and appreciate the feel of a book aiming to work with a mixture of materials.

Modern technologies have dazzling capacities. It is now possible, using **digital editing**, to make it seem as though Marilyn Monroe and Brad Pitt are playing a scene together or that Arnold Schwarzenegger can 'morph' into an android before our eyes; to broadcast such scenes simultaneously across continents; and to accompany it with music created entirely by a computer. The **Internet**, a global 'Information Superhighway' has been touted, like many technologies in the past, as a kind of Utopian space where information about 'the universe and everything' is readily available and all questions can be answered.

Two major fallacies have evolved as a result:

- All you need to know about is how to press the buttons on these amazing technologies. Theories and histories are now irrelevant.
- Especially irrelevant are theories that allow us to understand why such technologies are unequally distributed both geographically and between rich and poor. Or, why they take the forms they do.

Yes, the technologies are terrific, and this is what makes modernity an exciting yet possibly disturbing experience. But we hope you find our sections on their histories, distribution and ways of working useful, rather than a diversion from the delights of simply celebrating 'virtual reality'. And, however convincingly you have Monroe and Pitt in the same **frame** together, however much information is at your fingertips on the Net, you can't rely on virtual decisions about what dialogue they will speak, or how they will be lit, framed, and directed to move. Nor can you make use of the Net without some sense of what information you need. For this we all need theories and histories of how stories, images, and music have been made, told, and sold in the modern media and before.

Media Studies is still a young subject area and the syllabuses – the official definitions – offered by the various examining and awarding bodies are still being developed. The media industries are also growing and developing rapidly and the academic subject can't afford to get left behind. We hope we've covered all the basic *concepts* you will encounter and quite a few of the *debates* or issues which are addressed by Media A-Levels, the new GNVQ Advanced in Media: Communication and Production, BTEC and City & Guilds Media courses, and by Access courses and many undergraduate media units as well. *Media theories* have also influenced work in other subjects including Sociology and Cultural Studies. *Media production practice* increasingly spills over into art, design and photography. Our 'target audience' includes many different groups of students and so don't be surprised if you find things that aren't on your syllabus. Dip into them anyway: you'll probably find that they increase your understanding of the key concepts (and they may well be required for the next course you take).

We haven't included any essay questions as such, because we haven't targeted any one particular syllabus and we would rather try to support your basic understanding of concepts and debates. We are conscious that Media Studies needs to be approached in an integrated way and so we have tried to indicate links between the chapters whenever possible and to think of activities that require you to be 'active' in your learning.

The two of us, over the last fifteen years or so, have worked in most levels of further and higher education, and in media education generally. We 'entered the field' because we enjoyed popular culture in all its forms and we recognised its importance in contemporary society. Most of all, we love movies and that gives this book a special flavour. We have also tried to indulge an interest in radio as well as all the other media you would expect to find. We hope that our enthusiasm comes through in the writing – Media Studies should be challenging *and* fun. Whatever your interest, in passing an exam or simply understanding the 'media society', we hope you will enjoy reading and working with the book. Let us know, by writing to the publishers about your ideas for improving it.

How the book is organised

There are two types of material in the book. The main chapters carry the key theoretical ideas and concepts which are explained and contextualised in general terms. The case study chapters allow us to explore applications of theory or more specialised theoretical points in detail.

Case studies are distinguished by page design. Where main chapters use a single column and a margin for extra material, case studies are presented in two columns without margins. We expect you will need to keep 'dipping in' to the main chapters, but that you might read the case studies straight through.

Finding material

The book isn't organised like a 'set text' – there is no correct way to use it. Instead it serves as your support, so it is important that whatever you need, you can find it easily. At the start of all chapters and case studies is a list of main headings. In chapters, the appropriate headings are repeated in a computer-style menu at the top of each page. 'Running heads' on each page always let you know where you are.

If you want to find a key term, look in the index and you will find one or more references to explanations and definitions. The first time a key term appears in a chapter it will be presented in **bold type**.

References

As all media researchers will tell you, good references are invaluable. They provide evidence of the origins of material and they point to further sources which could be used. We've adopted a number of strategies. Whenever we quote another writer, we have placed a name and a date in the text, e.g. (Barthes 1972). This refers you to a book written by Barthes and published in 1972. Sometimes the page reference is also given (e.g. Barthes 1972: 182); here 182 indicates the page. The full reference (which includes title and publisher) is then given at the end of the chapter/case study. You should learn to list this full reference, for any books you use, at the end of your essays.

The list at the end of a chapter includes the sources we have used and perhaps some other material we think relevant. Some of our sources are quite difficult, both to obtain and to read, so we don't always expect you to go to them direct. At the end of the book we have included a 'selected' list of important (and accessible) texts which we do recommend you to look at.

The titles of films, television and radio programmes, newspapers and magazines are usually given in *italics*. Again, this is a convention that you might usefully copy, especially if you word-process your work. It makes it much easier to read essays. We have given the country of origin and the date of release of films to help you find them in reference sources (the Movie Database on the Internet is very good). We have tried to use film examples which are well referenced, so even if you've never heard of them, you should be able to find out more.

Activities

Dotted through the book you will find suggested activities. The book is designed as your guide, not as a class text, so where possible the exercises and activities are those you can undertake yourself at any time. Sometimes, especially for production-based activities, you will need others to help you.

1 Images and languages

The media work with words, images, sounds, or a mixture of all three. These have their own rules and conventions, but it is only when we experience the breaking of their rules, or stop to think how many of those rules we know, that we question the 'naturalness' of the image and sound combinations we have learned. We spend years at home and at school learning how to read words, and, before that, how to speak them. Because such effort is needed, it should be easier to be aware of language as a matter of **codes and conventions**. Yet we lose this awareness too as everyday usage makes language seem natural or 'transparent'.

When the media were first seriously studied, in the late 1950s, existing methods of literary and art criticism were applied to them. But it soon became clear that simply to discuss a film or TV programme by such methods (the valuing of 'good dialogue' or 'convincing characters' or 'beautiful compositions') was not going to allow certain kinds of engagement. People began to question the critical terms used in such discussions and ask : 'good' or 'convincing' or 'beautiful' according to what criteria? For whom?

We don't want to lose a sense that attention to language is important in media work. Scripts, single lines, soundbites in news, T-shirt slogans, headlines: the verbal is a key component of most media. But we need first to outline an influential and less literary way of studying such meaning systems, called **semiotics**.

Semiotics

Also called 'semiology', this is the study of **signs**, or of the social production of meaning by **sign systems**, of how things come to have significance or meaning. Though not all of its terms are used all the time in media analysis, its approaches are now very much part of the subject area, and are ones you need to understand, despite important criticisms in recent years.

Drawing on the work of the linguist **Saussure**, semiotics argues that language is one of many systems of meaning. Others include clothing,

Stuart Hood recounted once that the BBC announced the Russian invasion of Afghanistan with the newsreader standing. Scores of people rang in to ask if war had broken out, simply because the newsreader was standing rather than sitting behind a desk.

Ferdinand de Saussure (1857–1913) French linguist who pioneered the semiotic study of language as a system of signs, depending on codes and structures. He distinguished between **langue** as a system of rules of speech (which children, for example, have to learn), and **parole** as acts of speaking. Other theorists, such as **Volosinov** put more emphasis on the difference and creativity involved in everyday speech acts.

'Dress is a form of address' (Erving Goffmann).

 rose
or
ROSE

Figure 1.1

Roland Barthes (1913–80) French linguist who pioneered semiotic analyses of cultural and media forms. Most famous for *Mythologies* (1972), a collection of essays applying his theories wittily to ads, wrestling, Greta Garbo's face, and so on.

gesture, facial expressions, haircuts, etc. These work by means of signs, which have a twofold nature:

- First, a sign has physical form (words, either in the form of marks on paper (R-O-S-E), or sounds in the air; a haircut; a fingerprint; a photo). This is called the **signifier**. A sign must be understood as referring to something other than itself. This is called the **signified** and is a concept, not a real thing in the world. The word 'rose', spoken or written, refers to the concept of a certain kind of flower. **Barthes** would call it 'roseness', and like other semioticians would emphasise the distinction between this concept, the signified, and the **referent**, which is what is referred to: real roses, in all their difference.

  This is a useful way of remembering that words do not directly label or depict the world but instead divide it into imaginative categories. It is easy to forget this, since we have normally come to use language easily and unselfconsciously. If you hear the word 'cat' or 'mother', a particular animal and woman are likely to spring to mind, and it's easy to imagine you are much closer to the world through language than in fact is the case.

- Second, these categories, into which verbal and other languages divide the world, work by means of differences. This is an emphasis which semiotics shares with **structuralism** (see below).

Signs are only fully understood by reference to their relationship to, or difference from, other signs in their particular language system. This relationship is sometimes as important as their relationship to the rest of the real world.

Examples

Once sound becomes possible in cinema, the potential meaning of silence is changed. The same is true of black and white in relation to colour. It signifies differently to produce a photo or a film in black and white once the choice to make it in colour is an available one. Black and white can then signify 'seriousness' or 'pastness'.

The part of the natural colour spectrum between blue and black is called purple and often signifies imperial power, or mourning. But in cigarette ads, under severe health warning restrictions, 'purple' signifies Silk Cut, just as 'red' signifies Marlboro cigarettes in others, and the yellowy colour called gold signifies Benson and Hedges in yet others.

ACTIVITY 1.1

The word 'man' may seem the simplest kind of label. But it usually signifies within a particular structure of meaning. A 'man' is not a 'boy'/a 'woman'/a 'god'/a 'beast'.

- Try creating sentences, questions where these different meaning-structures are implied, such as 'Is it a man's jacket you want?' (rather than a woman's, or a boy's). (Sometimes you will be able to signify your meaning by vocal emphasis.)

Once the extent to which languages are composed of material signs is grasped, it becomes easier to see that signs have relationships among themselves, as well as in the ways they **represent** the world.

Denotation and connotation

Signs **denote** or signify or point towards different aspects of our experience, the world. The word 'red' denotes a certain part of the colour spectrum, which involves differentiating it from other parts, such as 'blue' or 'pink'.

But signs also **connote**, or link the things they denote by association with other things. (Signs themselves can also relate to each other, most obviously through characteristics like words rhyming, shapes on screens resembling each other.) These **connotations** give overlaid meanings from personal or social history and experience. (We would argue this always happens, though Barthes' division of signs into 'denotative' and 'connotative' suggests a purely denotative sign is possible.)

We are likely to have experienced red in blood, sunsets, excited complexions, fires – which perhaps indicates why, in certain cultures, the colour has connotations of fierceness, passion, danger. But then these meanings get built into further signs: traffic lights, flags, phrases like 'paint the town red', 'like a red rag to a bull' and AIDS-awareness ribbons, which draw on and themselves reproduce these connotations.

Unintentional puns can often remind us of this capacity of words to float free of intended meanings. For example, when drafting the case study on westerns and The Searchers' treatment of images of Native American characters, I first wrote: 'The film uses these with some reservations.' I quickly amended it (Gill Branston).

Example

Take *Pretty Woman* (US 1990) or *Don't Look Now* (UK 1973), or any other film/TV drama/ad where red is important.

Q What do you think the colour red connotes in them?

A In *Pretty Woman*, Vivien/Julia Roberts wears a red dress (after first wearing her multi-coloured hooker's gear, and later a black dress) at a point in the film where it seems to signify a growing confidence and passion in her feelings about her relationship with Edward/Richard Gere.

Gold is another good example. It denotes either a certain part of the colour spectrum, or a metal of that colour. But its connotations within certain cultures (not an arbitrary matter, but one deriving partly from its prizing for jewellery, special ceremonies, and as a currency) are much wider, as in such phrases as 'golden opportunity', 'good as gold' and so on.

Sounds also signify. They are used in TV and cinema ads, as well as radio, where very quick, concentrated messages are constructed, drawing on heavily conventionalised signs: the chirp of a cricket signifying tropical climates; the creak of a door, sign of possible horror or mystery; a click of a cricket bat, and perhaps the coo of doves, signifying an English summer cricket match; and so on. (See Chapter 15, 'Realisms' for more on 'sound images'.)

Polysemy

polysemy (from the Greek, *poly* = many, *semeion* = a sign) having many meanings.

Though red may be a widely recognised sign within western culture, its meaning is by no means either fixed or single but **polysemic**. Just because red has featured in many contexts, as part of several **codes** or ways of combining signs, it is possible, for example, for some viewers to read Julia Roberts' dress as signifying danger, or socialism, or as part of the director's liking for the colour red (if the director were Scorsese) or as a colour within the fashion system (more fashionable than, say, turquoise). This is a result of two main factors:

'Text' and **'reader'** in ordinary life refer exclusively to written work, often holy or official. But in Media Studies they refer to anything capable of having meanings, written or not, highly valued or not (e.g. an ad, a piece of rap music, a cartoon). The 'reader' refers to anyone making a meaning in everyday encounters with such 'texts'.

- The inherent ambiguity or instability of signs once they are in contact with **'readers'** (which they have to be to produce meanings at all). Price (1993) quotes Hodge and Kress (1988) on amber traffic lights, whose official meaning is intended as 'slow down for red light' but which many motorists understand as 'speed up to avoid red'. 'Rose' signifies the idea of 'rose-ness' but each of us may well conjure up a different image of a particular rose, with very different associations. With more complex signs, like national flags, let alone movies, the range of audience interpretation is even wider.
- Most of the signs we encounter (photos, newspaper front pages, pop videos) have many elements (images, written words, colours, sounds, music), each capable of signifying in multiple ways, which compounds the possibilities for polysemy.

The 'Sleau lunch' ad (see Figure 1.2) was the first of a series used in summer 1995 to sell Perrier mineral water. If we consider the ad at a denotative level it sounds merely baffling: a snail made from what appears to be green glass with drink labels stuck on it? A description involving connotative meanings might describe it as using a crafted glass snail (a subdued green colour in the original), full of tiny bubbles, to signify a pleasantly leisurely meal, and perhaps also offer the generally agreeable connotations of 'green', ranging from summer countryside to mildly ecological politics. The caption 'Sleau lunch' will signify 'witty play on

SLEAU LUNCH

Figure 1.2

words' to a readership that has basic French (which may be assumed of those the agency has tried to reach by placing the ad in papers such as the *Guardian*). The French language is often used as the signifier of sophistication, though snails, eaten as a delicacy in France, often act as signifiers of the strange customs of 'Those Others across the Channel'.

ACTIVITY 1.2

To explore a range of French language connotations:
- Note how many cosmetics and fashion brand names trade on this connotation.
- Collect some other ads where snatches of French seem to offer meanings of 'sophistication'.

So the snail itself may signify 'Frenchness', in all its **instability** as a signifier, along with the Perrier label (which does not even show the full name 'Perrier', though a few descriptive words, again in French, are visible). Clearly, for xenophobes viewing the ad, even the connotations of sophistication will not be positive ones.

If you live near to the countryside, or are a gardener, the connotations offered by an image of a snail might be very different: this particularly large snail looks as though it's looking for its lunch – i.e. your plants. Indeed, it's perhaps only when such a possible horizon of meaning, as it is sometimes called, is brought into play that the work of the ad in trying to cut off possibly unpleasant connotations becomes clear. This work is partly attempted by the way the ad is styled, photographed, gently coloured (cool clear glass rather than dark sticky slime), but also in the appeal, through its placement, to a metropolitan or city-dwelling audience. It is worth remembering that for readers in continents where snails are rare, if not unknown, the ad would have very different meanings.

The next ad in the series is shown in Figure 1.3. See if you can make a similar analysis of this image and caption.

Figure 1.3

Anchoring

One way in which control will be attempted over the potentially disruptive polysemy or ambiguity of images is through the use of captions. This is called **anchoring** because of the similar way in which an anchor will try to limit the movement of a boat or ship in the sea.

ACTIVITY 1.3

Look at the next striking news photograph you notice and see how the caption attempts to limit the range of potential meanings or connotations which the photo might otherwise have for particular readers.

● Blank off the caption and see what is the most extreme but credible caption you can devise for the image.

Iconic, indexical, arbitrary and symbolic signs

A key distinction is made (initially by **Peirce**) between **iconic, indexical, arbitrary**, and **symbolic signs**. Verbal language, spoken and written, is mostly composed of arbitrary signifiers in the sense that there is no necessary resemblance between the black marks on the page 'rose' and those plants in the rest of the world that share the name 'rose'. Any pronounceable combination of letters could have been originally decided on to signify 'roseness'. The only exceptions are words (when spoken) called 'onomatopoeic', where a sound resembles what it signifies, like 'rumble' or 'hiss'.

Iconic signifiers, however, always resemble what they signify. There is a physical similarity between a photo, or a good drawing of a rose, and our ideas or experience of those flowers, and for this reason the photo is called an iconic signifier of 'roseness'. Sounds are often iconic signifiers. This is a useful distinction because it draws attention to the ways that photographs, film, TV images and so on, though often seeming to be simply a record of the real, are as constructed as verbal accounts. They only seem like 'a window on the world' (as recent developments in special effects technologies suggest).

Indexical is used of signifiers that act as a kind of evidence: smoke of a fire; sweat of effort; spots of measles and so on. Or to use the distinction (see Chapter 18 on Technologies) of analogue and digital, a sundial or barometer is an indexical sign of heat or of time passing, whereas digital technologies (translating music into signals, which are then reassembled) act like arbitrary signs.

Symbolic is used of visual signs that are only arbitrarily linked to referents. The diamond hats often worn by monarchs for example, are called crowns, and symbolise monarchy. Thirty years ago the road sign to warn drivers about a school was the image of the 'torch of learning' (see Figure 1.4): it was meant to stand as symbol of the place where that learning happened. But this conventional (i.e. socially agreed) meaning

Charles Sullivan Peirce (1839–1914) American pioneer of semiotics, usually quoted for his distinctions between different kinds of sign.

Icon usually refers to visual emblems or portraits of saints rather than their written or spoken names.

rose
or
ROSE

A rose by any other name?

Figure 1.4

Figure 1.5

became unfamiliar, and the sign was changed to the 'two children crossing' sign (see Figure 1.5). In other words, it was changed to a more iconic sign.

It's worth emphasising that the same sign can be iconic, indexical and symbolic. Imagine a photograph (like the famous one of the Democracy Movement demonstrations in Tiananmen Square) of a demonstrator in front of a tank standing with shirt open and arms outstretched as if making a cross. This would be at one and the same time:

- an iconic sign (it is a photograph of a real man in a square: the sign resembles its referent)
- an indexical sign (light on the body and the shadow act as a kind of evidence, telling us the time of day)
- a symbolic sign (his pose suggests or connotes the crucifixion, especially for western readers). The photo would be understood by them to have resonances of 'making a sacrifice').

'Language is not a neutral medium that passes freely and easily into the private property of the speaker's intentions; it is populated – overpopulated – with the intentions of others ... forcing it to submit to one's own intentions and accents, is a difficult and complicated process', Volosinov, Russian linguist active in the 1920s, who 'disappeared' in the Stalinist purges of the 1930s. Some argue he also published under the name of Bakhtin.

How arbitrary are signs?

So there are important senses in which signs, far from naturally just labelling things, are arbitrary. However, signs must also be used and recognised or shared by people in order to produce meaning. This may consist of children having to learn how to use certain words, or of a culture which has come to use 'rose' in certain contexts to signify 'romantic love'. Correspondingly, agreed meanings will differ both between cultures and over time. The words 'cool', 'wicked', and 'bad' have, in some contexts, completely lost or even reversed their previous meanings in the last few years.

This need for social agreement about the work of signs means that meanings are not fixed, or 'arbitrary' in the sense of 'imposed'. There are 'struggles over the sign'. The best-known example is probably debates over how TV and print newsrooms should describe certain acts: are they performed by terrorists? Freedom fighters? Patriots? The Union Jack has usually stood as symbol of the unity of the British Isles, and of the monarchy that rules them. But for Republican groups in Wales, Ireland or Scotland, it will be used and understood in quite other ways. Is an announcement about redundancies in a particular industry to be worded as 'massive job losses', 'rationalisation', or 'slimming down the workforce'?

'We're not killjoys, that title belongs to people who drink and drive and who kill other people's joy, not just for a couple of hours, but for ever' (Chair of Action on Drink and Driving, November 1986).

ACTIVITY 1.4
- Look at the next news headlines or lead stories you encounter with an eye to such constructions. Think how else particular events could be signified.

Codes

Semiotics further stresses that we learn to read signs in different kinds of combinations or codes, often without being conscious of it. Examples would include:

- the combinations through which different colours signify for particular cultures: the choice of white for innocence in the west, for instance, relates to knowledge of the ways colours are coded here. In many Asian cultures, white is associated with death and mourning.
- The *codes of expression* and gesture (clearly open to analysis when operated by actors) such as: raised hand in combination with certain facial expressions = threat. Though expressions of grief, apprehension, etc. seem broadly shared across cultures, less immediate codes such as gesture seem culturally variable: nodding the head can mean refusal, for example.
- The *codes of lighting* mean we often read shadows as signifying menace or mystery, rather than simply 'evening'.
- It comes as quite a shock to realise that most cinema combines its shots in a system called **continuity editing**, which includes several different codes: sound, camera movement, ways of signalling transitions, etc. Audiences have learned to read these so fluently that they simply seem natural. (See Chapter 3, 'Narratives').

Let's explore a couple of examples to try to make this clearer. Figure 1.6, used for the National Lottery launch in 1994, uses a number of different codes. The camera is placed at a low angle, part of the positioning available to photographers, often signifying a kind of awe. In this it is partly iconic, since as children we have to look up to adults; the

Figure 1.6 Ad for National Lottery launch in 1994

arrangement of ceremonies often puts those of high status above the rest of the event, and we even have a phrase, 'high and mighty', which links power to physical elevation. (But a low camera angle does not always or inevitably produce these meanings. In *Psycho*, for example, the camera is sometimes placed just below Norman Bates's head, at an extreme angle, as he talks, and has the effect of accentuating his bird-like angularity and strangeness. This is very far from an impression of awe or status.)

In the ad (Figure 1.6) the starry hand (a warm golden colour in the original) with its pointing finger may signify and connote differently for different people. It would be very difficult, within western culture, to avoid the association with 'the hand of God', even if you object to this usage, or do not believe that God exists. Audiences are also likely to make the connection 'finger of fate', and some may recall the finger of E.T. in Spielberg's movie, which itself draws on this range of connotation. Of course a child may misread these offered meanings, and see this as a frightening or puzzling or funny image. Meanings can never be guaranteed to be understood in particular ways by audiences, nor can they simply be 'read off' like a secret code to be cracked.

It is also worth pointing out the use of **cropping** here. The house has to represent or stand in for an ordinary house in order for the implied message ('Even you [ordinary person] could be a winner') to work. But the scale of the possible win is enormous, so the base of the house (its ordinary street-ness?) has been cut off, and it seems to signify as

See *The South Bank Show*'s use of the strikingly similar Michelangelo painting of the finger of God delivering life to Adam in the myth of the Creation (Figure 27.1).

something out of a fairy tale, or perhaps a Gothic tale with a happy ending, given the clouded sky.

ACTIVITY 1.5

Look at a few newspaper or family album photographs and cover part of them so as to give the effect of cropping or focusing on one area of them.

● What difference does this make to the meanings they seem to suggest?

Look at Figure 1.7. Try to describe what it represents. Comment: You will probably have drawn very quickly on your knowledge of codes of

Figure 1.7

dress, expression, movement, gesture, location as well as the codes of photography (when black and white is used; why the angle of the photo). Indeed, you may have jumped immediately to the interpretation 'this photo shows a child being taken away from its mother'. Try to 'rewind' and play more slowly your processes. Did you understand it partly through your knowledge of other codes such as:

- those related to photography (lighting; type of film stock used; whether black and white or colour; camera angle and focus; amateur or professional photographer?)
- those related to context or genre. You are, after all, encountering it in a book on Media Studies, which cannot afford the luxury of colour images (so it might originally have been in colour), in a chapter on Images. So the meaning may not be as straightforward as it seems. You are also encountering it at a historical moment when the issue of 'lone parenting' is quite high on the media and political agenda.

Had you come across it at an exhibition, or in a friend's photo album, or used as the cover of a magazine (or perhaps at a different moment in history?), your interpretation would be slightly different. In a newspaper, the caption might have 'anchored' its meaning for you.

The photo is a production still by Paul Chedlow for the Ken Loach film *Ladybird, Ladybird* (UK 1994) and represents a moment in the film where the central character's child is taken away from her by social workers. The woman running out is not the mother. Do you think this explanation accounts for the angle of the shot?

Martin Barker (1989: 263) argues that Volosinov sees structuralism, and by extension semiotics, as treating 'language as a dead thing... [because it argues] we do not *understand* language [which involves being socially involved in it], we *decode* it' (our emphasis).

An important note

We have tried to suggest the usefulness of semiotics in analysing the range of meanings at play within texts. At the same time we've tried:

- first, to refute the implication that all of the available meanings are always 'working on' audiences. Many early applications of semiotics fell into this trap. In their eagerness to show what the approach offered, and to deconstruct what were seen as oppressive systems such as advertising, some analyses came close to suggesting that by listing as many signs, codes and connotations as possible, they had the key to how audiences were Really Being Brainwashed.

To avoid this, we suggest you try to use terms like 'offer' or 'suggest' or 'invite readers to' when analysing the signs within media products, since signs, being social processes, can always be interpreted differently, even though some **discourses** (see Chapter 11, 'Ideologies') offer meanings which circulate much more powerfully than others (such as awareness of images of God in the National Lottery ad).

● Second, we have also tried to analyse texts with audiences and readerships in mind. It is significant that the Perrier ad was placed in the *Guardian*, and thus hoped to address a certain kind of middle-class, educated reader. Equally, the National Lottery ad had a much wider 'spread' and sought to address a broader audience with less specialised signs. We have tried to build such contexts into the discussion of the ads, as most of us do when encountering signs in life outside this book. See Chapter 5, 'Genres', to see how meanings are determined by familiar contexts.

Intention, meaning, value

The *intention* to communicate, so crucial to other approaches, need not apply in semiotic approaches. Though the wearer of a baseball cap may have considered 'Americanness' when he or she first bought it, they do not have to be thinking of, or intending, this meaning in every social encounter. Nevertheless, it may well act as a sign, be 'read','give off' meanings, signify even in situations where the wearer is not intending that.

To use the word *signify* rather than *mean* can emphasise the extent to which meanings are ultimately uncontrollable by their originator. To say something 'means' this or that usually claims only one interpretation and, further, claims that this is the correct one. Semiotics is part of modern 'structuralist' developments within language, which emphasise the ways in which language structures are not simply controlled by their speakers, but often work to determine their meanings.

Another unfamiliarity of this kind of approach to media texts is that structuralist/semiotic analysis is not interested in questions of value – how good is this or that song, or film? It holds these off in order to investigate how meanings have been produced, or to **deconstruct** text, programme, film or photo, into its component signs. It is further often interested in trying to imagine how these meanings could be different. This can be tricky for people in a culture, like the British, that lays heavy emphasis on evaluating literary texts, and which tends also to be suspicious of theory or analysis, seeing it as 'destructive' or negative.

When performing a semiotic analysis of a text, we are deconstructing it, and the word **construction** is frequently used in connection with, and is almost a sign of, semiotic approaches, since it puts a distance between the analysis and the often natural seemingness of the film or piece of radio, etc. being explored. This brings us to structuralist approaches, which in fact preceded semiotics.

Structuralism

Structuralism is a set of early twentieth-century ideas and positions which broadly emphasised that:

- all human organisation is determined by large social or psychological structures with their own irresistible logic, independent of human will or intention
- meanings, whether linguistic or **anthropological** can only be understood within these systematic structures.

Freud and **Marx** in the nineteenth century can be seen to have begun to interpret the social world in this way. Freud argued that the human psyche (the conscious and unconscious mind) was one such structure, making us act in ways of which we're not aware, but which are glimpsed in the meanings of some dreams, slips of the tongue and so on. Marx argued that economic life, and particularly people's relationship to the means of production (do they own them, or do they work for the owners of them?) was another.

The structuralists mentioned most often in Media Studies are Saussure, Peirce, Barthes and **Lévi-Strauss**. They emphasised the importance of **structuring oppositions** in myth systems and in language. To deconstruct an ad or a film is to see what parts of it seem to be in systematic opposition and then expose the extent to which one side of that opposition is always valued less than the other, or even repressed and ignored. (See Chapter 3, 'Narratives' for fuller explanation.)

Anthropology The study of human groups, often used of other cultures than that of the researcher. **Structuralist anthropology** might study the ways that a culture organises its rules on food as a system: by rules of exclusion (the English see eating frogs and snails as a barbaric French custom); by signifying oppositions (savoury/sweet for example); and rules of association (steak and chips followed by ice cream, but not steak and ice cream followed by chips).

Sigmund Freud (1856–1939) Austrian founder of **psychoanalysis** or the theory and practice of treating neuroses, and the theories of 'normal' unconscious mental processes obtained from its procedures.

Joke: With psychoanalysis, it's not what you say, it's the way you don't say it.

Claude Lévi-Strauss (b. 1908) French anthropologist (not the inventor of denim jeans). Most active from the 1950s, studying myths, totems and kinship systems of tribal cultures in North and South America.

ACTIVITY 1.6

See if you can apply some of what you have learnt in this chapter to the four ads in Figure 1.8. Points to look for:

- What meanings do the ads seem to be offering?
- Why are they initially puzzling?
- Are the images iconic? Symbolic?
- Why are the glasses of beer altered in various ways: by huge amounts of very thick foam, etc.?
- Do these images work rather like metaphors in speech – 'as bright as a button', for example?
- What is the role of the (arbitrary) signifiers of language in the ad? Do they anchor the meanings?
- Do any other social contexts also anchor the meaning, such as the ways contemporary cigarette ads are required to operate?
- In what contexts would these ads have to try to seize your attention?

VANISHING CREAM.

Boddingtons. The Cream of Manchester. Brewed at the Strangeways Brewery since 1778.

Figure 1.8a

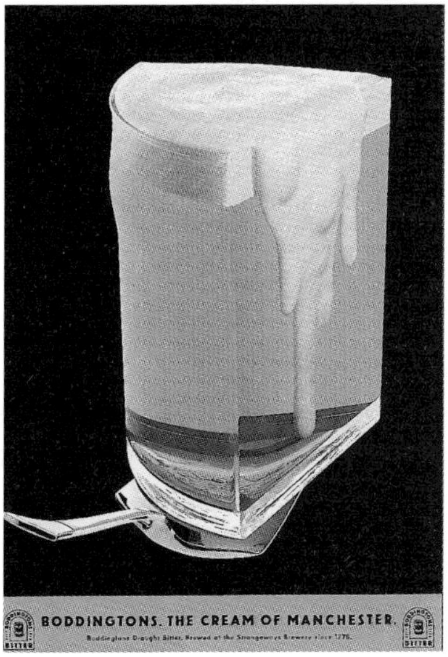

BODDINGTONS. THE CREAM OF MANCHESTER.

Boddingtons Draught Bitter. Brewed at the Strangeways Brewery since 1778.

Figure 1.8b

BODDINGTONS. THE CREAM OF MANCHESTER.

Figure 1.8c

THE CREAM OF MANCHESTER.

Boddingtons Draught Bitter. Brewed at the Strangeways Brewery since 1778.

Figure 1.8d

Finally ... a cautionary note

These approaches help us remember that languages and codes, especially those of images, are never as natural as they look, or come to feel. They are socially constructed and understood, and can in turn be socially shifted.

We have tried to emphasise that signs are not simply or only arbitrary, 'read' purely by means of differences between them, as a self-contained system. This was part of the legacy that semiotics inherited from structuralism's emphasis on 'deep' or basic structures, argued to exist across cultures. But people also learn to understand and use signs by association (for example, with a parent's tone of voice; with danger or with relaxation) and within different social contexts, histories and power relations.

Semiotic and post-structuralist emphases have often been taken up as part of a crippling sense of powerlessness in the face of modern political and social developments. Language, especially in post-structuralism, is often emphasised as being *only* untrustworthy, slippery, and of very limited use in understanding the world.

At the same time, the explanations offered by semiotic approaches have been accused of using the language of exploration and discovery, but actually finding what they set out to find in the text's structuring oppositions, connotations, myths. As Strinati (1995) and others have asked of semiotics' pride in discovering latent or hidden meanings in a text:

- Why privilege the latent over the surface meanings?
- Why presume that once the preferred meaning is discovered, there are no more meanings to be found which are even more 'hidden'?

An important criticism is also that semiotic approaches are often very uninterested in **empirical** research into what actual audiences make of texts. As you test out the usefulness of the approach, try to bear in mind and also test out these questions, too.

Empirical Relying on observed experience. A controversial word, used by opponents to imply an approach opposed to any kind of theory, and relying on sense experience alone. Yet no experience is raw, all experience is to some extent mediated through assumptions, cultural habits and so on. (See Raymond Williams, 1976.)

Test of whether you've understood this section – an obscure joke: 'I would still earn my living as a semiotician even if it was called something else'. (Umberto Eco, semiotician).

References and further reading

Barker, Martin (1989) *Comics: Ideology, Power and the Critics,* Manchester: Manchester University Press (especially Chapters 7 and 12).

Barthes, Roland (1957) *Mythologies* (trans. 1972), London: Paladin.

Culler, Jonathan (1976) *Saussure,* London: Fontana.

Eagleton, Terry (1983) *Literary Theory: An Introduction,* Oxford: Blackwell (esp. Ch. 3).

Hawkes, T. (1977) *Structuralism and Semiotics,* London: Methuen.

Hodge, D. and Kress, G. (1988) *Social Semiotics,* London: Polity.

Price, Stuart (1993) *Media Studies,* London: Pitman.

Strinati, Dominic (1995) *Introduction to Theories of Popular Culture,* London: Routledge.

Williams, Raymond (1976) *Keywords: A Vocabulary of Culture and Society,* London: Fontana/Croom Helm.

Williamson, Judith (1978) *Decoding Advertisements,* London: Marion Boyars.

Reading a voice
The characteristics of
speech radio

2 / Case study: Speaking on radio

'Image analysis' is a common activity in media education and usually involves studying still images such as magazine covers, documentary photographs, etc. Sometimes it is applied to individual images taken from films or television, but surely not to radio?

> *image* n. likeness: ... a picture or representation (not necessarily visual) in the imagination or memory
>
> *Chambers Twentieth Century Dictionary*

Radio is **coded** and it **signifies** in ways as complex as a photographic image. We learn to read these levels of signification very quickly, but it is difficult to discuss what we hear in the same way as what we see. After decades of developed analysis, the visual image is more readily recognised as 'made up', and there exists more detailed terminology with which to discuss it than there does for the **sound image**. This short case study attempts to provide some starting points.

Reading a voice

You can't see a person, but you can hear their voice. What do you know about them, just from the voice? What are the codes which are at play in this process of speaking and listening?

- **pitch**: is the voice 'high' or 'low'?
- **volume**: 'loud' or 'quiet'?
- **texture**: 'rough' or 'smooth', 'soft' or 'hard'?
- **shape**: 'round' or 'flat'?
- **rhythm** or **cadence**: does the voice rise and fall or keep a continuous tone?

All of these are **formal** properties of a voice – someone could be speaking an unknown language yet they will be communicating something to you simply by the sound of the voice. We can recognise these codes at a **denotative** level, but what do they **connote**?

ACTIVITY 2.1

Take a cassette recorder and a good quality external microphone and tape several different people talking in a variety of situations (in the classroom, in the pub, at home). Play back the recordings and in the first instance trying to ignore what they say, just listen to the sound of the voices.

- Can you recognise any of the codes listed above?
- Can you describe the sound of any one voice?
- What does the sound mean to you?
- Can you relate it to the age or gender of the person? You may be surprised to find that some 'old' voices sound 'young' and vice versa – suggesting perhaps that it is something else which confirms the 'old person's voice'.
- Do some voices sound more attractive, more interesting? Why? Could you imagine any of them on the radio? Doing what?

We speak of someone being 'photogenic' – looking good in photographs or on film, often better than they do in 'real life'. Marilyn Monroe was said to fall into this category. In the same way somebody could be 'audiogenic' – sounding good on radio with a voice that suits the medium. Others can be trained to work well on radio – rhythm can be added, pitch, texture, shape, etc. altered. Nevertheless, radio professionals would probably tell you that some voices are never going to make 'good radio' and that others are 'naturals'. Let's test this out:

ACTIVITY 2.2
Tape a variety of radio voices from different stations, some local, some national. Try to include presenters (DJs, newsreaders) and interviewees.
- Can you tell which is the trained 'radio voice'? If so, what makes it different? What distinguishes the national as against local broadcaster or the presenter from the interviewee?

So far, we have distinguished one set of codes: the formal qualities of the voice itself. Next we might consider the **technical** quality of the radio voice, the coding of the voice, which depends on the radio studio engineer and the 'production' of the voice. You may think that a voice on radio, especially in news and current affairs, is broadcast 'as is', but in all cases what we hear on the radio is a *reproduction* of the original voice. This reproduction is dependent on:
- the **acoustics** of the studio: a room with hard, shiny surfaces will produce a harsh, 'bright' edge to the voice; a studio with absorbent surfaces will soften the voice;
- the choice of **microphone**;
- the engineer's **processing** of the signal.

This last point requires some explanation. Each radio station will have a particular target audience and, apart from a minority of BBC stations, will be heard on a set wavelength. For instance, Radio 5 engineers know that most of their listeners will hear the low frequency Medium Wave or AM (Amplitude Modulation) signal in cars in busy traffic. They therefore 'compress' the signal, taking out the highest and lowest frequencies, and boosting the middle frequencies to produce a 'loud and clear' range of voices. By contrast, Radio 3 and 4 listeners are expected to be listening to the FM (Frequency Modulation) signal on a good quality radio or hi-fi system, where they can appreciate the full range of sounds. If the Radio 4 voice was broadcast untouched on Radio 5, it might be difficult to hear everything clearly.

The trick of altering sound according to the listening conditions was famously 'discovered' in the 1960s by the record producer Berry Gordon, founder of Tamla-Motown. He realised that the record buyers heard his releases on tinny transistor radios and cheap record players, yet the engineers mixed the sound so it sounded good on expensive studio monitors. He brought cheap radio speakers into the studio and changed his mixing style so that it sounded how he wanted it through the radio speakers.

No matter how good the engineering and the equipment and how natural the voice, the microphone **technique** is very important. Radio training helps presenters to learn to breathe properly, so that they don't garble words, and to speak at the correct distance from the microphone to avoid sibilance (the 'sss' sound) and 'pops' on plosive letters like 'p' and 'b'.

We can now turn to the content of radio speech – what is actually said. Even so, we can decode *how* it is said rather than what the direct message may be. We can define a set of **cultural codes**:
- **accent**: British voices are particularly characterised by accents. Accents are about pronunciation (and about rhythm, cadence, etc.) and inflection. We can tell a great deal through the recognition of flattened or extended vowels, missed consonants, etc.
- **dialect**: everyone in the UK speaks a dialect, a sub-language which differs from a notional 'standard English'. So-called 'received pronunciation' or 'BBC English' is the dialect of the Southern English middle class. All dialects will have particular vocabulary and syntax as well as pronunciation differences. In the UK, dialect and accent combine to provide that definition of class origin which is fundamental to British social life.

Voices and class

'So important indeed is the question of the use of h's in England … that no marriage should take place between persons whose ideas on this subject do not agree.'

(from *How to Choose a Wife* (1854), quoted in Mugglestone 1995)

In the 1930s many working-class cinemagoers were irritated by the 'cut-glass' accents of British actors and this helped the popularity of American films:

'They want to cut out the Oxford accent and speak more King's English.'

'The absence of the 'Oxford accent' brings them [American films] more on working people's level.'

(Bolton cinemagoers quoted in Richards and Sheridan (1987))

● **language register**: most of us are capable of changing the vocabulary and syntax we use to suit particular circumstances. We shift language registers when we shift from talking to a neighbour to addressing a formal meeting. (See Chapter 11 on Ideologies for discussion of **discourses**.)

These cultural codes are tremendously important on radio. One of the recent successes in radio has been the revamped Radio 5 and much of that success can be traced to the fresh new voices of the presenters, especially those with distinctive regional accents. Callers to Radio 5's phone-ins sound as if they represent a wider cross-section of the public than those on Radio 4.

Could industrial working conditions affect the way people speak? Geoffrey Macnab, in *Sight & Sound*, March 1994, discusses actors from South Wales such as Stanley Baker and Richard Burton. He quotes 'popular wisdom', suggesting that their rich voices are partly explained by a way of speaking which involves deep breathing and pinched nostrils to compensate for coal dust in the air. For more on this and other ideas about actors' voices see Branston (1995).

ACTIVITY 2.3

Run up and down the array of stations on your radio dial. Stop at each voice you hear for a few seconds only.

● Do you recognise the station immediately? Does the combination of cultural codes give you instant clues?

● Can you draw any conclusions about how radio presenters are selected?

● Consider local radio in particular. We tend to feel that BBC Local Radio uses more recognisably 'local' voices and that the commercial stations are more likely to be staffed by presenters with an all-purpose 'music radio' voice.

● Do you agree? Why do you think this might be the case?

Finally, we can define codes of **context**:

● What comes before and after the voice? Does the station use jingles or **idents** (see below) or music in between speech presentation?

● Are 'live' reports presented with lots of 'atmosphere' or with a 'flat' background?

● are voices carefully distinguished, each with its own space, or do the presenters interrupt and talk over each other or their interviewees?

The characteristics of speech radio

What really marks out the difference between Radio 4 and all the other stations that carry substantial speech-based material is the privileged status of the presenter's voice. Apart from Radio 3, every other station uses a call-sign or ident (identifying logo or sound image) to remind us who we are listening to (in much the same way that European television stations carry an ident in the corner of the screen).

What do we make of the use of music in what are ostensibly speech-based programmes of the 'magazine' or documentary type? The producers would probably argue that they add interest to the overall sound. Critics argue that they detract from what is being said, devaluing its importance (whereas the chimes of Big Ben are seen to confer dignity and authority). The use of popular songs to illustrate items on Radio 4 is the source of great angst to supporters of the service – during the writing of this paragraph an item on removing male body hair has played on *The Locker Room* on Radio 4. The closing remarks were accompanied by Sade singing 'Smooth Operator'. This might be a witty coda to an unusual piece or possibly a completely unnecessary 'filler' detracting from the more serious issues in the programme.

ACTIVITY 2.4

Tape news and magazine programmes from different stations on the same day. Try to find the same news items on each station.

- How are they presented differently in terms of context? Ignore, if you can, *what* is said for the moment and concentrate on *how* it is presented.
- Does the presentation add or detract from the story? Which one do you find most interesting and what is it that holds your attention?

The use of 'atmosphere' on live reports has re-emerged as an issue since the advent of Radio 5 'Live' and the general arguments about 24-hour radio. To some extent this is part of the rebirth of radio generally. Many of the major events of the past twenty years have been very much television events (Tiananmen Square, The Gulf War, the Berlin Wall coming down). Twenty-four-hour radio can't hope to compete with the very big stories which justify the use of expensive satellite time and the break-up of TV schedules, but it can bring us a continuous flow of second-division stories. How should it present these? Increasingly, reports from 'the front-line' feature reporters shouting above the noise or sending reports down crackly phone lines. It is harder to hear what they say, but is it gripping because it sounds 'vivid' and is coded as 'real' and 'immediate'?

Radio 5 Live won its first Sony Award in 1995 for an item which combined a serious and important content with what we might see as a realist style of presentation. During an otherwise routine magazine programme, a news reporter came on air to announce the ceasefire declaration in Northern Ireland. The news was so fresh that the reporter was still out of breath from running up and down stairs. The judges clearly felt that this added to the excitement of the announcement.

Chris Evans transferred from the *Big Breakfast Show* to its Radio 1 equivalent, and has been very successful, playing not only with sound effects, but also with openly made 'mistakes' combined with a degree of squabbling between presenters. He occupies a place somewhere between 'music radio' and the 'magazine' programmes on more formal 'speech radio' stations.

- Can you describe his approach to 'speaking on the radio' using the terms outlined here?
- Can you explain his appeal?

This takes us into the realism debate which is addressed in detail in Chapter 15, 'Realisms'. We will finish here by noting that the overlapping of voices on radio (i.e. everyone talking at once) on discussion programmes like Radio 4's *The Moral Maze* may be seen as representing a 'lively debate'; on the other hand, it makes following the debate rather more difficult.

If you follow up these brief introductory ideas about a 'semiotics of radio', you might find yourself listening quite carefully to the radio in future and thinking about how you will approach recording voices for your own productions.

References and further reading

Branston, Gill (1995) 'Viewer, I Listened to Him' in P. Kirkham and J. Thumim (eds) *Me, Jane,* London: Lawrence & Wishart.

Crisell, Andrew (1994) *Understanding Radio,* London: Routledge.

Goffman, Erving (1980) 'The Radio Drama Frame' in J. Corner and J. Hawthorn (eds) *Communication Studies,* London: Edward Arnold.

Lewis, Peter (ed.) (1981) *Radio Drama,* London: Longman.

Mugglestone, Linda (1995) *Talking Proper: The Rise of the Accent as a Social Symbol,* Oxford: Clarendon Press.

Richards, Jeffrey and Sheridan, Dorothy (eds) (1987) *Mass Observation at the Movies,* London: RKP.

Scannell, Paddy (ed.) (1991) *Broadcast Talk,* London: Sage.

Wilby, Peter and Conroy, Andy (1994) *The Radio Handbook,* London: Routledge.

3 Narratives

- Making narratives, or stories, is a key way in which meanings get constructed in the media – and outside them.
- Both factual and fiction forms are subject to this shaping.

Most of us tell stories all the time: gossiping about friends; telling jokes; filling family photo albums with appropriate events and some highly constructed characters: the proud graduate (never the hard-pressed student); the happy (never fraught) groups on holiday. All cultures seem to make stories as an involving and enjoyable way of creating sense and meanings in the world. Two points are worth bearing in mind as we attempt a systematic study of narrative in modern media:

- narrative theory suggests that stories in whatever media and whatever culture share certain features;
- but particular media are able to 'tell' stories in different ways.

General theories of narrative

Narrative theory studies the devices and conventions governing the organisation of a story (fictional or factual) into sequence.
The names of **Todorov**, **Barthes**, **Propp**, and **Lévi-Strauss**, working mostly with myths and folk tales, are ones you will come across in discussion of media narrative processes. Here are the bare bones of their influential **structuralist** approaches to narrative.

Tzvetan Todorov Bulgarian structuralist linguist publishing influential work on narrative from the 1960s onwards.

Todorov argued that all stories begin with what he called an **'equilibrium'** where any potentially opposing forces are 'in balance'. This is disrupted by some event, setting in train a series of events, to **close** with a second, but different 'equilibrium' or status quo. His theory may sound just like the cliché that every story has a beginning, a middle and an end. But it's more interesting than that. His 'equilibrium' labels a state of affairs, or a status quo, and allows us to think about how this is 'set up' in certain ways and not others. 'Nurses today decided to reject a pay offer of 1%', for instance, begins a news story with a disruption to an equilibrium, but we only know about one side of the balance. We don't know who has offered the pay rise and what has gone before. How, where and when *else* could the story have begun are always good questions to ask.

Barthes suggested further that narrative works with five different **codes** which activate the reader to make sense of it. Of particular interest is the idea that an **enigma code** works to keep setting up little puzzles to be solved, to delay pleasurably the story's ending: e.g. how will Schwarzenegger get out of this predicament? What is in the locked room? An **action code** will be read by means of accumulated details (looks, significant words) which relate to cultural knowledge of our (often stereotypical) models of such actions as 'falling in love' or 'being tempted into a robbery'.

Such approaches have been applied not just to fiction forms, but also to long-running news stories to see if narrative structuring 'sets up' certain expectations and puzzles. ITN's *News at Ten* often works by teasing us with enigmatic summaries of stories before the ad break. Newspaper billboards work in similar ways. In the stories themselves, disruption to the status quo (say in a war, or strike, or demo story) is often narratively attributed to one group or person, rather than to others whose actions before the 'story' started might have been equally provocative, but are less frequently tied into a story opening (see examples below). This can mean that more complex historical and political explanations are structured out of the story-telling, both at the beginning and in the final 'equilibrium'.

Propp examined hundreds of examples of one kind of folk tale, the 'heroic wondertale' to see if they shared any structures. He argued that whatever the surface differences, it was possible to group characters and actions into:

- eight **character roles** (or 'spheres of action' as he called them to indicate how inseparable are character and action)
- thirty-one **functions** (such as 'a prohibition or ban is imposed on the hero' or 'the villain learns something about his victim') which move the story along, often in a highly predictable order. For example 'the punishment of the villain' always occurs at the end of a story, and the 'interdiction' or forbidding of some act, always comes at the beginning. What is apparently the same act can function in different ways for different narratives. For example, the prince may build a castle as:
  - preparation for a wedding
  - defiance of a prohibition
  - solution of a task set.

Roles or spheres of action, he argued, make sense of the ways in which many very different figures (witch, woodcutter, goblin, etc.), could be

The five codes are: the **action or proairetic**; the **enigma or hermeneutic**; the **semic**; the **symbolic**, and the **cultural or referential** code. For more detail, see Barthes (1977).

Vladimir Propp Russian critic and folklorist whose influential book, translated as *Morphology of the Folk Tale,* was first published in 1928.

reduced to eight character roles – not the same as the actual characters since one character can occupy several roles or 'spheres of action'. These are:

1 the *villain*
2 the *hero*, or character who seeks something. ('Hero' is one of those terms that does not mean the same within theory as it does in life outside, where 'hero' and 'heroic' have moral connotations of 'admirable' or 'good'. Here it's much closer to describing an active way of carrying the events of a story.)
3 the *donor* who provides an object with some magic property
4 the *helper* who aids the hero
5 the *princess*, reward for the hero (see above) and object of the villain's schemes
6 her *father*, who rewards the hero
7 the *dispatcher*, who sends the hero on his way
8 the *false hero*.

Examples of a woman hero in traditionally male genres would be *Tank Girl* (US 1995), *Aliens* (US 1986), *Thelma and Louise* (US 1991), and in television, *Prime Suspect* (UK 1994). Can you think of others?

Such work on stories is inevitably bound up with the times and social orders which produced them. For example, it's worth noting that the hero can now often be a female character, as in *Blue Steel* (US 1990), especially since the word 'heroine' (Propp's 'princess') implies a character who hangs around looking decorative until the hero is ready to sweep her away. (Many commentators prefer to use 'the sought-for person' instead of 'princess'.)

Yet since fairy tales, or versions of them (like *Pretty Woman* (US 1990) or *Star Wars* (US 1977)), are still current for most of us, it is perhaps not surprising that Propp's approach continues to be useful. The general aim of trying to uncover structures beneath the surface differences of widely circulated, popular forms such as fairy tales, TV serials or movies, has been very influential. It reminds us that though characters in stories may seem to us very 'real' (especially in cinema and TV), they must be understood as constructed characters, who have roles to play for the sake of the story. They do indeed often act as 'hero', 'villain', 'helper' and so on. It's striking how quickly, as readers, we settle into such expectations of characters. We feel it very sharply when the person we thought was the hero or helper turns out to be the villain, as in *Coma* (US 1978) or, indeed, in *Psycho* (US 1960) where, to the shock of its first audiences, the female hero (and star) is killed off a third of the way through the film, and the shy young man who seemed to be a helper turns out to be something very different.

Yet other narrative forms, such as the *Mahabharata* from Indian culture, or indeed western 'women's' forms such as romance, or the musical, take pleasure in much less action-driven narratives, with convoluted patterns (often circular), several climaxes, and scenes of spectacle and humour given real narrative weight.

ACTIVITY 3.1

Check that you can identify narrative roles in a favourite fictional media text. Then try watching for the way that media language will often attribute narrative roles and thus construct 'characters' even in non-fiction forms. Weather forecasts will sometimes characterise, or rather narrativise natural forces: winds, isobars and so on may be called 'the villain' or 'to blame'; a warm front is 'coming to the rescue'. Or in discussions of crime, the word 'villains' may be used instead of 'criminals'.

- What difference might this make ?
- What narrative images might it evoke?

Figure 3.1 '...and the rain will move in from the South West, threatening the Test Match at Edgbaston by early afternoon'

Paradigm A class of objects or concepts.
Syntagm An element which follows another in a particular sequence. Imagine choosing from a menu. Paradigmatic elements are those from which you choose (starters, main courses, desserts). The syntagm is the sequence into which they are arranged. Or think of it as vertical and horizontal structures.

See Chapter 5 'Genres'; Chapter 6, 'Going West'. **Native Americans** were of course usually called Indians, in the end because Christopher Columbus made the mistake of thinking he had landed in India and named them accordingly.

Lévi-Strauss argued that an abiding structure of meaning-making was a dependence on **binary oppositions**, or a conflict between two qualities or terms. Less interested in the order in which events were arranged in the plot (called **syntagmatic** relations), he looked 'beneath' them for deeper or **paradigmatic** arrangements of themes. This theory was applied to the western genre in the 1970s. Writers suggested that the different sheriffs, outlaws and **Native Americans** not only existed in Proppian narrative terms, but could be seen as making up systematic oppositions, among others:

homesteaders	Native Americans
Christian	pagan
domestic	savage
weak	strong
garden	wilderness
inside society	outside society

Let's apply the work of these four theorists:

- Though news is a 'factual' media form (see Chapter 12, 'Selecting and constructing news'), it's striking how, especially in radio and TV, the programmes themselves take on a narrative shape. Watch the start of the evening news programme on BBC or ITV for signs of a kind of 'once upon a time-ness' in: the studio set-up, title music, signs of authority in newscasters' dress, voice, bearing, position and so on.

- Once a 'story', or an individual life, is closed (as by Kurt Cobain's suicide or River Phoenix's drug overdose), events before it will be told in the light of that ending as narrative **closure**, and often seen as 'leading up to it'.

- Reporters are trained in how to **construct** a 'good story'. This, especially for **tabloid** forms, involves shaping along the lines of suspense, a clear beginning and ending, and heroes and villains.

- Headlines, especially in tabloids, will often dramatise by 'character' names familiar from other media, as in the use of the word 'psycho' in stories of community care tragedies, or the title 'Peter Sutcliffe, the Yorkshire Ripper' (see Figure 3.2).

- **Close-ups**, particular words or emphases in the reporter's account ('he *seems* distraught at the prospect . . .'; 'looking radiant, she announced . . .') will often signal the parts of Barthes' action or enigma codes.
- Longer news stories are even more interesting. When an event is first constructed as news, it can be 'played as' a number of stories, without clear hero or villain roles. But if it goes on for long enough, it's striking how often it will be structured as a narrative. In the process, complex historical events and motives will often get left out for the pleasures of a good story. A good example is the Gulf War of 1991.

Applying Todorov However outrageous Saddam Hussein's invasion of Kuwait was, the way many news organisations treated it meant that other factors motivating his behaviour were structured out of the story, such as

Figure 3.2

the power of the big western oil companies, the previous price fixing which threatened catastrophe for Iraq's economy, and the military support that oil-hungry western powers had given to other despotic but oil-rich regimes. Much better, for story and war purposes, was an emphasis on his individual villainy or despotism as prime cause of the war.

Applying Propp In fact, 'Saddam' was structured very clearly as the villain role, with 'Stormin' Norman' (the US General Schwartzkopf) and the Allied Forces together carrying the hero role (John Major as 'helper'?). Of course, this does not exist in isolation from other processes of meaning construction. Long-standing stereotypes constructing 'the Orient' as full of cruel despots; patterns of censorship during wartime, and the difficulty of constructing a big story around pictures of night-time bombing raids could also be said to contribute to this particular narrative emphasis.

Applying Todorov Wars end, eventually, but how do the media structure those endings? Even though repercussions and related events will go on happening (post-traumatic stress syndrome; long recovery from injuries; oil pollution; boundary disputes . . .) the deep satisfaction of a narrative

AS THE FLAG RISES AGAIN IN THE WEST

Our brave young men

BRITAIN'S fighting men won warm praise from their commander on the Falklands yesterday.

Major-General Jeremy Moore, the man who accepted the Argentine surrender, sat in Government House in Port Stanley and paid tribute to the young soldiers whose determination, toughness and skill had brought victory.

'If anyone back home is complaining about the youth of Britain then by golly they should have seen them here,' he said. 'I cannot speak highly enough of the training, dedication, toughness and capability of the young men who made up the landing force.'

In the last three days of fighting, 33 British troops were killed and 140 injured.

General Moore said: 'One always feared the casualties could have been heavier. The fact that they were not is due to the quality, determination and fighting effectiveness of the units themselves.'

The 'man of the match,' he said was Brigadier Julian Thompson, officer commanding 3 Commando brigade.

He praised the Royal Navy. 'They demonstrated the fighting quality that has been their tradition through the centuries back to Nelson and Drake. It has been a marvellous sight to behold.'

General Moore also spoke of the achievement in keeping the force supplied 8,000 miles from Britain.

'The enemy thought we could not do it. But our logistics people did it—and the fact that they did is a near miracle.'

But he had no praise for Argentine officers who had treated their young conscripts inhumanly. He said : 'Some conscripts, perhaps the majority, did not want to be here and were not enjoying it. Some of them were kept in the trenches by having bullets fired through both feet.'

WE'RE back—to stay. The men of 40 Commando Royal Marines raise the Union Jack again at Port Howard, on West Falkland. The small settlement's unforgettable moment came the day after the surrender at Port Stanley

Figure 3.3

shape is part of what pushes newsrooms to mark, to *celebrate* 'an ending', a 'new but different equilibrium' – and often to signify it by some happy or domestic event, suggesting a return to normality – very like 'And so they all lived happily ever after'. The tanks roll home, the soldiers talk of their pleasure at a job well done, and eventually there is the welcome home by the women and children. Parts of the media may signal scepticism, through focusing on possible long-term damaging effects.

Applying Lévi-Strauss Is it possible to group together, in two opposing lists, the qualities which get structured into the story as belonging to each side? For the Gulf War these might include:

east	west
barbarism	civilisation
despotism	democracy
Scud missiles	Exocet missiles
backward technology	futuristic technology
the past	the future

ACTIVITY 3.2

Take any story, preferably a long-running one, from recent news and consider:
● How has the initial equilibrium been set up?
● How has the disruption to that been constructed?
● How do you think this narrative will 'end' or 'close', and what will be left out of that ending?
● How else could the story have begun, with what other 'equilibrium'?
● How have the people involved been constructed as characters with narrative roles such as hero, villain, donor, etc.?
● Are there any signs of 'action' or 'enigma' codes being set up?

'The fourth goal makes it a happy ending for Villa ...'; 'Fowler, the hero of the match ...'; 'the never-ending story of the Olympics, symbolised by this athlete carrying the flame to be lit again ...'; 'giant killers Keighley ...'

Sports programmes also work with narrative forms. There are the 'stories-so-far' of stars which we're invited to bring to bear on particular performances. The processes of winning and losing, so central to sport, are told as narratives. Study the ways in which camera placing, freeze frames, action replays, and commentary work with these narrative underpinnings in the next event you watch on TV.

Narration, story and plot

The term **narration** describes how stories are told, how their material is selected and arranged in order to achieve particular effects with their audiences.

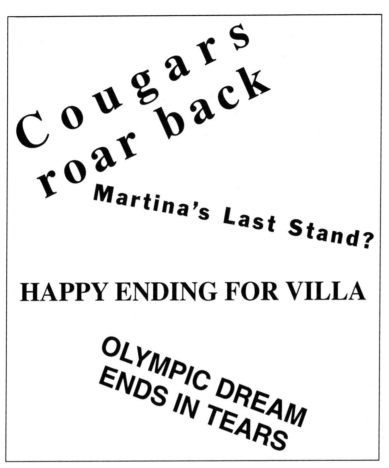

Figure 3.4

Plot and **story** are terms often used in this context, though another useful distinction is the one used by Russian theorists in the 1920s between **syuzhet** and **fabula**. (These foreign terms are used instead of plot and story because the meanings of plot and story are often slippery, and they often get confused with each other.)

Story, or fabula, is helpfully defined by Bordwell and Thompson (1990: 56) in relation to film, though you can think about how it works in other forms, such as magazine stories, comic strips or radio. They argue it consists of: 'all the events in a narrative, both explicitly presented and inferred'. This would include routine events, such as visits to the bathroom, which we assume carry on happening during a story, but would be tedious as part of the plot. It may also include material we only find out by the end of the story, having been busy trying to piece things together throughout, such as Norman's mental condition in *Psycho*.

The plot, or syuzhet, is: 'everything visibly and audibly present in the film before us; in other words those highly selected parts of the story which the narrative puts before us' (Bordwell and Thompson 1990). Detective fiction is a good example of the rules of such combination. We should feel at the end of a good detective story that we have been adequately puzzled, so that the 'solution', our piecing together of the story in its proper order out of the materials offered by the plot, will come as a pleasure. But we should not feel that the plot has cheated; that parts of the story have suddenly been revealed which we couldn't possibly have guessed at. The butler cannot, at the last minute, suddenly be revealed to have been a munitions expert.

ACTIVITY 3.3

Take one of your favourite stories and tell it in flashback form.

● What effect does this have on how you get to find things out, how your sympathies flow?

One example might be the story of Red Riding Hood:

● Who would have to be speaking, and to whom, to tell this story in flashback? The wolf in 'A Wolf's Afterlife'? Red Riding Hood herself?

● What effects would this have on suspense?

Another part of the construction of narratives involves the voice telling the story. A first-person narration will use 'I' as the voice of the teller, and should not give the reader access to events which that 'I' could not have witnessed, or known of. Spectacular cheats are possible, as in the film *Sunset Boulevard* (US 1950) where we discover, at the end, that the first-person narrator who has been telling the story is in fact dead – that it seemed a flashback when it couldn't possibly have been one.

Figure 3.5 Nineteenth-century illustration of 'Little Red Riding Hood'. What if the story began here?

A third-person or impersonal narration refers to a story which seems to 'get itself told', as in 'Once upon a time there was a kingdom . . .' Cinema and many TV/video narratives are impersonally narrated; they seem to just unfold before us.

ACTIVITY 3.4

Look at a few ads from TV. Ask yourself of each:

● Is this a narrative?

● If I think it is, why do I think so? How do I know?

● If I think it's not, why is this so?

Using narrative form, an ad will often:

● group its events in cause and effect order. Non-narrative ads won't do this. They may simply consist of a set of claims about a product, as in supermarket ads which list prices, or ads setting up a mood and linking it to the product, like the antics of the popular Anchor butter dancing cows.

● even in a few seconds, create a sense of characters and action or enigma codes through economical use of signs and stereotypical traits.

These work as Propp suggests: the same traits that help us build up a sense of them as 'real people' are also crucial for the action, the furthering of the plot. There will be a discernible 'hero', and often a villain and possibly donor. (An interesting line of enquiry is to ask yourself: how far is the product the hero?)

There will be, as Todorov suggests, some sense of an initial situation, which is disrupted or altered in some way and then happily resolved at the end; usually, of course, through the magical intervention of the product being sold.

You will also probably be able to distinguish syuzhet and fabula. Even if flashback is not used, try to imagine the same events told differently, from the point of view of another character, for example, or with different amounts of time, and therefore emphasis, given to different segments of the narrative.

Applying Lévi-Strauss's approach, TV ads can often be analysed so as to show a systematic grouping of recurring signs, situations or characters in opposition to each other. Levi's jeans ads (not named after Lévi-Strauss), for example, often group qualities as the following sets of oppositions. Check to see if the latest example is still using them:

young	old
hip	uncool
young generation	parental figures
sexy	asexual
rule-breaking	rule-enforcing
Levi's jeans	not Levi's

Narratives in different media

When stories are told in modern media, they are the products of highly diversified and sophisticated industries. These have divided up their output into different types or genres (horror, musical, news . . .) and researched their audiences carefully. Narrative theory can be applied to these stories. But part of what also happens is that media genres can be activated in audiences' minds in ways not directly to do with the explicit, summarisable events of a narrative. A friend may tell you about a scene and then say 'I can't quite explain why, but it was really frightening/funny/moving.' They may well have registered, though be unable to point explicitly to, the way a certain kind of lighting may have signified a horror or thriller story, so that a detective fiction, or a TV sitcom, suddenly changes its tone quite strikingly.

For example, a setting like the American desert in a movie will tend to evoke the western, or road movies like *Paris, Texas* (US 1984) rather than the Gulf War. In a woman's film like *Thelma and Louise* (US 1991), this will partly account for what we expect of the two central characters. They become somehow 'buddies' in a western, with an 'old timer' gradually initiating the younger buddy into certain attitudes. They become heroic, larger than life figures in a CinemaScope genre; 'outlaws' – but outside laws involving rape rather than those of the western's robbery or killing, and so on.

ACTIVITY 3.5

Take any Levi's jeans ad, from magazines or TV, and decide what genre the style of filming or photography evokes.

● How does this help you to identify the nature of the 'characters' within this very brief narrative?

If there are certain structures which seem to govern all story-making and story-telling, these have to work differently in different media, and for different cultures. You should consider this if you're involved in a project which asks you to choose a medium for a story: what can 'x' medium do (strip cartoon, say) that 'y' cannot, and vice versa? These differences are partly due to the nature of different media.

Photography This might seem an odd example of a narrative form, since it deals in frozen moments of time (like stained-glass windows in earlier times). But often the impact of a powerful news or advertising photo lies in what it makes us imagine has gone before, or is about to happen. In this sense narrative is often quite clearly signalled, depending on angle, information given, construction of imagined characters – and whether or not black and white film stock is involved. The difference between black and white and colour often signals 'pastness' and 'presentness', which is of obvious use to a story-teller in light.

ACTIVITY 3.6

Look for ads which use the black and white/colour contrast in the way suggested above.

- How do they invoke narrative expectations and knowledge ?

Figure 3.6 Cover image from *Vertigo* magazine: a still from *Ladybird, Ladybird* (UK 1994)

ACTIVITY 3.7

Look at Figure 3.6 again.

- Do you begin to construct a story which might explain what these figures are doing?
- Do they have characters for you in that story? On what evidence or signs have you begun to build these characters ?
- What is the situation? How do you know?

Comic strips (and by extension animation) tell their stories by a compelling combination of:

- words (including thought bubbles)
- line drawings. These can streamline characters and events more than even the highest budget movie. You never have to worry about spots on the star's face, or problems with lighting in comic strip or animation
- flashpoint illustrations of key moments involving extreme angles and exaggerations in ways that TV and most cinema has not done. (Interestingly, an important moment in modern cinema was when such stylised composition entered the western through the influence of comic books on the so-called 'spaghetti' or Italian western. It is now very familiar through films like *Batman* (US 1989) and *The Mask* (US 1994).

Cinema This quite quickly developed into an entertainment medium which above all else tells stories, shown on big screens, lasting 90 minutes to two hours. Like video and audio recordings, it's a 'time-based' medium, depending on the manipulation of time and space (rather than image or words alone) to tell its stories. This average length, and the way audiences pay to see it all at one sitting, can give it some of the intensity of a short story, and arguably lead to a different experience than that of longer fictions like novels, or soaps, which are read or viewed over days, weeks, even years.

Shot A series of frames produced by the camera uninterruptedly. It can be as short as a few frames or as long as there is film in the camera. Try watching a film and tapping every time you spot a cut where shots are combined by editing.

Early cinema quite soon shed the assumption that all the camera needed to do was to film actions as though they were theatre, from a fixed position in the stalls. Film-makers quickly elaborated an audio-visual language in **shots** which supplemented, though usually included, that of words.

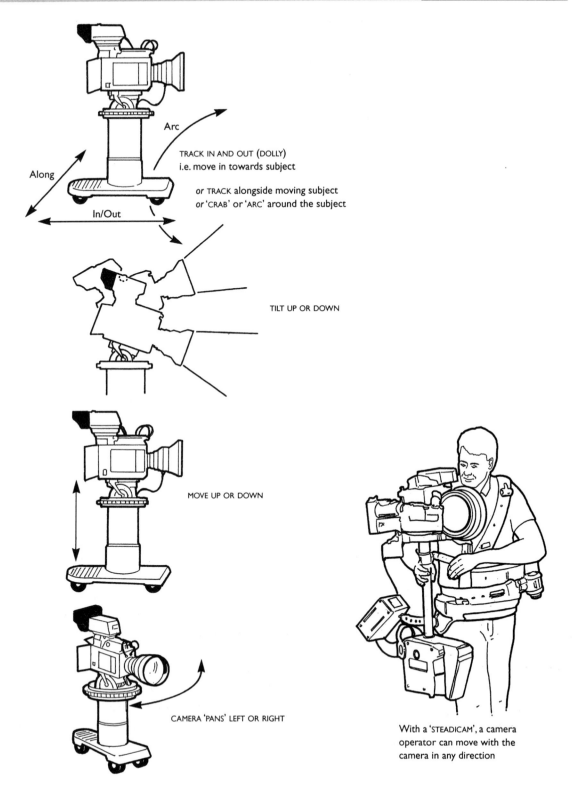

Arc

TRACK IN AND OUT (DOLLY)
i.e. move in towards subject

or TRACK alongside moving subject
or 'CRAB' or 'ARC' around the subject

Along

In/Out

TILT UP OR DOWN

MOVE UP OR DOWN

CAMERA 'PANS' LEFT OR RIGHT

With a 'STEADICAM', a camera
operator can move with the
camera in any direction

Figure 3.7 Camera movements

Try to develop an awareness of this, and avoid talking about characters in a film as though they were either real people or characters in a novel, where dialogue and description are supremely important. It's worth emphasising here the importance of script and basic story design. Much comment on cinema/TV, wanting to distinguish it from literature, has downplayed the role of the writer. You certainly need to spend as much time as possible on the writing stage of audio-visual story projects, as well as thinking about their audio-visual qualities.

Camera movement became an important way of telling stories, whether a **track** (where the camera seems to move through space) or a **pan** (where it swings smoothly around its axis, up or down) or a lens movement like the **zoom** (a close-up movement which gives the effect of the camera 'eye' having picked something out).

Framing, the decision as to what the shot frame should include, involves choices around how much audiences see of a character or situation, and therefore how they are invited to engage with a scene. The most familiar example is probably the tight framing on a character's hand opening the door to the mysterious darkened room in a horror film. The audience can be expected to know that Something Nasty is waiting, and to be wanting to see it, but the film-maker deliberately frames so as to withhold that knowledge. This is both pleasurably frightening, and may well pull our identification towards the character doing the exploring.

Mise en scène The staging of an action for the camera, including aspects of cinema which overlap with theatre: lighting, costume, sets and the behaviour of figures. In some accounts camera movement is included, which broadens the term to mean something like 'direction' itself.

Mise en scène or the setting up of a scene is another term for discussing how stories are being told in cinema and TV. It originated in theatre (around the staging of a scene) and is used to describe many of the ways in which audio-visual media differ from literary forms. Some writers use it to describe all the visual elements, including camera movement, which make up shots which are then combined together through editing. Others, perhaps more helpfully, use a separate term to include discussion of camera movement and choices around colour balance, lens, angle, etc: **cinematography**.

If you think of your favourite scene from a movie, and the role of mise en scène within it, you will find that it has been an important part of your sense of the narrative. Take a film like *Fatal Attraction* (US 1987): the mise en scène repeatedly constructed the 'good wife' in glowing, warm, soft colours, in comfily cluttered domestic spaces, with the actress's hair softly framing her face. The 'evil woman' however was given a flat next to a slaughter house, which was painted in harsh whites, minimally decorated, unwelcoming, while the actress playing her, Glenn Close, was given a hairstyle evoking serpent tails, and was repeatedly shot and lit in harsh, angular ways.

Figure 3.8 ▶

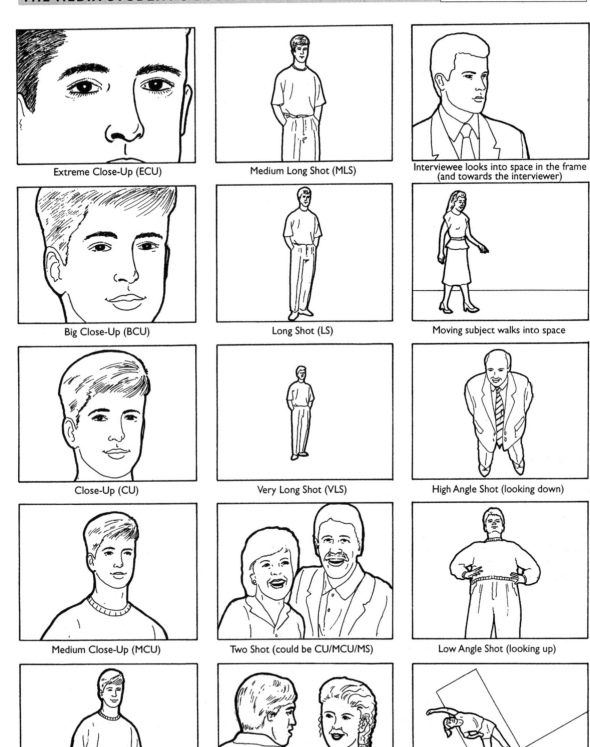

Extreme Close-Up (ECU)

Medium Long Shot (MLS)

Interviewee looks into space in the frame (and towards the interviewer)

Big Close-Up (BCU)

Long Shot (LS)

Moving subject walks into space

Close-Up (CU)

Very Long Shot (VLS)

High Angle Shot (looking down)

Medium Close-Up (MCU)

Two Shot (could be CU/MCU/MS)

Low Angle Shot (looking up)

Medium Shot (MS)

'Over the shoulder shot'

Tilted Frame

Narrative time and space, then, can be manipulated (for the purposes of suspense, identification, withholding of knowledge, etc.) by:

- the initial script and story
- the choices made in **mise en scène, camera framing and movement**
- **editing**.

Unwritten rules of editing (the combination of shots) soon developed, and came to be called **continuity editing**.

- a section of a film or TV fiction usually begins with an **establishing shot** which sets up the whole space in which the next part of the narrative will happen, helping us to identify where figures are in relation to each other, what significant 'marks' are, and so on.
- The camera tends to stay on one side of an imaginary '180° line of action' which can be drawn through any scene (common examples are a car chase, or a conversation between two people). Again, this is intended to draw us into the story by minimising the effort needed to imagine ourselves within its space. And, for example, when cutting between two people looking or moving towards each other, failure to observe the rule can mean they will seem to be looking in the same direction.
- Shots are generally co-ordinated with each other by cuts, or a simple splicing together, and the rules observed in this process are meant to aid the audience's absorption in the narrative. For example, conversations will be filmed by the '**shot/reverse shot**' system. Here,

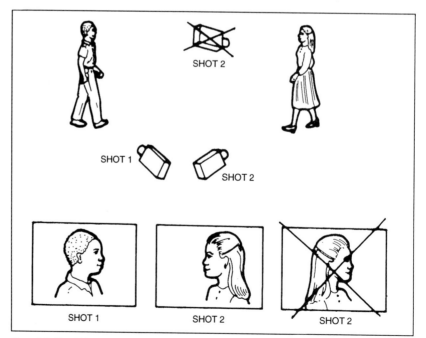

Figure 3.9 The 180 degree rule is designed to prevent confusing transitions

once the 180° **line** has been set up, the camera will cut back and forth
from one end of that line to the other, involving, in a conversation, for
example, a position close to one character, looking at the second, then
with the second character looking at the first.

- **Cross cutting** is another way of telling a story through the
  manipulation of space in editing. It refers to the placing together of
  shots which actually belong to different spaces of the narrative.
  Audiences have learnt to read these as happening simultaneously – as
  in chase scenes.
- The passage of longer amounts of time in editing will be signified by a
  dissolve or **mix** (video term) – the effect of one shot dissolving into
  the next – or by fades – one shot fades out to black, and the next
  gradually 'fades up'. These are often ways in which flashbacks, so
  useful in the arrangement of syuzhet or plot, are signalled.

Though this system was never written down as a set of rules, it is
surprising how powerfully entrenched it is in our expectations of cinema
and television. One way of becoming aware of the rules is to watch them
being broken in comic forms in films by directors like Mel Brooks or
Woody Allen.

A further, much underestimated part of film is sound. This will be as
carefully organised as images and editing to serve the narrative.
Particularly helpful is the way that sounds can be continuous across visual
cuts, thus 'carrying' the audience across the cut and making editing less
obvious and the narrative appear less disjointed.

ACTIVITY 3.8

Take any scene from a recent film or TV fiction; or you could look at a Levi's TV ad
again. Take notes on:

- how it has been edited;
- how the mise en scène contributes to the narrative.

Now examine the sound track.

- What are the components of this track: music? voices? noises? sound effects
  including distortion? How have they been chosen and arranged? Are some louder
  than others? Why do you think each has been included? Do any seem accidental?
- How have they been shaped around the action, or talk in that scene? How
  close do the voices seem, how have they been chosen, or constructed? How
  does all this help construct the narrative?

Radio This medium uses sounds and silence. This affects the way it can
handle narrative, constructing through voices, noises, sound effects and

'I prefer radio to TV because the pictures are better' (anonymous young listener).

silence the illusion of space between characters, and time between segments. It cannot give up much narrative time to features on which cinema might want to spend time (say the display of visual special effects). Characters cannot stay silent for long periods of time (like the Tim Roth character, often silently dying 'onstage' in *Reservoir Dogs* (US 1992)), since they would seem to have 'disappeared'. Since its signifiers are relatively cheap and easy to produce however, it is free to construct the most bizarre and exotic stories, from time travel to a play set in the memories flashing through the head of a drowning woman in her last moments.

Institutions and narratives

Differences between the ways stories get told in different media are partly, then, to do with the material (sound, celluloid, line drawings, image and sound, words alone) of that medium. But they are also to do with institutional or industrial shaping.

Look at the following chart suggesting some differences in how closed and open narratives work in those different media institutions, 'cinema' and 'television':

Closed narrative, e.g. cinema	**Open narrative,** e.g. soap opera
1 'Tight' reading involved, with audience aware it's watching a two-hour story and therefore reading with the likely end in mind.	1 Casual reading, without the sense of an ending. Soaps proceed as though they could go on forever.
2 Relatively few central characters; huge range of 'depth' of audience knowledge, even interior voice-overs giving characters' thoughts, hallucinations etc.	2 Many more characters, naturalistically represented and producing a **multi-strand plot**.
3 Characters arranged in a 'hierarchy' (central, cameo, supporting roles, extras etc.).	3 Characters not usually in a marked hierarchy but shift in and out of prominence.
4 Often with audience invited to make 'verdicts' on them, identifying narrative roles, as in Propp: hero, villain, donor.	4 Characters shift also in and out of narrative function. Today's villain may be next week's helper.
5 Time usually very compressed: two hours of screen time constructs	5 Time usually corresponds to 'real world time' *within the segments of*

events as happening over months, years, sometimes centuries.

6 Time and events are usually special to this particular story, and need have no resemblance to the viewer's world. Flashbacks and even flashforwards are possible.

7 Reader/viewer usually only has evidence about the characters from this single text, plus star, publicity and genre expectations.

8 The same audience can be assumed to watch the film from beginning to end.

9 Often elaborate visual image, and music as integral part of the narrative.

each episode, though across it time is compressed, as in cinema. Flashbacks are rare.

6 The difference between time in the serial and outside it are blurred. Episodes may make reference to real life events going on at the same time, such as elections, Christmas.

7 Audiences are assumed to have different kinds of memory, and knowledge of a long-running soap. Magazines and the press often speculate about the fate of actors' contracts, and thus the characters they represent. Many different kinds of reading are therefore available.

8 Each episode has to try and address both experienced and new viewers.

9 Relatively rare use of music, especially in British soaps, and relatively simple visual image.

'"The Royals" is the longest-running soap opera in Britain ... [it] is based on the same narrative structure as *Dallas* ... Like *Dallas* it is the long-running story of an extremely wealthy and powerful family ... The fact that "The Royals" is loosely based on reality only adds to its fascination.'

(Coward, 1984: 163)

The open-ended serial form (soap) developed first on US radio in the 1930s as a cheap way of involving audiences often composed of housewives, whose buying choices detergent manufacturers wanted to influence. It was later an ideal form for commercial TV, keen to sell the promise of audiences' regular attention to advertisers. The BBC also sought to boost its early evening audiences with soaps. This is partly in the hope they will stay with the channel that evening, and also to help the BBC produce large audience numbers when it makes its arguments for the level of the next licence fee.

Though soap is one of the most familiar and discussed forms of media, remember it is not just 'one thing': there are Australian, American and British soaps, to name but three, on British TV, and these in turn divide into high and low budget forms, and have different relationships to documentary, glamour, sitcom, romance, regional identities, and now even male audiences. Nevertheless, we can generalise that one of British soap's attractions for its producers is that costs can be kept down and the narrative can be centred on a few key locations (the square, pub and cafe in *EastEnders*) which are meeting places and one of the staples of the narrative. They are argued to involve the Utopian pleasure of imagining yourself a part of the soap's community. They are also key to soaps' production needs, since soaps cannot rely in the same way as feature films on suspenseful manipulation of time. Even though a soap has to go out for two or three nights a week, particular storylines swing in and out of prominence, allowing:

- time for rehearsals, holidays, the covering of actors' illnesses, pregnancy, etc.;
- a wide appeal through choice of several stories designed to involve different sections of the audience. If you're impatient with one 'strand', you know that another, which interests you more, will probably be along in half a minute or so.

Soap narratives may also change as a result of attempts to shift the composition of their audiences – and advertisers, in the case of ITV. After the huge 1990s franchise restructuring, Granada charged more for expensive ad slots in *Coronation Street* than ever before. Regular viewers detected an 'upmarket' move in sets, situations and some character types which are part of the attempt to get more expensive ad slots sold to advertisers. After the success of *Brookside,* other soaps have tried to attract male audiences to this traditionally female form by means of 'tough' story lines and characters.

ACTIVITY 3.9

Make notes on an episode of your favourite soap.

- How many storylines does that episode contain?
- To which sections of the audience might they appeal?
- Which are the main storylines? The same as a few weeks ago? Why do you think this is?
- How is time managed in the episode?
- How many sets are used? Why have these places been chosen?
- Are there any rumours circulating about the fate of particular characters/actors, in the press, on TV, or fanzines?
- How does your knowledge of these affect your viewing? Does it add to your pleasure? How?
- How does the soap story try to address both experienced and new viewers? How are repeated use of characters' names, repeated updatings of the storylines and so on managed so as to inform new viewers, yet not bore regular ones?
- If it's on a commercial channel, what do the ads before, during and after suggest about the expected audience?

Other forms fall interestingly between these two narrative shapes, such as series, mini-series and serials (including 'classic' serials), designed to meet particular scheduling needs. Series (such as *Northern Exposure, er* or *Casualty*) may last many weeks but will signal a sense of an ending (unlike soaps, which proceed as though they will never finish). Series will feature the same characters, and some long-running stories involving them in a multi-strand narrative, but each episode will have a central story which will be concluded at the end of the hour. *The Bill* is interesting here, proceeding like both a male-centred soap and a series.

References and further reading

Barthes, Roland (1977) *Introduction to the Structural Analysis of Narratives,* London: Fontana.

Bordwell, David and Thompson, Kirsten (1990) *Film Art: An Introduction,* London: McGraw-Hill.

Buckingham, David (1987) *Public Secrets: EastEnders and its Audience,* London: BFI.

Coward, Ros (1984) *Female Desire: Women's Sexuality Today*, London: Paladin.

Crisell, Andrew (1994) *Understanding Radio,* London: Routledge.

Eagleton, Terry (1983) *Literary Theory: An Introduction,* Oxford: Blackwell, Ch. 3.

Geraghty, Christine (1991) *Women and Soap Opera,* London: Polity Press.

Lévi-Strauss, Claude (1972) 'The Structural Study of Myth', in De George, R. and F. (eds) *The Structuralists from Marx to Lévi-Strauss,* New York: Doubleday Anchor.

O'Sullivan, T., Hartley, J., Saunders, D., Montgomery, M. and Fisk, J. (1994) *Key Concepts in Communication and Cultural Studies,* London: Routledge.

Perkins, Victor (1990) *Film as Film,* London: Penguin.

Propp, Vladimir (1975) *The Morphology of the Folk Tale,* Austin: University of Texas Press.

Todorov, Tzvetan (1977) *The Poetics of Prose,* Oxford, Blackwell.

Turner, Graeme (1993) *Film as Social Practice,* London: Routledge, Ch. 4.

4 / Case study: Telling *Psycho*

Applying Todorov, Propp,
Barthes and Lévi-Strauss
Story and plot in *Psycho*
Psycho as a film narrative
Synopsis

Psycho (US 1960) is one of the most celebrated films ever made, which is why we chose it for this case study. However, if you have somehow missed seeing it, first read the synopsis of the plot at the end of this case study.

ACTIVITY 4.1

In fact, have a look at this synopsis even if you have seen the film. Note how different the verbal account is to a movie.

- Do you have any disagreements with particular emphases?
- Begin writing your own synopsis. How would you do it? Where would you begin?
- How much knowledge would you release to your reader? When?

Applying Todorov, Propp, Barthes and Lévi-Strauss to *Psycho*

Q How would you describe the initial situation or equilibrium (i.e. after **Todorov**)?

A It consists of a secretary and her lover (Marion and Sam) who want to marry but cannot afford to.

Q And the disruption to this?

A Marion's decision to steal the $40,000 her boss asks her to bank.

We are partly prepared for this (**Barthes**' action codes), not just by the lovers' conversation about money but also by the dates which are superimposed on the film's opening shots:

PHOENIX, ARIZONA, FRIDAY, DECEMBER THE ELEVENTH, TWO FORTY-THREE P.M.

This plays with narrative construction, and also generic markers such as the precise time — often signalled in films where a crime like a theft is important. It's a kind of visual cheat, since by the end of the film the theft has ceased to matter at all. It was a 'red herring', though important for our sense of Marion's change of mind just before she's murdered. When, to our surprise, this happens, a second equilibrium is set up. The surprise is partly one that would occur in whatever medium the narrative were told. Using **Propp**, Marion was the hero or central figure (with her boss as dispatcher) and we expect her to carry that role for most of the story.

But Marion/Leigh's death is also a play with the conventions of cinema: Janet Leigh, who plays Marion, is the star of the film and we expect stars to play in the film to the end. After her death, the hero role is split between Sam and Lila (with Arbogast as helper). The audience's attitude towards Norman probably changes, but is always partly formed as Propp and Barthes suggest.

Viewers/readers do seem to try to make sense of characters by exactly the kinds of 'spheres of action' which Propp offers:

- Is Norman going to turn out to be a helper/victim, as the scene clearing up the shower suggests?
- Is he the false hero for a while, when we may suspect he's clearing up after his mother's killing, and we

anticipate the film may turn out to be about his defence of his mad mother?

Psycho, like any detective or mystery fiction, depends on setting up characters, **codes of enigma**, and **codes of action** which mislead the audience. These will work with stereotypical features of characters' actions (whether or not a text is estimated as 'popular' or 'arty'). Does Norman's angular appearance, accentuated by lighting and camera angles in his encounters with Marion, signify 'shy young man' or 'strange neurotic'? We busily read the signs or clues, as Barthes suggests, puzzling about what's going on, what will happen next, and expecting, as Todorov suggests, the pleasure of solution with the final equilibrium or **closure**. In the case of *Psycho*, this consists of:

- Norman incarcerated and diagnosed by the psychiatrist as criminally insane
- Lila and Sam safe, but knowing now Marion is dead
- an unknown number of bodies, including those of Marion and Arbogast, in the swamp, as well as the $40,000, which the audience has probably forgotten about, just as viewers are likely to have forgotten the other secretary (played by Hitchcock's daughter) at the beginning of the film.

Story and plot in *Psycho*

Q Think back to the initial **equilibrium**. What changes would occur to the narrative if this were constructed around Norman?

A Sympathy and identification would be affected: the illusion that Mrs Bates is still alive would have to go, and Norman's madness would have to be signified. Sympathy and identification would be affected by this rearranged knowledge: for example, the plot or syuzhet could hardly begin with the arrival of Marion at the motel, since she would not yet be a character known to us, and her death would not therefore invite as much identification, and horror.

To focus on plotting and time shifts, we need to make notes on moments when the film goes into 'real time'

(i.e. when the length of time taken by events on screen corresponds almost exactly to the length of time they would take in real life). When does this happen, and why do you think it happens?

One example: when Norman discovers Marion's body, and begins to clean up the bathroom. The scene begins with his cry 'Mother! Oh God! Mother, Mother! Blood, blood!' over shots of the house and his running from it towards the motel. This comparatively long scene seems partly constructed to allow audiences to recover from the shock of the killing. The audience reaction was much more extreme when the film was first released, indeed according to Anthony Perkins, the entire scene in the hardware store following the shower murder was usually inaudible thanks to leftover howls from the previous scene. Hitchcock is even said to have asked Paramount to allow him to remix the sound to allow for the audience's reaction.

The scene also swings suspicion away from this 'nervous young man'. If audiences suspected too early on that he was the killer, it might spoil some of the 'finding out' pleasures of this mystery/thriller/horror movie.

Clearly the careful arrangement of events in the plotting is crucial to most films, even ones that don't proceed by flashback. Here, if the plot's ordering of events corresponded exactly to that of the story, we'd have a quite different kind of film, something like a psychological study of Norman. Our point of view would be affected: we'd be 'with' Norman at the beginning, and he could less easily function as the 'monster' in a horror movie, outside understanding and sympathy (a narrative role the word 'psycho' evokes in newspaper headlines).

Instead we'd be offered the pleasures of a developing understanding of this 'case history'. Knowledge, sympathy and of course possible styles of filming would be affected. In other stories using flashback, the moments when the plot goes into the past often try to elicit sympathy. In the novel *Wuthering Heights*, for example, much is revealed about Heathcliff's childhood towards the end of the narrative, when he seems almost monstrous, and the insight into his treatment in childhood suddenly swings our sympathies right round, back to him for a while (see Figure 4.1).

ACTIVITY 4.2

- Try to draw a graph or chart which will show how *Psycho* has been plotted in terms of time shifts. Draw a line that runs across the top of the graph to represent the actual time covered by the story (i.e. from Norman's childhood to his monologue in the police station. We're told he killed his parents ten years previously).

- Then draw, as the side of the graph, a line roughly representing plot or syuzhet time. This, of course, will be much less than the 10–15 years of the story. Try to proportion it according to the sections of the film, e.g. Lila and Sam set out about halfway through.

- When does the film go into flashbacks? Remember that events can be represented verbally in a film narrative, through conversations.

- What effects might these have on audience knowledge of events, or sympathy towards certain characters?

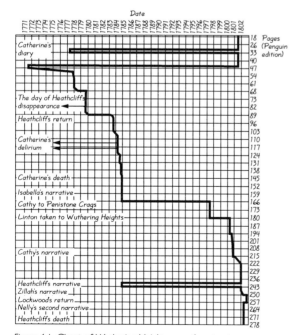

Figure 4.1 Chart of *Wuthering Heights* narrative structure

Applying Lévi-Strauss

Lévi-Strauss is less interested in the chronological plotting of a story than repeated elements and their systematic relationship, usually across many stories.

ACTIVITY 4.3

Jot down any repeated oppositions which strike you in this film, such as: dead/alive; mother/son; the past/the present.

- Do they seem to fall into a pattern that might help to account for the movie's power?

Comment Lévi-Strauss's approach has been fruitfully applied to film and TV so as to reveal their underlying patterns over a series, or whole genre (the western; *Dallas*; the gangster movie). But it is more problematic when applied to a single film such as this. Still, you may feel it helps you to understand how the plot has been structured. It might support the feeling that Mother is set up as the 'real' villain. She's the only main character (remember they can be constructed offscreen, by verbal accounts alone) whose story, or presence, or point of view we're not given. We only know her through the psychiatrist's account (very sympathetic to Norman), with phrases like 'His mother was a clinging, demanding woman' and 'Matricide is probably the most unbearable crime of all – most unbearable to the son who commits it.' Pretty uncomfortable for the mother too, but the film's plot gives us little room to feel this. Lévi-Strauss might help us see if mothers, or the malign powers of dead women, are constructed in this way in other films by Hitchcock.

Psycho as a film narrative

Like most movies, this one is told in an 'impersonal' way. The camera work and plotting do not position us with any one character's point of view. (Try to imagine it told from the point of view of Marion, or Norman, or Lila.)

And, working in the classic **continuity system**, events mostly just seem to unfold.

There are a few exceptions which prove the rule, when the camera seems to be telling the story in a more emphatic way. In the scene just after Marion has been entrusted with the $40,000, we see her dressing, the money lying on the bed. The camera, with suspenseful music on soundtrack, moves from the money to her handbag and back again, as though to offer her temptation. It's like the moment after the murder, when Norman takes a last look round the bedroom and the camera tells the story, reminding us of the money lying wrapped in a newspaper.

Though different media tell stories in different ways (what would be the literary equivalent of these shots?) some narrative effects can be shared by different media.

- The repetition of certain compositions, or musical themes, or phrases in film and TV. In *Psycho* Bernard Herrman's score works with two main repeated themes, one signifying flight and pursuit, the other resembling a series of screams (most famously in the shower scene). These are an important part of how we read the 'clues' of the narrative. They also provide formal pleasures over and above that, as we register 'a story well told', as a joke can be well or badly told.
- The repeated use of certain compositions (such as a full-screen menacing face in *Psycho*) is both a narrative and a broader formal device, rather like the use of rhyme in poetry to point up connections and contrasts, or like refrains in songs.

It may be that when we see the full-screen face of Mother near the end, it's disturbing partly because it is reminiscent of the face of the traffic policeman, his eye sockets replaced by huge sunglasses, who gives Marion (and the audience) a nasty shock early on in the movie. It's also reminiscent of Norman's face, when lit so as to hollow out his eye sockets. The two sets of associations or connotations are brought together in the final shots of the film where, if you look carefully, you will see Norman's face merge with Mother's mummified one,

then both dissolve into the image of a car being lifted from the swamp.

Critics have suggested the final shots are particularly satisfying because at the end of such a puzzling narrative we suddenly have explanation, and also an image of something coming into the light of day after so much repression and darkness. At any rate, it is a very *cinematic* narrative moment.

ACTIVITY 4.4

Look at other ways in which film and TV construct narratives (such as lighting, costume) and see how they work in this movie in a particular scene. How would you represent this scene, and these elements within it :
- on radio?
- in written form?

'Norman Bates heard a noise and a shock went through him. It sounded as though somebody was tapping on the windowpane …'

This is how the novel on which *Psycho* was based begins. How would you continue from here? How would you preserve suspense, especially around the mother's identity?

ACTIVITY 4.5

Look at the poster for the film (Figure 4.2) and say what expectations you think audiences might have had as they began this narrative.
- What is your evidence for arguing this?

Now look at the advertising hoarding for a shop sale in Vienna depicted in Figure 4.3.
- What does it suggest about the 'image' of Hitchcock, and therefore the way it works now in posters and the films themselves?

Figure 4.2 The poster used in the re-release marketing campaign which emphasised the importance of the narrative opening

Figure 4.3 Hoarding advertising the SCS store in Vienna. It reads: 'Horror prices or . . . SCS'

Synopsis

Marion Crane (Janet Leigh) and her lover Sam (John Gavin) meet in her lunch break in a hotel room, as happens whenever he can come to Phoenix. He is divorced, working in a hardware store, and since he's paying maintenance to his ex-wife, and for his father's debts, he feels they cannot afford to get married. She goes back to her work as a secretary, where her boss entrusts her with $40,000 in cash, asking her to bank it.

Later, she drives out of Phoenix with the money. After being stopped by a patrolman and exchanging her car to evade detection, she stops at a motel, run by Norman Bates (Anthony Perkins) whose mother can be glimpsed and heard in the house nearby. Unbeknown to Marion, Bates watches her undressing through a concealed hole in the wall. She seems about to return to Phoenix to confess to the theft and return the money, but is brutally stabbed to death in the shower. Norman, finding her body, puts it into a car (unwittingly also putting the money with her) which he pushes into a swamp.

Lila, Marion's sister, arrives at Sam's workplace and they begin the hunt for Marion, at the same time as Arbogast, a private detective investigating the missing $40,000, arrives on the scene. Arbogast questions Norman, who at first denies Marion's visit to the motel. Returning later to investigate further, Arbogast is brutally stabbed to death.

When he fails to return, Lila persuades Sam to accompany her to the deputy sheriff who tells them Mrs Bates has been dead for ten years, having poisoned the man she was involved with when she discovered he was married, and then killing herself. The bodies were found by Norman. We hear Norman speaking to his mother and insisting on taking her down to the cellar.

Lila and Sam check into the motel and begin to search it. Lila is shocked to discover a woman's stuffed corpse in the cellar and Norman, dressed in old-fashioned woman's clothing, enters, trying to stab her. Later, a psychiatrist explains that the now incarcerated

Norman is schizophrenic, and had murdered his possessive mother two years after his father died, as he was jealous of her lover. He had then taken on her personality, especially at times when he was attracted to a woman, as he had been to Marion.

References and further reading

Anobile, R. (ed.) (1974) *Alfred Hitchcock's* Psycho, London: Macmillan.

Cook, Pam (ed.) (1985) *The Cinema Book*, London: BFI. (See section on Narrative.)

Modleski, T. (1988) *The Women Who Knew Too Much*, London: Methuen.

Rebello, S. (1991) *Alfred Hitchcock and the Making of Psycho*, New York: Harper Perennial.

Williams, Linda (1994) 'Learning to Scream', *Sight & Sound*, December 1994.

A video of *Psycho* is available from CIC Video at 4th floor, Glenthorne House, 5–7 Hammersmith Grove, London W6 0ND. Tel. 0181 741 9773.

5 Genres

Introduction

The term 'genre' is a French word for type or kind, as in biological classifications of plants and animals. In study of the media, it involves some long-standing debates about the status of popular forms.

> Q How many folk singers does it take to change a lightbulb?
> A Four. One to change the bulb and three to sing about how good the old one was.

However simple, a lightbulb joke depends on the same kinds of knowledge and expectations as any genre product. Unless you've never heard one before, as soon as you hear the question you are likely to begin thinking in certain directions rather than others for the answer.

> Q How many Latin American secret policemen does it take to change a lightbulb?
> A Twelve. Two to change the bulb, four to shoot the witnesses, and six to deny it all to the international media.

In other words, the question will be *framed* or *categorised* for you in a certain way; it announces itself as a joke, a fiction, not a mathematical or electrical puzzle, or a serious comment on all folksingers.

> Q How many Real Men does it take to change a lightbulb?
> A Real Men aren't afraid of the dark.

If you enjoy lightbulb jokes, you will both know and not quite know what to expect from it. In other words, a *system of expectation* is set up around it, one which involves both **repetition and difference**, as in other art forms.

> Q How many psychoanalysts does it take to change a lightbulb?
> A Only one: but the lightbulb has to really want to change.

The repetition is of the bare framework: a lightbulb, a group of people about which certain stereotypes exist, and a number which relates the two in an amusing way. The difference lies in how the particular connection between those elements will be made *this* time. It's the particular combination of the three, rather than something called 'difference' alone, which makes the new joke enjoyable. As the genre becomes established, play can be made with its conventions, as in the Real Men and psychoanalysts versions. And though these jokes are not a very serious comment on folk singers, part of their pleasure is their satirical reference to well-known stereotypes, and thus to your feelings about real world groups which you may not personally know.

Media genres

Media products are divided into genres or types because production organised thus helps to minimise risk and predict expenditure in particularly volatile and unpredictable industries. TV companies, for example, depend on predictable annual income from the licence fee (BBC) or advertising (ITV companies) and find it convenient to divide up budgets according to departments like Light Entertainment, Drama, News and Current Affairs. Commercial TV also needs to be able to promise advertisers the attention of audiences at predictable times of day and night, for which regularly scheduled genre slots are invaluable.

Genre	Number of films	1993 Units shipped (000)	Sales ($m)
Action adventure	17	3,115	186.3
Comedy	47	6,554	392.1
Drama	71	9,020	539.7
Family/animation	8	1,500	89.7
Foreign-language	19	257	15.4
Horror	13	1,695	101.4
SF/fantasy	3	625	37.4
Thriller	24	3,940	235.7
Western	3	1,005	60.1

Figure 5.1 US video releases by genre in 1993

Source: Paul Kagan Associates, published in *Screen International* 21/10/94

So in terms of economics, audiences for genres are created as targets for advertising, or for other kinds of profitability. But they are not thereby rendered the helpless mass, duped into consumption, as some theories suggest. They quickly develop sophisticated (though usually implicit) expectations of the genres they enjoy.

In an attempt to target ever more specialised, small segments or niches of the potential audience (see Chapter 9, 'Advertising, Marketing and Fashion'), media forms have become more and more cross-generic recently, as different kinds of music, TV and film clash and mix genres which were previously held apart: comedy-horror, cyberpunk. Nevertheless, media products are still marketed according to generic categories.

ACTIVITY 5.1

Next time you are in the book or music sections of two major book retailers, W. H. Smiths or Menzies, note the different genres announced by album/CD covers and book categories: romance, gardening, thriller and so on.

● What seem to be the **signifiers** of particular genres?

Zap through the channels on your TV or radio. Look at title sequences.

● How quickly are you able to tell what kind of programme or music is on offer?
● How were you able to tell? What kinds of differences get signalled through music, colours, kinds of dialogue, voices, pace of editing, etc.?

Try turning down the sound on the title sequence of a TV genre and substituting another kind of music.

● What difference does this make?
● Can you tell gardening programmes from motor racing coverage just by the title music for example?

Why study genre?

Though most of us are able to operate *genre awareness* in this quick and easy way, media theorists have been interested in the idea of genre because of:

● its importance in understanding the *low status* of mass-produced media products in relation to *higher status* art forms;
● its capacity to help us understand the nature of **categorisation** and the role of repetition and difference in this;
● its focus on how *entertainment* or **escapist** forms might work to organise and perhaps narrow the frames, the expectations through which we understand and imagine the world and its social possibilities. But where does the term 'genre' come from?

The term 'genre'

The first person to use the term in the context of art was the Greek philosopher **Aristotle**, who tried to divide literary output (which then consisted mostly of performances) into groups or types (tragedy, comedy, drama, epic, lyric) and then to rank them.

Unlike many modern writers, he was not interested in ranking according to difference (as we are, implicitly, when we come out of a movie praising it for being 'a bit different from your average action adventure/ horror/ romance ...'). Aristotle was much more interested in valuing a performance, not for its novelty, but for how well the genre's rules had been *obeyed* or acted out.

This remained a major standard of classical value in European art for many centuries, though by the late eighteenth century, ideas of novelty and originality were becoming bound up with higher artistic valuations.

A good example of the battles for the right to claim cultural status for mass media products is the history of the term 'genre' in Film Studies. By the time it entered this field, in the mid-1960s and early 1970s, it was a term used *of* (though not always *by*) the Hollywood studios to describe the organisation of their production and marketing. It is easier to co-ordinate huge business ventures if resources are categorised into production lines: musicals, horror films, comedy and so on. In turn, such categories mean that the publicising and reviewing of films can be more efficiently organised, even down to particular **stars**' associations with certain genres: Meg Ryan as promise of slightly 'kooky' romantic comedy for instance.

Repetition, art, industry

One of the most widespread ways of dismissing genre, entertainment or **popular** forms is the charge that 'They're all the same' or 'If you've seen one, you've seen them all.' It's easy to feel this about genres that don't engage us. The accusation bolsters suspicion of popular media in several ways.

Movies, pop music, TV are seen as being a lower kind of cultural production to 'true art' simply because they involve industrial production. Critics and academics, especially in Britain, have long been suspicious of such capitalist industries, and have implied that 'true art' takes place outside them. Such suspicion still surfaces (along with imagery from the low-status activities of women in the kitchen) in the metaphors used to dismiss genre products, emphasising repetition and sameness, as though films were just like the output of any other factory – or kitchen. It's a suspicion based not in (often valid) objections to the ways profit-led industries tend to treat the people who work for them, but in nineteenth-century images of a Real Artist or Author as someone working alone, often against the grain, and in a pre-industrial way. (See 'Independents and Alternatives', Chapter 27.)

ACTIVITY 5.2

Look at the review section of any current newspaper or magazine.

- How many terms like the following can you find: run of the mill/recipe/served up/fodder/staple diet/stock/formula/junk food culture/pap/the Dream Factory/churned out like baked beans ...?

'The hedonistic but passive barbarian who rides in a fifty horsepower bus for threepence to see a five million dollar film for one and eight is not simply a social oddity; he is a portent.'

(Hoggart, 1958)

a 'shiny barbarism'... 'the ceaseless exploitation of a hollow brightness'... 'a spiritual dry-rot'... a 'Candy Floss World'

(Hoggart, 1958)

'The musical has always been my favourite film genre. It has the peculiar capacity to create bubbles in time: there are people, going about their business, then suddenly erupting into song and dance in extravagantly expanded moments of emotion while the narrative stands still.'

(Williamson, 1987)

Ernst Bloch (1885–1977)
German Marxist cultural theorist of Utopian impulses in art *(The Principle of Hope*, 1954–59, written during exile in USA).

Mikhail Bakhtin (name thought by many to have been adopted by V. N. Volosinov during the Stalinist purges of 1930s and 1940s) wrote on sixteenth-century carnival as expression of desires to 'turn the world upside down', as a moment of Utopian celebration.

Added to such long-established stereotypes, Hollywood had the disadvantage, for British and European critics, of being American. It was part of an increasingly successful competitor for world markets, and a nation often perceived as composed of upstarts and emigrants from Europe who couldn't quite speak proper English.

Because its products (like those of TV, or the pop music industry) were intended above all to entertain audiences for an evening between one day's work and the next, rather than to be pondered over for all time, Hollywood was assumed to be incapable of producing anything worthy of serious attention, let alone anything artistic or realistic. Genre films were also, contradictorily, felt to be *both*:

- the carriers of capitalist **propaganda** or ideology *and yet*
- pernicious because they encouraged audiences to escape from serious questions via fantasy.

Dyer (1973) argued that entertainment or genre forms are pleasurable (the hostile term would be escapist) precisely because they allow a kind of fantasy escape from a reality experienced as full of scarcity, alienation, into a world coded as abundant, energetic, transparent, intense and with moments of community. Following the Russian literary theorists **Bloch** and **Bakhtin**, he called them **Utopian** pleasures, not in the sense that they literally represent or speak about Utopias, but that key moments and qualities of the genres represent parts of the fantasy of such escapes from grinding reality. This need not always be into the obvious escapism of the musical. Dyer argued that in westerns, for example, Utopian elements might consist of chases, pounding music and fights exemplifying *energy*; the expansive landscape as *abundance*; the 'face out' and much of the confrontational dialogue might make up *intensity*, while the morally unambiguous hero of most 'classic' westerns embodies *transparency*. Finally, the townships and the cowboy camaraderie he argued make up the Utopian category *community*.

ACTIVITY 5.3

Look at the chart in Figure 5.2. Using these categories:

- Can you find any or all of these Utopian qualities in a contemporary genre product?
- See if they seem to work for morning DJs or hospital drama series, for example.

social tension/inadequacy/absence	utopian solution
Scarcity (actual poverty in the society; poverty observable in the surrounding societies, e.g. Third World); unequal distribution of wealth	Abundance (elimination of poverty for self and others; equal distribution of wealth)
Exhaustion (work as a grind, alienated labour, pressures of urban life)	Energy (work and play synonymous), city dominated (*On the Town*) or pastoral return (*The Sound of Music*)
Dreariness (monotony, predictability, instrumentality of the daily round)	Intensity (excitement, drama, affectivity of living)
Manipulation (advertising, bourgeois democracy, sex roles)	Transparency (open, spontaneous, honest communications and relationships)
Fragmentation (job mobility, rehousing and development, high-rise flats, legislation against collective action)	Community (all together in one place, communal interests, collective activity)

Figure 5.2 Dyer's Utopian chart (1977)

Jane Tompkins (1992) has argued that the Utopian pleasures of novels and films of 'the west' (for women as well as men) are bound up with the offer of seriousness, of imagining yourself in a boundary situation, in a place that will put you to some kind of ultimate test. The 'escape' here is argued as being from an existence where work is not serious or satisfying enough. This is a point worth thinking about in connection with assertions that some genres are more **realistic** or serious than others, which are 'simply' escapist, and therefore **trivial**.

Others, like Jackie Stacey (1993), have argued Dyer's categories need to be thought through more specifically, in relation to gender, class, ethnicity and different historical periods. But they are still a valuable way to understand the pleasures of genre or entertainment forms.

Trivial From the Latin *tres*, meaning three, and *via* meaning way, trivia originally referred to the place where three roads met …The modern sense of trivial – commonplace, ordinary, of small account, trifling, inconsiderable – may have been influenced by the crossroads being a place where women met to exchange news.

(Mills 1991)

Repetition and difference

The 1960s and 1970s justifications of Hollywood were often achieved either through claims that directors could be seen as authors, just like 'real' artists, or through claims that 'the real world' was somehow allowed to speak through certain particularly important and unusual films. Such positions allowed **Hollywood cinema** to be taken seriously, but produced a very negative view of film genres, seen as just the studio's requirements for repetition ('we need another western') which the True Author would have to struggle to subvert.

A key term here is repetition. There's clearly some truth in the charge that genre production works to repeat and contain certain elements or combination of elements within forms. Hollywood studios were economically driven from the early twentieth century onwards, via the link-up between banks and film studios, to guarantee a regular flow of production to ensure cinemas full of paying customers ready to come back again for more.

Very few of us go to the cinema, or buy CDs, or watch soaps simply for the reassurance of repetition. However pleasurable it is to see or hear a well-loved convention, or track played out, or to feel 'I knew that was going to happen', the entertainment industries have to balance repetition and difference to produce the **pleasure**, which is what we buy when we purchase a new CD, or a ticket to the cinema.

> Even the satisfaction of feeling 'I knew that was going to happen' surely depends on it not seeming all that obvious?

ACTIVITY 5.4

Take your favourite **soap**, record an episode and when you play it back, stop the recording at a key moment for the plot. Now try to predict, to write the script for what happens next.

● How easy was it to do this?

● Were you right in your prediction?

● What does this suggest about repetitiveness and genre products?

Critics of popular forms often imply that they would prefer each product to be utterly different. But if any story, or video game, or melody were utterly different to all others, we would have no means by which to understand it.

Example

Reservoir Dogs (US 1992) was praised for its 'difference' and 'originality' when it came out. But these were dependent on generic sameness. It played with and against the expectations of the male-centred action adventure movie: a crime; intense relationships exclusively between men; violence. Within this context, the pacing and arrangement of the plot, the importance given to a quirky kind of dialogue, the handling of violence, the use of pop music and so on could be experienced as comprehensible 'difference'.

Repetition as a 'boo word' is mostly used against entertainment forms, or of 'failed' high cultural forms. Shakespearean tragedy, or opera, is said to have 'conventions', 'archetypes', and to 'brilliantly rework' already existing stories.

Myth and genre

In the 1960s popular narratives (like the James Bond films and books) began to be read, via the structuralist approaches of **Lévi-Strauss** and **Propp**, as though they were the myth systems of modern societies (see Chapter 1, 'Images and Languages'). Jim Kitses in *Horizons West* (1969) and Will Wright in *Six Guns and Society* (1975), for example, worked on the western assuming that:

- films work like myths which seek to explain a society to its members
- in such storytelling, certain patterns emerge, especially oppositions, which reveal how a society feels about issues important to it at certain times.

Jim Kitses, using Lévi-Strauss's approach to the myths of pre-industrial cultures via 'structuring oppositions', studied the western for such categories as Wilderness vs. Civilisation, Individual vs. Community, Nature vs. Culture and so on.

ACTIVITY 5.5
Jot down any ways in which the last genre product (film, TV serial, album track) you encountered worked with such oppositions.

Will Wright (1975) took a group of commercially successful westerns and assumed because they were box office successes they could be treated as working like myths. He argued a progression through changes in their typical plots, analysed according to Propp's functions and roles (see Chapter 3, 'Narratives'). The **classical** western (such as *Shane* (US 1953)) corresponded to the individualistic conception of society underlying a market economy, where the loner will happily come to the aid of 'society'. The later *vengeance plot* (as in *The Searchers* (US 1956)) begins to reflect changes in that economy, with society becoming less worthy of defending. Finally (for 1975) the *professional western* (Italian or 'spaghetti westerns' – see 'Going West' case study, Chapter 6) was argued to reflect the values of a planned, corporate economy where only a mercenary professionalism counts.

Such ambitious studies were attempts to have popular genres taken seriously, though many important problems have since been raised about them:

- If the stories in any genre are reduced to a single list of common, supposedly mythic functions, what happens to the specific pleasures of such genres – music, actors, voices, whatever?
- The term 'reflect' is often a sign that the actual, complex linkages between something called 'society' and something else called 'art' or 'culture' have not been fully argued. There are several 'intermediate' levels, such as star images, changes in audience composition, the relationship of a particular genre to technologies, the availability of texts and so on, which make a simple connection of 'society' to 'myth' unsatisfying.
- In particular, there is the difficulty in arguing that box-office takings (with different prices, publicity campaigns, other attractions, etc.) can be a direct and reliable indicator of a film's myth status for something as complex as modern social orders.
- Wright seems interested only in some myths, not in others. Where, for example, is there any consideration of gender in his account of the western?

Mythic approaches can sometimes seem like a variant on the 'sameness' or 'repetition' emphasis on popular cultural forms ('They're so much the same that we can treat them all as one slowly evolving mythic story').

Repertoires of elements

The most important recent development in thinking about familiar entertainment genres was to put them into the context of audiences' understandings and activities. Genres are no longer seen as sets of fixed elements but as working with '**repertoires of elements**' or fluid systems of conventions and expectations. These are shared by film-makers and audiences, who are *both* active on *both* sides of meaning-making, though often in ways that go unvoiced, until they are studied and thought about.

These conventions and expectations include the areas of:

- narrative
- audio-visual codes (for which the term **iconography** is often used)
- ideological themes.

For example, science fiction (comics, books, TV series, films, video games) will often (though not always) work through narratives whose starting point, or initial disruption, will be a situation set up in terms of global themes and **ideological** issues such as those raised by a highly technological and class-stratified future, perhaps posing questions like:

'It's unusual for a woman who starts out wearing pants, carrying a gun and riding a horse to be still doing so at the end of the movie. Suitably re-clad in dress or skirt, she prepares to take her place in the family, leaving adventure to the men' (Buscombe 1988: 241). Is this still true of westerns?

Iconography comes from art history. There it refers to emblem books of the fifteenth and sixteenth centuries guiding artists as to the correct colours, gestures, facial expressions, etc. with which to encode Christian doctrine. Since cinema and TV work with music, lighting, editing as well as gesture, etc., the term 'signification' is probably more useful.

What is the difference between a human being and a cyborg? How is the law to be enforced in such social orders ? This narrative will probably proceed in the manner of an action adventure or detective fiction, with violent encounters between adversaries, chases, fights, puzzles to be solved, often to do with technology, and an ending which resolves a mystery or defeats a villain associated with hi-tech.

In the area of the audio-visual, the experienced reader of the 1990s may reasonably expect certain kinds of spectacle, often to do with hi-tech machinery, futuristic cityscapes, or visualisations of the results of global

Figure 5.3 Comic book dystopic still

pollution (as in the *Robocop* films (US 1987, 1992) or *Judge Dredd* (US 1995). Part of the excitement or mysterious atmosphere will be created by particular types of music, often electronic. Certain stars, usually, though not always male, and associated with 'high action' movies, may also be linked to the genre, like Schwarzenegger or, more recently, Stallone.

On the other hand, the **romance** genre, whether in novel, or photoplay, TV or film form, will work with narratives whose starting point will often be the arrival into the life of the female hero of a male who, shall we say, interests her romantically. This sets in play issues such as the nature of intimate relations between men and women, and expectations about the family, work and marriage. The narrative will often proceed by means of intimate conversations and encounters, coincidences, mistakes and so on, delaying and thus intensifying the audience's desire for the couple(s) to 'get it together', and usually ending happily in terms of the central, romantic relationship. *Casablanca* (US 1942) plays with the elements in combination with those of a political thriller, and a male central character, while *The Piano* (New Zealand 1993) is an example of an 'art' film by an independent female director which also uses these generic elements.

At the level of the audio-visual, there are different traditions than for science fiction: lavish clothes and domestic settings; much greater use of close-ups, especially focused on the eyes, for male and female actors; less use of fetishised shots of women's bodies; certain styles of intimate acting and dialogue; use of female stars in strong roles; all amplified by a particular kind of music: sweeping chords, piano and string sections of the orchestra.

A famous moment from a key **gangster** movie captured in Figure 5.4 illustrates the crystallisation of elements from the gangster repertoire, some the result of the pressure of censorship bodies on Hollywood to 'punish the gangster' (a very popular figure in Depression America's cinema) by public death (usually on the street).

- The policeman represents this public calling to account, while the woman, often cradling the gangster's head or otherwise mourning his fate, perhaps embodies our own affection for him, as well as being an echo of the ethnically marked (Irish or Italian) mother of earlier gangster films, worrying about his violent career.
- The church steps have, for experienced gangster film fans, the resonance of repentance from earlier years of the genre, as well as providing a sumptuous setting for a tableau or frozen expressive moment, which Hollywood inherited from stage melodrama.
- In the moments just before this death, the Cagney character has climbed them partway, then staggered down them, perhaps acting out

In 1982 alone 250 million women bought a Mills and Boon book. Though this trend sems to have peaked in the mid-1980s, in 1987 a quarter of all books read by women in the UK were 'romance fiction'.

Figure 5.4 Death tableau from *The Roaring Twenties* (US 1939)

the rise-and-fall narrative structure so often shaping gangster films, sometimes for reasons of censorship. (See Jenkins (1982).)

Art cinema is often viewed as the place where individual directors manage to express themselves in non-US national cinemas far from Hollywood. But some critics have suggested that art cinema can be approached as a genre itself, though one whose defining feature is that it tries not to look like genre cinema, in fact it is defined by its difference to whatever Hollywood is defined as being at the time. The repertoire of elements which make up this cinematic genre could be cited as:

- less action-oriented styles of shooting, editing and narrative
- unresolved narratives rather than the closure of entertainment forms
- an emphasis on the director's authoring presence
- self-conscious reference to Hollywood.

'If it's in focus it's pornography; if it's out of focus it's art cinema' (graffiti).

Genre boundaries, culture, ideologies

Any categorisation, like genre, makes a difference to interpretation.

ACTIVITY 5.6

Discuss in a group, if possible, what your response would be to watching someone being beaten up:

- in a cartoon film
- in an action adventure film

- on the TV news
- in a documentary.

What does the discussion suggest about genre knowledge and interpretation?

Some genres are surprisingly difficult to separate. Science fiction is closer to horror than might appear at first sight by the different iconographies or audio-visual resources of each: futuristic hi-tech special effects in one; gore and monstrous bodies in the other. But both share

Figure 5.5 Frame from *Judge Dredd* (US 1995)

elements such as mad scientists, terrified victims, bizarre experiments, monsters. And both have been amenable to comic strip representation, not needing big budgets to imagine possibly grotesque developments, exaggerated characters and action sequences.

The bulk of this chapter has tried to argue that cultural forms require **innovation** and not simply repetition. Yet a key question remains: what kinds of innovation are unacceptable in commercial genres? And acceptable to whom? Hollywood is often said to have been simply interested in 'telling a good story'. So what about the point made by some critics that genres actually work to 'police' the boundaries of what audiences can enjoy or connect? Might genre conventions take the pressure off film and TV makers to find unconventional answers to the often acute problems symbolised in film or TV narratives? Such 'obvious' boundaries can make us accept statements like: 'The audience wants a happy ending' or 'But you can't have a political film ending like that.'

Censorship operations exist not only in the HUAC (House UnAmerican Activities Committee) investigations of leftist work in Hollywood during the 1940s and 1950s, or TV's controllers banning programmes. They also consist of a spectrum of assumptions about acceptable activities within particular genres which can be invoked to suppress or dismiss. During the years of struggle against apartheid and its effects on sport in South Africa, it 'just wasn't done' for cricket commentators to bring such politics into their coverage. Some generic mixes, such as **drama-documentary** or the related form **'infotainment'** (where information and entertainment forms are mixed, as in *Oprah Winfrey* style chat shows), often provoke anxiety in critics and audiences, especially if controversial areas are being explored through them. Censorship can take place in 'the nicest possible way', by such forms being called a 'mishmash' or 'inappropriate mix' (of generic conventions). Certain genres have been taken as the place where some but not other closely related kinds of activity are fictionalised and handled. In TV, for example, recent events in the real world are categorised as part of the **news genre**. After a certain time, though, such events are classified as 'history' and come under quite different rules, notably involving less need for impartiality.

ACTIVITY 5.7

Do you think it is right to talk of 'the news genre'?
- If so, list its repertoire of elements.
- What variations are possible within them?

A cultural or ideological approach to genres is interested in these questions. It asks whether the repetitions within genres, and, equally important, the imaginings they exclude as well as the ones they encourage, reinforce dominant and sometimes oppressive sets of values. Much **feminist** work has been interested in how genres have been given very different valuations, partly depending on the sex of their majority audiences. This often involves economic and studio power to command budgets (more westerns have been made than any other kind of film) and perhaps in turn to construct greater respect for such male genres. The 'woman's film' or photoplay or romance TV series, however, is still mostly ridiculed by critics. Yet this is one of the few genres where it is possible to imagine dilemmas and changes in a key part of most people's lives: the area of intimate emotions. This has arguably contributed to the sense that 'the private' and 'the public' are completely separate, and have very different kinds of importance.

On the other hand, such fictions have been argued to limit the extent to which women are allowed to imagine themselves as assertive, as involved in politics or public life, for example (see Chapter 7, 'Representations').

A note on verisimilitude

Although all genres, from TV news to heavy metal music, are constructed, working with codes and conventions, some of them are perceived as having more **verisimilitude**, or connection to the 'real', than others. This makes a key difference to assumptions as to what their ideological work might be. For example, the first step taken by many media campaigners on excessive violence on TV is to mistake how connected to reality are genres like cartoons for their audiences. (See Chapter 15, 'Realisms' and Chapter 29, 'Audiences'.)

This 'real-seemingness', the ways that media forms will use systems of what seems 'real', 'likely' or 'probable' in texts, involves two areas:
- the genre's relationship to expectations about the rest of the real world
- sets of expectations which are internal to the genre, such as how a 'proper' or 'real' police series or strip cartoon should proceed, or what realistic acting consists of. (See the rather mannered appearance of early Method performances, hailed at the time as breathtakingly realistic.)

The writer of *Underworld* (1926), Ben Hecht, had once been a journalist and wrote: 'As a newspaper man ... I had learned that nice people ... loved criminals, doted on reading about their love problems as well as their sadism.'

In relation to the real world, for example, the gangster film or 'courtroom drama' has always been taken more seriously than, say, the musical, because it makes more reference to public/political events in the historical world outside the film, by using newspaper headlines, naming real-life politicians or criminals, and so on. In its style of filming, the gangster genre has traditionally worked in black and white (often seen as closer to the codes of documentary and history), and until relatively recently (it is part of how *The Godfather* films reworked the genre) made little use of the flamboyant colour, camera angles and movements enjoyed by fans of the musical (and felt to be 'unrealistic' by non-fans). Similarly the happy ending of a 'real' musical is not felt to be realistic in a gangster movie, even though it seems many real-life gangsters are alive and well and living in expectation of a comfortable death. (Though *Goodfellas* (US 1990) was felt to revive the genre partly by representing this situation.)

What complicates things even more is that in a media-image saturated culture, the conventions of fictional genres are often used not just in advertising, but also to make news stories more vivid. The alleged serial killer Frederick West's home is called 'The House of Horror' in tabloid headlines, triggering that genre's resonances. News and documentary stories of the struggles against the Mafia in Italy in 1994–5 regularly used references to, music from, even shots that resembled *The Godfather* gangster films, in order to add glamour to the story in a ratings-conscious TV system. Such images often feed back into the 'reality effect' of the next gangster movie or TV series, and so on, in the process called **intertextuality**.

References and further reading

Altman, Rick (1989) *The American Film Musical,* London: BFI.

Barker, Martin (1989) *Comics: Ideology, Power and the Critics,* Manchester: Manchester University Press.

Bourdieu, Pierre (1980) 'The Aristocracy of Culture', reprinted in R. Collins, J. Curran, N. Garnham, P. Scannell, P. Schlesinger, and C. Sparks (eds) *Media, Culture & Society: A Critical Reader*, London and Beverly Hills: Sage.

Buscombe, Ed (ed.) (1988) *The BFI Companion to the Western,* London: Andre Deutsch/BFI.

Dyer, Richard (1973) 'Entertainment and Utopia', in *Only Entertainment* (1992), London: Routledge.

Feuer, Jane (1982) *The American Film Musical,* London: BFI.

Gledhill, Christine (ed.) (1987) *Home Is Where the Heart Is,* London: BFI.

Goodwin, Andrew and Whannel, Gary (1990) *Understanding Television,* London: Routledge.

Hoggart, Richard (1958) *The Uses of Literacy,* London: Pelican.

Jenkins, Steve (1982) *The Death of the Gangster,* London: BFI.

Kaplan, E. Ann (ed.) (1979) *Women in Film Noir,* London: BFI.

Kitses, J. (1969) *Horizons West,* London: Thames & Hudson/BFI.

McArthur, Colin (1972) *Underworld USA,* London: BFI/Secker and
Warburg.

Mills, Jane (1991) *Womanwords*, London: Virago.

Neale, Steve (1990) 'Questions of genre', *Screen,* vol. 31, no. 1.

Pirie, David (ed.) (1981) *Anatomy of the Movies,* London: Windward.

Stacey, Jackie (1993) *Star Gazing: Hollywood Cinema and Female
Spectatorship,* London: Routledge.

Tompkins, Jane (1992) *West of Everything: The Inner Life of Westerns,*
Oxford: Oxford University Press.

Williamson, Judith (1987) 'Music While You Work', *New Statesman,* 27
March.

Wollen, Peter (1992) *Singin' in the Rain,* London: BFI Classics.

Wright, W. (1975) *Six Guns and Society: A Structural Study of the Western,*
Berkeley: University of California Press.

6 / Case study: Going West

More westerns have been produced than any other kind of studio film. Their echoes have become a naturalised part of jeans, fashion and cigarette advertising imagery, as well as country music, novels, and American language.

'a great sense . . . of this as a new frontier . . . there aren't any frontiers except this one . . . and this is a frontier that's expanding every day . . .'
   (Kevin Kelly of *Wired* on the Internet, *Guardian*, 15 May 1995)

'Greg May lives in a tunnel under a fashionable part of Manhattan: "I'm a survivalist, a frontiersman."'
   (*Observer*, 'Life', 16 July 1995)

Each episode of *Star Trek* began: 'Space – the final frontier.'

They seem a good area to test out your understandings of the issues raised by theories of genre.

Applying 'repertoires of elements' to westerns

Like any genre, the western is not composed of fixed plots, locations, characters, etc. but of repertoires or collections of elements and expectations. Typical **narrative** patterns begin with an act of violence as disruption to status quo or initial equilibrium. This sets in flow events often focused on **ideological** themes such as conflicts around law and order, especially as these involve questions of gender (perhaps in the form of 'protecting the women') or of nationhood (America usually defined and defended against 'the Indians'). The enigmas of the narrative will rarely be, as in a detective film, a matter of 'Who did it?' but probably 'How will he take revenge?' Typical narrative situations within this might be 'the shoot out' on the street, the conflict between two kinds of women ('saloon-girl' and 'school marm') for the hero, the letter from far away which arrives and is followed by a flashback to the writer – and so on.

In the area of the audio-visual, typical historical setting and costume for the western often stretch from 1840 to 1890 or so, while the location can be almost anywhere – except for East Coast city streets. Certain stars, such as Clint Eastwood, are strongly associated with the western and its terse-lipped dialogue and acting styles. Familiar objects accruing resonance (sometimes called iconography) in westerns include, unsurprisingly, guns, stetson hats, horses. The overall 'look' of the genre has often been 'high, wide and handsome', employing **CinemaScope** or other widescreen **formats**, sometimes using **deep-focus** lenses, and a golden tinted, **Technicolor** look – all of which help to display to advantage the landscape, which acts almost like another character.

Music for westerns is often a combination of 'military' or 'state occasion' rhythms, instruments and chords, as in the 'New World' Symphony of Dvořák, with perhaps the gentler sounds which signify 'campfire', and voices reminiscent of the related country music genre.

These typical features represent the broad predictability of the genre. But what about difference? For every item on the list you could probably think of exceptions. Some celebrated westerns such as *High*

Noon (US 1952) or *The Left-handed Gun* (US 1958) have been in black and white. Recent westerns, partly targeting a female audience, have centred on female heroes, such as *Even Cowgirls Get the Blues* (US 1994) or *The Ballad of Little Jo* (US 1993). Interestingly, once this happens, the narratives often take on a very different shape, much less focused on the climactic male violent shoot-out. And so on.

Sometimes, for experienced audiences, the smallest changes can signal connections to contemporary issues. *The Outlaw Josey Wales* (US 1976) is one of the first westerns to call Native American characters 'guerrillas'. The brutal treatment of Native American guerrilla characters in *Ulzana's Raid* (US 1972) was also taken by many to be referring to America's involvement in Vietnam.

Let's look at how such issues work in a famous example of the genre.

Example 1: *The Searchers* (US 1956)

If you have not seen *The Searchers*, here is a synopsis:

Texas 1868 (i.e. three years after the end of the Civil War). Ethan Edwards/John Wayne returns to his brother Aaron's home, evasive about what he has been doing in the intervening years. While he is out with a posse to investigate the presence of 'marauding Indians', the homestead is attacked, Aaron and his wife and son are killed, and their two daughters abducted by the Comanches. Ethan and his adoptive nephew Martin pursue Scar and his Comanche band for several years, Martin becoming increasingly worried that Ethan's desire for revenge will mean the death of his niece Debbie, whom Ethan sees as polluted and no longer related 'by blood' by having become one of Scar's squaws. Helped, albeit incompetently, by the US cavalry, the two attack the Comanche camp where Scar is first killed by Martin and then scalped by Ethan. Ethan pursues Debbie but instead of killing her takes her home, though he himself returns to his solitary wanderings.

Comment on synopsis

When you have seen the movie, you will realise how much this verbal account (as with any film: recall the *Psycho* case study (Chapter 4)) reduces its meanings and pleasurable processes. Genre forms are often dismissed by plot summaries: witty TV reviewers summarising the events of a soap episode outside the context of fans' close knowledge of the characters for example.

In many ways the film does seem to contain the 'stock' or 'classic' (depending on your valuation of the genre) elements of the western. These include:

1 **narrative**
- centred around a strong and violent male, played by John Wayne
- initiated by an act of violence against that male or which comes to concern him
- shaped by revenge, ending in a bloody but visually compelling climactic shoot-out, plus a final, brief, more domestically centred but less compelling coda.

2 **ideological** *themes* such as
- the defence of 'America' against the 'Other' in the form of the Comanches
- gender assumptions, such as the unspeakable acts the Comanches are constructed as perpetrating on 'white women', as well as the confinement of women to the home and domestic sphere, while men inhabit the film/genre's central area of the exciting but dangerous wilderness
- questions of law and order, especially in the conflicts between Ethan and other characters (such as Martin Pawley/Jeff Hunter and Rev. Clayton/Ward Bond) about how far he should go in his pursuit of vengeance.

Audio-visually it works with the familiar elements of Monument Valley and other desert settings. Though the shots of Monument Valley are particularly spectacular, and composed in very 'painterly' ways, the mixture of long shots and close-ups is typical of many westerns, and works in combination with the kinds of music and voices described above.

Yet it is clear that simply listing elements to tick them off against an imaginary list of components of 'the ideal western' is not only boring, but does not begin to explore the different ways those elements can be combined or articulated together differently. Nor, when the movie is considered in detail, can the neat listing of elements explain how it actually moves and 'works'.

> 'Articulation' is a term used to involve a play on both senses of the word: articulate as in 'speak' or even 'make clear', and also articulate as in 'articulated lorry', where there is a sense of different parts being combined in particular ways in order to move together.

Ethnicity

Take, for example, the treatment of 'Indian' or Native American characters. The conventions of many westerns were bound up with mythologies and brutal practices that confirmed white America's 'destiny': the right to drive out and even exterminate the original inhabitants of the continent. The original Americans are often represented as marauding savages with very little access to either soundtrack, culture or good sense.

ACTIVITY 6.1
The next time you see a 'classic' western (i.e. produced between 1930 and 1960), make notes on how Native Americans are represented in it. As with any group whose representation (see Chapter 7 on Representations) you are studying, look at the following points:
- How much access are they given to soundtrack and dialogue?
- Is there subtitling when they are signified as speaking their own language?
- Are they given full characterisation or set up as minor, highly stereotyped figures?
- If characterised, along what lines? Rational? Honourable? Intelligent? Attractive? Worthy opponents?

- Or are they constructed as 'deserving' their fate?
- Is the audience invited to identify with them by means of camera positioning, plot construction, casting, etc.?

But *The Searchers*, released in 1956, seems to deploy these conventions with some criticisms. For example, it seems at first that the attack by Indians on the small white band early in the film will proceed as it does in *Stagecoach* (US 1939) and scores of other westerns: motiveless Comanches swoop from their (unfairly advantaged) site high in the mountains, making incomprehensible sounds, and being defeated by the vastly outnumbered whites. Here, however, though they do appear from 'on high', they make a long march alongside the whites before breaking into an attack. This, and the cross cutting between the two sides over the river, including discussion of religious rituals, gives some sense of two parallel cultures. As does the first meeting between Scar and Ethan, where some weight is given to cultural difference via the need for translation.

Again, later in the film, Indian prisoners are shown being taken into camp, as the soundtrack music modulates from jaunty cavalry march to a sadder version of the same, as though from the Native Americans' side.

ACTIVITY 6.2
Before going on to consider Ethan/Wayne's role, make notes on the rest of the film, considering how far you think it challenges conventional representations of the Native Americans, using the list from Activity 6.1.

Ethan/Wayne is certainly the Proppian hero figure, both by the narrative/audio-visual structures which centre on him, and the casting of a major star in the role. But the character has been called an 'anti-hero' and is *partly* criticised as racist, with Wayne's acting style much less genial than in some earlier films. Ethan is antagonistic to his companion, Martin, on grounds of his mixed race, and expresses such knowledge and hatred of the Comanches that some critics have suggested a fascination bordering on obsession with them, and even described Scar as being like a 'crazy mirror of Ethan's desires' (McBride and Wilmington 1974).

The Searchers: genre and authorship

A familiar way of dismissing genre products is to argue that the 'good' ones are only ever made by remarkably gifted authors who have struggled successfully *against* genre conventions. John Ford was one of the first beneficiaries of this position, and *The Searchers* is argued to exemplify his innovations. Certainly he had such a long track record in the western that changes within his own work and in the genre are almost impossible to disentangle. A synopsis making these authorship emphases would begin:

> Ethan/Wayne returns to his brother's house in 1868. Neither cavalry officer nor community leader, possibly a criminal, he is John Ford's first anti-hero. A suppressed love is implied between Ethan and his brother's wife – unthinkable in earlier Ford – but brother, wife and a son are killed.
>
> (Slightly adapted from Buscombe 1988.)

Such an approach underestimates the contributions of the 'stock company' which Ford gathered round him (actors, writers, etc.) and the networks of contributions from, but also other ways of accounting for a film's 'differences' from, the supposed norm. For example, it was produced by one of the independent production companies – C.V. Whitney Pictures Inc. – becoming more common in Hollywood as a response to economic uncertainty and the competition from TV in the late 1940s.

> 'The flavour will be relished by your patrons satiated with the mediocrities of television.'
>
> (Warner's campaign book to exhibitors of *The Searchers*)

Massively advertised, the film was marketed as the start of 'The American Series' of films from the new company about American history, and was categorised not as a western (which was then still a despised genre) but as a drama. C.V. Whitney Pictures also emphasised its desire to make 'art' and 'finer entertainment', which perhaps enabled/necessitated a certain difference in the film's treatment of established elements, and the use of such high status workers as Max Steiner, whose musical score is key to the film's sweeping power.

Maximilian Raoul Steiner (1888–1971) Composer on many of Hollywood's most celebrated movies, including *Gone With the Wind, Now, Voyager* and *Casablanca.* His career exemplifies some of the crossover connections of high and popular (or genre) forms in the years of the studio system. A musical prodigy, he graduated from Vienna's Imperial Academy of Music at 13, after completing the eight-year course in one year. He studied under Mahler, became a professional conductor aged 16, then emigrated to the US in 1914 to orchestrate and conduct Broadway musicals and then Hollywood films.

Also part of this competitive 'difference' was the decision to make it in the then new **VistaVision** screen format (see Chapter 19, 'Developing widescreen technology'). This clearly provided an impetus to the film's spectacular use of landscape, which in the western anyway is often imbued with connotations of American history.

When the film came out, however, some puzzlement was expressed at Ethan's character. Some critics seemed to be struggling to describe attitudes (racist) outside the political vocabulary of the time. Brian Henderson (1985) has argued that we need to explore the film's *historical context* to understand its resonances for some 1956 US audiences. It is an adaptation of a novel (written by Alan LeMay) published in 1954. During the time the screenplay was being written, an important event in the

Civil Rights struggles of Afro-Americans was taking place: the so-called 'Brown vs. Board of Education of Topeka' decision, in which black students won the right to the same education as whites. Implementation was postponed for a year, and during 1954–5 there were heated debates and massive resistance in the southern states. These involved fears of intermarriage in a continent where twenty-nine states still had statutes forbidding it.

Henderson argues that, certainly for US audiences, these heated debates would have resonated in the film, and are emphasised in the change from novel to screenplay. Examples include: an extended conflict between Martin and Ethan over the importance of Debbie's 'blood' (i.e. white race); the fact that in the novel Martin is '100% white' so there is no question of conflict with Ethan on the grounds of race. He suggests that it is a film about 'black–white' relations round about 1956 via a story of 'red–white' relations.

ACTIVITY 6.3

View *The Searchers* with Henderson's suggestion in mind.

- How does it affect your understanding of it?
- Does it seem a convincing suggestion?
- If so, could it be 'proved' or investigated? How?

Example 2: 'Spaghetti westerns'

These films were made in the 1960s as co-productions between American companies with tax money to gain by European production, and Italian companies with a large home market of avid cinemagoers which TV had not yet fully reached. Several differences are again made possible by such a production context:

- Because they were shot in Europe (mostly Italy and Spain), Monument Valley, with all its heroic connotations of moral testing and extreme possibilities of danger and ambush, was not a feasible

location. Often much more bleached-out desert locations were used, crucially shifting the genre away from celebration of a specifically American landscape.

- Because they were initially low-budget Italian productions, and extras cost dear, massive 'Indian' attacks were not possible, but then neither was the insulting treatment of such characters common in westerns. (Massed Mexican armies, and associated stereotyping, were often used however.)

- Sergio Leone, the director of several of these films, argued the importance of Italy and Spain's experience of modern war, while American territory has never been occupied or invaded in modern times. This, he suggested, makes the Civil War narrative of a film like *The Good, the Bad and the Ugly* (US 1966) engage with the degradations of occupation, and the grimly comic reversals of fortune in war in a way that US westerns had never been able to until then.

- The inclusion of bizarre sounds as part of Morricone's music, and an extreme, comic-book approach to

Figure 6.1 The 'spaghetti western' *The Good, the Bad and the Ugly* (US 1966), United Artists

camera angles and framing was also enjoyed by many as part of a sarcastic, modernising approach taken to the audio-visual traditions (and by implication the 'all-American' values) of the western.

Representation and westerns: gender

The western is often argued, through its representations of male and female characters, to have contributed to the strength of ideologies of gender. Certainly in its peak years, the 1940s and 1950s, it seems to have shaped the expectations of many viewers about 'what a [white] man's gotta do' to be a Real Man. Young male audiences for such films, watching them regularly on cinema and then on TV screens, playing 'cowboys and Indians', being given toy guns, and being told 'Big boys don't cry', have spoken and written of watching with great attentiveness the ways in which the cowboy conducts himself, his physical style and how that embodies lessons about 'real' and 'inadequate' masculinity in the film's narrative.

'I grew up watching westerns. At four I had a cowboy suit ... and "playing cowboys" is a dominant memory from my early years. In the late 1950s as a middle class boy living on the northern edge of London, I followed *The Lone Ranger*, *The Cisco Kid*, Matt Dillon, *Cheyenne* and the other serial westerns on the TV ... I absorbed their styles. For years their movements shaped my own. Not surprisingly, when later ... I saw Jon Voight in *Midnight Cowboy* pose in front of a mirror in stetson and tasselled leather jacket, I recognised the gesture with a shock of embarrassment.'

(Pumphrey 1988)

Generic elements which repeatedly stage such informal lessons include:

- the long saloon bar along which insults can be traded
- the cool glances given and received, perhaps over a game of poker
- the emphasis on a strong male silence, often opposed to the 'gabbling' or probing of emotions or desire for articulacy from the main woman character

- usually at narrative climax, the breaking of this 'manly reserve', allowing the eruption of an exciting and often intricately filmed violence.

'Western heroes have usually restricted themselves to a pitiably narrow range of activities. They can't daydream, or play the fool, or look at flowers, or cook ... or ... make mistakes.'

(Tompkins 1992)

- Do you think this is true?
- How are such activities handled when western male heroes do undertake them – as comedy? Oddity?

Representation and westerns: ecological politics

A few years ago it would have been rare for viewers of westerns to complain at the treatment of the animals in them (apart, that is, from campaigning to stop stunts which might injure horses). But the rise of political movements for ecological awareness has made these parts of the film newly visible, just as happened with Civil Rights struggles and images of Native and Afro-Americans in them. It has become much harder to ignore the final purpose of the cattle runs to the big slaughterhouses and refrigeration centres of the eastern cities which are celebrated in many westerns, and which gave the cowboy his original name.

'The Wild West of the cowboy began in 1866, when post-Civil War eastern cities' demand for beef encouraged open-range Texas ranchers to drive their herds north to the Kansas railheads. Falling profits, overgrazing, the advance of farmers fencing the land and the terrible winter of 1885–6 ended the open range as quickly as it had begun. During those 20 years the typical cowboy was no more than an uneducated young migrant Southerner, in a job that was always exhausting, monotonous and ill-paid.'

(Murdoch 1985)

Such attitudes towards the natural world perhaps make natural other, related feelings (towards subjugation, dominance). As Jane Tompkins (1992) points out, in westerns the horse makes every man (or woman, in some westerns) a master. It brings into the western long-established resonances of chivalry, lordly privilege, as well, perhaps, as fulfilling a longing for a different kind of pre-technological existence with fantasies of bodily freedom and easy, expansive movement. These are deeply seductive Utopian pleasures for many audience members, and have been drawn on by the advertisers we mentioned at the beginning of this case study. The problems are, as with any media form:

- At whose expense, and from whose position are such fantasies played out?
- Can audiences enjoy the fantasies without also being involved in the naturalising or rendering invisible of other feelings which the fantasies involve?

ACTIVITY 6.4

- Ask yourself if you agree with the above.
- What changes have there been in the genre in your experience?
- Across what areas have these changes occurred?

Read Chapter 11 on Ideologies for a sense of how challenging these questions are.

References and Further Reading

Buscombe, Ed (ed.) (1988) *The BFI Companion to the Western,* London: BFI/Andre Deutsch.

Caughie, John (1981) *Theories of Authorship,* London: BFI.

Cook, Pam (ed.) (1985) *The Cinema Book,* London: BFI, pp. 64–72.

Frayling, Christopher (1981) *Spaghetti Westerns: Cowboys and Europeans from Karl May to Sergio Leone,* London: RKP.

Hardy, Phil (1987) *Encyclopaedia of the Western,* London: Aurum.

Henderson, B. (1985) '*The Searchers*: An American Dilemma', in B. Nichols (ed.) *Movies and Methods,* vol. 2, London: University of California Press.

Kitses, Jim (1972) *Horizons West,* London: Studio Vista.

McBride, Joseph and Wilmington, Mike (1974) *John Ford,* London: Secker and Warburg.

Murdoch, David H. (1985) 'The Western Myth', *The Listener,* 10 January.

Neale, Steve (1990) 'Questions of Genre', *Screen,* vol. 31, no. 1.

Pirie, David (ed.) (1981) *Anatomy of the Movies,* London: Windward.

Pumphrey, Martin (1988) 'Why Do Cowboys Wear Hats in the Bath?', *Critical Quarterly,* vol 31. no. 3.

Pye, Douglas (1972) '*The Searchers* and Teaching the Industry', *Screen Education,* no. 17.

Tompkins, Jane (1992) *West of Everything: The Inner Life of Westerns,* Oxford: Oxford University Press.

Wright, Will (1975) *Sixguns and Society: A Structural Study of the Western,* Berkeley: University of California Press.

7 Representations

One of the key terms of Media Studies is 'representation': a word with several possible emphases:

- It can signal the way the media re-present events, reality. However realistic looking their images or sounds are, they never simply present the world. They are always a **construction**, never a transparent window (see Chapter 15, 'Realisms', and Chapter 1, 'Images and languages').

- But 'representation' goes further than the word **construction**. It prompts the question: how have groups, or possibilities that exist outside the media been represented by media products? This relates to the 'How?' of different media and **genres**, but also has broadly political implications:

  - Representation reminds us of the world of political representatives. The media give us images, ways of imagining particular groups which can have material effects on how those groups experience the world, and how they get understood or even legislated for by others.

  - This is partly because the major mass media have the power to re-present, over and over, some images, some assumptions, and to exclude others, and thereby make them unfamiliar or difficult to engage with.

Stereotyping in this context has been a key issue, and you should read the case study accompanying this section (Chapter 8). To briefly summarise, it raises such questions as:

- Do the media, in the images and understandings they so powerfully circulate, suggest to large audiences that x or y character is typical of that group, and therefore that the whole group should be viewed in certain ways?

- Are these ways best described as negative?

- If that seems to be the case, how might those understandings and images be altered?

Representations and gender

One of the richest areas of discussion of representation and media forms exists around gender identities. Though there are often confusing differences in the ways the terms are used, we find useful the distinction between **sex** and **gender**. Sex in this context is not the same as sexuality (which refers to people's sexual orientation, their object choice, sexual activities and imaginings). *Sex difference* we will use to refer to the division of people into male and female, depending on physical characteristics such as sex organs, hormonal make-up and so on.

Gender differences are culturally formed. They exist on the basis of the biological, but build a huge system of differentiation over and above it. So whereas your sex will determine broadly whether or not you can bear a child, for example (though even this is not a universal truth), gender-based arguments have insisted that because women bear children, therefore they should be the ones to stay at home and bring them up. 'It's only natural' says a whole social system of regulations, tax arrangements, childcare and so on.

> To put it another way sex says 'It's a boy'; gender says 'Oh, good' and gets out the blue baby clothes, the train set and toy guns, and a whole set of assumptions.
>
> (adapted from Branston 1984)

ACTIVITY 7.1
- How can you tell which of the very simply drawn characters in Figure 7.1 is male and which female?
- Which lines on the drawing told you?
- What does this suggest about the ease with which assumptions of gender difference circulate in our culture?

Figure 7.1

Some of these assumptions are circulated through the media, and **feminist positions** keen to challenge them have developed approaches that are key for the debate on representation of any group. **Content analysis** is a valuable starting point. It assumes that there is a relationship between the frequency with which a certain item (say 'women in the kitchen') appears in a media text and the intentions of its producers, as well as the responses of its audience.

Such studies of gender roles in magazines and advertising have shown that women are still represented according to long-standing cultural stereotypes. Gill Dyer, researching them in 1981, reported that they are repeatedly shown 'as housewives, mothers, homemakers' while men are often represented 'in situations of authority and dominance over women'. The use of a male **voice-over** (traditionally a position of authority on the soundtrack), of men as scientists, or at least as knowledgeable about the product while women were more often consumers – all these typify the situation in ads. In 1978, 13 per cent of central characters in UK ads were women while 41 per cent of UK employees were women.

Ten years later, in 1990, Guy Cumberbatch found that there were twice as many men as women in ads; the male voice-over was still predominantly used, even in ads for women's products; the women in ads were usually younger and more conventionally attractive than the men, who were twice as likely to be shown in paid employment as women – and so on (see Strinati 1995).

ACTIVITY 7.2

Conduct your own random survey across a day's ads. Take a category such as age, ethnicity or gender and try to discover how it has been represented according to:

- the numbers of characters in ads who belong to the group
- how they are represented in the ads – as narrative heroes? As consumers or as experts? With or without dialogue?
- Do the voice-overs seem to belong to one of the group?
- Are they repeatedly shown in some situations but not others, e.g. at work or in the home; as people preoccupied with their appearance?

Such evidence is striking and demands careful thought. But various objections have been made to the methods of content analysis (see Chapter 29, 'Audiences') and by extension some of the simpler forms of stereotyping and representation approaches. In the case of gender and representation we need to note:

- the assumption that what is needed are more realistic portrayals of women since the media are said to reflect society, and such reflections should always be accurate ones
- the relative neglect of wider structures of economic and political power, which might make it arguably realistic to show more women than men active in the home, for example
- the assumption that only irrational or ignorant prejudice could account for such stereotyping
- the assumption that the media have huge powers to socialise people into beliefs, roles and behaviour. Yet people are not always successfully socialised in this way.

Representations and the real

Such approaches imply that media forms have a responsibility to be realistic or to produce positive images of disadvantaged groups. But media texts belong to genres and forms that don't have a straightforward relationship to the rest of the real. To say that a media text is 'distorted' or 'unrepresentative' may ignore the following points:

'At least one study ... found that high-viewing children were more sceptical in a Stereotype Acceptance Test.'

(Durkin 1985)

- It is a representation in the other sense of the word: a construction with its own formal rules and fascinations, working in a particular material, whether that be celluloid images, or words sung to bass guitar rhythms.
- Its images may belong to a genre (crazy comedy, or horror) which is not experienced in the same ways as, say, the news. Audiences' degree of familiarity with its conventions clearly becomes important here.
- The idea of reflection is in any case always problematic for cultural forms. It implies a far too straightforward, mirror-like role for fantastic forms such as horror or science fiction. It suggests there is a fairly simple thing called 'reality' to be 'reflected' in a one-to-one, undistorted way (see Chapter 15, 'Realisms', and Chapter 12, 'Case study: Selecting and constructing news').

Comedy provides interesting debates in this area. When Les Dawson said the line: 'I knew it was the mother-in-law 'cause when they heard her coming, the mice started throwing themselves on the traps', there were several pleasures on offer: his delivery, voice and timing; the verbal surprise; comic exaggeration; and the economic elegance of a good joke. This economy is only able to work because a quickly recognisable stereotype is in play. The stereotype (here of the Mother-in-Law) could be said to offer the pleasure of community, of feeling a 'we' and a 'them'-ness for a moment.

The questions that usually need asking of such a joke include:

- from whose point of view is it being told? Whose point of view is excluded; who is the 'them' outside this cosy community?
- How is the audience positioned, not only by the joke but by the context in which it is told: all male club/TV show/radio documentary?
- How does the group on the receiving end of the joke seem to be treated in the rest of representation? Does that change how we might experience the joke?

To make this last point clearer: in the case of mothers-in-law, we may feel OK to laugh, since this is rather an outmoded target. Changes in family structures have eroded the considerable power of the mother-in-law of working-class couples who had to live in her home for the first few years of married life. We may even feel the degree of exaggeration itself is signalling the joke's distance from reality. To put it in *semiotic* language: pleasure is more from the play of the signifiers than from agreement with the way the *sign* represents its **referent**.

'I'm not prejudiced. I make anti-Irish jokes too.'
(Bernard Manning, club and TV comedian)

However, you might feel differently if you were an older woman, and the object of a great number of contemptuous jokes and comedy sketches (or you might not!). And when jokes centre in a less exaggerated way, perhaps on a group that is being abused on the streets, for whom there are very few 'communities of feeling' to enter, it becomes a much less easy thing to laugh along with it.

There are other differences in relationships to the real (see **verisimilitude** section of Chapter 5, 'Genres'). The cartoonist Posy Simmonds once wrote that when she drew black or Asian figures they seemed to be readily taken to represent their whole ethnic group. To draw a black or Asian man as fat, drunk, foul-mouthed and lazy, she said, would probably cause offence, whereas if the 'same' kind of character appeared as one of Lenny Henry's stage sketches there would be far less likelihood of offence. This is partly to do with the nature of cartooning as opposed to live performance. It is often used in political contexts where we're used to seeing points made about a whole group of people, and it tends to use very broad strokes and situations to achieve its comic work. Furthermore, the two authors or originators of the messages – the white female cartoonist and black stand-up comedian – are likely to have different relationships to the group being represented.

Questions of positive and negative images

History suggests that once an oppressed group, such as women, perceives its political and social oppression, it begins to try to change that oppression at the level of representation. This often involves trying to replace 'negative' with 'positive' images. This, however, is a complex process, involving the following areas:

- the effect of employment practices in the media on such images
- debates around how to define the 'community' being represented
- questions of what is to count as 'positive' representations
- the differences that the understandings of different audiences will make to the meanings of certain kinds of images, including genre competence, religious beliefs, etc.

Groups that are heavily stereotyped (as 'problems') are likely to have less **access** to influential positions in the media, or to other kinds of power. This can set up a vicious circle of unemployment; it may also mean there may be few images or stories that centre on them sympathetically (as opposed to ones where they feature as villainous or untrustworthy. See Chapter 6, 'Case study: Going West'). This may be the result of violent historical processes, including wars or colonialism, which have left a long legacy of trivialising or insulting images.

When images of the group do begin to be produced, they have to bear what has been called the burden of representativeness. This involves two main aspects:

- What is taken to be the object of representation. It is always crucial to ask: what is the 'reality' being represented? For huge groups such as women, or British Asians, which members of the group are doing the defining of 'the community'? Or what is positive and what negative about an image? To imply that 'Asian British' is a homogeneous group, all sharing the same experiences of age, class, gender, sexuality and so on, is clearly foolish.
- There is also the question of how to construct characters belonging to the group, if they have been relatively absent from media images previously, and may therefore be read by many as 'representative'.

Because for many years there were so few images of black British on TV, or because the images were of 'problems', when black characters *did* appear on soaps or in dramas, they were often felt to 'stand in for' or represent the whole of their particular 'community'. This sometimes resulted in a feeling that a character could never 'behave badly' because of its representativeness. As a result, some members of such groups felt that being represented in various and ordinary ways would be a positive step.

The Cosby Show, with the upper-middle-class respectable Huxtable family and some assured comic performances as its focus, gained high TV ratings in both the US and Britain in the late 1980s. It is an example (along with the very different series *Roots* (US 1977) which treated the slave history of US African-Americans) of the impact of US images of ethnicity on British audiences. Justin Lewis (1991) interviewed black and

'When the safari hunters from the BBC or TV companies drive into Brixton or Brent they've already decided what they want to say. Out come the cameras and the anxious directors, looking over their shoulders for trouble; out come the zoom lenses ... out come the bubbling production assistants, eager to ... chat up a Rastafarian to give an interview on camera.'

(Tony Freeth in Cohen and Gardner 1982)

'I longed to be an actress. Unfortunately, the only role models I had, the only visible Asian women in the media, were a barely literate woman in a sari in the sitcom *Mind Your Language*, who spent most of her time saying "Golly gosh" and knitting bootees ... and a young beautiful presenter on a kids' show.'

(Syal 1994)

white American audiences to explore how far this sitcom's cosy picture of black professional life was socially **progressive**. White viewers seemed to identify in a 'colour-blind' way with black characters, who perhaps confirmed for them 'the American Dream', i.e. that colour is not a barrier to 'making it'. Black viewers, while perceiving the absence of references to racism or unemployment, nevertheless liked the show partly because they saw it as compensating for the lack of sympathetic images of African-Americans on US TV.

Afro-Caribbean British characters were mostly absent from films, ads, TV in the 1960s (hence the pleasure taken when *Roots* was screened). When they were present, it was often as 'problems': as criminals, or as suffering from family breakdown. 'Positive' images of them reversed this, and sometimes produced characterisations of strict parents, near-noble teachers and so on. But this was still a narrowing of the range of representation compared to the roles available to white characters.

In such a context, for example, the *EastEnders'* variety of black characters – some involved in petty crime, some parents coping with family difficulties, some in love and so on – was welcomed by many. Others, in the mid-1980s, picketed the film *My Beautiful Laundrette* (UK 1985) because of its images of gay and drug-dealing Asian British characters. 'Negative' images are not always best opposed by (someone's idea of) 'positive', but by the availability of a range of fuller ways of being imagined. This is arguably easier in a soap opera than a feature film, and is certainly easier when plenty of the group in question are employed in the meaning-making industries (especially media).

> A different group and approach: there's a lovely moment at end of the film *Sleep With Me* (US 1995) involving a character who throughout the film has been a keen card player, always impatient at delays to the card sessions. Only in the very last shot do we see him away from the card table, and suddenly realise he is in a wheelchair. Without any reference to disability, he has been constructed for most of the film as 'just the same as the other characters'.

There is another, quite different attitude towards 'positive' and 'negative'. Supposing a group with good grounds for surliness, and for lack of co-operation with a social system or situation (slaves in plantation conditions, as imaged in *Gone With the Wind*) are represented as always smiling and whistling contentedly at their lot? They may well wonder if this image is 'positive' only for those who want to be reassured that all is well with an unjust set-up.

'Cosby has said of this charge: "To say that they are not black enough is a denial of the American Dream, and the American way of life. My point is that this is an American family ... and if you want to live like they do, and you're willing to work, the opportunity is there."'
(Dyson, quoted in Lewis 1991: 162)

'Pictures of perfection make me sick and wicked.'
(Jane Austen)

'There are no such things as negative images. There are just undeveloped stories which give the result, not the process.'
(Ayoka Chenzira, Edinburgh Film Festival 1985)

Sometimes groups heavily stereotyped by comedians, cartoonists and so on have responded by taking on the denigrated identity that the stereotype or abusive nickname gives them. Examples would be black groups calling themselves 'niggers'; gays calling themselves 'queens' or 'queers'.

In fact, there is no such thing as the '100% right on text' or 'positive image' which will guarantee to change audiences in progressive ways all on its own. Texts have always to be understood in the context of audiences, and of production practices. And it seems to be the case that fictional entertainment texts have an extremely complex relationship to audiences' sense of the real.

'Taking on the previously denigrated identity is a way of wrong-footing bigoted opponents.'
(Andy Medhurst 1994)

'The "flight" into a fictional fantasy is not so much a denial of reality as a playing with it. A game that enables one to place the limits of the fictional and the real under discussion, to make them fluid.'
(Ang 1985: 49)

Other ways of changing representations

It is important that debates over representations should not keep simply to the level of textual analysis. Various vehicles and issues are crucial in shifting taken-for-granted assumptions. These include:

- political change and the ways it can widen (or narrow) imaginings and the range of images possible (such as 1960s and 1970s feminist movements, or the Civil Rights struggles in 1950s and 1960s USA)
- employment patterns and production achievements in media industries
- access to dissenting mechanisms like the Right to Reply

Figure 7.2 Published in the *Guardian*, spring 1995

- audiences' ability to come across, and feel comfortable with a wide range of media experiences.

It may seem odd to suggest that dominant **discourses** can be shifted at the level of production, simply by having women or blacks making certain kinds of films, TV, or music. But the assumption that a woman would be too frail, or scatty, or feeble to get together an action surfing thriller is dispelled by Kathryn Bigelow's achievement in making *Point Break* (US 1991). Similarly, racist assumptions about African-Americans' organisational and creative abilities may be countered by Spike Lee's success in getting big projects together.

Figure 7.3

Affirmative action or *equal opportunities* policies usually apply to less illustrious positions, and simply mean that wherever possible, people from particular groups (such as women, or those with disabilities) will be appointed to jobs if their suitability is more or less equivalent to that of other candidates. For groups so far marginalised in media jobs this can open up the following possibilities:

- Crude stereotypes can be countered by the presence of members of such groups in the workforce. If you have people with disabilities working on a newspaper, it makes it much harder to resort to the stereotype that 'disabled people are always helpless victims'. Several black journalists have commented that racist headlines by **tabloid** papers would be harder to justify in the newsroom if there were more non-white British journalists employed there.

- Such media workers may well (though not inevitably) be more alert to, or simply know about 'angles' on news stories, or have ideas for credible storylines about members of that group. *Cagney and Lacey* and *French and Saunders* partly resulted from such inputs from women in media.

'The presence of six black journalists in the *Sun* newsrooms would do more good than any number of disciplinary actions against them for racist reporting.' (Lionel Morrison, one of the first black journalists to work in Fleet Street, *New Society*, 2 Oct. 1987)

STATEMENT ON RACE REPORTING

1 The NUJ believes that the development of racist attitudes and the growth of fascist parties pose a threat to democracy, the rights of trade union organisations, a free press and the development of social harmony and well-being.

2 The NUJ believes that its members cannot avoid a measure of responsibility in fighting the evil of racism as expressed through the mass media.

3 The NUJ reaffirms its total opposition to censorship but equally reaffirms the belief that press freedom must be conditioned by responsibility and an acknowledgement by all media workers of the need not to allow press freedom to be abused to slander a section of the community or to promote the evil of racism.

4 The NUJ believes that the methods and the lies of the racists should be publicly and vigorously exposed.

5 The NUJ believes that newspapers and magazines should not originate material which encourages discrimination on grounds of race or colour as expressed in the NUJ's Rule Book and Code of Conduct.

6 The NUJ recognises the right of members to withhold their labour on grounds of conscience where employers are providing a platform for racist propaganda.

7 The NUJ believes that editors should ensure that coverage of race stories be placed in a balanced context.

8 The NUJ will continue to monitor the development of media coverage in this area and give support to members seeking to enforce the above aims.

Race Reporting

Only mention someone's race if it is strictly relevant. Check to make sure you have it right. Would you mention race if the person was white?

Do not sensationalise race relations issues, it harms Black people and it could harm you.

Think carefully about the words you use. Words which were once in common usage are now considered offensive, e.g. half-caste and coloured. Use mixed-race and Black instead. Black can cover people of Arab, Asian, Chinese and African origin. Ask people how they define themselves.

Immigrant is often used as a term of abuse. Do not use it unless the person really is an immigrant. Most Black people in Britain were born here and most immigrants are white.

Do not make assumptions about a person's cultural background – whether it is their name or religious detail. Ask them, or where this is not possible check with the local race equality council.

Investigate the treatment of Black people in education, health, employment and housing. Do not forget travellers and gypsies. Cover their lives and concerns. Seek the views of their representatives.

Remember that Black communities are culturally diverse. Get a full and correct view from representative organisations.

Press for equal opportunities for employment of Black staff.

Be wary of disinformation. Just because a source is traditional does not mean it is accurate.

Reporting Racist Organisations

When interviewing representatives of racist organisations or reporting meetings or statements or claims, journalists should carefully check all reports for accuracy and seek rebutting or opposing comments. The anti-social nature of such views should be exposed.

Do not sensationalise by reports, photographs, film or presentation the activities of racist organisations.

Seek to publish or broadcast material exposing the myths and lies of racist organisations and their anti-social behaviour.

Do not allow the letters column or 'phone-in' programmes to be used to spread racial hatred in whatever guise.

GUIDELINES ON TRAVELLERS

X Only mention the word gypsy or traveller if strictly relevant or accurate.

X Give balanced reports seeking travellers' views as well as those of others, consulting the local travellers where possible.

X Resist the temptation to sensationalise issues involving travellers, especially in their relations with settled communities over issues such as housing and settlement programmes and schooling.

X Try to give wider coverage to travellers' lives and the problems they face.

X Strive to promote the realisation that the travellers' community is comprised of full citizens of Great Britain and Ireland whose civil rights are seldom adequately vindicated, who often suffer much hurt and damage through misuse by the media and who have a right to have their special contributions to Irish and British life, especially in music and craftwork and other cultural activities, properly acknowledged and reported.

Figure 7.4 National Union of Journalists codes on race reporting

'**Right to Reply**' policies are also important. The stance of newspapers such as the *Sun* during Mrs Thatcher's years in power is an example of a large institution which had far more power than most of us to keep circulating headlines, employing cartoonists, buying photos and stories maintaining hostile images of groups such as the GLC with its 'Fare's Fair' policies for low-priced transport in London. Such targeted groups had far less power to circulate the opposite political assumptions and often had positions discredited by allegations which were unfounded, and were retracted later in an obscure part of the newspaper. The Right to Reply lobby asks for the reply to such stories to be given equal prominence to the original story. Thus an untrue front-page headline would have to be corrected on another front page.

ACTIVITY 7.3

The success of attempts to shift assumptions through such policies will also always depend on audiences.

- How much chance do they have of access to, and confidence with a wide range of images, entertainment forms, information and arguments?
- For example, how close are they to a Regional Film Theatre or a big book shop where they can come across a range of books, postcards, magazines, music?
- How likely are they to feel easy with the assumptions, codes, discourses of '**alternative**' or controversial forms (see Chapter 27, 'Independents and alternatives') trying to challenge dominant codes?

'We must do something for the understanding of new works. Besides being popular there is such a thing as becoming popular.'
(Brecht 1978: 11)

References and further reading

Ang, Ien (1985) *Watching Dallas*, London and New York: Methuen.

Baehr, Helen and Dyer, Gillian (eds) (1987) *Boxed in: Women and Television*, London: Pandora.

Bogle, Donald (1992) *Toms, Coons, Mulattoes, Mammies and Bucks: An Interpretative History of Blacks in American Films*, New York: Continuum.

BFI Education Dept. (1982) *Selling Pictures*, London: BFI.

Branston, Gill (1984) *Film and Gender*, London: Film Education.

Brecht, Bertolt (1978) *Brecht on Theatre*, ed. J. Willett, London: Eyre/Methuen.

Cohen, Phil and Gardner, Carl (eds) (1982) *It Ain't Half Racist, Mum*, London: Comedia in association with Campaign against Racism in the Media.

Dunant, Sarah (ed.) (1994) *The War of the Words: The Political Correctness Debate,* London: Virago Press.

Durkin, Kevin (1985) *Television, Sex Roles and Children*, Milton Keynes: Open University Press.

Goffman, Ervin (1976) *Gender Advertisements,* London and Basingstoke: Macmillan.

Lewis, J. (1991) *The Ideological Octopus,* New York and London: Routledge, esp. Chapter 7.

Pines, Jim (ed.) (1992) *Black and White in Colour: Black People in British Television since 1936,* London: BFI.

Seiter, E. (1986) 'Feminism and Ideology: The Terms of Women's Stereotypes', *Feminist Review,* no. 22.

Strinati, Dominic (1995) *An Introduction to Theories of Popular Culture,* London: Routledge.

Syal, Meera (1994) 'Bhaji on the Beach: PC: GLC' in S. Dunant (ed.) *The War of the Words*, London: Virago.

8 / Case study: Discussing stereotypes

What are stereotypes?
Stereotypes and media
Stereotyping and the real
How do stereotypes change?
Cause and effect in stereotypes

Stereotyping has been part of key debates over representation in Media Studies such as:

- Do the media, in circulating images that involve particular kinds of people, suggest to large audiences that x or y character is **typical** of certain groups, and therefore that the whole group should be viewed in certain ways?
- Are these ways usually inadequate?
- Are 'negative' and 'positive' useful terms for such discussion?
- Is there a difference between information and entertainment or fiction forms in such debates?

What are stereotypes?

Stereotypes are not actual people, but widely circulated ideas or assumptions about particular groups. They are often assumed to be 'lies', and to need to be 'done away with' so we can all 'get rid of our prejudices' and meet as equals. The term tends to be much more derogatory than 'type' (which means very similar things). We want to suggest other ways of thinking about them.

Stereotyping is a process of **categorisation** (see Chapter 5, 'Genres' chapter) necessary to make sense of the world, and the flood of information and impressions we receive minute by minute. We are all prejudiced, in its root sense of 'pre-judging' in order to carve our way through any situation. We all make mental maps of our worlds to navigate our way through them, and maps only represent parts of the real world, and in particular ways.

- We all employ typifications in certain situations.

- We all belong to groups that can be typified, and stereotyped.

For example, if you were being interviewed by a man wearing a pin-striped suit and waistcoat, with an English upper-class accent, you would probably, quite fast, make certain deductions about him, and maybe modify your behaviour accordingly. After ten minutes, you might have changed your attitude towards him, because of his behaviour, but you would still be interpreting him through stereotypes or categories on the basis of certain signs. This would be a perfectly reasonable procedure on your part. We all make sense of people on the basis of gestures, dress, voice and so on, very much as we construct a sense of characters in the media. In other situations you might make certain deductions on first meeting someone dressed in a particular way which are equally a categorisation, but a *sympathetic* rather than a *negative* one (depending on your taste in clothes). Stereotypes are not always negative.

Though a dominant assumption in our culture is that we are all unique individuals (which is in some ways true), it is equally true that we share certain broad structures of social experience: around age and gender for example. These make it possible to understand many of the experiences we have as being typical. Indeed, it's arguable that our differences are due not to 'unique essences' but to the particular ways that very typical forces (such as class, gender and ethnicity) have intersected in our unique instance. This broadens the opportunities both for understanding other people's experiences, and perhaps for changing the social structures that produce them.

The usual trap in thinking about stereotyping is to feel that all typing is bad, and that all characterisations that present themselves as being complex are good. But complex characterisations, to be recognisable at all, need to relate in some way to the 'typical'.

ACTIVITY 8.1

Think of a character whom you consider to be complex (perhaps one in a long-running **soap opera**, or Jane Tennison/Helen Mirren in *Prime Suspect*).

- Consider how far that complexity is a collection of attributes, many of which are typical of particular groups.
- If you chose a soap character, consider how the length of time available for its 'building up' across the serial will be important. (Look again at Propp and the idea of character as *action* in Chapter 3.)
- If you chose a star performance, how far were you partly reading the character through the star's history?

Stereotypes and media

It is often argued that stereotypes are an unavoidable part of mass media representations. **Hollywood cinema**, for example, grew out of an early film industry aimed at illiterate, multi-ethnic American audiences. It soon learnt how to communicate via quickly established visual stereotypes (often adopted from theatre melodrama, with its silent frozen tableaux and polarised virtue/vice characterisations). Costumes condensed various stereotypical meanings: the vamp (slinky low-cut gowns); 'the shop girl' (ordinary daywear); mother (modest dresses); good cowboy (white hat); shady Mexican (moustache, unshaven) and so on. The recourse to stereotypes is useful for such widely circulated entertainment products.

Such examples are often used to suggest that all stereotypes are very simple, and only open to fixed interpretations. As Gillian Swanson (1991) has suggested though, even such an apparently simple stereotype as that of the **Dumb Blonde** turns out, on closer examination, to be quite a complex cluster of characteristics. We might produce a list such as:

strange logic/innocence/manipulativeness/humour/ blondeness and other characteristics emphasising the body/childlike nature/adult knowingness

---

ACTIVITY 8.2

Take some media 'Dumb Blondes' (e.g. Marilyn Monroe, Barbara Windsor) and see if the list applies to them.

- How many of the elements are contradictory?
- Which elements are repeated, which are combined differently in particular actresses?
- Which of them change over time? Barbara Windsor in *EastEnders* is a particularly interesting example.

As Swanson points out:

Mask-like make-up, for instance, can simultaneously suggest vacancy and cluelessness, glamour and attractiveness, as well as a certain class position through connotations of brashness and overt sexuality. It may equally suggest a deliberate refusal to be accessible, as in more recent stars such as Annie Lennox and Madonna.

(Swanson 1991: 133–4)

She goes on to argue that it is not so much that some images of women 'escape' the stereotypes, but that in the ways they combine typical and atypical elements, they change the terms in which the stereotypes can be understood. This is rather like the way that repetition and difference work in genres (see Chapter 5, 'Genres').

In addition, the processes of watching apparently stereotyped fictional situations may turn out to involve shifting patterns of identification. Swanson cites the example of a rape scene shown through the eyes of the male perpetrator:

Girls and boys may not identify with him in quite the same way, however. If the only way to participate in the suspense of the narrative is to adopt the male point of view, female spectators may be able to do so by their familiarity with the *conventions* of this kind of story. But the clash between the social formation of our identity (here, female) and the position we are asked to occupy to get pleasure (here, male) may produce anxiety in our viewing and response.

(Swanson 1991: 125)

Stereotyping and the real

So stereotypes, like genres, can be said to exist, even if their elements shift over time as well as within and across particular media, and even though audiences understand them in often ambiguous ways. They have been argued to have the following characteristics:

- They involve both a categorising and an *evaluation* of the group being stereotyped.
- The evaluation is often, though not always, a negative one.
- The group being stereotyped often has few means of affecting, of having a say in these representations.
- Stereotypes change over time. O'Sullivan *et al.* (1994: 127) give the example of the 'cloth-cap worker' of the 1950s who became the 1980s 'consumerist home-owner who holidays in Spain'.

Stereotypes work by taking some easily grasped features presumed to belong to a group, putting them at the centre of the description, and implying that all members of the group always have those features. They also suggest that these characteristics, which are often the result of a historical process, are themselves the cause of the group's position.

One of the strengths of stereotypes is that they can point to features that appear to have 'a grain of truth', which we could indeed say are, or have been typical of, particular groups. But even if such apparent evidence exists, the stereotype then repeats, across a whole range of media and informal exchanges, that this characteristic is *always* a *central* truth about that group. Let's take an example. Women are still often powerfully stereotyped as erratic and dangerous drivers. This stereotype can be

seen as relating to historical and social factors:

- In order to drive well, a relatively expensive investment needs to be made in a car; in time, petrol and training to drive it; and in experience of using it. These are all more easily available to people in reasonably paid jobs, which have traditionally been occupied by men rather than women.
- Part of this historical disadvantaging of women are **discourses** around technology and gender which have constructed 'the truly feminine woman' as unable to cope with technology – or driving.
- Since there are many poor drivers on the road, there's a fair chance that women actually will compose a number of them, and can thus be pointed to as examples of the truth of the stereotype. But it is the stereotype that makes the *perception* of such a connection likely in the first place.
- There is a kind of formal pleasure in the jokes to be made, even by women, about women drivers. They can be made in such a way as to distance the teller

Figure 8.1 Cartoon by Posy Simmonds published in the *Guardian* in the 1970s. Stereotypes of groups of women work within larger discourses about 'what women are like'

from the 'truth content' of the joke. This relates to the capacity of some fictional **genres**, with their repetition of certain entertaining elements (such as the 'scatty woman driver' in comedies) to keep negative stereotypes going, and to appear simply 'harmless', so anyone objecting to these repetitions seems 'humourless'.

How do stereotypes change?

If this sounds like a 'no-win' situation for women, it's interesting to note that this stereotype seems diminished over the last fifteen years.

- Active lobbying for less demeaning images of women have had some effects across the cultural industries which represent them.
- Relatedly, more women have entered the workforce and gained experience in driving. In fact 42 per cent of drivers were women in 1994, though they still started driving later than men, and drove fewer work-related miles.
- If you have access to minority publications, such as insurance companies' journals, or even some business pages of newspapers, you will see that some insurers charge women lower premiums, considering them a lower risk than men.
- The stereotype has shifted partly because women have been more targeted recently as potential car buyers. The ecology lobby may also have had an effect, making the display of machismo through gas-guzzling power play in big cars less acceptable. (For one thing, advertising agency workers are highly media-literate metropolitans, used to tuning in to trends and new ideas. They do not want to appear to hold 'Jurassic' prejudices.)

As a result of these processes, images of competent women drivers are produced and widely circulated (even though they are rarely imaged as in charge of the big, authoritative saloon cars advertised on a Sunday night's TV).

A **pluralist** position (see Chapter 11, 'Ideologies') might argue that this shows there are no such things as

powerful stereotypes. But it is important to remember that major **institutions** such as advertising and the **tabloid** press have much more power to circulate inadequate, as well as new or challenging stereotypes and assumptions. So the mere existence of counter-stereotyped images has to be judged in relation to where, and how often, they are likely to be seen and accepted.

ACTIVITY 8.3

Collect and study ads and news stories involving women drivers. Test the above suggestions. Look at health and safety ads on the dangers of drunk driving.

- How do they gender such drivers? Is/would it be a shock to see a woman represented thus?
- How would you discuss such an image in relation to positive and negative images debates ?

Even though you may feel it is simply 'changes in the real world' which shift stereotypes, struggles around representations are always also needed. Representations, discourses, stereotypes of the real, are an inextricable part of the real world, never just an add-on extra.

Cause and effect in stereotypes

Another key point about stereotypes is that they can take something that is an effect of a group's situation and encourage audiences to feel it is the cause of that group's low status. For example, for a long time in Hollywood cinema and other discourses, black slaves working on cotton plantations before the American Civil War of 1861–5 were often stereotyped through such signs, among others, as:

- a shuffling walk
- musical rhythm, and a tendency to burst into song and dance readily
- (in characterisations of female house slaves) bodily fatness, uneducated foolishness, and childlike qualities (*Gone With the Wind* (US 1939) contains two notorious examples in 'Mammy' and Prissy).

Figure 8.2 Scarlett and Mammy in *Gone With the Wind* (US 1939)

To say that these demeaning stereotypes embody a grain of truth may seem in itself insulting, but consider the following facts:

- Slaves on the Southern plantations in the nineteenth century would have had their calf muscles cut if they tried to run away from slavery (the shuffling gait of the stereotype).
- Slaves were given hardly any educational or cultural opportunities. (Hostile use of the stereotype demeans efforts to make music and dance out of very simple resources to hand. It attributes 'rhythm' to primitive, animal qualities, thus justifying slaveowners' positions like 'they couldn't benefit from education anyway'.)
- The women were often treated simply as breeding stock by the slave owners. When this function was over, once they had given birth to numbers of new slaves and their bodies were perhaps enlarged by repeated pregnancies, they were often moved into the main house and used as nursemaids to the white children. Again, hostile use of the stereotype invites us to account for the Mammy's size in terms of physical laziness or ignorance rather than her exploitation at the hands of the slave system.

ACTIVITY 8.4

Next time you see *Gone With the Wind*, note the ways in which the slave characters are constructed.

- Do you agree with the points made above about the female slaves?
- Are male slaves constructed according to different stereotypes? Why might this be?
- How does the narrative construct the Mammy character?
- Why does she have no family, no history or presence at the end of the film?

A final note: though you may feel that large, historically oppressed groups such as black American slaves, or Irish people have been heavily stereotyped, this usually happens through more than one stereotype, and it is possible to imagine them being used sympathetically, as in black reformist **propaganda**. More usually, though, even if there is often a grain of truth in particular stereotypes at some moments in history,

THERE WERE THESE THICK PADDIES........

Figure 8.3 (By courtesy of Leeds Postcards)

they keep being circulated long after the end of the situations that gave rise to them. *Gone With the Wind* was released in 1939, not 1839.

This may partly be due to the pressures from tourist and heritage industries for marketable, nostalgic imagery, often coming out of successful media products. *Gone With the Wind* is a huge source of souvenirs, theme parks, tourist attractions in Georgia. These offer pleasures that are analogous to the shifting fascinations of entertainment forms: updatings of the South's history, ingenious spectacle, fun, lighthearted engagement with the heavy tales of slavery.

'Towering at least 20 feet above the ground (in Natchez, Mississippi) is a vast, grinning, turbanned, earringed, tray-carrying Mammy. At first sight she appears to be a monument, until you see the signs for a petrol station, public phone and cafe . . . you enter a door in her voluminous skirts and order your hominy grits and black-eyed peas within her warm and welcoming body.'

(Taylor 1989: 168)

It becomes difficult but necessary for black groups, as for any group trying to align political issues of representation to the entertaining pastimes of the media, to object that the nostalgia is for an order founded on slavery, mostly perceived from the white plantation owners' point of view.

References and further reading

BFI (1982) *Selling Pictures Teaching Pack*, London: BFI.

Bogle, Donald (1992) *Toms, Coons, Mulattoes, Mammies and Bucks*, New York: Continuum.

Dunant, Sarah (ed.) (1994) *The War of the Words: The Political Correctness Debate*, London: Virago.

Geraghty, Christine (1991) *Women and Soap Opera*, London: Polity Press.

O'Sullivan, Tim, Dutton, B. and Rayner, P. (eds) (1994) *Studying the Media. An Introduction*, London, New York, Melbourne and Auckland: Edward Arnold.

Perkins, Tessa (1979) 'Rethinking Stereotypes' in M. Barrett, P. Corrigan, A. Kuhn and V. Wolff (eds) *Ideology and Cultural Production*, London: Croom Helm.

Pines, Jim (ed.) (1992) *Black and White in Colour*, London: BFI.

Seiter, E. (1986) 'Feminism and Ideology: The Terms of Women's Stereotypes', *Feminist Review*, no. 22.

Strinati, Dominic (1995) *An Introduction to Theories of Popular Culture*, London: Routledge.

Swanson, Gillian (1991) 'Representation' in David Lusted (ed.) *The Media Studies Book*, London: Routledge.

Taylor, Helen (1989) *Scarlett's Women: Gone With the Wind and its Female Fans*, London: Virago, esp. pp. 174–80.

9 Advertising, marketing and fashion

Advertising has important connections to the study of representation and of media audiences. To **advertise** simply means 'to draw attention to something' or to notify or inform someone of something (Dyer 1982). It is now the media form most often encountered, most of the time: on urban billboards; on commercially funded TV; in magazines and newspapers; or pushed through front doors.

ACTIVITY 9.1

How many forms of advertising have you encountered this week?

- Where?
- What are the main differences between them?
- What difference did their location make to the ads, and to your engagement with them?
- Have you ever advertised? In which medium?

Advertising has drawn the attention of generations of analysts, especially in work on the effects of mass commercial culture. Objections to it have included the following allegations:

- Its processes are deceitful promises, designed to promote materialism, waste, hedonism and envy.
- It acts as an unnecessary business expense, which adds significantly to the costs of goods for customers. Large monopolies such as Proctor and Gamble spend millions advertising their own products (such as soap powders) against their own subsidiaries.
- It leads to barriers to competition and to oligopolies because young companies cannot afford the huge costs needed to break into markets.
- Its glamorous images lead to conformity, especially in relation to already powerfully stereotyped areas such as gender, class, ethnicity and age.

'Remember the consumer isn't a moron, she is your wife'
(David Ogilvy, founder of one of the largest ad agencies in the world, Ogilvy and Mather).

History

Advertising can arguably be found as far back as Greek and Roman public criers, shouting the wares of local traders and shopkeepers. But its recognisable modern form appears around the seventeenth century when newspapers began to circulate and announce fairs, shipping lists and miraculous cures (Dyer 1982).

It was in the USA, with its huge late nineteenth-century expanding capitalist economy, that consumers began to be educated (informally, of course, by ads) into the possibilities and attractions of mass consumption. For many years ads were described as though they operated in a trivial and irrational way, and as though they had the most pronounced effect on women (because femininity is traditionally constructed as irrational and as bound up with consumption not production). Nevertheless, real gains and freedoms, especially for women, were represented by modern products, sold by the department stores in safe shopping districts, and later by supermarkets which introduced the revolutionary idea that shoppers could choose for themselves the nature and number of items they would buy.

> Quite intentionally, shopping was linked with individual choice and pleasure. In well-lit, airy stores, goods of all descriptions were displayed for inspection. Prices were fixed. There was no obligation to buy. Where traditionally retail had been men's business, the department stores became downtown women's clubs with restaurants, rest rooms and polite personal attention. Their opulence and displays of luxury made them 'schools for consumption'.
>
> (Pumphrey 1984: 182)

Such developments also brought women increased work opportunities, though unionisation for working rights was slow, and they often found themselves in low-skilled, low-paid jobs. (Similarly the advantages of huge super- and hypermarkets, and multiplex cinemas, are now being set against the levels of car ownership which they assume and encourage.)

ACTIVITY 9.2

Find some writings on advertising which put a heavy emphasis on its power alone, outside these retailing contexts, to influence people into buying certain goods.
- How would you want to qualify them?
- Note when you next visit your local supermarket, its careful **mise en scène**. (Slightly pink lighting over the meats? Smell of bread enticing you through the store? Sweets for tired children at check out? Muzak pacing your visit, depending on time of day?)
- Think how you would relate its attractions to the power of ads.

By the end of the 1920s US advertisers, consciously or unconsciously, began to try to transform the buying habits of a national audience of consumers (largely women). They realised that to do this they could not simply reject traditional assumptions about gender roles. The success of the American government's **propaganda** during the First World War convinced them that they could also use **social psychology** or **behaviourism** as research into human motivation and ways of associating came to be called (see Chapter 29, 'Audiences').

Lifestyle advertising developed, going beyond a simple outline of a product's uses to encouraging potential buyers to associate it with a whole desirable style of life, and to feel that not owning the product would involve personal failure, unpopularity, loneliness. Along with this, the idea of fashion (that is, democratic, not high fashion), and keeping up with fashion through consuming goods, was newly emphasised. We may see this now as related to unequal distribution of resources, or to obsessive and expensive attitudes encouraged in even young children towards wearing the 'right' trainers or jeans, or having the 'right' body shape. But in the 1920s the positive connotations given by fashion to change, novelty and youth undermined traditional attitudes which tended to celebrate 'thrift, self-sufficiency, home cooking, family entertainment, hand-made and hand-me-down clothes' (Pumphrey 1984).

These attitudes often had oppressive consequences for women, generally the ones expected to do the 'making' and the 'handing down'. So the figure of *The Flapper* in films, magazines and books offered a challenge to nineteenth-century constructions of femininity on the level of style, image and consumption rather than in other areas such as conventional politics. As Pumphrey describes her, the Flapper's 'unencumbered simplified clothing, short hair and boyish figure, rebellious lifestyle and pursuit of pleasure . . . [along with] her hectic social life' made her a key cultural figure, though one with as many silences as some contemporary advertising images: Where does she work? Where does her money come from? What will happen when she grows older? What else is she interested in? How does she relate to the political women's movements of the 1920s?

The other major figure to which women were invited to relate was apparently very different: *The Housewife*, constructed as having sole responsibility for keeping the home clean. Yet she too was set up as a modern figure. Ads, even those encouraging the most paranoid levels of anxiety about germs in the home, did not treat their addressees patronisingly. The Housewife was constructed as having a serious responsibility (keeping the home clean and safe); as democratically

'To banish fashion from the realm of truth . . . is to imply that there exists a wholly other world . . . in which . . . meaning . . . is transparent and immediately obvious. But not only would that be a world without fashion, it would be a world without discourse, a world, that is, without culture or communication.'

(Wilson 1985)

Figure 9.1

'Dirt is matter out of place.'
(Douglas 1966)

joining 'hundreds of thousands of American women' who have also benefited from this or that product. She was therefore encouraged to think of herself as, in a way, both a public and a private figure, who was being offered the opportunity to take advantage of modern, labour-saving devices; in other words to be connected with technological advances.

As with the Flapper though, there are gaps in this construction or myth. Why should such labour-saving devices actually mean more work for women, via the much higher standards of cleanliness expected of them? If women's work in the home is so important, why is it not counted or paid as work? Why cannot men, or some children, share responsibility for this work within the family? Are, or could, these questions be related to political change?

For both these mythical figures, advertisers constructed a kind of *self-surveillance* in which women were repeatedly invited to take part, asking questions about how clean, how safe was their bathroom/kitchen/cutlery/toilet, and how appealing was their hair/skin/figure/personal aroma?

ACTIVITY 9.3

Look through TV ads during programmes which might be assumed to attract audiences of mainly women (e.g. morning or afternoon TV).

- Do you think such self-surveillance is still invited? How can you tell?
- How does the camera position viewers in relation to the women in the ads?
- Are there any ads addressing men in ways that encourage self-surveillance?
- What kinds of questions are women shown putting to themselves in ads for:
  - cosmetics, clothes?
  - household cleaners?
- Are the ads significantly different in their use of:
  - fantasy situations?
  - irony, wit, playfulness?

Hollywood movies from early on were an important arm of American exports. As early as 1912 English and German manufacturers became alarmed at the decline in demand for their goods, which they attributed to American goods being displayed in Hollywood movies. Fashions and furnishings were showcased, establishing **tie-ins** with manufacturers. In the mid-1930s sketches of styles to be worn by specific actresses in films were sent to merchandising bureaux, which produced them in time for the film's release, then sold them in Macy's Cinema Fashions Shops, among others. The American 'Woman's Film', usually set in the home, often featured very lavish, gleaming, up-to-the-minute kitchen technology and furniture, and again, it either set the fashion for such consumer goods or influenced design of them.

Synergy is often taken to be a very modern term, referring to the **marketing** across different media of figures such as Donald Duck or Judge Dredd by **conglomerate** corporations like Disney (in cards, games, T-shirts, theme parks, mugs and so on, sold in the chains of shops recently opened in the UK). Today it is a highly focused part of the film industry, with companies like Coca-Cola and Pepsi having their own in-house divisions dedicated to **product placement** in Hollywood, including the influencing of scripts (Wasko 1994; Chapter 20, 'Industries', this volume). The history of advertising, fashion and Hollywood suggests such link-ups have been around for some time.

'Want a Coke?' (Eliot to E.T.)
'Gimme a Pepsi Free' (Michael J. Fox in *Back to the Future*).

ACTIVITY 9.4

- Next time you see a 'classic Hollywood' film, watch for the use of:
  - fashion shows
  - narrative shapes (such as the Cinderella story)
  - 'flapper' characters (e.g. Joan Crawford's roles in the 1930s films as aspirational working-class girl who makes her way up the social ladder but ultimately turns her back on it for True Love).
- How do these enable the showcasing of clothes specially lit, framed, and moving 'like liquid light' (Eckert) – and available at a shop near most members of the audience?
- Can you think of any contemporary movies that work in similar ways? *Pretty Woman* (US 1990) or *Working Girl* (US 1988) are obvious examples, but you will probably be able to think of others (*Baywatch?*) whose narratives give glamour to certain products.

These tie-in products as they are now called, were controversial as early as the 1920s. Exhibitors (cinema owners) were sent press books offering window displays and other product information for goods shown in films. Maria La Place (1987) describes a whole set of messages to exhibitors about how the 'transformation' of Bette Davis in *Now, Voyager* (US 1942) could be used to sell fashion goods, slimming diets, hairstyles, cosmetics and so on. The cigarette industry regularly lobbied performers to smoke on screen. By the late 1930s Hollywood occupied a privileged position in the advertising industry.

Figure 9.2 Bette Davis as Charlotte Vale in *Now, Voyager* (US 1942) is transformed from (a) a plain spinster to (b) a fashionable woman and, finally, to (c) a woman confident in her own identity. Her clothes reflect this transformation

Marketing

Such histories make visible the close connection between advertising and marketing, as well as the surrounding cinematic fantasies into which, say, the latest Levi's or Nike ad fits.

Marketing can be defined as the sum of the ways in which a product is positioned in its particular market. This includes pricing, physical availability in shops, by mail order, etc., and often the 'brand' image of the product, which may be constructed by its placement in movies, pop videos, TV serials, or in association with stars or sponsorship deals (such as that of *Inspector Morse* and Beamish beer, or Spike Lee's deals with Nike shoes).

PR or **Public Relations** (see Chapter 12) is a related area, involving the selling of persons or companies, using many of same techniques as advertising, though depending on arranged incidents, 'spontaneous' happenings, etc. being reported by the media as news (by such publicists as Max Clifford). Though these processes have always been linked, the connections have never been as powerful as they are now.

MTV, for example, is a TV channel devoted to music videos, which are themselves both ad (for particular albums) and product (a purchasable video) as well as TV (selling audiences' attention to more advertisers). In many cases tie-ins (such as Michael Jackson's $15m deal with Pepsi on the 'Bad' album) further commoditise the whole operation.

The effects of advertising

It is important to have a sense of how these areas work together since many accounts of advertising (semiotic, deconstructive, **Frankfurt School,** political-economic) analyse particular ads outside the full marketing and indeed cultural context in which they 'work'.

'In post-war West Germany, women were constrained to search beyond national boundaries for female cultural forms untainted by aftertastes of Nazism. To don the accoutrements of an American female ideal – nylon stockings, scarlet lipstick, narrow skirts and high-heeled shoes – was in part to register a public disavowal of fascist images of femininity: scrubbed faces shining with health, sturdy child-bearing hips sporting seamed stockings and sensible shoes.'

(Carter 1984)

See also Hebdige (1988: chs 3–5) on the 'threat' of American style in Britain of the 1950s, also treated in Chapter 5, 'Genres'.

Huge powers are then attributed to the ads themselves. As used in some classroom teaching, it can lead to the feeling that the class can coolly examine the ways that advertising works *on the rest of* its audience, while they personally stay above all that. This approach coincides at some points with the claims of **advertising agencies** who are in the business of making and 'placing' or circulating ads for particular clients.

'Where [some writers] cite the success of Marlboro through media manipulation, my memory … is that the brand was launched in the UK with a six-month low-price campaign that captured many smokers of budget brands. Likewise … the "Reaches the parts …" campaign for Heineken lager, happily coincided with the hottest summer of the century in the UK, with pubs running out of the traditional bitter, and the punters switching forcibly to lager.'

(Cubitt 1986)

Even in the 1980s, when study of the media moved to look at broader histories of advertising, there was still a tendency to take for granted the **effects** of individual ads. To some extent such work was taken in by the overconfidence of advertising itself. By 1989 the advertising bubble had burst and recessionary times, including a tighter market for advertising, set in. It is now worth trying to understand both the limits of ads as individual texts, and the powers of advertising as a system of representation.

ACTIVITY 9.5

Have you ever seen a major ad (with prime-time placement on TV, for example) for a product which it has been difficult to obtain? Choose a prime time ad and research:

● How easy is it to find the product?
● How does its pricing relate to its marketing?
● Does its image relate to any current movies, fashions or songs? If so, how?

It is not necessary to agree with the extreme global pessimism of the Frankfurt School and its successors to argue for some key effects of the advertising system:

- the power of the identities which advertising invites us into
- the consequences of increasingly ad-funded TV and other cultural systems
- the persistence of older-style effects in some parts of the world. Despite the ironic self-awareness and regulation of western advertising, many older-style ads and marketing ploys are still used in the 'Third World' and Eastern Europe, as well as in poorer areas of the 'First World'.

Cigarette companies for example, are rushing to ensure their brands are known in Russia before health restrictions on advertising are imposed. Western women are now encouraged, for health reasons, to breast feed their babies: mothers in Third World countries are often encouraged in hospital to begin the habit of buying expensive packeted baby food milk.

'[In India] ... television has brought the lifestyle of the urban middle class – with its electric kitchen gadgets, motor scooters and fancy furnishings – to villages where women still collect cow dung to fuel their cooking fires ...Though [washing machines and fridges] have little practical use in a farm hamlet with no running water and only a few hours of electricity each night, they have become status symbols in one of the world's fastest growing consumer markets.'

(*Guardian*, 4 January 1995)

Identities and advertising

Advertising has always been keen to locate and profit from the cutting edge of cultural fashions and change. In the last twenty years this has involved processes like **focus groups** (See Chapter 30, 'Selling audiences'). Advertisers have also often learnt from developing knowledge and discussions about the media. Media Studies, after all, started some forty years ago, and many of its assumptions are embedded in journalistic and other popular discourses.

Certainly major advertising agencies, such as Bartle, Bogle Hegarty (BBH), can claim successes like their work for Levi Strauss Europe. The jeans were 'relaunched' in 1982 via campaigns to change the image of the 501s from 'the sort of thing bank clerks would wear – middle-aged ones, at weekends'. A fourteen-fold increase in volume sales of Levi's 501s between 1985 and 1991 and a market share in Europe 4.2 times that of its closest competitor are quoted by the brochure which BBH produces to sell itself to potential clients.

Agencies achieve successes like this campaign partly by tapping into the very latest changes in riskable attitudes, all that 'edge' cultural activity we sometimes call 'fashion' or 'trend'. One recent Levi's ad featured a transvestite wearing the jeans. Though it was quickly taken off British TV, it was seen as a Benetton-style attempt to maintain the reputation of Levi's for striking ads at a time when the 'pink pound' or gay community's spending power is being sought by advertisers.

Such ads are neither simply irresponsible, as the NVLA (National Viewers and Listeners Association) have claimed, nor an abstract stand for a liberalisation of sexual attitudes. The processes of advertising's necessary attempt to keep up to the minute means that it will be driven to take such risks, which many would applaud as giving visibility to groups whose very existence has previously been censored.

Yet most ads will in the end represent us to ourselves as shoppers, as consumers. In the end they promise to solve all the cutting-edge dilemmas and imagery they conjure up by acts of consumption. In the process some rich contradictions are thrown up. Magazines will produce articles and even campaigns around topics like pollution; date rape; women's guilt at their supposed inadequacy as mothers, wives, homemakers; child abuse; the dangers of sexualising very young girls in advertising imagery and so on. It's precisely on such topicality that they can sell themselves to advertisers. But the bulk of their pages will be full of ads which sell products to their readers on the basis of feelings like guilt, images of sexualised toddlers, 'perfect' bodies and the thrill of fast cars, even if many of these are dealt with ironically and with a sense of humour.

ACTIVITY 9.6

Look through your favourite magazine and see if there are any contradictions between the messages of articles and editorials and the images offered by the ads.
- Make notes on any groups of people who seem invisible in those ads.
- What is the age range beyond which desirability for **mainstream** fashion ads seems to end?
- Can the homeless or disabled easily feature in ads?
- Are there magazines where such groups can be represented in advertising imagery? Which groups? Where?

The Advertising Standards Authority Monthly Report, May 1995, reported that a spot-check of ads in the national press in July 1993 showed that 38 per cent of questionable ads were for health and beauty products. Nearly 64 per cent of slimming ads broke the ASA Codes in January 1994.

To take a few specific examples of the possible *effects* of advertising:
- Research into anorexia suggests that young women's understandable absorption into representations of fashion can very easily lead to dissatisfaction with, and an inability to imagine as desirable, any but the most conventional (usually thin or at least adolescent) body.
- Research into housewives' attitudes to their work quickly reveals enormous amounts of guilt about the cleanliness, or tidiness of their homes, even if they feel they are quite able to laugh at, or with, individual ad representations.
- Many men would argue that the most compelling advertising representations of masculinity are ones that produce real levels of

anxiety and inadequacy, even if male culture, with its emphasis on strong silences or loud camaraderie, makes it difficult to talk about or explore such feelings.

- The tobacco industry spends around £50m a year on advertising in the UK (*Media Guardian*, 29 May 1995), £35m of which goes on posters which, with their huge health warnings against using the product, embody the contradictions of this deadly and addictive commodity.

ACTIVITY 9.7

The **ASA** (**Advertising Standards Authority**) is an industry-funded body which oversees non-TV and cinema advertising. Take a recent ad which you find offensive or misleading for whatever reason, and write a letter of complaint to the ASA.

- Discuss the replies you receive with fellow students in the context of the issues raised in this chapter.

References and further reading

Barthes, Roland (1972) *Mythologies,* London: Cape.

Bartle Bogle Hegarty Pack, obtainable from them at 24 Great Pulteney Street, London W1R 4LB. Tel. 0171 734 1677.

Berger, John (1970) *Ways of Seeing,* London: Penguin.

Carter, E. (1984) 'Alice in the Consumer Wonderland' in A. McRobbie, and M. Nava (eds) *Gender and Generation,* London: Macmillan.

Coward, Ros (1984) *Female Desire: Women's Sexuality Today*, London: Paladin.

Cubitt, Sean (1986) 'Reply to Robins and Webster', *Screen,* vol. 27, nos 3–4.

Davidson, M. (1992) *The Consumerist Manifesto,* London: Routledge.

Douglas, Mary (1966) *Purity and Danger: An Analysis of the Concepts of Pollution and Taboo*, London: Ark.

Dyer, Gillian (1982) *Advertising as Communication,* London: Methuen.

Eckert, C. (1990) 'The Carole Lombard in Macy's Window' in J. Gaines and C. Herzog (eds) *Fabrications Costume and the Female Body,* London: Routledge.

Goffman, Erving (1976) *Gender Advertisements,* London: Macmillan.

Hebdige, Dick (1979) *Subcultures: The Meaning of Style,* London: Methuen.

—— (1988) *Hiding in the Light,* London: Routledge.

La Place, Maria (1987) 'Producing and Consuming the Woman's Film' in C. Gledhill (ed.) *Home Is Where the Heart Is,* London: BFI.

Lee, M. (1993) *Consumer Culture Reborn,* London: Routledge.

Leiss, Klein, Jhally (1986) *Social Communication in Advertising,* London:
Marion Boyars.

Marcuse, Herbert (1964) *One Dimensional Man*, London: Routledge &
Kegan Paul.

Mattelart, Armand (1991) *Advertising International,* London: Routledge.

Myers, G. (1995) *Words in Ads,* London: Edward Arnold.

Myers, Kathy (1986) *Understains: The Sense and Seduction of Advertising,*
London: Comedia.

Orbach, Susie (1993) *Hunger Strike,* London: Penguin.

Packard, Vance (1979) *The Hidden Persuaders,* London: Penguin.

Pumphrey, Martin (1984) 'The Flapper, the Housewife and the Making of
Modernity', *Cultural Studies.*

Wasko, Janet (1994) *Hollywood in the Information Age,* London: Polity Press.

Williamson, Judith (1978) *Decoding Advertisements: Ideology and Meaning in
Advertising,* London: Marion Boyars.

—— (1985) *Consuming Passions,* London: Marion Boyars.

Wilson, Elizabeth (1985) *Adorned in Dreams: Fashion and Modernity,*
London: Virago.

Background to the *Keighley News*
Producing the editorial material
Selling advertising

10 / Case study: Local advertising and newspapers

In one sense, a local paper is a public service. How else is a small community to discuss issues and exchange useful information? (Local radio could provide discussion space, but not the range of information.) Without a commercial newspaper, the community would have to finance some form of newsletter. In practice most communities find that there is enough advertising revenue available locally to support a regular paper. In small communities this will be a weekly, in larger areas a daily evening and in one or two large cities a morning daily and possibly a Sunday paper.

This chapter looks at an example of local advertising and you should read it in conjunction with Chapter 9, 'Advertising, marketing and fashion'.

Background to the *Keighley News*

Keighley is a small town in West Yorkshire which, with its surrounding rural areas, has a population of around 70,000. It supports a weekly newspaper, the *Keighley News* (henceforth *KN*), which claims to be 'read by two out of three local people' – a very high **market penetration**. The next small town, 9 miles away, is Skipton – also with a weekly paper which overlaps the potential circulation area slightly. During the week Keighley readers receive up to two free papers (depending on the efficiency of delivery) and many residents will also buy an evening paper, most likely a local edition of the *Bradford Telegraph and Argus* (*T&A*) which circulates throughout the whole Metropolitan District of nearly 500,000. The *T&A* is less successful in persuading everyone to buy a copy and sells around 60,000 copies, Monday to Saturday. A small proportion of Keighley residents will buy the *Yorkshire Evening Post*, published in Leeds (15 miles away) and again with a series of local editions. There is also a 'regional morning daily' from the *Yorkshire Post*.

In this fairly saturated media market, keeping a weekly newspaper afloat is difficult. So, how does the editor of the *Keighley News* face his task and what kind of publication does he produce?

The 'spec' for the **Keighley News**

The *KN* is a **broadsheet** paper with two main parts plus at least one, and sometimes two, half-size supplements. The issue published on Friday, 26 May 1995, which we will analyse here, comprised a total of 40 full pages (two 20-page main sections) including 4 pages of colour (the outside covers). The half-size TV Listings Guide and 'Class of 95' supplement were both 16 pages, again with colour on the outside covers.

ACTIVITY 10.1

From these descriptions can you calculate the paper requirements at the printworks? Assume that a double spread of broadsheet pages is printed at one pass (and that they are cut in half to produce pages for the half-size supplements).

● How many double sheets are required altogether?
● How does this affect the choice for the number of pages in each part?
● What would be the problem in having a supplement with 14 pages or 15 pages?

A rough survey of this particular issue reveals the following breakdown of the use of space in the two main parts of the paper:

Editorial	45.5%
Display Advertising	19.5%
Classified Advertising	35.0%
The Listings Supplement	
Editorial (Listings and Previews)	67.0%
Display	33.0%
The 'Class of 95'	
Editorial (School Photographs)	80.0%
Display	20.0%

The task of the editor now begins to get clearer. He must produce enough interesting **editorial** material to attract readers at a set price (in this case 30p) and sell enough space to balance the production costs when taken in conjunction with the revenue from sales through newsagents.

Producing the editorial material

The *KN* employs sixteen editorial staff – a relatively high number for a paper of this size (some have wider

The *KN* is published by Bradford and District Newspapers, which also publishes the *Telegraph & Argus*, the local free sheets and, like most regional groupings, the other smaller papers in the district as well. The *KN* competitors are therefore mostly papers within the group. Printing takes place in Bradford, saving the cost of a dedicated printworks. Keighley is the 'backup' base for the group with modern accommodation and extra staff. Bradford and District Newspapers are part of the Westminster Press Group, one of the five major regional newspaper groups in the country. Westminster Press is in turn owned by the Pearson Group (*Financial Times*, Penguin Books and shares in Yorkshire/Tyne Tees TV and BSkyB).

responsibilities). It also benefits from being part of a larger group of newspapers and overall appears well equipped to provide the necessary material.

The job roles of some of the staff give a clue to the nature of the editorial material used by the *KN*. A *business editor* is essential. Keighley is still very much a manufacturing town and every week there are enough small news items to justify a business page. Big stories concerning the town's major employers such as Peter Black – suppliers and distributors of footwear and accessories to department stores – occur every few months and in the edition under review the *KN* editor had joined local business people on a trade mission to the United States.

Every local paper will have a *sports editor* who will be responsible for a considerable amount of sports news – in Keighley all the local amateur teams plus the town's very successful Rugby League team. Sport provides guaranteed **copy** week in, week out. One of the editorial team is responsible for entertainment covering local theatre and music and another for co-ordination of reports from 'village correspondents' – these are essential in an area with a large number of small communities which, although close to each other, are also proud of their separate identities and keen to find news about themselves in the local paper. *Community news* also gets a page of events and meetings in the form of a Noticeboard in Section Two of the paper.

In the centre pages are a number of features which you will certainly find in your local paper. The editorial column includes a statement about the independence of the paper and its proud tradition (the paper started in 1862, when there was a growing band of newspaper readers – Charlotte Brontë came down from Haworth to collect the papers in Keighley in the early part of the nineteenth century). Local independence is an important feature. Although many local papers will actually have quite evident political party leanings, expressing them too clearly might backfire in a small community and prevent the paper following up important stories, or risk alienating a proportion of readers.

The 'leader' in this issue reflects on the fate of a local road safety campaigner killed in a traffic accident. You might want to reflect on the listing of 'news values' in Chapter 12, 'Selecting and constructing news' and consider what makes important 'local' news. Issues like road safety tend to be very important and this leader would be read by many people as a contribution to the debate. Alongside the editorial are three 'columns' by local writers. These often revolve around nostalgia (one is written here by a retired local librarian who has become the recognised archivist for the town and seems to have an endless supply of vintage photographs) or something 'folkloric' or dialect-based ruminations on the world from the perspective of a local person. Where the national columnist is urbane and sophisticated, local columnists must to some extent cater for the sensibilities of local culture. On this occasion the two other KN columnists are both dealing with universal issues but there have been occasions when a traditional Yorkshire influence was evident in their stance. (Interestingly, one of the major reasons, revealed by **reader research**, for residents *not* buying the paper was because they were 'not from Yorkshire' – so a local identity cuts both ways.)

Opposite the columnists is the **letters page**, the source of passionate interest in both short-term and long-term debates. A long-running local saga concerns the siting of wind turbines on the moors, while the latest big story has been Rupert Murdoch's Rugby 'Super League'. The KN became very involved in the battles over Super League status for the town team and this produced a very lively letters page.

In Section Two of the KN, the editorial content comprises the entertainment coverage and wedding photographs plus advertising features and the Noticeboard mentioned above. The rest of Section Two is taken up by **classified** ads.

Many parts of the paper are 'predetermined' each week. Out of 20 pages in Section One, 7 are for 'news' and the other 13 are concerned with 'business', 'sport', 'letters', etc. The reporters have all week to collect news stories. 'News' will last that long if no-one else reports it and so getting the editorial material together is not really like the frantic rush of the daily paper (although that will happen if local news breaks, as it did with Super League) – it is more a question of getting the details right and making sure that all parts of the community are properly covered.

ACTIVITY 10.2

Analyse your local paper and divide the news and features up as we have done above.

- Does your paper work in the same way?
- Do you have any particular local features not commonly found?
- What kinds of issues feature in the letters page and editorial?
- What is the difference (if any) in terms of news values between these issues in your local paper and those commonly found in national newspapers?

Selling advertising

There are a number of separate issues to consider. How do you produce quality editorial material, and present it attractively, without raising costs too much? How do you increase advertising revenue without deterring readers who don't want to feel overwhelmed by the ads – there is nothing worse than the publication which seems to be all ads and no news or features (unless, of course, it is *Exchange & Mart*).

Advertising and editorial are interdependent. Advertising space sells because of the promise to reach the readers. If the editorial quality falls and circulation falls with it, advertising revenue will also fall. If advertising revenue falls, the cover price must rise, but this in turn will drive more readers away and so on. This is the vicious whirlpool of decline every publisher dreads. Get it right and it works the other way. New readers mean more advertising revenue and in turn more resources for editorial.

Masthead

Publishing information (blue)

Lead story

Secondary leads

Display ad

Banner

'Puff' or 'blurb'

Filler

Colour photograph

Menu

Display ad

Blue strip

Weather

Bar code

Small display ads

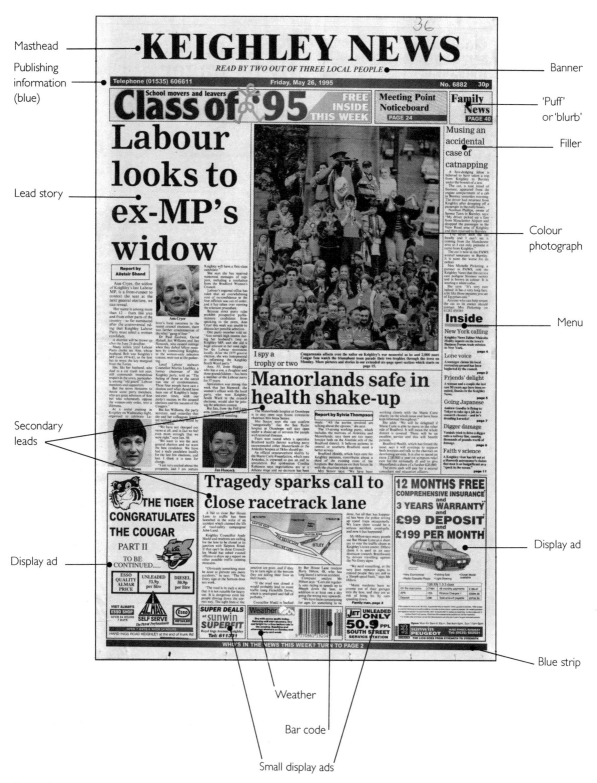

Figure 10.1 Front page of *Keighley News*, 26 May 1995

Analysis of front page

You can tell a great deal about a newspaper by looking carefully at its front page and in particular at the design features. We've identified a number of specific features on our example issue of the *KN* and we will attempt to read each separately, before attempting an overall view.

Masthead The *KN* has a very simple and straightforward title (blunt and Yorkshire): KEIGHLEY NEWS in a traditional serif typeface. Beneath in the same upper-case serif, but italicised, is the **banner** 'READ BY TWO OUT OF THREE LOCAL PEOPLE'. Nothing else appears in the masthead. This is unusual. A common practice is to include a small ad in each corner, known as 'earpieces' or 'title-corners'. These are usually taken by a well-known local company and can carry a very high ad rate. The argument is that when the newspaper is folded for display on the shelves, these ads will always be showing. Check your own paper. On the *KN* these title-corners have moved to the bottom of the page. Beneath the title a blue band carries the date, issue number, price and contact telephone number – a neat presentation of all the necessary cover information.

Puffs Underneath the masthead in a prominent position is a set of 'puffs' – promotions for what is inside. These are in colour and highlight the major attraction this week – the School supplement.

Lead story The main story is usually placed on the left-hand side of the page, where we tend to look first. It carries a headline in the same size as the masthead (about 62 points). This particular story is perhaps more 'national' than 'local', highlighting the problems of the local Labour Party being forced, against some local feeling, to select a woman candidate. The twist is that the frontrunner is the widow of a highly-respected past MP for the town. There are only three small 'pen-pictures' to go with

the story. The editor had hoped to interest the national press and television in the story, but he was upstaged by the death of former Labour Prime Minister Harold Wilson. All the London journalists who were heading for Keighley were diverted to Wilson's home town of Huddersfield.

Colour photograph Colour has arrived only recently in the *KN* and every effort is made to find an interesting (if not always particularly 'newsworthy') image for the front page. In this issue there is a large image of the celebrations for the local Rugby League team which has just won the 2nd Division Championship. This image fulfils all the picture editor's aims. It is colourful (most fans are wearing the Cougars' red, green and white); it shows dozens of local people involved in an historic moment for the town; and it has a composition built around a statue of a sailor on the war memorial, allowing a punning title – 'I spy a trophy or two'.

Secondary leads The bottom half of the page carries two important local stories. Look carefully at the layout. Can you work out why one is in three columns and the other in four?

Filler Down the right-hand column of the page is a classic 'filler' story – a cat which travelled under the bonnet of a taxi. This isn't hard news – it could go anywhere in the paper to provide a little light relief. Here it is used just to fill space which is not big enough for a lead story. Because nothing in the story is 'essential', it can be shortened to fit any space quite easily. Editors always need a stock of filler stories available.

Menu Most publications carry a menu on the front page of what is inside. This serves a different purpose to the puff. None of the items in the menu is likely to persuade the casual reader to buy the paper, but the information is helpful in locating items (and it also acts as another front page filler).

Display ads The bottom corners and strip of the front page are sold as display advertising. The two small ads in the bottom bar are really the missing earpieces which have slid down and combined with a weather chart and a bar-code to assist check-outs in supermarkets and garages. The main design feature here is the use of the second colour, blue. The strip at the foot of the page matches that at the top which neatly frames the whole page. The colour is also available as a second colour to the display ads, improving their visibility. Note also that the ad on the left, for an Esso Garage, picks up on the Rugby League success 'the tiger congratulates the cougar' – this is an increasingly important feature of local sponsorship. The team's success has been closely linked to growing public support, including business support. Rugby League is very much a 'community sport' and there is genuine mutual benefit for local businesses and supporters in the continued success and the promotional opportunities for the town.

Design of the front page

The *KN* at this time (changes are promised) is a traditional broadsheet. The front page works on an eight-column grid. The photograph and the second lead story break up this grid by stretching three columns across a four-column part of the grid.

How many typefaces are used? At first glance it looks like just two – a serif face for all the body text and main headlines and a sans-serif for the reporters' by-lines and some of the information headings. (A **serif** is a bar across the end of any of the 'arms' of a character, which are known as 'ascenders' or 'descenders'. **Sans-serif** is 'without a serif'). Look more closely at the the the masthead and the headline for the lead story. Check out the 'L'. The masthead uses a face with much more tapered serifs – those in the main part of the paper are chunkier and squarer. The masthead is an older and more traditional face.

By modern standards the *KN* presents a traditional-looking local paper with splashes of colour and quite a 'clean' and open presentation. This is spoiled to some extent by very untidy boxes for the reporters' by-lines and some of the outlines around stories. The editor explained that although all the technology for page make-up was available locally, there were still glitches in the process of organising printing in Bradford, so that he wasn't able to monitor the layout decisions easily.

Sans-serif faces are thought to suggest a more modern, 'younger' look to a paper and we might expect to see more of them in the *KN*. However, the editor knows his market and he doesn't want to move too fast. The readership profile and reader research suggest that too much change could alienate readers. (The sister paper in Skipton has a very 'old-fashioned' look and is extremely healthy.) Overall, the 'look' of the *KN* probably suits its readership – a balanced age-profile, cautious about change but not uninterested, and expecting value for money and open, honest comment.

- What does your local paper look like? Do you think it matches the expectations of its readers?

Display advertising

Most of what we think of as advertising is **display advertising**, although in Section Two of the *KN* as in many papers, local and national, the majority of space goes to classified ads. The easiest way to distinguish between the two is to remember that classifieds are usually just a few lines of text in a tiny standard print size, whereas display ads can be any size, but will be in their own separate space and may use any typeface or graphics they choose in order to stand out or 'display' on the page.

The most obvious users (i.e. the biggest ads) of display space in local papers tend to be local supermarkets, furniture warehouses, garden centres, etc. Display ads cost a great deal and therefore in order to justify their cost they must reach a high proportion of potential buyers of the products being advertised. This explains why nationally available products are rarely advertised in local papers. There is little point in advertising a particular brand of car in a local paper since the ad would be seen by only a fraction of the potential national market. Advertising in every local paper would not be as good value as advertising in one or two national papers. However, advertising a car as part of an ad for a local garage makes sense in a local paper, if 'two out of three' potential buyers at that garage get to see the ad.

Classified advertising

Hundreds of tiny two-line ads doesn't sound very glamorous and 'selling classifieds' might be thought of as a very routine job. In fact, a successful classified section is often the basis for the overall success of a newspaper. This is true of local and national papers. One of the strengths of the *Guardian* is its different specialist classified sections for each day of the week. Classifieds offer a very important service and they may be the sole reason some people buy the paper.

We can split the classified section in a local paper into different functions. First there are 'official announcements'. Fortunately for the paper's owners, there are certain public announcements which must be made by law and the local paper is the perfect place for them: these comprise planning notices, licence applications, etc. Then there are the more personal announcements, the 'hatched, matched and dispatched' as they are often known (births, marriages and deaths). We are all interested in what happens to friends and neighbours and these are often the most eagerly scrutinised part of the paper. In Keighley, the convention has grown up whereby when someone has a birthday such as a 40th or 50th, friends or relatives will put in a photograph of said person when they were, say, 5 or 15 years old. This increases the fun and the interest and is the kind of custom warmly encouraged by the paper.

The third function of the classified section is to

advertise local products and services and here again there are strong links to the local community. The local council is likely to be a big advertiser in relation to job vacancies and this may create difficulties if the paper is also running investigative stories on the council. There have been several instances, especially in London and other large cities, where paper and council have fallen out so badly that the council has refused to advertise in the local paper. Both sides suffered badly in such disputes. The paper lost advertising revenue and the council found recruitment much more difficult. This is a good example of how commercial necessity might constrain (or help maintain) local press relations.

A successful classified section will generate good business for the paper if it convinces readers that the goods and services on offer are worth pursuing, i.e. that everyone offering something uses the classifieds to sell it. The classifieds manager dreams of the situation where eager punters are waiting for the paper to appear so they can be the first to apply for the job, bid for the second-hand car, etc. It might not be such a rush on a weekly paper like the *KN* (which offers free classifieds for the sale of items under £50), but in big cities where the evening paper may have several editions starting at around 11 or 12 noon, the first edition is likely to be bought either by people chasing jobs or flats or by gamblers checking the afternoon racing.

Advertising features

Part way between advertising and editorial copy is the advertising feature and this issue of the *KN* carries two such features: one is a food and drink column and the other a piece on a local fair. These features are designed *directly* to attract advertising. The newspaper produces a general article, usually with the aim of giving information about a particular topic, and invites businesses with some link to the topic to advertise on a special deal basis. There are a number of standard ploys. For instance, when a new restaurant opens or is refurbished, a piece may be written about the opening and advertisements sought from the drinks suppliers, builders, furnishings suppliers, etc. associated with the opening. Most of the parties concerned benefit from the arrangement. The paper sells space, the advertisers get a good deal and a little extra attention because of the focus on the page, the restaurant gets free publicity, and even the reader gets useful information in terms of knowledge about a new facility. In order to preserve its ethical position, the paper will print 'Advertising Feature' at the head of the piece to signify that what follows is not a news report or a food and drink 'review'. The reader must then accept that the information in the piece, though not factually inaccurate, will not be as objective as in other parts of the paper.

A comprehensive advertising sales and promotion policy

Many aspects of selling advertisements are, like the news itself, relatively fixed. Many of the classifieds and even some of the regular display advertising are placed week in, week out. However, in order to maintain a high level of ad revenue and to deter competitors, it is important for the paper to be 'selling' space and not just 'renting' it out. In other words, the paper must employ people to contact firms and persuade them of the value of advertising. We've already noted the appearance of advertising features and in this issue of the KN we have a whole supplement, 'The Class of '95' which is little more than a collection of group photographs from local schools. This ensures that all those featured will buy the paper as a souvenir, but also gives an opportunity for school outfitters, local newsagents, etc. to advertise.

The most competitive area of advertising is in the classifieds and here the paper must be sure that it is efficient (and accurate) in taking copy, i.e. it provides a good service to users, but also it must sell new ideas and new deals to business users of classifieds like the estate agents and motor dealers. A new deal such as discounts for long 'runs' over several weeks or for bigger displays within the classified section can make a dramatic impact. There is also a 'production constraint' factor.

Selling advertising space (and from the other side buying space – known in the industry as **media**

Imagine you are the editor of a local paper and you plan a 40-page issue with 18 pages of classifieds. The deadline for copy to go to the printers arrives and you have all the editorial material sorted out, but you only have 17 pages of classified ads. What do you do?

There are a number of options, but you certainly can't leave the page blank. You can't drop the page because pages come in fours, at least. You could spread the material more widely and lose the space, but this will mean that you have lost potential revenue. The best move is to phone round your regular advertisers and offer lower and lower rates until you persuade them to buy the remaining space.

Can you see any drawbacks in this? If you do it too often, the advertisers may start to think you are in some kind of trouble – or they might decide to withhold their ads until your prices fall.

buying) requires specialist knowledge and skills. A whole separate industry has grown up which supports the process and you can get a good flavour of the business if you read the trade publication Media Week, which carries advertisements by newspapers themselves targeting media buyers and presenting information about their circulation figures (usually as audited by the Audit Bureau of Circulation (**ABC**)) and their reader profile (i.e. the percentage of AB, C1, etc.). You may also come across reports from **media research** organisations who log the effectiveness of advertising campaigns in different media. Local newspapers want to show that they offer better value to advertisers and they may commission research to prove it. This wouldn't normally be done by a single title, but may be undertaken by a newspaper group as a whole. The KN receives material produced by a national market research organisation commissioned by the group. This is followed up with local **reader panels**.

The nature of media research is such that what may appear insignificant details can be crucial in persuading advertisers. For instance, the *KN* has recently learned that it has a completely balanced **age profile** (i.e. the same percentage of each age group reads the paper).

ACTIVITY 10.3

Think about the way people use local newspapers.

● How long do they spend reading them?
● How long do they keep a weekly paper in the house?
● How reliable and accurate do readers feel local news is compared to national or regional news?
● Why do they read the paper? Why do some people not read it?
● What kind of research findings would best persuade advertisers that local newspapers offer a good deal? Try to mock up an ad for the group that owns your local newspaper, to appear in *Media Week*.

Advertising managers need to be constantly up to date in terms of how advertising is changing and what kinds of new products are being sold. A new arrival in 1995 was the National Lottery and many newsagents took to buying small display ads to let local residents know that they were selling tickets.

The saturated media market and advertising spend

So far we have discussed only newspaper advertising and noted the different types of newspaper circulating in a local area. We have also made the point that the total advertising spend in any locality is probably relatively fixed, i.e. there is a limit to how much businesses or individuals are prepared to spend on advertising at any one time. Therefore if a new medium or a new competitor in the same medium comes along, the same spend will be spread further and divided up between a greater number of media products. (This point seems to have escaped the pundits who suggest that we may have all kinds of new media services offered and that many of

them will depend on advertising revenue.) If this is the case, the new media will initially offer very inexpensively produced products, because there is no guarantee the advertising revenue will be forthcoming.

So what competition might prove a threat to a local newspaper? The two obvious contenders in the current climate are local radio and cable. Radio stations have been opening in several new localities recently, and cabling of much of the country is either completed or underway at the time of writing. The threat from radio is immediate. Radio is undergoing something of a revival in commercial terms, but in a small town like Keighley the impact has not been great. The local commercial station in Bradford broadcasts across the whole metropolitan district and tends to compete with the *Bradford Telegraph & Argus*. Nevertheless, the *KN* is watching the franchises on offer carefully.

Broadcast radio can't target small districts directly, but cable can. Yorkshire Cable does not carry local advertising, but other cable companies have experimented with very local schemes. It is possible for a cable company to send advertising material down the cable to just a handful of streets. This could be highly attractive to supermarkets, since they could promote a special offer at a local store at a very low cost to just a few people who live close by, while a different ad went out to customers on the other side of town. Such ads would obey our rule of reaching a very high percentage of the target group. The *KN* has worked closely with Yorkshire Cable, who sponsored the TV listings supplement. Reader research discovered this was not valued, so it has since been dropped and other supplement ideas tried. The editor is well aware of the need to keep ahead of the market.

The *KN* can't act unilaterally and decisions about the relationship with other media are taken at group level. Local papers may be one of the oldest media, but they have survived by adapting to new conditions. The *KN* is already stored on CD-ROM and is prepared to offer new services to businesses and individual readers when the market is proved to be there. Who knows, in a few years time local newspapers may act as 'network servers', distributing business information down **ISDN** lines and providing everyone in the neighbourhood with up-to-date listings of events and a library of local history information for schools. And won't such a service still carry a 'hatched, matched and dispatched'?

References and further reading

The most important material for study in this area is the spread of local newspapers in your local area and, if possible, some contact with the people who produce them. Most textbooks and manuals are geared more towards the national press:

Evans, Harold (1978) *Pictures on a Page: Photojournalism, Graphics and Picture Editing,* London: Heinemann.

Keeble, Richard (1994) *The Newspapers Handbook,* London: Routledge.

Moore, Ben (1992) 'Hold the Front Page!', *In the Picture,* no. 17, summer. (This provided the basis for the Front Page Analysis exercise in this chapter.)

11 Ideologies

Marxist approaches
Challenges to Marxist
  approaches
Pleasure
Discourses
Critical pluralism

The concept of **ideology** has been a key one in shaping the field of Media Studies. Though currently rather unfashionable, it still underpins some important debates. The term refers to:

- sets of ideas which give some account of the social world, usually a partial and selective one
- the relationship of these ideas or values to the ways in which power is distributed socially
- the way that such values are usually posed as 'natural' and 'obvious' rather than socially aligned.

Some ideas, though they form a system and are quite rigid, don't fall into the area of the 'ideological'. Someone may have obsessive ideas about personal cleanliness, and relate them systematically to every area of their life, but these would not necessarily be called ideological.

Nor is **ideology** the same as **propaganda**, though politicians will often use the two as though they were interchangeable. Propaganda is a **genre**, or particular kind of discourse, which announces itself openly as wanting to persuade its audience of something. Though it usually urges political positions, such as voting for a particular party, propaganda may carry apolitical messages (e.g. not to drink and drive). The methods of advertising and propaganda can be quite close.

Government propaganda is used at moments of 'national emergency' (e.g. wars), when it will attempt to control and shape public perceptions in particularly coercive ways such as:

- direct **censorship** of reports, especially of casualties or enemy successes
- only allowing a certain 'pool' of approved journalists into a war zone (Falklands and Gulf War)
- banning fiction and entertainment material which it perceives as related to the war (*Carry On Up the Khyber* was pulled from the schedules during the Gulf War).

Such examples could be argued as simply the taking to an extreme of quite routine processes, such as MI5 vetting of staff in the BBC until very

Propaganda was first used as a term in the Roman Catholic Spanish Inquisition (the Society for the Propagation of the Faith). O'Sullivan, Hartley *et al.* (1994) define it as: 'the intentional control, manipulation and communication of information and imagery in order to achieve certain political objectives' and advise careful use of the term.

ITN explained to a Parliamentary Defence Committee on the reporting of the Falklands War (not a war of national emergency, when censorship may be justifiable) that it tried to give 'a nightly offering of interesting, positive and heart-warming stories of achievement and collaboration born out of a sense of national purpose'. The BBC stated that an impartial approach was felt to be 'an unnecessary irritation'.

recently, or the occasional direct pressure on news and current affairs, let alone the key everyday processes of news shaping by official sources.

Q Is propaganda then the same as ideology?

A The relationship is better seen as that of one end of a spectrum to the rest. Ideology is used of positions which are not so explicitly visible, and which may be at work in both propaganda and advertising as well as in routine media processes.

For instance, **sociobiology** provides 'taken for granted' assumptions coming out of arguments that the natural world, or sometimes simply the study of genetics, proves that all human beings are 'naturally' acquisitive, competitive and selfish. A counter view would be interested in:

- suggesting examples from the natural world that provide other images of a non-competitive kind
- tracing whether sociobiology's particular emphasis seems to accompany the rise of positions celebrating (or stating as natural) a ruthless 'survival of the fittest' version of capitalism in the 1980s and 1990s.

Marxist approaches

In France, in the period leading up to the 1789 Revolution, it was argued, scandalously, that some ideas had a systematic relationship to social power, rather than simply existing 'freely'. This was part of the long replacement of feudal world views by more modern ones – in other words, it was itself ideological.

The Western European feudal (roughly tenth to fifteenth centuries) world view was that the earth was made by God, with the sun revolving round it, and that everything on earth had its natural place in a divinely designed order which could not be questioned. Most discussion of ideology in Media and Cultural Studies comes out of the work of **Marx** who also, but in the nineteenth century, questioned a supposedly natural, inevitable order of things. He tried to understand and challenge the power of the rising class of industrial manufacturers or capitalists (the bourgeoisie as they were sometimes called) within a new profit- and market-dominated system – capitalism. He was especially interested in their relationship to their employees, the working classes who, he argued, had the power to change history by their united action.

He used the concept of ideology (which he never defined 'once and for all') to account for how the capitalist class protected and preserved its economic interests, even during years of unrest and attempted revolutions. Marx emphasised the importance of **class difference**, or people's relationship to the means of production: do they own factories, banks, country estates, or do they have to earn their living by working

---

The statement 'the sun revolves around the earth' now ludicrous, was once highly ideological, key for the dominant position of combined religious and secular powers. Galileo was shown 'the instruments of torture' by the Roman Catholic Church in 1616 to prevent him establishing that the earth moved round the sun, a position which threatened the foundations of a world view putting established (western) earthly power at the centre of the universe.

Karl Marx (1818–83) German political intellectual and activist, analysing and seeking to overthrow by revolutionary means the emerging industrial capitalist social order of nineteenth-century Europe.

'The ideas of the ruling class are, in every age, the ruling ideas: i.e. the class, which is the dominant material force in society, is at the same time its dominant intellectual force. The class which has the means of material production at its disposal, has control at the same time over the means of mental production.'

(Marx, *The German Ideology*, 1845/6)

together for the owners of factories, banks and so on? Two of his emphases have been particularly important for Media Studies:

- He argued that the **dominant** ideas (what might be called the '**common sense**') of any society are those formulated by the ruling class to secure its rule or dominance. This was argued to be the key to why the meaning-making bodies (which now include the media) in any society represent political issues as they do. It implies that the working class needs to develop its own ideas and struggle for the means of circulating them if it is successfully to oppose the capitalist class.

- Related to this, he formulated what is called a **base–superstructure** model of the social role of institutions such as the media. This assumes that the base of a social order (its ways of materially reproducing itself: by industrial capitalist, or feudal–rural relations, for example) determines its superstructure, its 'secondary' ideological and political institutions, such as religion and cultural life. Such a model is also often called **economic determinist**, since the economic 'base' is seen to crucially determine, not just influence, cultural and political activity.

More recently, **political economy** approaches such as those of Peter Golding and Graham Murdock, or of the Mattelarts in relation to **media imperialism**, have tried to develop Marx's emphasis on the determining role of the economic, against what has been argued as media theory's overemphasis on textual or cultural elements. They emphasise the extent to which those who own and control huge proportions of the media (such as Rupert Murdoch or Ted Turner) share in the privilege of the dominant class. In turn this group will ensure that the social imagery and knowledge which is circulated through the media is broadly in its interests and reproduces the system of class inequalities from which it benefits.

This does not necessarily deny that **alternative**, even radically **oppositional** ideas (such as those of Greenpeace, or of Noam Chomsky's anti-imperialism) don't struggle for **access** to the media, often with some success. They argue the need for a sense of the interplay between the economic (especially ownership patterns) and cultural or symbolic levels of the social order. But they strongly emphasise the increasing concentration of power in the hands of a very few media conglomerates, suggesting this leads to:

- a decline in the range of material available, e.g. in satellite and cable TV programming, as global capitalist forces exclude all but the commercially successful

- an exclusion of those lacking economic power or resources both as voices in the media and as consumers of the new technologies

- the prevalence of 'easily understood, popular, formulated, undisturbing, assimilable fictional material' (Golding and Murdock 1991).

'To make a film about racism, Hollywood uses the buddy movie.' (Smith 1988: 30 on *Mississippi Burning*)

Among the objections to this position is the extent to which any economic determinist account of the media can choose to argue for merely the *interplay* of economic and cultural. It is also important to consider why popular cultural products such as films, TV and music are popular without writing off the audience as dupes. (See Strinati 1995 for more detailed discussion.)

Antonio Gramsci (1891–1937) Italian marxist activist who took part in complex political struggles in the Italy of the early twentieth century, involving Church and State, north and south, peasants and modern industrial workers.

Gramsci's term **hegemony** became important in thinking about how dominant value systems change through struggle. It moved away from an emphasis on the power of *one* dominant ideology, and the absolutely determining power of the economic base. Instead, a struggle for dominance (or hegemony) in the area of ideas and values was argued to be waged by alliances of key groups that have achieved control over the 'decisive economic nucleus'. The concept of hegemony varies over time in Gramsci's writings from *coercive control* (direct force or threat) to *consensual control,* arising when individuals 'willingly' take on the world view of the dominant group.

It is a useful distinction or refinement on the original formulations of Marxism. For Media Studies the crucial emphasis has been that people are not forced against their will into a **false consciousness** of the world, but that they have their consent actively fought for all the time, nowadays almost exclusively through the media. This position provides a space in which to argue for debate and change, not simply to feel that those who own the cultural industries (more concentratedly than ever before) can control everything that occurs within and as a result of them.

Let's apply these positions to contemporary struggles imaged by the media. These will often involve words as well as images. As was often said of him, and of others, when Nelson Mandela was in prison, 'Yesterday's terrorist is today's freedom fighter and tomorrow's government leader.' Well-circulated terms like 'benefit scroungers' are argued to deflect attention away from huge structural inequalities of wealth and from the causes of dependency, and on to relatively minor or exceptional cases of benefits fraud. On the other hand, terms like 'the over-developed or First World' are much less familiar than 'developing countries or Third World'.

One of the many contradictory sayings of 'common sense' is the proverb 'The Lord helps those who help themselves.'

The word 'famine' for food crises in the 'Third World', for example, has been argued to work to obscure financial–political relations, and their colonial histories, by conjuring up Biblical, pre-industrial images of mysterious scourges coming from God, or Nature. These obscure very modern processes such as:

- western food mountains
- price fixing of harvests
- the policies of the IMF (International Monetary Fund) and other big banks
- the 'futures' speculation on commodities (i.e. crops) on western Stock exchanges.

Images of the victims of such shortages have often worked with a particular visual rhetoric: the camera usually above the pitiful victim, preferably a child, who is given no name, or access to the soundtrack or translation facilities if seen on TV. This invites western audiences to think of them as existing in a victim's dependency relationship to the west (whereas it is the west that is dependent on raw materials, at a certain price, from the 'Third World').

Such images are also argued to perpetuate the situation by excluding images of such people as potentially or actually active in their own fates – by developing appropriate technology with the west, or arguing for 'Third World' debt to the IMF to be cancelled in order to kick-start their economies – and possibly economies in the west, as trade grows in consequence.

ACTIVITY 11.1

Can you think of an occasion when the media have seemed to act out the kind of struggle for hegemony which Gramsci describes?

- Jot down what struggles you think were taking place over the issue in any of the media forms you came across. Examples might include debates over entry into the 'European Union'; over 'single mothers' and the idea of benefits fraudsters, or over any big charity telethon.

If you can study the 'Live Aid' tapes, or other material campaigning for help to the 'Third World', see if you agree that it is structured in the way suggested above.

- Does it seem to be trying to introduce some of the political arguments around debt, appropriate help, etc.?
- What seem to be its systematic emphases and exclusions, including its performers?
- Why do you think this was?
- How would you construct a charity ad for such an appeal?

(Recently there have been attempts, in both the US and UK, to ridicule such struggles over representation, working with a powerful term which sets up an imaginary stereotype: 'political correctness'.)

Figure 11.1

Louis Althusser (1918–90)
French philosopher who
developed a structuralist version
of Marxism. His ideas are most
clearly laid out in 'Ideology and
Ideological State Apparatuses' in
*Lenin and Philosophy and Other
Essays* (1971).

The other name you will come across in Media Studies is that of
Althusser who tried to 'establish Marxism as a science and to rid it of
economic determinism' (Strinati 1995: 147). He argued that economic
determinism works only in 'the last instance', and that parts of the
superstructure are 'relatively autonomous'. Ideology, in his theories, is a
force in its own right. Class rule is said to be sustained by two kinds of
organised power, which operate in a structurally related way. The
Repressive State Apparatus (RSA) includes the army, police, prisons

and law courts. It wins and maintains state power by force. The **Ideological State Apparatus (ISA)** is argued to include education, the church, party politics, the family and the media, and to maintain power at the ideological level, in people's minds. It does this partly by naturalising, making into 'just common sense', assumptions and ideas which are ideological in that they manufacture and maintain consent to the existing social order.

ACTIVITY 11.2

Look again at Figure 5.2 (p. 59) in Chapter 5.

- Apply the exclusions (class, patriarchy, race) which Dyer suggests it habitually operates, to any contemporary media entertainment text.
- How does this help understand the ideological workings of entertainment forms?

Althusser's approach is different to the classic Marxist emphasis on cultural or media forms as expressions of, or forces determined by, the economic base. But an objection to his scheme is that it implies there can be 'no way out' of ideology, and that this, of course, fails to account for the work of Althusser, since in theory he is outside its grip in order to be able to write about it at all.

Challenges to Marxist approaches

Several important changes in the world since the heyday of these Marxist theories of ideology are worth noting:

- the collapse of Eastern bloc state socialism
- accompanying this, the renewed power of consumer capitalist 'free market' emphases, including their media theory equivalents: celebration of audiences' power in relation to the media
- the challenge of newer politics (based on gender, ethnicity, sexuality and environmentalism) to the class- and economics-focused analysis of Marxism
- a growing scepticism about the claims of science to absolute truth. This matters, since science had often been appealed to as the opposite of 'ideology' in Marxist-derived theories. Some **postmodern** positions have abandoned any kind of attempt at a rationally accountable or improvable world.

Since we still live in deeply unequal, class-divided societies, driven by the classic capitalist logic of profit and competition, Marxist interest in economic power and its relationship to ideology and to social transformation has continued to be relevant for attempts to change that logic. But several qualifications need now to be made:

- To talk of one dominant ideology implies an improbably coherent, argument-free ruling class, smoothly making the rest of us go along with its view of the world.
- Such ideological analysis risks making very patronising assumptions about anyone other than the person doing the analysing. If the wheels of ideology roll so perfectly smoothly to produce conformity, how has the person analysing their workings come to have a position outside that system?
- Althusser's formulations in particular, as applied to Media and Film Studies, have been argued to have been applied in ways that hugely overstress the power of texts to determine people's actions (see Chapter 15, 'Realisms').
- A renewed exploration of the role of ownership and political-economic structures in general is needed in Media Studies. But a Marxist analysis is more than this: it argues the determining power of the economic base. Yet if ideas and culture can affect that base (as in religious fundamentalism, struggles over free speech, Live Aid, environmentalism and so on) how can the distinctive emphasis of Marxist approaches be retained?
- The weighting given to 'the *dominant ideology thesis*' was more recently challenged by writers (Abercrombie, Hill and Turner 1980) insisting that though dominant ideologies do exist, they are not the most important means for making social orders hang together. Indeed, the existence of huge state bodies for surveillance and armed control, as well as the rise of racism and religious fundamentalism, suggests we do not inhabit unified social orders, running smoothly along. Abercrombie *et al.* suggest that the 'dull compulsion of the economic' as well as the power of state force leaves us little room, time or power to challenge systems of values which most people disagree with, or feel to be personally irrelevant.

Pleasure

Within Media Studies more specifically, important early studies of news processes (see Chapter 12) were replaced by an interest in fiction, entertainment and fantasy forms. These are much less amenable to an ideological approach which often sees as the 'sugar on the pill' the pleasures which audiences take in entertainment forms. It can also underestimate audiences' capacity to compare media with non-media experience.

Of course, 'pleasure' is not just one thing, nor are pleasures value free. Apart from formal pleasures (the elegance of a script or a set of special effects) or even erotic ones (the turn of a face or body on screen), the media offer cognitive pleasures, related explicitly to sets of values. There are pleasures of hearing a marginalised position given stirring expression, or of being offered an image (whether documentary or soap opera character) which suddenly seems to help us understand a situation.

Nevertheless, such pleasures are not always found where you might expect. Dahlgren (1985) and Stam (1983) among others have argued that focusing on 'pleasure' in relation to the news suggests that far from audiences absorbing the '**bias**' or 'dominant ideology' in TV news, they often slip in and out of attentiveness to its messages, and more regularly take pleasure in its form and the sense it gives them of being 'up to the minute', and in its reassuring tendency, however horrendous its stories, to flatter them into a sense of being privileged witnesses, of having the world scanned and under control. The newscasters chatting together at the end of the bulletin, for example, is reassurance that 'we' can all return to the 'normal' world of the domestic – and the ads.

In such an emphasis, the major ideological effect of the big TV news bulletins (daytime ones are slightly different) is argued to be the way they avoid provoking the viewer into political action (which could be assumed to be a reasonable response to some of the stories), thus contributing to a passive and acquiescent citizenry/electorate.

Figure 11.2 The pleasures of reassurance?

ACTIVITY 11.3

How much of a routine or ritual is watching the news in your household?

- Does it seem to have a reassuring function?
- What seem to be the markers of such reassurance, and of 'up to the minuteness' in news programmes?
- Does this differ between local and national news items?
- How do you think this relates to the issues raised in this chapter?

Discourses

Where have we got to? The argument that there are dominant ideologies (connected to gender, ethnicity, etc.) rather than one dominant ideology (dependent on the economic base) was a step away from Marxism. The term **discourse**, associated with the work of **Foucault**, involves yet another, slightly different emphasis in thinking about the relationship between socio-political power and the media. A discourse is any regulated system of statements or language use which has rules, conventions and therefore assumptions and exclusions. Foucault takes this broadly linguistic definition further by exploring how discourses organise knowledge in the context of serving particular kinds of power relationships. The ways that children are defined by intelligence and aptitude tests is a good example of power as knowledge. So is the well-funded research of commercial TV into its audiences as **consumers**.

Discourses are rather like language genres or categorisations, especially within media (see Chapter 5). They are different to both 'jargon' and 'language in general'. Discourse analysis is interested in exploring what values or ideas about the world are contained, prevented, or perhaps encouraged by the practices and (often unspoken) rules of a particular discourse and their different **registers**. For example, the media overwhelmingly report pay negotiations in terms of management's 'offers' and union's 'demands'. If a strike occurs, the story will begin with the union's 'refusal' of an offer. But, of course, such events could equally be signified in terms of management's 'demand' in response to workers' 'offers'. Discourse analysis is interested in seeing how widespread such different habits and arrangements are, and how they might relate to other social power structures.

We all inhabit and work with various discourses. The way you would write a letter to your teacher as an apology for absence, to a bank manager asking for an overdraft, or to a close friend will employ different discourses or kinds of socially situated language. Some (the semi-legal

Michel Foucault (1926–84) Post-structuralist philosopher, sociologist and historian of knowledge. He is celebrated for work on the relationship of power to knowledge, involving the power of discourses, especially in the areas of madness and sexuality.

Discourse 'a socially produced way of thinking or talking about a topic' (John Fiske in Allen 1987: 268).

Register A variation in a language according to its context or situation, rather like a fine tuning. See O'Sullivan et al. 1994.

A note on jargon and discourse

Media Studies has its own discourse, which is sometimes accused of being a jargon. Such accusations are often made when one area of expertise meets another. My technical vocabulary, whether as a football enthusiast or a film fan, is **jargon** to you – and vice versa. But subjects like Media Studies and Sociology are about things we deal with in our everyday lives. So they either speak the language of common sense and run the risk of seeming to state the obvious, or they interpret, analyse and use more specialised sets of knowledge, but are then seen as using an excluding, elitist jargon for something 'we all know about'.

discourse of the letter to the bank manager) will have more social power than others.

If you have studied science at school you will have employed a scientific discourse to describe experiments. 'The bunsen burner was lit', for example, is one of a number of ways in which 'scientific impersonality' will be marked in writing up an experiment. The account will ideally seem to come from nowhere (no mention of the person who lit the burner), and therefore to conceal its human fallibility in favour of a kind of authority. British TV news often operates in a similar way.

ACTIVITY 11.4

The next time you watch the evening news note:

- the imposing high-tech studio
- the decision to seat newscasters behind a large but uncluttered desk
- the absence of many signs of the hustle and business of news processes
- the 'casting' of people with Standard English accents
- the use of impersonal language, even tones, semi-formal dress and so on.
- Does this seem like a discourse, with rules, exclusions and assumptions?

This is quite different to the discourse of **tabloid** news, which is much less formal, more jokey and aggressive, and will often 'call out' in its headlines, as in the notorious examples of the *Sun*'s 'GOTCHA' in the Falklands War to the sunken Argentinian warship *Belgrano* and its 400 plus crew, or 'UP YOURS DELORS' during European negotiations. A particular layout, typography, use of photographs and captions will also structure this discourse.

Each of them emerges from different histories and therefore relationships to established power: BBC news from the changing history of British **public service broadcasting**; tabloid news from the commercial history of journalism, especially recent multinational price wars and globalisation.

Critical pluralism

It may seem that these developments away from classical Marxism, culminating in discourse analysis, come close to an account of the media which floats free of power, such as exists in many **pluralist** models. These emphasise the diversity and choice in media forms, and argue that if certain values are dominant, it is because they are genuinely popular.

> Think about the suggestion that if there is a dominant ideology in the late 1990s, it is this: 'Everything is relative. There are no big power structures. We all have lots of freedoms. There is no such thing as a dominant ideology.'

Golding and Murdock's political economy approaches (see p. 119) emphasise both the importance of economic power, and the ways that alternative, even radically oppositional ideas circulate in the media. Such **critical pluralism** acknowledges that there may be struggle between competing discourses, but insists that it is not an amicable free-for-all (as in pluralist theories and the 'free market' values they so closely relate to). Some discourses are backed by greater material resources and have easier access to the major means of publicity and policy making. Examples include:

- 'the commercial speech of the consumer system' (**marketing** and advertising) and its emphases (see Chapter 9, 'Advertising, marketing and fashion')
- the conservative political positions of right-wing ideologues such as Newt Gingrich in the USA. These have power to legislate changes in media ownership and **deregulation**, or to encourage right-wing 'shock-jocks' in circulating certain 'limit' political positions, like outright racism, and so on.

This approach is a useful corrective to some applications of Gramsci's term 'hegemony', which give little weight to habitual and repeated access to images and knowledge, rather than the more exciting flare-ups of hegemonic struggles over strikes, or wars, or other 'moments'.

In 1995 a federal government building in Oklahoma City was bombed, involving nearly 200 dead and harrowing scenes on TV news.

For days there was speculation about who the bombers were. But only hours after the bombing a tiny agency, Inter Press, pointed the finger at the American far-right militia movement. They worked not on inside information, but on simple deduction, involving

- the date (the anniversary of the ending of the Waco siege, highly significant for the militias)
- the fact that a government building was bombed (given the militias' hatred of central government)
- the proximity of Oklahoma to Waco.

'According to [the agency bureau chief] the episode speaks volumes about the ...American media. "When they think terrorism, they think Middle East," he said.'

(*Guardian*, 1 May 1995)

Discussion

Given the historical involvement of the USA in the Middle East oil states and the recent turns that history has taken, the assumption that Middle Eastern terrorists might be to blame for Oklahoma City is not totally unreasonable or unlikely. But it seems that one ideological position had very little speedy access to the minds of journalists: one which would have connected the bombing to the rise of extreme right-wing armed movements inside the USA, to the easy availability of weapons as promoted by the National Rifle Association (NRA) and so on.

ACTIVITY 11.5
- When did you last see a film where the villain role was a Middle Eastern terrorist? (*True Lies* and *Back to the Future* are a couple of examples.) How widely circulated was that film?
- When did you last see a film where the villain role was a right-wing American militia member? How widely circulated was that film?

Much contemporary advertising takes an apparently surprising 'Green' ideological position. The growth of struggles over the future of the global environment has led to ads attempting to co-opt them for their purposes, often trying to suggest that it is possible and desirable to unite ourselves with 'nature', and that certain products, from shampoo to cars, can help us do this (e.g. see Figure 11.3). Such ads clearly relate to widespread fears about the ruination of the planet by overproduction and

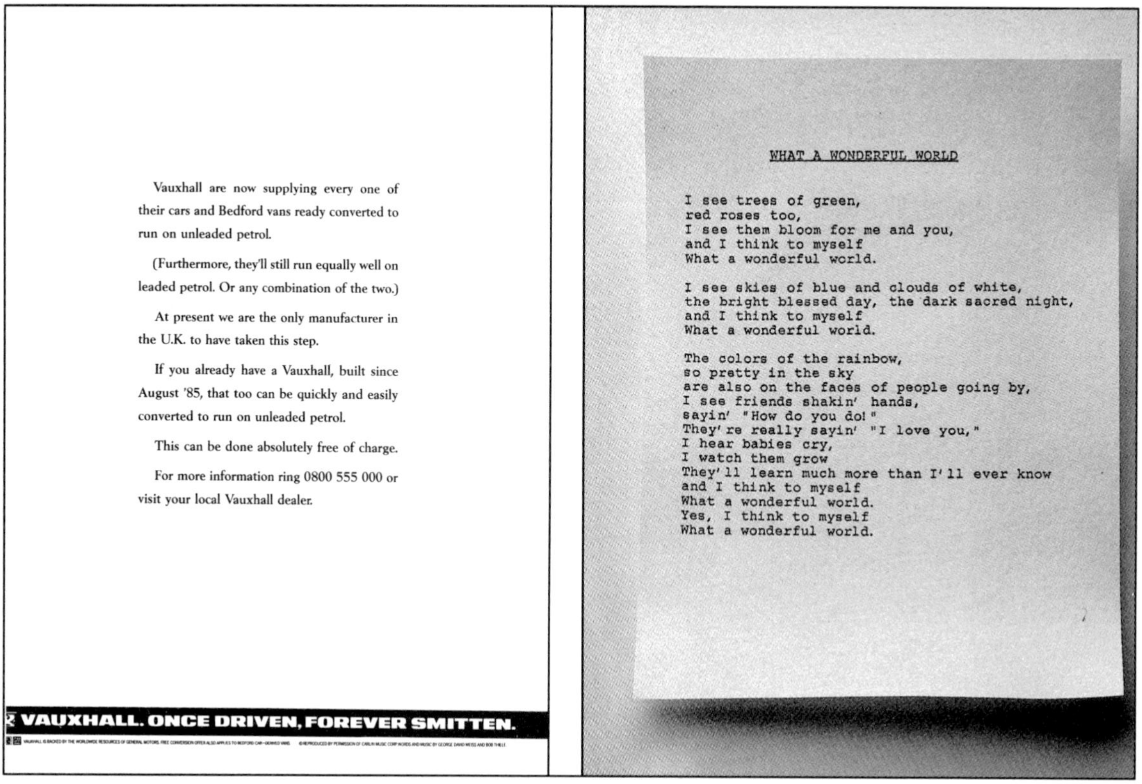

Vauxhall are now supplying every one of their cars and Bedford vans ready converted to run on unleaded petrol.

(Furthermore, they'll still run equally well on leaded petrol. Or any combination of the two.)

At present we are the only manufacturer in the U.K. to have taken this step.

If you already have a Vauxhall, built since August '85, that too can be quickly and easily converted to run on unleaded petrol.

This can be done absolutely free of charge.

For more information ring 0800 555 000 or visit your local Vauxhall dealer.

VAUXHALL. ONCE DRIVEN, FOREVER SMITTEN.

WHAT A WONDERFUL WORLD

I see trees of green,
red roses too,
I see them bloom for me and you,
and I think to myself
What a wonderful world.

I see skies of blue and clouds of white,
the bright blessed day, the dark sacred night,
and I think to myself
What a wonderful world.

The colors of the rainbow,
so pretty in the sky
are also on the faces of people going by,
I see friends shakin' hands,
sayin' "How do you do!"
They're really sayin' "I love you,"
I hear babies cry,
I watch them grow
They'll learn much more than I'll ever know
and I think to myself
What a wonderful world.
Yes, I think to myself
What a wonderful world.

Figure 11.3 A very restrained car. What *could* it be suggesting?

overconsumption, especially in the overdeveloped world. Yet they produce a reassuring but crazy answer: consume more!

Other discourses have worked differently in this area. The successful 1995 consumer boycott of Shell petrol stations in protest at the decision to sink the Brent Spar oil platform into the North Sea suggests that alternative discourses can struggle quite powerfully through the media. Greenpeace's intervention in news imagery, particularly through the *Rainbow Warrior* sailing to areas of environmental crisis, has been important here (though you might like to consider what has to be excluded, and what emphasised, in that image).

Related to these objections is the Marxist position that ads make products appear as if by magic, obliterating the central importance of questions of production rather than consumption: Who produces these goods? Under what conditions? In what relationships to the profits and policies of the company?

The Co-operative Bank in 1994 began to advertise their product (banking) with various promises that they would change their relationships to oppressive, exploitative and polluting regimes or companies (see Figure 11.5). Their stark black and white, comparatively

Figure 11.4 (By courtesy of Leeds Postcards)

low-budget TV commercials, initially run on Channel 4, more than
doubled their recruitment of customers. They were fronting a critical,
'alternative' position on the capitalist industry in which they are
involved. They were also, in classic capitalist fashion, seeking to signal a
crucial market difference between themselves and their competitors,
rather like the 'pink pound' (the market for gay consumers) which
advertising experts were discussing at about the same time, or the
controversial Benetton campaigns using risky photos.

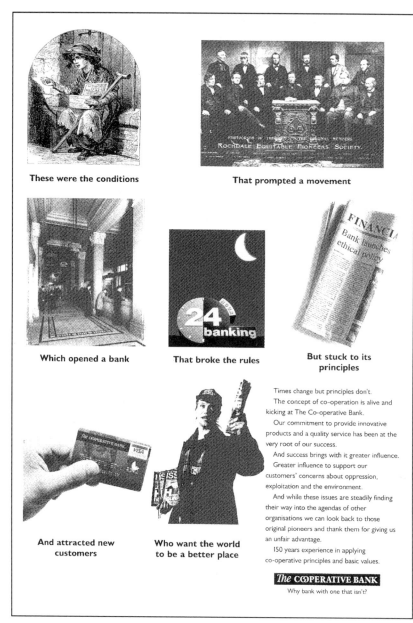

These were the conditions

That prompted a movement

Which opened a bank

That broke the rules

But stuck to its principles

And attracted new customers

Who want the world to be a better place

Times change but principles don't. The concept of co-operation is alive and kicking at The Co-operative Bank.

Our commitment to provide innovative products and a quality service has been at the very root of our success.

And success brings with it greater influence. Greater influence to support our customers' concerns about oppression, exploitation and the environment.

And while these issues are steadily finding their way into the agendas of other organisations we can look back to those original pioneers and thank them for giving us an unfair advantage.

150 years experience in applying co-operative principles and basic values.

The **COOPERATIVE BANK**

Why bank with one that isn't?

Figure 11.5

ACTIVITY 11.6

Taking the Co-operative Bank advertisement outlined above (Figure 11.5):

- How far does this break the rules of advertising and of Marxist expectations of the media?
- Is this ad an example of how discourses that were previously considered ideologically **alternative**, or 'outside' the mainstream begin to enter and to change it?

- Or is this an example, on the other hand, of incorporation, a term used (by the Frankfurt School especially) to describe the capacity of capitalism endlessly to absorb even movements and positions that are deeply critical of it?
- How does this relate to questions of ideology raised in this chapter?

References and further reading

Abercrombie, N., Hill, S., and Turner, B.S. (1980) *The Dominant Ideology Thesis,* London: Allen & Unwin.

Allen, R.C. (ed.) (1987) *Channels of Discourse,* Chapel Hill and London: University of North Carolina Press.

Althusser, Louis (1971) 'Ideology and Ideological State Apparatuses', in *Lenin and Philosophy and Other Essays*, London: New Left Books.

Barker, Martin (1989) *Comics: Ideology, Power and the Critics,* Manchester: Manchester University Press.

Dahlgren, P. (1985) 'The modes of reception: for a hermeneutics of TV news', in P. Drummond and R. Paterson (eds) *Television in Transition,* London: BFI.

Eagleton, Terry (1981) *Walter Benjamin or Towards a Revolutionary Criticism,* London: Verso.

Goffman, E. (1976) *Gender Advertisements,* London: Macmillan.

Golding, Peter and Murdock, Graham (1991) 'Culture, Communications and Political Economy', in J. Curran and M. Gurevitch (eds) *Mass Media and Society,* London: Edward Arnold.

Hall, Stuart and Jacques, Martin (1983) *The Politics of Thatcherism,* London: Lawrence & Wishart.

O'Sullivan, T., Hartley, J., Saunders, D., Montgomery, M. and Fisk, J. (1994) *Key concepts in Cultural and Communications Studies* (2nd edn), London: Routledge.

Sarup, M. (1988) *An Introductory Guide to Poststructuralism and Postmodernism,* Brighton: Harvester Wheatsheaf.

Smith, Gavin (1988) 'Mississippi Gambler', *Film Comment*, vol. 24, no. 6.

Strinati, Dominic (1995) *An Introduction to Theories of Popular Culture,* London: Routledge, esp. chs 2 and 4.

Thompson, J.B. (1990) 'Ideology and Modern Culture: Critical Theory,' in *The Age of Mass Communications*, Stanford, Ca.: Stanford University Press, p. 7.

Williamson, Judith (1978) *Decoding Advertisements,* London: Marion Boyars.

Alternative media are defined (O'Sullivan, Hartley *et al.* 1994) as: 'those forms of mass communication that avowedly reject or challenge established and institutionalised politics, in the sense that they all advocate change in society, or at least a critical reassessment of traditional values'. (See also Chapter 27, 'Independents and alternatives'.)

12 / Case study: Selecting and constructing news

'News professionals'
News values
Impartiality in news
The question of objectivity
News now

News is a globally important media form. We hope this section helps you to understand both

- its relationship to **dominant discourses** and **ideologies** and
- how these are negotiated as parts of media **institutions**.

Two points are often made about news within Media Studies:

- It is not transparent, not the 'window on the world' it often sets itself up to be.
- Its constructed versions of events are not unbiased and usually serve dominant interests. This matters particularly with TV news, from which most people get their sense of the world's happenings.

The work which pioneered such views is now some twenty to thirty years away. At the end of this chapter we suggest how it now needs to be qualified. Nevertheless, it is still true that BBC and ITN's two prime-time news bulletins claim enormous authority and to some extent objectivity for themselves as purveyors of news. They may not have power directly to affect people's beliefs and behaviour but ideologically they can set the **agenda** of issues which we find ourselves thinking about. This may encourage those who are already confident of majority opinion to become increasingly vociferous, while those who perceive themselves to be in a minority fall increasingly silent. News is also often able to set the agenda for current affairs and investigative documentaries teams.

An **agenda** is a list of items to be discussed at a meeting, usually drawn up by the person chairing the meeting, who has the power to arrange them in order of importance. Terms such as 'hidden agenda' or 'agenda setting' in relation to news suggests such powers are being exercised covertly by those in control of it.

ACTIVITY 12.1

Watch the title sequence of ITV or BBC evening news bulletins. How do these title sequences announce the nature of the programme to follow? Note such features as:

- the kinds of imagery and music used (science fiction? an emphasis on futuristic, speedy news-gathering technology?)
- the dress, demeanour, accent, tones of the presenter
- the set up of the studio
- how the items chosen relate to power centres such as Westminster and Washington.

Do you agree that such arrangements are above all trying to claim *authority* for this news bulletin?

Two secretaries in lunch break:
'Did you see the News at Ten?'
'Yes, awful wasn't it? That necklace with those earrings ...'
    (Sketch from *The Victoria Wood Show*, BBC, 1988)

Make a note of a day's major news **headlines**. Think if they affect what you and your friends talk about. Then note the headlines a few weeks later.

- Do you wonder what happened to stories which, in the first set of headlines, seemed urgent and important?
- When did they recede into less important status?
- Does this mean that you and your friends forgot about them to some extent – that they went 'off the agenda'?

'Royal' stories; which qualities are being valued by professional awards, and promotions, and so on).

'In the 1950s, women reporters interviewing people on the streets were assumed to be soliciting. More recently Associated Press reporter and Vietnam correspondent Edie Lederer had to get an "I am not a prostitute" certificate from the authorities before she could travel in Saudi Arabia to report the Gulf War.'

(Sebba 1994)

'News professionals'

The argument that news does not exist, free-floating, waiting to be discovered in the world outside the newsroom, has accompanied the development of theories of **news values**. These are argued to **construct** rather than simply accompany the *gathering of news*. They are not consciously held values. Indeed, many journalists would say their main professional ideal is the achievement of **objectivity**, an ideal which some would call an *occupational ideology.*

The theory of news values sees news as the end product of a complex process which begins with a systematic sorting and selecting of events and topics according to *professionalised news values:* 'the professional codes used in the selection, construction and presentation of news stories in corporately produced press and broadcasting' (O'Sullivan *et al.,* 1994). They are professionalised in the sense that they have to be acquired in order

- to become a journalist, through training on the job, or achieving qualifications
- to function effectively as a journalist (which may involve less formal learning contexts, such as canteen gossip about who's in and who's out, and why; what is now the 'house style' of your paper or radio station; whether, like the *Sun*, it employs no foreign correspondents, or, like the *Independent* tries to avoid

It is often argued (Schlesinger 1987) that like most TV professionals, journalists make programmes for other TV professionals, partly because their sense of the rest of their audience is very slim. 'They won't understand it', 'We'd love to run the story but the public just don't want to hear about it' are statements often made on the basis of very little systematic attempt to find out exactly what audiences might want.

Schlesinger (1987) also pointed out that news teams quickly develop a sense of 'who to rely on' which involves *'hard stories'* full of facts, statistics and quotes from official sources. They will prefer items which don't risk libel action, which come from 'accredited sources' such as one of the big world **news agencies**: Reuters, Press Association, Associated Press and United Press International, which send stories directly into the computer systems of bodies like News International. These, and the press office of a corporation or government department rather than a campaigning leaflet, are the preferred sources of news or its *primary definers.* They don't even need seeking out, but are sorted so that 'copy tasters' can select items to be used. Most newsrooms scan the morning newspapers and listen to the radio from early in the day. This is now more of a two-way street than it once was, as up-to-the-minute TV news, and even TV news pictures, often constitute newspapers' headlines the next day. But whatever the direction of the flow, such news structures will tend to favour those who already have enough power to employ press officers, print press releases and publicity, and hire Reuters to make up a VNR (Video News Release).

REUTERS
TELEVISION

QUESTIONS AND ANSWERS
VIDEO NEWS RELEASES

WHAT IS A VIDEO NEWS RELEASE?

A VNR is just the same as a written press release, except that it is produced on video. It means that broadcasters can be supplied with news pictures without the need to send out their own film crew or correspondents. A VNR is paid for by the corporate client - broadcasters get it free of charge.

WHAT IS THE REUTERS TELEVISION VNR SERVICE?

We use the unique global resources of Reuters to deliver VNR's to broadcasters in the most cost-effective way possible. No other VNR supplier has resources to match.

We provide VNR's to broadcasters in the same way that we provide any news story, except that we identify the item as a VNR and say who the client is. VNR's are normally between four and ten minutes long, often with a short voiced version called an 'A' roll.

WHY SHOULD REUTERS TELEVISION HANDLE MY VNR?

Because our service works. We are already known and trusted by broadcasters everywhere, so that when news editors receive an offer of free pictures from us, they give the story proper consideration. We already have the delivery system running smoothly, so we can keep costs down.

HOW MUCH DOES IT COST?

That depends on what we are asked to do. We always prepare a detailed price estimate, but as a guide, an average cost of production, distribution and monitoring in a single European country is between £6,000 and £10,000. A Europe-wide service concentrating on national broadcasters costs £10,000 to £15,000, and world-wide distribution costs about £20,000.

WHO USES REUTERS FOR VNR WORK?

Recent clients include the European Space Agency, Smirnoff, SmithKline Beecham, the Corporation of London, Glaxo, Johnnie Walker whisky, Chemical Bank, BT, the London Docklands Development Corporation, McDonalds, Beefeater gin, the Diamond Information Centre, P&O and Du Pont.

Figure 12.1

Examples

Far fewer foreign correspondents are now permanently employed to develop expert, intimate knowledge of a particular country. Covering 'sudden' foreign stories (the 'fireman' approach), 'packs' of journalists are often parachuted into an area together, stay in same hotels, share information and stories

rather than investigate for themselves, while also competing for 'the big story'.

> CNN came within seconds of announcing George Bush's death when he publicly collapsed at a banquet in Japan. They were nearly the victim of a hoaxer who rang in pretending to be Bush's doctor – as well as of the institutional drive to be first with the news rather than sure of it.
>
> (Described in Rosenblum 1993)

This tendency may be intensified by the ability of news agencies to arrange speedy satellite transmission of such instant judgements – itself a good example of the priorities of much modern TV journalism. It is also, of course, intensified by the sheer danger of certain assignments.

> 'On 31 December [1994] at least 103 journalists had been murdered – the highest figure in the history of the profession.'
>
> (Opening statement, Reporters Sans Frontières, 1995 Report)

Correspondents may also learn a professional, authoritative language with which, for example, to sanitise wars (see any number of accounts of the 'smart bombs', 'usherettes', 'carpet bombing' and so on in the Gulf War). Financial news, on the other hand, will be habitually described through phrases like 'the pound had a bad day' or 'getting the economy back on the rails', none of which is language to demystify the already mysterious workings of stock exchanges.

Frenzied circulation and ratings wars between organisations have tended to accelerate the professionals' emphasis on being 'first with the big story' rather than 'the one that got the story right'. This trend is accentuated by new technology, such as digitalised cameras, which means a reporter can input a story with photos into a newsdesk terminal almost as soon as it is written.

ACTIVITY 12.3

- Are some interests rather than others served: for example, in the habitual use of certain phrases rather than others (see above)?
- How would you relate these institutional news processes to the debates about dominant ideologies and discourses? This is best attempted once you have read Chapter 11, 'Ideologies', and Chapter 24, 'Institutions'.)

News values

There have been many different definitions of **news values** since Galtung and Ruge laid out a now famous pioneering list in 1965 (Galtung and Ruge 1981). The most important, adapted from their list, are:

- **Frequency** Those events which become news stories will be of about the same frequency as the news bulletins, i.e. of about a daily span. An oil spillage will be perceived as a news story; the slow work over time of legislation which makes it less (or more) likely to occur will not feature as news.
- **Proximity** Since news is circulated on the whole by national broadcasting organisations, news will consist of items that relate to that nation. Many people may be involved in a boat capsizing in Thailand, but until the number reaches hundreds, it is not likely to compete with a motor crash involving four people on the M25 in British headlines. Since these 'First World' stories often constitute much of the material of the big news agencies, which get sold to 'Third World' broadcasting stations, the circle can be a rather vicious one. Broader processes of language in news (and outside) carry the same kinds of skew: why are military commanders called 'warlords' in the 'Third World' (or Bosnia) but 'Chiefs of Staff' in the west?

ACTIVITY 12.4

The point is often made that the radio can cover foreign news much better than other media, especially through its correspondents.

- Listen to the BBC World Service (and/or watch CNN or Euronews if you can) for a few hours, and see how different is the news agenda of such services.

- **Threshold** or the 'size' of an event that's needed to be considered 'newsworthy'.
- **Negativity** 'If it's news, it's bad news' sums up the feeling that long-term, constructive events are much less likely to feature as news than a catastrophe. It is also suggested that news takes the normal for granted, and so is driven to make stories out of the **deviant**: crime, dissidence, disorder. In turn, news processes will add to stereotyping and scapegoating of 'out' groups, because of the ways it feeds on the thrill of their deviancy. It may also shape news coverage of 'Third World' issues in terms of 'coups, crises and famine' since they fit more dramatically into existing understandings of those areas than do items about small initiatives (such as adapting bicycle technology to help a village, or new drugs to reduce disease).
- **Predictability** If the media expect a kind of event to happen, it will be reported as having occurred. The most famous example is Halloran's case study of coverage of a large anti-Vietnam war demonstration in 1968 which was very peaceful, but had been expected to be violent. The few skirmishes that occurred were heavily focused upon, so the event was reported, as predicted, as 'violent'. The same used to be true for the Notting Hill Carnival, and is sometimes true of football matches.

    Another meaning for predictable is that events which are termed 'news' are often known about years in advance, such as conferences, anniversaries, annual reports, book or film launches and so on. (Though, of course, predictable famines are not part of the diary for coverage.) 'The news should really be called the olds' as someone once put it.

ACTIVITY 12.5

Regarding the predictability of news events:

- Note from current news how many items are of this kind.
- Why do you think journalists favour them?

- **Unexpectedness** Oddly enough, given the above, news is *thought* to consist of the unexpected, even though this can only occur within broad patterns of what is expected, even predicted. An important consequence is that where there are big issues, such as unemployment, Third World impoverishment and homelessness, there's a feeling that though it does go on happening, the journalist cannot keep on writing the same story, and so looks for a 'twist', perhaps a way of personalising or even sensationalising it, or simply leaves it as 'not news'. Hence news items suddenly focus on homelessness at Christmas, while treating it as 'not newsworthy' the rest of the year. 'By the time the pictures are horrific enough to move people, it is almost too late', as one journalist put it.

- **Continuity** If an event is big enough it will be covered for some time, and often even 'non-events' which are part of that story will be covered. 'Nelson Mandela has still not arrived back in Soweto after his release from jail.' 'All was quiet today at the Waco siege.'

- **Unambiguity** 'News' is constructed as something clear, not needing subtle interpretation even if it fits into a complex situation, like a war. (Though often listed as a news value, this can be argued to be a feature of the way a story gets told rather than of the event itself.)

- **Composition** The 'story' will be selected according to the editor's sense of the balance of the whole bulletin, or page. If many foreign stories have been

used, even a fairly unimportant 'home' story may be included. This may also affect the way items are juxtaposed.

ACTIVITY 12.6

Look at the balance of items in a bulletin. Again, using **broadsheet** papers as your source of a fuller news agenda, see if you feel the composition has been adjusted as suggested above.

- Within the bulletin, do certain items seem ordered so as to be grouped together, either for contrast, or to suggest connections?
- List the items in an order that would invite different connections.

- **Personalisation** Wherever possible, events are seen as the actions of people as *individuals*. Thus NHS cuts may be put on the agenda by 'Baby X' not getting the operation s/he needs. This links closely to two areas not part of the classic area of news values, but of larger drives: narrativisation and visual imperatives.

- **Narrativisation** of news. Items are from the start called 'stories' (see Chapter 3, 'Narratives') and when they become long-running 'sagas', the individuals on whom the spotlight has been focused often become characters: 'Maggie and Arthur' slog it out in the Coal Strike. Often these characters inherit, and re-jig, parts of older stories. The Falklands War coverage, for example, drew on an existing repertoire from Second World War films, with themes such as 'War is Hell but it makes Heroes', 'The Women Wait while the Men Fight', and with the Argentinian leader, Galtieri, represented as being a 'little Hitler', a 'tinpot dictator'. As Hartley comments, 'News is a matter of fitting unknown facts to known narratives' (Hartley 1992).

- **Visual imperatives** are said to be especially important in TV news (and unimportant in radio, where sound codes are key). They drive towards stories that have strong pictures, whether of Princess Di in a bikini or of 'Biblical' looking famines.

Increasingly, if wars are heavily censored or inaccessible to picture technology, computer-aided graphics will be used to give a sense of what might be happening. The argument needs critical consideration.

- First, radio's agenda is very similar to TV's, despite the absence of pictures.
- TV or press stories that are deemed important will have computer-aided graphics to assist visualisation, so the pictures do not always 'lead'.
- 'Less newsworthy' controversial or speculative stories, or ones involved with long-term processes are rarely helped in this way, even though they could be. Again, the visual imperatives tend to follow, not lead existing news priorities.
- 'Soundbites' or vivid short phrases used over and over in coverage of some stories, could be argued as equally important, and as deriving from verbal, radio-related forms. Yet they do not get celebrated in the same way as visual determinants. Why?

ACTIVITY 12.7

Watch a few TV news bulletins.

- How have 'visuals' been used? What do they contribute to stories?
- Do you agree with the suggestions on 'visual imperatives'?

ACTIVITY 12.8

List the stories featured on BBC, ITN and radio news during a day. Then list the spread of stories in two of the broadsheet papers.

- Are there any overlaps in the choice of TV and radio stories? Do these follow the priorities of news values?

Figure 12.2 One story that was deemed worth visualising (*UK Press Gazette*, 27 March 1995)

Impartiality in news

Broadcast media in Britain are legally required to be politically **impartial**, i.e. broadcasters cannot express a point of view on 'major matters' but, in a linked phrase, have to make balanced reports. But a balance is always between certain forces, and these tend to be those points of view that are assumed to reflect existing public opinion. Thirty years ago, this was defended as reflecting the Labour–Conservative axis of parliamentary politics, with a stopwatch eye to how much time each party was given on TV.

Now, the political spectrum stretches further, even in the number of parliamentary parties, though opinion that falls outside 'parliamentary democracy' is still deemed unacceptable. News was not allowed to balance Mrs Thatcher's ideas on the poll tax with those who argued for (illegal) non-payment, though after the withdrawal of the tax, such views were given news coverage, as a kind of 'historical background'. The same is true of the initial censorship and then much fuller post-1995 peace initiative coverage of the IRA.

The major critics of news in this area from the 1970s onward have been the **Glasgow University Media Group** (GUMG). They have employed **content analysis** (see Chapter 29, 'Audiences') involving hundreds of hours of recorded news broadcasts, focused mostly on industrial items such as strikes. They argue that the news consistently favours the interpretations of the already powerful. This is because journalists share assumptions about the real world which are rarely seriously questioned, such as the view that strikes are harmful and disruptive. Furthermore, they rely on official sources to an extent that systematically outlaws different accounts of events. In the 1984–5 Coal Strike for example, news settled into two themes, both of which favoured the Thatcher government's determination to defeat the strike:

- the return to work by those giving up the action
- violence used by pickets against police and non-striking miners.

GUMG criticised TV news for relying heavily on, and often using the words of, the employer's (NCB) press releases. Philo (1990) later suggested that such headlines and footage, whatever else people viewed on TV at the time, formed the news memories most people now have of the strike. Similarly the 'Winter of Discontent' (strikes of low-paid public sector workers in 1979) became solidified into a few phrases and images ('the dead unburied'/'rats on the streets') which:

- greatly exaggerated the effects of the strikes
- hardly ever suggested the strikes were a kind of evidence of the crucial nature of public service workers' labour.

These phrases were being quoted nearly twenty years later as dire warning of the excesses of trade union power.

Other *frameworks* or *horizons of explanation,* GUMG argued, were absent from the agenda set by news during the Coal Strike. There was hardly any discussion of the Conservative 'Ridley plan' from years before to defeat the miners as a way of closing the pits and weakening trade union power generally. Debates on the destruction of communities, or the need for British-based, non-nuclear energy sources in the future, as well as suggestions that the police provoked strikers, were also marginalised. (These latter were given thirteen times less coverage than violence attributed to pickets.)

ACTIVITY 12.9

Have another look at the section on critical pluralism in Chapter 11, 'Ideologies' (p. 128) and say how it can be related to such processes.

GUMG's critics (notably Alastair Hetherington (1985) and Martyn Harrison (1986)) argued that both ITN and BBC provided fair or impartial accounts of the strike, hampered only by the pressures under which journalists always have to operate. Arthur Scargill, for example, was argued to have been given many more hours coverage in interviews than were government representatives.

GUMG replied that the interviewing style was generally a very aggressive one, which undermines the impression given by simply quoting hours of coverage.

The question of objectivity

Objectivity is an impossible goal for any statement or story for the following reasons:

- To decide to feature a statement or story on the news is to make a decision about other events that cannot be told, and therefore to prioritise, or set a value on it.
- Since there are always several positions from which to tell a story (see Chapter 3, 'Narratives'), and it is impossible to produce an account from completely 'outside', a position on it will eventually have been chosen.
- To say objectivity is possible is to imply that an unarguable interpretation of an event exists prior to the report or story.

Nevertheless, if we adopt the position that news can and should be *as adequate and informative as possible for particular purposes*, then when a national audience needs to be informed about the justification for and conduct of, say, a war or major industrial confrontation, it is right to object to unnecessary government censorship, or a reliance on news sources that favour one side or the other.

Schlesinger (1987) cites a Finnish experiment with news (1965–70) which tried to engage and stimulate further demands for background information. Traditional notions of balance had to go, for, the Finns argued, 'new news is bound to be partial in favour of the suppressed of society'.

ACTIVITY 12.10

Think about how you would like to see news organised.

- Would it work better within an openly argumentative or **'biased'** current affairs system, with each programme having a stated position (green/ feminist/free market/socialist, etc.) which they argued in publicly accountable ways? This would need a built-in '**right of reply**' mechanism, and proper regulation to ensure there was no gross imbalance towards one tendency or another, across TV channels.
- How would news then function?

News now

Finally, questions and criticisms like these still have much power to explain news processes and their relationships to dominant discourses and ideologies, but you should also remember that:

- 'News' exists not just as BBC or ITV news, as was the case when some of the pioneering critical accounts were written. Most people now have access to at least four TV channels, if not 24-hour cable and satellite news through Sky and CNN. However limited the agenda they often keep to, they are driven to offer somewhat different accounts of events. CNN in particular has posed interesting problems for news managers, given its ability to deliver 24-hour-a-day news during, for example, the Gulf War. Radio offers more sources of news, as well as news-related forms such as phone-ins. The **Internet**, said to be unpoliceable and unregulatable, is a growing source of news stories and ways of organising around them, as the opposition to the Gulf War in the USA showed. And as long as investigative documentaries are funded, audiences have another source of information on which to form news judgements.
- Newspapers, far from cultivating a transparent, 'unconstructed' style, do not have words like 'impartiality' in their charters, and often try to entertain and galvanise their readers as much as (some would say less than) to inform them. This sometimes makes them appear like an arm of the PR (**Public Relations**) industry, at other times it produces an attractive irreverence many miles away from the BBC house style.

THE Sun

23p

Thursday, April 27, 1995   23p   Audited daily sale for March 4,134,571

SEX CONFESSIONS OF TAKE THAT
See Pages 12 & 13

FREE
2 Tickets to Alton Towers
Token 4 on Page 19

Sun EXCLUSIVE

PAM V SAM
See Page 15

£100m FORGED NOTES RACKET BUSTED BY COPS

By DAVID WOODING
and MIKE SULLIVAN

£100million international forgery racket was smashed yesterday when cops seized a record haul of fake bank notes from a lock-up garage.

Bundles of perfect £50 and US $100 counterfeits with a total face value of £18million were stashed under a pile of baby booties.

The swoop was a triumph for officers who spent two years tracking a ring that has flooded the world with forgeries in many currencies.

Five detectives of the South East Regional Crime Squad raided the £5-a-week garage in Bow, East London — and were astonished at the size of the cache.

Eight large boxes were stuffed with £10million in £50 notes, the biggest-ever seizure of fake sterling.

Another three cartons contained £8million in $100 bills, the second biggest haul of forged US currency in Britain. The forgeries were in bundles of 500 tied with plastic bands. Police
Continued on Page Seven

WINSTANTS CHURCHILL

Fury as MP scoops Lottery cash for Winnie's wartime papers

TORY MP Winston Churchill faced outrage last night after the Government used £13.25million of National Lottery cash to buy his grandfather's wartime papers.

Mr Churchill, 54, will personally make several millions after negotiating the sale of 1.5 million documents held by his family.

He exploited a loophole in Sir Winston's will to clinch the deal.

The MP's payout is like winning the Lottery's Instants jackpot dozens of times over.

But last night the sale was branded "a shabby trick." Oxford University history professor Norman Stone said: "It's like

By TREVOR KAVANAGH
and PASCOE WATSON

selling the great wartime leader in a raffle.

"This is another sign of the sheer bloody tackiness of this country.

"The Government should have rushed an Act through Parliament to make them available
Continued on Page Four

Under fire . . . Winston Churchill

Figure 12.3

ACTIVITY 12.11

Look at the front page illustrated in Figure 12.3.

- How are 'information' and 'entertainment' values in play here?
- How does this whole front page address its readers?

- The argument that TV news is constructed, not transparent, is no longer surprising. Even the 'rule' that music is never to be used as accompaniment to stories is occasionally broken in humorous or satirical stories. TV programmes such as *Drop the Dead Donkey* or *It'll Be All Right on the Night* take for granted, and add to, audience knowledge of news codes and constructions. Do they, however, help audiences to understand and even help to change the broader processes of news construction?

- The analysis of news for dominant values and assumptions is important, and far more telling than a few funny 'out takes' on *It'll Be All Right on the Night*. But it is clear that the effect of news on audiences is far from all-powerful. This is made vivid through events such as the boycott of the *Sun* on Merseyside when it libelled Liverpool soccer fans after Hillsborough, or in examples like the following, on understandings of the Gulf War:

'the survey demonstrates that most viewers believed oil supply was a main reason for the hostilities, while television's favourite explanation was "to liberate Kuwait", followed by "to uphold international law". Oil featured in 4% of BBC's reports, 3% of BBC 2's and 5% of Channel 4's.'

(Georgina Henry in the *Guardian*, 20 Jan. 1992, reviewing David Morrison's *Television and the Gulf War*, John Libbey and Co.)

References and further reading

Eldridge, J. (ed.) (1995) *News Content, Language and Visuals*, Glasgow University Media Reader, vol. 1, London: Routledge.

Galtung, J. and Ruge, M. (1981), 'The Structure of Foreign News: The Presentation of the Congo, Cuba and Cyprus Crises in Four Foreign Newspapers', extract in S. Cohen and J. Young (eds) *The Manufacture of News*, London: Constable.

Glasgow University Media Group (1976) *Bad News*, London: Routledge & Kegan Paul.

—— (1980) *More Bad News*, London: Routledge & Kegan Paul.

—— (1982) *Really Bad News*, London: Writers and Readers.

—— (1993) *Getting the Message: News, Truth and Power*, London: Routledge.

Golding, Peter and Elliot, P. (1979) *Making the News*, London: Longman.

Goodwin, Andrew (1990) 'TV News: Striking the Right Balance?', in A. Goodwin and P. Whannel (eds) *Understanding Television*, London: Routledge.

Harris, R. (1983) *Gotcha! The Media and the Falklands War*, London: Faber.

Harrison, M. (1985) *TV News, Whose Bias?*, London: Policy Journals.

Hartley, John (1982) *Understanding News*, London: Routledge.

—— (1992) *Tele-ology: Studies in Television*, London: Routledge.

Hetherington, Alistair (1985) *News, Newspapers and Television*, London: Macmillan.

May, A. and Rowan, K. (1982) *Inside Information: British Government and the Media*, London: Constable.

O'Sullivan, T., Hartley, J., Saunders, D., Montgomery, M. and Fisk, J. (1994) *Key Concepts in Cultural and Communication Studies* (2nd edn), London: Routledge.

Philips, D. (1992) *Evaluating Press Coverage*, London: Kogan Page.

Philo, Greg (1990) *Seeing and Believing,* London: Routledge.

Pilger, John (1992) *Distant Voices,* London: Verso

Reporters Sans Frontières (1995) *Report: Freedom of the Press throughout the World,* London: John Libbey.

Rosenblum, Mort (1993) *Who Stole the News?,* New York: John Wiley & Sons.

Schlesinger, Philip (1987) *Putting 'Reality' Together,* London: Methuen.

Sebba, A. (1994) *Battling for News,* London: Sceptre.

13 Global and local

The international media
  market
'Media imperialism'
Changing contexts in the
  1990s

Who are the best-known personalities across the world? The Pope? The
US President? Perhaps, but a safer bet might be Madonna or Denzel
Washington. If we are surprised to find a Michael Jackson cassette in an
African market, perhaps that says more about our stereotypical view of
'other' cultures than anything about the tastes and aspirations of the local
population. The information and communications technology industry is
rapidly becoming the biggest and most powerful enterprise in the world
and we should not be surprised that it has an impact everywhere.

If Hollywood stars have universal appeal, what of local or regional
stars? How are the lives of people in Africa, Asia and Latin America
represented in their own media and across the world? Can there be a
viable media industry in every country? And will it concern itself with
local issues? These are important questions for Media Studies, which have
been tackled from several different perspectives. We will attempt to
survey these and then study one example in detail.

A useful starting point is to think about media production and
consumption in global and local terms.

- Media corporations are increasingly thinking globally and some media
  theorists believe we should concentrate on looking at the impact (usually
  detrimental) of these major producers on the media environment in
  'poorer' countries – this is the so-called **media imperialism** model.
- More recently, a number of writers have alerted us to the development
  of local media production in many different parts of the world in
  which mixing 'traditional local' and 'global' styles and techniques
  creates new kinds of product. This position sees the media imperialism
  approach as outdated and unhelpful. We can recognise here the
  influence of **postmodernist** ideas (see Chapter 17).

The international media market

We set out in Chapter 20, 'Industries', the extent to which, through
vertical and horizontal integration, the major multinational media
corporations have come to dominate the international media market.

Hybridity is a term used by
postmodernist critics to describe
media products that mix different
sets of formal properties and
cultural values. In the UK music
market we talk of a 'crossover hit'
when a generic product is
accepted in another genre.
Hybridity is about crossovers and
national cultures.

> MTV has very quickly become one of the most recognised media brand names (rivalled only by the BBC and CNN) and is now available in one-quarter of all television households in the world (according to the president of MTV International, quoted in the *Independent on Sunday*, 28 May 1995). MTV is owned by Viacom, recent acquirers of Paramount and major players in American television.

How is this international market organised? It is not, of course, a 'free market' with many buyers and sellers of media products. Media industries operate as **oligopolies** – a few large organisations dominating the market. The media corporations that control the market are owned by American, European and Japanese capital and this is evident in the importance of **European languages** across the world. The corporations divide the world into a series of regional markets, listed in descending order of market importance:

1 North America (US and Canada)

2 Western Europe, Japan and Australia

3 Developing economies and regional producers (including India, China and Brazil, and Eastern Europe)

4 The rest of the world.

(These categories are based mainly on film and television distribution, but they provide a useful indicator for all media markets.)

There are many media producers, located in groups 2 and 3, who are able to operate in different regional markets – very effectively in many cases. However, they have little chance of penetrating the major market in North America. American corporations, in contrast, can market effectively in all the markets, including the poorest. The most important single institution operating worldwide is 'Hollywood', represented in film terms by the MPAA (Motion Picture Association of America), but also by the individual studios in relation to television and music sales. The other major axis of American media power, New York, has a similar role in advertising and publishing.

European languages are both 'oppressive' in many parts of the world – their use pushes out local languages and local culture – and potentially useful in enabling communication across linguistic barriers (although in some areas, such as East Africa with Swahili, other regional languages could serve this purpose).

The legacy of colonial rule can result in some unexpected difficulties – ex-French colonies, for instance, found themselves with the SECAM colour television system, which initially made distribution of programme material to neighbouring PAL (ex-British colonies) or NTSC (American) system countries more costly.

ACTIVITY 13.1

Which producers can sell abroad?

Test the UK cinema market in terms of the origin of films. You can find statistics in reference sources such as the *BFI Film and Television Handbook*. Alternatively, you could survey the films that appear on your local cinema screens – or perhaps interview the cinema manager to gain access to a list of films shown over the year. If you do this, make sure you balance the local multiplex with a BFI-supported Regional Film Theatre.

- If you have access to cable or satellite television, look and see what kind of programming UK and European services offer.
- If you are lucky enough to be on holiday anywhere in the world outside the UK, buy a local paper and check the cinemas and television listings.
- How do your findings match up to the ranking of the regional markets/producers outlined above?

Rigging the television market

Once a television series has been distributed to the various markets in North America, it will be offered to every broadcaster in the world at differential rates. These rates are based on audience size in 'developed' countries (Europe, Australia, etc.), but in Africa the rates are lowered dramatically so that they can be virtually given away for a few dollars per showing. Rates are so low that many African broadcasters cannot hope to produce programming of a similar technical quality at a lower price – they cannot afford *not* to buy in. Somewhere in the world, someone is still watching *Dynasty* or *Hawaii Five-0*. Other major television producers benefit in similar ways. 'Telenovelas', **soap operas** produced in Brazil, are popular in Portuguese-speaking parts of Africa (and in many other markets as well).

Local broadcasters have two main problems: training and equipment. Training needs to be 'on the job' for at least part of the time and should be undertaken on expensive broadcast quality equipment. Media production assumes an infrastructure. Most of the readers of this book will take for granted access to such things as videotape, batteries, cables, etc. Broadcasters in some parts of the world may be hundreds of miles from a reliable supplier. Equipment designed for broadcast use in North America, Western Europe and Japan will not necessarily perform efficiently in tropical conditions (where in any case a reliable source of mains electricity may not be available). The upshot is that trainees are sent to North America or Europe or the training is offered by the equipment manufacturers on their terms. The broadcasting authorities in the poor countries find themselves in a weak bargaining position in a rigged market. The media corporations work to maximise their market share and to exclude potential competitors wherever they operate.

'Media imperialism'

Imperialists build empires in which they are able to control 'subject peoples'. In the nineteenth century, European nations (and later the United States) consolidated imperial power, which had been achieved by conquest (and deceit), through economic exploitation. Each of the imperial powers had a different strategy. The French developed a system of 'cultural dependence' which saw colonial subjects educated in a formal system and inculcated with French cultural values. Later, after 'decolonisation', training and funding for media producers in the newly independent states induced them to stay within a French 'sphere of influence'. American policy has been less didactic and more clearly based on the spread of American popular culture which 'wins hearts and minds'. Many theorists saw that after 'decolonisation', many of the new states remained locked in a new colonialism of economic dependence and a 'colonisation of the mind' – in other words, local identity was difficult to assert in the face of the powerful media representations coming from the ex-colonial powers.

Some of the earliest work on this area was undertaken by Armand and Michèlle Mattelart, European academics who worked in the early 1970s on cultural programmes for the first elected Marxist leader in Latin America, Salvador Allende of Chile. The freshness of their approach is caught in one of their book titles, *How to Read Donald Duck*.

The Mattelarts' work was undertaken some twenty years ago, but it is still useful in informing debates in Media Studies. What makes their work important is a number of basic premises:

- recognition of the power of the multinational media corporations and the 'popular' media products they sell
- refusal to be pessimistic about political change and a belief in the importance of class struggle and cultural resistance
- recognition of the importance of issues about representation and about the imaginary and symbolic in different cultures
- refusal simply to portray the media corporations as 'bad' and the local producers as 'good'.

We can see here not just a critique of American and European culture, but a recognition of the importance of local or **indigenous culture**. The Mattelarts also stress the importance of struggle and the danger of falling into the trap of assuming that because the 'media imperialists' are powerful, we must study the ex-colonies as 'weak' and suffering from many 'problems' with no solutions.

Terminology is important in considering the international media environment. Who defines 'development'? Why do we assume one form of 'development' is best? One riposte has been to see Africa as 'under-developed', i.e. consciously starved of investment and exploited by the colonial powers. (See Chapter 11, 'Ideologies', for discussion of terms.)

Changing contexts in the 1990s

To a large extent, the media imperialism approach has been made redundant in the 1990s because of changing political conditions (the end of the Cold War and the collapse of the Soviet Union; the end of apartheid in South Africa, etc.) and because of developments in Media Studies itself.

> 'In 1990 it is clear that the international media environment is far more complex than that suggested by the "cultural imperialism" model whose depiction of a hegemonic pied piper leading the global media mice appears frozen in the realities of the 1970s.'
>
> (Annabelle Sreberny-Mohammadi in Curran and Gurevitch (1991))

In the context of some of the surviving oppressive regimes in the world, American television series can be seen to offer **progressive representations**. We discuss in Chapter 29, 'Audiences', how audiences can **negotiate** texts and we shouldn't assume that an African or Indian audience will necessarily 'read' imported media texts in a standard way. The impact of satellite television in India and Africa is a contemporary research task which will produce interesting observations (although collecting research data may prove difficult). One immediate outcome is that enterprising local pirates are illegally wiring up whole tenement blocks and creaming off much of the potential revenue which might go to News Corporation or other service providers.

We can identify two ways in which Media Studies can develop more positive approaches to the global and local media environment:

- look at the strategies which poorer countries can adopt in order to gain more control over local production *and distribution*. Very often, it is not production which is the major problem, but access to distribution. In many African countries, for instance, film distribution is almost entirely in the hands of overseas companies which are unwilling to distribute African films. Local producers are not lacking in creative ideas or production skills.

  Poorer countries could join together to build transmission (satellite) and distribution systems, especially with government support. The failure to do so often occurs at government level.

- theorists and critics could help to define the new **aesthetics** and the new products that have been developed locally. Examples of new approaches in cinema are touched on in Chapter 27, 'Independents and Alternatives'. Many of the examples cited in contemporary critical writing relate to music. Annabelle Sreberny-Mohammadi (1991),

Nigerian film producer and director Ola Balogun presented these 'strategies' for distribution at the Africa '95 Cinema Conference in London. He sees the airwaves as 'dominated by neo-colonialism' and argues persuasively for satellite and video distribution, controlled by local producers. Several speakers at this conference feared that the 'new South Africa' would dominate local producers, using powerful satellite transmissions in competition with French and American channels.

At the same conference, African-American academic Claire Andrade-Watkins observed that 'Africans don't "uplink" to satellites, they "downlink"' – this makes them consumers not producers.

suggests that Bedouin identity in North Africa has been revitalised through song and poetry recordings available on cassette, which have displaced the more commercial Egyptian culture in the region.

There is some tension between these two approaches (see Chapter 18 for discussion of potential conflicts over new technologies). 'Cultural theorists' tend to be suspicious of an overemphasis on technology or international agreements to improve the possibilities of local production. Their fears are founded on the experience of what have been termed **development media** strategies. Common in southern Africa and a legacy of British colonial attitudes in particular, these strategies privilege educational documentaries and 'social problem' films rather than allowing local cultures to be expressed.

Conversely, there is an argument that says that the potential value of indigenous production is not very great if the local population never gets to see or hear it. New production and distribution systems are needed and digital media technologies open up new possibilities.

The struggle over **representation** of a local identity is a complex issue and rather than try to cover a wide range of theoretical work, we have selected just one example of local media production which challenged the existing relationship of global/local. In our selection, we have been conscious of the 'other side' of colonial expansion in the nineteenth century – the **diaspora** of African and Asian peoples which has enriched cultural production all over the world and has created new cultures which challenge the global/local definition. The case study that follows looks at the Bob Marley phenomenon (and might be linked to the 'Making stars' case study in Chapter 23).

'Are you going to show programmes which are copies of western programmes, or programmes where the set is falling down?' This is the response Claire Monk received from a British 'media development academic' when she began to research a season of African television to be shown at the National Film Theatre in 1995. These attitudes and the reality of African broadcasting are explored in Monk (1995).

Diaspora originally referred to the 'dispersed community' of Jews after Babylonian captivity. Now it is generally used to describe the dispersed communities of any cultural group, particularly of African peoples in the Americas and Europe.

References and further reading

Mattelart, A., Mattelart M. and Delcourt, X. (1984) *International Image Markets*, London: Comedia.

Millier, Daniel (1992) 'The Young and the Restless in Trinidad: A case of the local and the global in mass consumption', in R. Silverstone and E. Hirsch (eds), *Consuming Technologies: Media and Information in Domestic Spaces*, London: Routledge.

Monk, Claire (1995) 'Small Screen Africa', *Black Film Bulletin,* vol. 3, no. 2/3.

Rodney, Walter (1972) *How Europe Underdeveloped Africa*, London: Bogle-L'Overture Publications.

Shohat, Ella and Stam, Robert (1994) *Unthinking Eurocentrism*, London: Routledge.

Sreberny-Mohammadi, A. (1991) 'The Global and the Local in International Communications', in J. Curran and M. Gurevitch (eds) *Mass Media and Society,* London: Edward Arnold.

Bob Marley and the rise of
reggae
Reggae as 'rebel music'
Marley and the pop
mainstream

14 / Case study: Bob Marley Superstar

Bob Marley and the rise of reggae

From the yards of Kingston, Jamaica, to the stadia of Europe and North America is a big step and a unique achievement. Millions of young people, from Zimbabwe to Australia, have been inspired in some way by Bob Marley's music. Yet, what was once 'rebel music' is now a CD boxed set and a nice steady earner for multinational record companies. The yards of Jamaica are just as poor (perhaps more so) as they were in 1960 when Marley's career began – the global/local issue in a nutshell.

Reggae as a musical form has probably been the most important catalyst in opening up the possibility of a genuine 'world music' (as distinct from the arbitrary category created by the music corporations). It represents a link between 'western' and African culture in the late twentieth century. As Stuart Hall (1991) remarks: 'All the most explosive modern musics are crossovers. The **aesthetics** of modern popular music is the aesthetics of the **hybrid** ... the aesthetics of the **diaspora**, the aesthetics of creolisation' (creolisation loosely refers to the mixing of European and African cultures in the Americas – food, language and intermarriage).

The original Wailers (Marley, Peter Tosh and Bunny Livingston) grew up in 1950s Jamaica in a rich musical environment which mixed traditional folk styles (derived from both the African culture of the transported slaves and the European heritage of the planters) and imported black American popular styles: swing, bebop, R&B and soul. Radio stations from the southern United States could be picked up in Jamaica and discs were

brought back by travellers to New York and played publicly by sound system operators at open-air dances.

By the early 1960s, this fusion was beginning to produce a new homegrown style, an original Jamaican popular music which evolved through different rhythms from ska and bluebeat to rocksteady and reggae. This wasn't just a performance music. Despite the generally poor infrastructure on the island (then still a British colony), a handful of record producers were able to produce records of increasing sophistication.

Many of the early hits were instrumentals with distinctive playing by jazz-influenced performers. Others, like the Wailers' first efforts, were covers of American soul hits. Gradually, however, aspects of the vibrant Jamaican street culture and the philosophies of the Rastafarian movement began to creep into the lyrics. (Rastafarianism is a religious movement drawing on the Old Testament, with a specific aim – the return of African peoples in the diaspora to Africa itself.) Here was a totally new musical form, developed in a country of only two million people but with the potential to influence millions more across the world.

Jamaican popular music was part and parcel of Caribbean emigration to Britain (and also to the United States and Canada). The British media associated the first immigrants with the music of the East Caribbean such as calypso, but during the 1960s a number of Jamaican artists made the British charts with what the (white) British public heard as accessible pop songs. By the early 1970s, reggae records were entering the charts on a regular basis and although the political message of reggae was beginning to emerge in the lyrics, the overall sound was still relatively light and 'poppy'. 'Israelites' by Desmond Dekker is a good example of a Rastafarian theme which was not recognised by most singles buyers, who made the song a UK No.1 in 1969. It lives on now as the music for 'Vita-Lite' margarine.

Within the British Jamaican community, however, reggae was getting 'harder' and 'heavier', the rhythm was slowing (with the steady intake of cannabis), the lyrics were more and more locked within the Rastafari culture of struggle with the forces of Babylon (i.e. the repressive forces of the British state). Jamaican patois was increasingly being used and eventually the lyrics would cease to be recorded at all or voices would become just another instrument. 'Dub versions' appeared in which instrumental 'parts' would be extended and repeated with endless variations. You can explore the cultural and political issues this raised in the writings of Dick Hebdige (1979; 1987)and Paul Gilroy (1982; 1987).

The Wailers were at this time still only Jamaican stars. Ironically, when they did finally make a breakthrough in Britain, it was not as reggae performers as such, but as part of the white rock business. They were signed up by Chris Blackwell, a white Jamaican based in Britain, who had already had some success with reggae artists, and saw the possibility of developing Marley as a rebel figure. The archetypal figure had already appeared in the Jamaican film *The Harder They Come* (1972), in which reggae star Jimmy Cliff played 'Ivan', based on the legendary 'Rhygin', a gunman and songwriter in late 1950s Kingston. Blackwell released the soundtrack to the film which became a cult album in Britain. The Rhygin legend produced a book also called *The Harder They Come* (Thelwell 1980); this tells (in a written Jamaican dialect) the full story of Ivan with more background detail.

It is at this point that the struggle over identity becomes crucial in the creation of the **star-image** of Bob Marley and where we can recognise a dilemma which is presented to anyone who puts a personal investment into 'cultural struggle'. Gilroy (1982) sees Blackwell and his Island record label using *The Harder They Come* and subsequent Island-backed reggae films to reach white rock audiences. The Wailers' first two Island albums 'Catch a Fire' and 'Burnin',

Figure 14.1

were largely remixes of earlier material and though they had a major impact with the growing numbers of black British reggae fans, they didn't attract white record buyers. It was not until the third album that Marley, now without Tosh and Livingston and with a slightly more familiar-looking (to white rock fans) backing band, attracted the broader British audience with 'No Woman, No Cry'. From then on, throughout the later 1970s and up to his death in 1981, Marley, despite remaining true to his Rastafarian beliefs, was gradually dropped by the more radical black youth and increasingly taken into the **mainstream** of international popular culture.

Reggae as 'rebel music'

The 'rebel' is a potent figure in media discourse and no more so than in texts designed for adolescent audiences. Most Hollywood 'rebels' are pretty 'safe' characters (James Dean?, Keanu Reeves?). The combination of 'rude boy' and 'rasta', which was how many white audiences (mistakenly) saw the early Wailers, was certainly not safe. The 'rude boy' character was a ghetto rebel stereotype, associated with crime and guns and resistance to authority and celebrated in songs like 'Johnny Too Bad'. As with American 'gangster' types, the rude boy continued to figure in popular culture, as a figure associated with dress codes and behaviour as well as rebellion, well into the Two-Tone period of the late 1970s. Later, the dancehall style with its sexist lyrics would take on some of the legacy. (Links are also visible to contemporary rap music.)

The Wailers were genuine in their Rastafarianism and its implications of resistance to white oppression in Europe and the Americas and a 'return to Africa'. The titles of the early Wailers' songs such as '400 Years', 'Burnin' and Lootin'', 'Get Up, Stand Up (For Your Rights)' illustrate the serious intent in the music. Other 'roots' stars were even more explicit in their references. Winston Rodney became 'Burning Spear' and another band called themselves 'Black Uhuru' – both these were names associated with Jomo Kenyatta, the successful leader of the Mau Mau uprising against the British in Kenya in the 1950s. The celebration of African heroes was a feature of roots reggae.

Marley and the new Wailers presented a 'sweeter' and more rock-orientated sound to go with a seemingly less aggressive stance. Where 'roots reggae' set out to exclude whites and to attract an aware audience, interested in rediscovering an African culture and African rhythms, Island was effectively **marketing** Marley as 'Bob Dylan or Marvin Gaye or both' (this was how Island A&R man Richard Williams remembers his impression of first meeting Marley).

Roots reggae survived as a vibrant form for many years and made a lasting impression on black British music. Whether it was because of the cultural stance, the practice of the sound system and the dub, or simply the example of black musicians struggling with a white industry, the influences are evident in hip-hop and soul in the 1980s. Massive Attack and Tricky in the 1990s are contemporary examples of a dub sound which owes something to 'roots'.

Reggae as a commercial black music has continued to develop through different styles such as lovers, dancehall and ragga and a number of **hybrids**, including the mix with bhangra music (a popular music derived from traditional Punjabi forms) which produced hits for Apache Indian in the early 1990s. We have discovered then a media form from the underdeveloped world which made an impact in Britain and America and produced, in the form of Jamaican record producers like Lee Perry, creative artists of international standing, as well as recording studios used by major American acts.

The commercial success of Bob Marley

The first major retrospective of Marley's career, 'Legend', released in 1984, has been one of the best-selling albums of all time with 10 million units sold worldwide. In America, 'Legend' still ranks No. 2 on the 'Pop Catalog' Chart in *Billboard* alongside the Eagles and Pink Floyd. In the UK, Marley hasn't been out of the Top 75 Album Chart since 1984.

Marley and the pop mainstream

The concessions to the white industry which Marley made have arguably allowed his music to have a greater impact both within the 'developed' and the 'underdeveloped' world. Gilroy (1987) suggests that Marley calculated that the price of changing his music to suit the tastes of both the white rock audience and the black American blues/soul audience was worth paying, if he could spread the ideology of Rastafari.

Gilroy goes on to consider some of the outcomes of Marley's success. With Marley as figurehead, the more mainstream reggae sound was effectively exported around the world. Marley himself performed at the Independence celebrations in Zimbabwe in 1980, an event of enormous significance and one which further encouraged musical disciples in Africa, Asia, Latin America and Australasia (i.e. Aboriginal and Maori performers). In Britain, Marley opened up a new space in the 'pop' mainstream which was exploited effectively by the mixed-race ska revivalists of 'Two Tone' and the anti-racist movement within popular music at the close of the 1970s (captured in text and images by Widgery (1986)). The Specials AKA's plea to 'Free Nelson Mandela' (1984) can be seen as a direct response to Marley's 'Africa Unite' (1979). Alpha Blondy from Ivory Coast, with a musical style modelled closely on Marley, produced 'Apartheid is Nazism' in 1986, neatly underlining the success of Marley's leadership in an international movement for African liberation.

Against this, Gilroy argues that after Marley's death, with no reggae star of equal stature to succeed to the leadership of this international movement, reggae was seized and emasculated by white musicians and despite the commercial success of the Marley legacy, a moment has been lost. For a while representations of the underdeveloped world were being offered on the world's media which were not totally controlled by the international media corporations. Towards the end of his life, Marley developed his own business interests – the Tuff Gong record shop, studio and recording studios. But the exploitation of Tuff Gong is still under the control of Island Records. Open the booklet in the latest Marley offering from Tuff Gong/Island ('Natural Mystic', 1995) and you will find adverts for 'Official Bob Marley Merchandising' (shirts and caps) to be sold throughout Europe.

ACTIVITY 14.1

Go into any record store and look at what is available from the Bob Marley back catalogue. Consider the images and text on CDs and vinyl records (if you can find any). Try to listen to a few tracks.

- Why do you think Marley has become such an international icon?
- Can you list any of the characteristics of his star-image which suggest a universality? (See Chapter 23, 'Making Stars' for more ideas about the star-image.)

'World Music'

The creation of a new category in the record racks is perhaps another legacy of Marley's success. The same record labels (Virgin and Island) which promoted reggae in the mid-1970s began to build a 'roster' of new stars from around the world during the 1980s. Perhaps they thought one of the stars they found in Nigeria, Senegal or Pakistan would become another Marley? Some, like Youssou N'Dour have indeed made hit singles and several have sold enough records outside their home territories to justify long-term contracts, but none as yet has found the universality that allowed Marley to reach such a wide audience (if that is what they want to do).

ACTIVITY 14.2

Try a role play idea. Imagine you are a performer in an African or Latin American country. You sell enough records and concert tickets in your own country to be a big star but your record label is local and can't promote you overseas. A representative from Virgin comes to offer you an international deal. What do you do?

- Try to compile a list of conditions you would like to place on a contract. (How much artistic control would you want? What obligations to your home fans would you consider?)
- Could you accept the contract and remain faithful to your 'roots'?

References and further reading

Much of the material on Bob Marley has been taken from *Mojo*, March 1995.

Gilroy, Paul (1982) 'Steppin' out of Babylon – Race, Class and Autonomy' in Centre for Contemporary Cultural Studies, *The Empire Strikes Back*, London: Hutchinson, pp. 297–302.

—— (1987) *There Ain't No Black in the Union Jack*, London: Hutchinson, pp. 160–71.

Hall, Stuart (1991) 'The Local and the Global: Globalisation and Ethnicity', in A. King (ed.) *Culture, Globalisation and World-System*, London: Macmillan.

Hebdige, Dick (1979) *Subculture: The Meaning of Style*, London: Methuen.

—— (1987) *Cut 'n' Mix*, London: Routledge.

Salewicz, Chris (1995) *Bob Marley: Songs of Freedom*, London: Bloomsbury.

Thelwell, Michael (1980) *The Harder They Come*, London: Pluto Press.

White, Timothy (1983) *Catch a Fire – The Life of Bob Marley*, London: Hamish Hamilton.

Widgery, David (1986) *Beating Time*, London: Chatto & Windus.

15 Realisms

Why 'realisms'?

Realism is a concept which writers and producers fight over – a politically charged term with a long and varied history, which needs to be controlled in some way if it is going to be useful for us.

What is in dispute? Look at any historical drama on television. A programme that depicted life at the court of Elizabeth I would be ridiculed if someone were wearing a wristwatch, but we accept that all the characters speak a recognisable English, even though we know that the people of the time spoke something we would find almost impossible to follow. The wristwatch breaks the rules of historical detail, but the dialogue translation is an acceptable realist convention – realism is something we have learned to decode.

A similar point arises with the selection of colour or black and white filmstock in an image. For older readers of texts, black and white photography often denotes realism. They are familiar with events from wartime, in which they have a personal emotional investment, being documented in monochrome in family snapshots or **newsreels**, whereas colour images of the same events seem like a fiction. Younger readers are likely to reverse this meaning and to take colour as real and monochrome as a style feature.

- Realism as a term draws attention to a desire to connect with the rest of the real world especially broad social questions such as unemployment, war, homelessness, etc.

However, you can't simply point a camera at such events and expect to produce realism:

- realism is an **aesthetic** construct which is produced by means of recognisable codes and conventions
- there is no single 'realism': different cultures and different contexts produce different 'realisms'.

The controversy around realism is explained by its direct connection to social issues – which themselves are often the basis for conflict – and by

Newsreels during the 1930s and 1940s were all presented in monochrome and remained as 'evidence' of the period until the 1970s and 1980s, when researchers discovered 'amateur' film footage of the end of the war, shot in colour.

Aesthetics refers originally to the 'principles of taste and art' or the 'philosophy of the fine arts'. It has come to be used to refer to an interest in visual style or 'the look' of something. A **realist aesthetic** is an approach to media production that consciously attempts to use a visual style that will help to produce a realist effect.

the contradiction inherent in its use as an approach to media production, i.e. that a **realism effect** requires careful preparation and perhaps considerable artistry on behalf of the producer – it is never just a case of 'simply capturing reality'. Two current examples:

- In the 1994 film, *Forrest Gump*, Tom Hanks shakes the hand of President John Kennedy, thirty years after Kennedy's death. We can now produce **photorealistic** images of events that never happened – not even as an acted-out scene, never mind as documented **actuality**. This technique was applied in an entertainment film and audiences were amused rather than threatened, but it does beg the question: 'If we break the link between concrete reality and its representation, where does this leave our trust in **documentary** evidence?' (see Chapter 18 on Technologies for more on this issue).

- Most viewers react to depictions of violence on the cinema or television screen, but some argue that 'realistic' violence is acceptable because it enables us to understand what the effects of violence really are, whereas 'cartoon violence' is simply gratuitous and likely to corrupt because it asks us to enjoy someone else's pain through a fantasy. Others argue the opposite – that because we know that some violent acts we see are a fantasy, they do no real damage, but realistic violence appeals to our prurient, voyeuristic nature.

Whether or not children can distinguish between the 'real' and the 'fantastic' in this context is an important consideration, but this point tends to be lost if the two sides don't understand how realism works. (See Chapter 5, 'Genres', and Chapter 29, 'Audiences', for comments on this issue and **verisimilitude**.)

Historical background

Realism as an artistic movement is associated with the rise of capitalism and the industrial revolution of the 1840s in Western Europe. As a movement in painting, it is seen as predominantly French, covering the period 1840–80 (Nochlin 1971). Some of the techniques used in realist painting (e.g. perspective and accurate scale) had been known since the Renaissance, but their application now coincided with the birth of photography – the first technology to offer a direct representation of 'reality'. Moreover at this time the writings of **Charles Dickens** and **Elizabeth Gaskell** (author of *North and South*) were being published (often first as serials) and these were notable for the attention paid to the **material conditions** of their characters' lives and to the social conditions of contemporary society at a period when two new classes, the industrial poor and the urban bourgeoisie, were becoming established. Earlier novelists had

---

Actualities was the name given to the first short films of 'real events'. The term 'documentary' appeared during the 1920s and has tended to be reserved for films of a certain length (perhaps 20 minutes).

Documentary 'The use of the film medium to interpret creatively and in social terms the life of the people as it exists in reality' – from the title page of *Documentary Film* by Paul Rotha (1939).

Charles Dickens and **Elizabeth Gaskell** both wrote about the new urban working classes during the middle years of the nineteenth century and helped to educate their readers about the 'condition of England'.

tended to use characters to explore either emotions or moral values (which isn't to say that realist novels were lacking discussion of values).

We can trace many of the contemporary debates around realism back to these two forms – the photograph and the 'bourgeois novel'. The two central issues might be the **use of technology** to get us closer to 'reality' and the debate about an aesthetic that constructs narrative time and space so that it seems *transparently* to represent the 'real world' to us as readers, inviting us to identify with an individual hero (rather than the 'everyman' of earlier stories).

Realisms and technology

Photography is a process involving drawing ('graph') with light ('photo') and the first photographic technology was used to help artists to draw more realistic pictures. The concept of a '**camera obscura**' (literally a dark room) into which light can be introduced through a tiny aperture to create an inverted image on a white background was first suggested by the Arab scientist Alhazen in the ninth century and 'rediscovered' in the Renaissance. In the late eighteenth century, portable 'light-boxes' with a focusing lens were introduced (known as 'camera lucida') and eventually the image was captured on light-sensitive materials – photography was born.

A photograph is a two-dimensional image of a three-dimensional reality and this requires an understanding of certain 'ways of looking' in order to understand how to 'read' the image as if it were 3D. We could argue that this is what visual realist conventions allow us to do.

The optical devices of the eighteenth century introduced artists to new ways of producing images which could be traced. They were particularly useful in enabling accurate reproduction of **monocular perspective**. Perspective describes the angle of view which changes as lines are drawn towards a point on the horizon. Monocular perspective implies a single point from which these lines are drawn – i.e. the representation is constructed so that a single viewpoint is allowed. The viewer is 'in control' of the world he or she surveys. In earlier painting styles, perspective was treated quite differently. If you go to an art gallery and look at pre-Renaissance paintings or those from non-European cultures (see Figure 15.1, Japanese print), you will find the size and placement of figures in a landscape presented in various ways. We are so used to the constructed sense of 'depth' in a photographic image that we find it difficult to 'read' these earlier images. Yet they serve to remind us that what we see in any representation is an artificial construction. The realist image is a 'learned' image – it is not something 'natural'. (See Neale 1985 for more on perspective.)

A Matter of Life and Death (UK 1946) is a famous fantasy film by Michael Powell and Emeric Pressburger. It includes a striking scene in which a country doctor uses a camera obscura to spy on his neighbours. Powell was a great 'anti-realist' fascinated by the camera as controlling eye.

Camera obscura are included in some museums or specially constructed towers and are worth visiting for the insight they provide into the pre-electronic 'world-view'. Try Edinburgh or Dumfries among others.

Figure 15.1 A fourteenth-century representation of samurai warriors from *Kitabatake monogatari*

Sound recording and realism

Much of the argument about realist aesthetics is taken up with visual codes, but we must not neglect 'aural realism'. The later nineteenth century saw the development of sound recording technology and with it a similar development of arguments about 'realist sound'. We can talk of the 'sound image' in much the same way as the visual image (see Chapter 1, 'Images and Languages', and Chapter 2, 'Speaking on Radio'). Our problem is that the terminology for discussion of sound images is not as well developed as that for visual images and as a consequence we are far less confident about discussing the realism of sound reproduction. A simple test will demonstrate the strangeness of discussing realist sound.

The sound of your own voice

Look at a recent photograph of yourself. Is it a good likeness? Most of us recognise ourselves in photographs. We might not like what we see, but we can accept it as a resemblance. Now listen to yourself recorded on tape. This is much harder to accept. Is that strange voice really you? Why are we so surprised to hear ourselves? Possibly, because our ears are less *trained to listen* to voices than our eyes are to look at pictures. There is also a physiological reason. When we speak, we push out or pull in air, which in turn creates sound waves. As a consequence we *feel* the vibrations from the act of speaking. When we hear our voice coming from speakers we don't feel anything (unless the speaker is so large and powerful that it makes the floor quake).

Perhaps this is what makes our own voice sound so alien – because it isn't accompanied by the familiar sensations of speaking. What would be even more strange would be to play a recording of ourselves backwards. This would be unintelligible. Yet, the visual equivalent would be to simply look in a mirror – a perfectly ordinary thing to do, but in fact an inverted representation of how we look, which we have learned to 'read'.

Tuning in to sound effects

Andrew Crisell (1994) makes the point that a particular sound on the radio works quite differently on television. The radio sound is more appropriately called a **sound effect**. Galloping horses being simulated by the production assistant banging together two halves of a coconut shell is a good example. On radio we accept this sound as a realistic representation. If we were offered an authentic recording of 'real' horses galloping along 'real' highways, we might not even recognise the sound, without its accompanying visual signifier. So, as well as the 'quality' of sound reproduction, we must consider the realist codes necessary to convey meaning.

For the visual image, realism would normally imply that most of the component signs were **iconic**, i.e. they physically resemble real-world objects they represent. A realist visual account of horse-riding would show real horses and would use the iconography of 'horse culture' – bridles, saddles, stables, etc. In the sound image, icons are much more problematic. All the associated sounds of horse-riding, such as the heavy breathing of the horse, the squeak of the leather saddle, the clomping of hooves, are 'mixed' within the sound image and we may be unable to distinguish one from another. Their resemblance to real sounds becomes a problem. We are more likely to respond to an identifiable sound (perhaps a single whinny followed by a snort of breath) which signifies the presence of a horse, than a realistic *mélange* of sounds. In this case the sound image is more **indexical** than iconic, an index being a sign that works by establishing a relationship between itself and reality rather than simply offering a resemblance. The horse sound tells us about the *presence* of a horse. This whole exercise serves to remind us that we also use abstract signs – a character could use the word 'horse', the sound of which has neither resemblance nor indexical relationship to the real animal.

The history of media technology during the twentieth century has been dominated by the drive for 'greater realism' and we consider one particular example in Chapter 19 on widescreen cinema. In one sense this is a technical challenge to the innovator, in another it is an aesthetic challenge to the producer, but it is always also a social and cultural issue about representing events and ideas.

Realism and social issues

The nineteenth century not only saw technological developments that allowed the detail of 'reality' to be represented to an extent never before contemplated, it also saw new industrial and social conditions which changed so quickly and so profoundly that they in turn prompted a demand for new ways of classifying and communicating the extent of that change. Journalistic writing and photography were developing alongside social investigations and industrial warfare. Two good examples would be the coverage of the American Civil War – documented in great detail by contemporary photographers and journalists whose work was recently used in the television series *The Civil War* (Channel 4, 1994) – and the work of Dr Barnado's in creating a photographic archive of the street urchins 'rescued' in Victorian London (exhibited in 1995).

The realist movement in painting and literature was over by the end of the century, but the use of photography and film to represent social issues has persisted and has produced fierce debates over 'realist aesthetics' during the twentieth century (see Chapter 17, 'Case study: A note on postmodernism' for more on this history). We will concentrate here on film and video, which will encompass sound and visual realism. Similar arguments can be explored in relation to still photography and sound-only recording.

Realisms in film and video

Cinema has developed over a hundred years with a constant tension between its twin roots of 'photorealistic' image technology, capable of documenting reality, and a fairground mentality of fantasy and magic. For every **Lumière** 'actuality' there is a **Méliès** fantasy with special effects and trick photography. This might suggest that the history of cinema is of documentary *or* fantasy, and of course it isn't. Instead, film-makers moved between the two and combined elements of both to present a remarkable range of different kinds of film texts (including documentaries with the appearance of fantasy and vice versa), in which the distinction between 'fiction' and 'fact' is not particularly useful (although to make this claim is still to create a political issue). This diversity is something to celebrate. We are discussing 'realisms' as part of a range of different approaches to the medium.

We've suggested that one distinguishing factor of realist film-making might be a concern with representing social issues. This would push out of the frame most **mainstream** films which, although they reproduce aspects of the real world accurately enough to signify a familiar location, are not interested in making use of the real events which might happen there every day. Instead, they pursue familiar story structures (providing the pleasures of genre) or special stories with 'larger than life' characters and unusual events. The level of realistic detail in a Hollywood film might be very high and the original story idea may have come from a newspaper or magazine story. A film like *Working Girl* (US 1988) might tell us something about New York office life and will certainly enable us as students to enter a discourse about 'women and work', but for our purposes here, it isn't realism.

One of two other elements must be present in a realist film:

● the film-maker is concerned to capture something about the experience of the real event, to represent it as faithfully as possible for the audience and to **mediate** it as little as possible; or

● the film-maker has something specific to say about the real world and has developed a specific style, using realist conventions.

The first of these is a pragmatic approach which tries to get as close as possible to an event in a physical sense and tends towards a documentary stance. The second is a more obviously 'political' position and is as likely to encompass realist fiction as documentary. Again, we might see the former as developing from photography and journalism and the latter from literature – but it isn't quite as simple as that. We will investigate three celebrated historical examples, selecting from a wide range of possibles. We think you need this detail in order to explore ideas about realism. All the examples have resonances in contemporary media production which we hope you will pick up, but please be careful not to take any of the three as representing 'fixed' positions about realistic aesthetics – this is one of the dangers of superficial studies which look for

Lumière brothers Auguste and Louis, French brothers often credited with the first cinema screenings in 1895. *Workers Leaving the Factory* and *A Train Arriving in the Station* were two of the 'actualities' of a few minutes' length which comprised the opening programme.

Georges Méliès was the first 'showman' of cinema. His short films in the first years of cinema included *A Trip to the Moon* (France 1902).

Dramadoc and **docudrama** are terms used to describe the mix of fact and fiction in modern television productions. Often a play will be written based on the transcripts of a 'real' courtroom drama or the memoirs or diaries of politicians etc. and using the visual techniques of documentary. Some critics get very agitated about the confusion between the documented fact and the written fiction – others see it as quite acceptable.

easy categorisations. You will find contradictions between the approaches, but also similarities, and their influence on contemporary work.

Direct Cinema

The high point of the 'direct approach to recording reality' came in the early 1960s and was known in America as **Direct Cinema**. Similar work (but with a different underpinning philosophy) was also carried out in France and an alternative title is **cinéma vérité** (cinema truth). You will recognise the modern term 'fly on the wall' and be aware of the standard television documentary techniques which enable viewers to eavesdrop on what appear to be 'real events' (i.e. not specially staged for the camera).

The simple premise of this approach is that a camera and microphone are as close to events as possible and that the film or tape is running continuously. Everything that happens is recorded. The film-makers have three main problems:

- finding camera and microphone technology that is lightweight and sensitive
- avoiding becoming part of the events and causing subjects to 'play to the camera'
- deciding how to reduce the hours of footage to a reasonable length for audiences (and avoiding a particular editorial position).

The early 1960s was the period when lightweight 16mm film cameras could for the first time be combined with good quality lightweight audio recorders for synchronised sound. With filmstocks sensitive enough to provide reasonable monochrome picture quality under most lighting conditions, including small hand-held lights, the documentary crew was ready to go almost anywhere – and they did.

The new approach began with *Primary* (US 1960), in which a crew followed presidential hopefuls John F. Kennedy and Hubert Humphrey on the campaign trail. The film was made by an independent television producer Robert Drew, working with three documentary film-makers who would become the core of Direct Cinema – **D.A. Pennebaker, Richard Leacock** and **Albert Maysles**. As Monaco (1980) points out, the aim of Direct Cinema was a sense of **'objectivity'** – the events and people who were the subjects of films were able to speak for themselves, avoiding voice-over narration (the conventional accompaniment to many documentaries up to that point).

Conventions can soon develop and become 'naturalised' as part of the medium. In the sophisticated 1990s we have become used to the presence of the camera in all kinds of unlikely places and we have also grown sceptical about the 'objectivity' of documentary approaches. In 1960 not only was the technology new, but the eavesdropping on ordinary lives was also novel. In many ways, Direct Cinema was less an *aesthetic* and more a *practice*, by which we mean it was less important that the films had a particular look or style and more important that the production was completed in a particular way.

The problem of subjects who 'played to the camera' and therefore behaved 'unnaturally' was partly avoided by selecting subjects for whom 'playing to an audience' was simply part of their usual behaviour. Politicians were followed by performers of various kinds, including Bob Dylan in probably the best-known and commercially most successful Direct Cinema feature, D.A. Pennebaker's *Don't Look Back* (US 1966), and the Rolling Stones in the Maysles Brothers' *Gimme Shelter* (US 1971).

Problems were faced by **Frederick Wiseman**, who began a series of 'institutional' documentaries in the late 1960s. Wiseman tackled a police force, a high school and various other welfare agencies. His aim was to spend long enough with his subjects, filming all the while, for them to begin to feel that he and his crew were 'part of the furniture'. When he eventually came to the editing stage he had miles of film to sift through and the question of mediation became crucial. The initial approach of Pennebaker and Leacock was to try to subordinate editing decisions to the flow of events – i.e. not to develop a particular viewpoint through selection of shots, but simply to show whatever the camera 'captured'. (Monaco makes a good point here when he emphasises this notion of 'capturing' rather than 'creating' images.) Wiseman couldn't do this with his hours of film – he was forced to make decisions and effectively to enter into the relationship between the camera and the subject, in other words to mediate.

Wiseman's films were controversial and it is worth considering the institutional aspects of this particular realist approach. The 'closeness to the subject' and the revelations that might ensue were associated with photojournalism – as were many of the technological developments in cameras, lenses and filmstocks. A parallel 'movement' to Direct Cinema was '**New Journalism**', a development in newspaper and magazine journalism in which feature writers began to adopt some of the strategies of realist novelists in order to present stories. This meant detailed descriptive writing and also the possibility that the journalist could become part of the story, recording how he or she felt. In a sense this was in conflict with the 'objectivity' of Direct Cinema. Yet, in another way, it shared what we might see as an immersion in the issue, especially following the Wiseman approach. Some of the better-known New Journalism pieces by Hunter S. Thompson and Joe Eszterhas (now well-known as the Hollywood scriptwriter of *Basic Instinct* etc.) belong to a

Shooting ratios for vérité documentaries are very high – 20 or 30 hours of film for a one-hour programme. The programme really is 'scripted' in the edit suite.

'counter-culture' view of America in the late 1960s and early 1970s and display the first signs of a coming together of television, cinema, rock music and magazine-writing which is now commonplace in 'style' magazines like *The Face* and television programmes like the *Rough Guides* series. A marker of this synthesis is *In Cold Blood* (US 1967), a Hollywood feature based on a New Journalism 'documentary novel', about a pair of murderers, by Truman Capote.

> 'Many of them seem to be in love with realism for its own sake ... They seem to be saying: "Hey! Come here! This is the way people are living now – just the way I'm going to show you! It may astound you, disgust you, delight you or arouse your contempt or make you laugh ... Nevertheless, this is what it's like! It's *all* right here! You won't be bored! Take a look!"'
>
> (Tom Wolfe on the 'New Journalists' in Wolfe and Johnson 1975)

> The 'excitement of the real' has been recognised by Hollywood film-makers who can use Direct Cinema techniques in features to add to the controversy of stories based on real events. Oliver Stone's films such as *JFK* (1991) and *Natural Born Killers* (1994) provide good examples.

The other important feature of Direct Cinema was that it was conceived in terms of television screening. The Drew Associates films were destined for television and Wiseman was commissioned by National Educational Television. Crucial features of television in the 1960s were:

- poor picture quality – fuzzy black and white
- the importance of the soundtrack: many theorists believed it carried more weight with audiences than the image track.

These two factors meshed with the approach to camera framings and editing – a direct style was suitable as any complex compositions and framings would be lost on the small TV screen while the jerky hand-held camera was acceptable – and the innovation of live 'direct' sound. The films were also assured a relatively large audience and one used to the 'live' feel of television.

This distinction between television and cinema in terms of audience involvement is important for the direct approach. A cinema audience, sitting in the dark in a secluded environment, can become immersed in the film, and experience a feeling of 'being there'. But where is 'there'? The cinema also suggests that the whole experience is 'magical' and 'special' and that the events we experience are somehow happening out of time. By contrast, the television broadcast suggests that we are able to eavesdrop on an event which is happening *now* in a place which we could visit.

By the early 1970s the Direct Cinema pioneers were already looking to video and the first portable 'rover' packs. Leacock in particular has continued to argue for more **access** to production for more people. The contemporary heirs of Direct Cinema are not too difficult to find. The early techniques quickly passed over into the current affairs documentary (*World in Action* in the UK) and then into both the 'safe' and the controversial **institutional documentary** series. The recent spate of *Video Diaries* and *Video Nation* style camcorder documents are in a direct line of descent, as are the series *Jimmy's* about life in a Leeds hospital and the ill-fated *Living Soap* about student life.

In this first example of cinematic (and televisual) realism, we have emphasised a number of factors:

- the role of technology
- the importance of a practice – how to do it in practical terms
- the importance of institutional links to other media forms (which in turn suggests something about how audiences will engage with the material).

ACTIVITY 15.1

- Where would you like to be a fly on the wall? Select a subject which you think would interest an audience and which you could visit with a camcorder. Ask yourself the questions posed by the Direct Cinema approach.
- Where would you place yourself to capture sound and image effectively? Could you capture all the material you would need to represent your subject to your satisfaction?
- What strategies would you use to ensure that your subjects did not 'perform' for the camera?
- Do you think your subject would automatically produce a story, or would you have to restructure the events during the editing process?

Formulating a realist aesthetic

Less pragmatic film-makers than the Direct Cinema group have at various times attempted to develop approaches that would combine an exploration of social issues using the full range of the possibilities of cinema. This is a less 'pure' and more sophisticated position than that of Direct Cinema in recognising that: 'Realism in art can only be achieved in one way – through artifice.' This assertion comes from the French

Institutional documentaries following the Wiseman lead have been popular on UK television. Mostly the exposure of institutions at work is informative or amusing, but those looking into the police and education have created great controversy – which probably says more about those institutions than about the documentary technique.

In the early 1970s, the leading 'fly on the wall' documentarist working in the UK, Roger Graef, found the BBC to be institutionally opposed to the **Direct Cinema** approach:

'The BBC published the Green Book on how to make documentaries: do a few days' research and then restage what was "typical". Such a process involved the invasion by a crew of technicians, moving the furniture and turning each location into a film studio.'
(Graef 1995)

André Bazin (1919-58) An influential critic whose essays are collected in two volumes published in English in the late 1960s under the title *What Is Cinema?* They are still in print (see Bazin 1967, 1971).

critic **André Bazin** (1971: 26) and it emphasises that realism is about a set of conventions. We shall discover that very different conventions can be made to serve similar ends.

The central issue is about how to involve an audience, not in terms of identifying with the individual hero of a conventional narrative, but in social issues, albeit played out in the lives of ordinary people. A realist film-maker is making a contract with the audience which implies a joint project to explore the real world through the medium of film. We've chosen to look at two influential historical figures and, in the case study of Chapter 16, at a controversial contemporary realist.

Roberto Rossellini

Roberto Rossellini (1906–77) A film-maker for forty years, constantly changing his approach to realism. Also an important teacher and lecturer on film and a major influence on younger film-makers such as Jean-Luc Godard.

Rossellini is best known as one of the founders of **Italian neo-realism** – an approach to film-making which flourished in the immediate aftermath of the Second World War and which was characterised by very low budgets, location shooting, non-professional actors and 'real' stories.

The subject of the neo-realism film is the world; not story or narrative. It contains no preconceived thesis, because ideas are born *in* the film *from* the subject. It has no affinity with the superfluous and the merely spectacular, which it refuses, but is attracted to the concrete . . . It refuses recipes and formulas . . . neo-realism poses problems for us and for itself in an attempt to make people think.

(Rossellini in *Retrospettive*, April 1953, reprinted in Overby (1978))

This presents an argument in favour of cinematic realism as a **progressive aesthetic** opposed to 'entertainment cinema' and in favour of education. (Rossellini was taken up by Marxist critics in the 1970s, but he remained a Catholic humanist intellectual throughout his life.)

Neo-realism represents a mix between the pragmatic (in 1945 the Italian film industry was, like the rest of the country, in ruins with abandoned studios and a lack of basic film-making materials) and the idealistic. The aesthetic had been developed first in France during the 1930s and later under the fascist regime in Italy, for which Rossellini began his career with documentary-style stories about the armed forces. The stylistic feature we want to highlight is the use of the long shot and the long take.

The **long shot** is the ideal framing device to show crowds and the movements of soldiers in battle. Its use in Hollywood tends to be restricted to **establishing shots** and genres like the western where 'figures in a landscape' are important. Usually, however, stories are told in mid-shot and medium close-up with attention paid to individual characters. Long shots are also difficult to organise on studio sets, where framing is often required to disguise the fact that a set is just a collection of 'flat' walls without a ceiling. Allied to the long shot is the use of **deep-focus**, which allows the film-maker to compose a shot in depth with objects in the foreground and the background, both in sharp focus. Different actions can take place within the frame and the audience can select to look at the foreground or background. Deep-focus requires plenty of light for the camera lens and studio sets have to have ceilings (which become visible with greater depth). Deep-focus works well on location and, like the long shot, was common in silent cinema before bulky sound equipment began to restrict camerawork.

A **long take** is any shot lasting longer than about 20 seconds (the Hollywood average throughout the studio period is about 12 seconds). For the film-maker, the long take poses problems because all the actions must be carefully worked out in advance. Long shots and staging in depth help because they give greater possibilities of movement in the frame. Alternatively, moving the camera by panning or tracking (see Chapter 3 for full explanation of these terms) allows greater freedom. The panning and tracking camera, shooting in long takes, is a feature of Rossellini's films at various times.

Shot length Various film scholars, including Bordwell, Staiger and Thompson, have undertaken surveys of shot lengths from a range of films and production periods.

Rossellini's first post-war film, *Rome Open City* (Italy 1945), shot under difficult circumstances on the streets of the newly liberated city, caused a sensation in France and the United States. However, it was the succeeding film, *Paisà* (Italy 1946), which perhaps best represents Rossellini's approach to realism in this period.

Paisà (the title refers to a colloquial Italian word for 'countryman' or simply 'friend') is concerned with the story of the Allied advance through Italy at the end of the war. Different characters appear in each of six separate episodes – there is no possibility of our identifying with an American hero who 'makes it through'. The story derives, in Rossellini's terms, from the concrete reality of the situation and the approach he takes to the production supports this aim. The six episodes are intercut with actual newsreel footage, titles and voice-over in such a way that it is difficult to distinguish 'real' from staged footage. The Americans in the film are professional actors (but not 'stars'), but many of the Italians are played by local people in the 'real' locations which Rossellini uses whenever possible. In the final episode, the incidents are very much based on events recounted by the 'real' partisans.

At the end of the final episode, which features Italian partisans and American and British agents fighting the Germans in the Po delta, the partisans are captured and shot and the protesting American leader is executed. The film ends with a partisan's body floating out to sea and a title explaining that the war ended a few weeks later. This bleak ending

Figure 15.2 A typical shot from the last sequence of *Paisà*. Note the camera angle which effectively mimics the partisans' view of their world and the long shot which encompasses the mixed band of partisans and British and American special forces, privileging no single character

would not be possible in a Hollywood film, but for Rossellini it is not the end of the 'story'. As Bondanella (1993) points out, for Rossellini the 'reality' is the triumph of the human spirit over adversity as understood in Christian philosophy.

The argument in favour of the long take and the long shot is demonstrated in the sequence illustrated in Figure 15.2. We are presented with a series of long takes in which the action unfolds, often in relatively long shot. The scenes are carefully orchestrated to flow almost seamlessly. Although there is clearly a 'leader' (the American officer), we are not forced to adopt his viewpoint. When mid-shots or medium close-ups are used, they pick out particular narrative incidents rather than develop individual characters. Most of all, the camera is used to create for us the viewpoint of the partisans who live in this unique environment. As Bazin writes:

> the horizon is always at the same height. Maintaining the same proportions between water and sky in every shot brings out one of the basic characteristics of this landscape. It is the exact equivalent, under conditions exposed by the screen, of the inner feeling men experience who are living between the sky and the water and whose lives are at the mercy of an infinitesimal shift of angle in relation to the horizon.
>
> (Bazin 1971: 37)

There are two important features about Rossellini's visual style in *Paisà*:

- The style attempts to 'reveal' the reality in the story, it doesn't draw attention to itself. It does, of course, 'construct' a representation of reality, but in doing so it fits Bazin's maxim that the representation of reality requires artifice.
- The relationship between film-maker and audience is such that the audience is invited to select where to look in the long shot composition and is allowed to follow the action in the long take. The director, by avoiding close-ups and cutting, is not shouting 'Look here!', 'Look at that!'

Fiction from fact

The basis of the neo-realism approach was neatly encapsulated by one of the main scriptwriters of the period, Cesare Zavattini. He referred to a typical starting point for a neo-realist film:

'A woman goes into a shop to buy a pair of shoes. The shoes cost 7,000 lire. The woman tries to bargain. The scene lasts perhaps two minutes, but I must make a two-hour film. What do I do? I analyse the fact in all its constituent elements, in its 'before', in its 'after', in its contemporaneity. The fact creates its own fiction...'

(Quoted in Williams 1980)

Zavattini did this to great effect in the celebrated **Bicycle Thieves** (Italy 1947) in which an unemployed man can't look for work unless he finds his stolen bicycle. In 1993, Jim Allen used a similar starting point for the Ken Loach film *Raining Stones* (see Chapter 16), which is based on an unemployed man who wants to buy a communion dress for his daughter. *Bicycle Thieves* was also a model for the first sub-Saharan African film, Ousmane Sembene's *Borom Sarret* (Senegal 1963) (see Chapter 28, 'African Cinema').

If you are interested in scriptwriting, trying out Zavattini's method is excellent practice. Take a simple action like the above and work backwards and forwards from it to create a story.

Rossellini went on in the 1950s and 1960s to explore ideas about realism in many different ways, but let's turn to another film-maker who had similar concerns, but very different and equally influential methods.

Sergei Eisenstein

Soviet Cinema in the 1920s was dedicated to celebrating and promoting the Revolution of 1917 and this produced a contradictory set of impulses. Films were at once experimental – part of the artistic work of a new society

Sergei Eisenstein (1898–1948)
A leading experimental director of
the Soviet Union in the 1920s as
well as a writer and teacher of film
theory. He gained considerable
recognition in the west and was
lured to Hollywood (not a
successful move).

Eisenstein quotes a 'miniature
story' by the American writer
Ambrose Bierce. In *The
Inconsolable Widow*, a woman is
weeping by an open grave. A
stranger approaches and comforts
her saying that 'there is another
man somewhere, besides your
husband, with whom you can still
be happy'. 'There was', she sobbed,
'but this is his grave.' The
juxtaposition of widow and grave
and our conventional reading are
all that is needed to make the
story (Eisenstein 1968: 15).

– but were also required to document and represent the successes of the
revolution. Most Soviet Cinema was therefore documentary in nature and
concerned with social issues. Later, in the 1930s, this contradiction would
be resolved in terms of a heavy '**socialist realism**' with a didactic narrative
and heroic characters, but in the 1920s much more variety was possible.

Sergei Eisenstein formulated a theory of '**dialectical montage**'.
Dialectics is the Marxist term for a process of analysis in which change is
identified as a struggle between opposites, which in turn produces a new
synthesis (expressed as thesis–antithesis–synthesis). **Montage** is the
process of putting images together so that new meaning is created
through a particular juxtaposition. If images are chosen carefully,
montage can 'represent' ideas quickly and dramatically. The shock of a
juxtaposition can be concerned with the *content* of the image (a starving
child juxtaposed with a gluttonous financier) or with *formal* differences
of size of shot or framing (a long shot of a crowd and an extreme close-up
of a face). Montage might result in a rapid succession of briefly held shots
in a sequence, whereby a 'real' process is speeded up, or a sequence of
shots which extends time by repeating images.

Eisenstein argues that montage is the best way to engage the audience
in a learning process. Through montage the film-maker exposes his or her
thought processes and this enables the viewer to participate in the process
of 'creation' of meaning which takes place through the juxtaposition.
This is both the opposite of Direct Cinema (*creating* images not *capturing*

Figure 15.3 Peter Kennard's comment on the end of the Cold War uses the contrast between
large and small juxtaposition/superimposition techniques to make its point

them) and a refutation of the Bazin/Rossellini method. Eisenstein says to his audience: 'Here is A, here is B, what do you make of putting them together? Yes, it's C isn't it?' Watching the film becomes a dynamic process of making the links and understanding the synthesis.

Eisenstein is best known for the films that tell the story of the Revolution and the struggles that went before. *October* (USSR 1928), which he co-scripted and co-directed with Gregori Alexandrov, was a tenth anniversary film about the Revolution itself. Photographed almost entirely in Leningrad (St Petersburg or Petrograd in 1917) the actors are largely local people – one similarity to the neo-realist approach. There is also the occasional use of long shot and 'very long shot' to show the mass of workers and soldiers. There the similarity ends. The montage film uses relatively short takes throughout and framings are designed not to 'reveal' actions but to present shapes and symbols that can be used to create interpreted meanings.

Often framings show us just faces – selected as being particularly suggestive of cruelty, jollity, etc. – or just hands, arms, etc. The strutting officers of the Tsar's guards are intercut with a mechanical peacock strutting and preening itself. As the mass of workers rush across the wide streets of Petrograd in very long shot like ants, they are intercut with two images of machine guns with a leering gunner gleefully firing way. These two images are of guns pointing in opposite directions and when they are shown in sequence for just a few frames each they appear to be flashing – a purely visual suggestion of the gunfire which is dispersing the workers and also an emphasis on the class betrayal by the soldier. Note here that *October* is a 'silent' film, which would usually have been viewed with some kind of musical accompaniment, and possibly sound effects.

At the start of the film, the workers' initial success is signified by a statue of Tsar Alexander III which literally falls apart – the head rolling off, the arms dropping off, etc. Later in the film, when the workers appear to be losing, Eisenstein and Alexandrov simply play the same sequence backwards and the statue is restored to power. Do these kind of tricks negate the 'realism' of *October*? Certainly some critics have taken montage to represent **anti-realism** or '**expressionism**' because of these exaggerated filmic devices. A debate about montage cannot divert us from the central point, however, which is that Eisenstein's aim is to explore a real historical event and to ask the audience to learn from it.

Conclusion

Realist media texts are predicated on the assumption that they say something about the real world. In the two case study chapters that follow, we explore what might be the place of such an assumption in the 1990s.

References and further reading

Bazin, André (1967; 1971) *What Is Cinema?,* vols I and II, Berkeley: University of California Press.

Bondanella, Peter (1993) *The Films of Roberto Rossellini*, Cambridge: Cambridge University Press.

Bordwell, David, Staiger, Janet and Thompson, Kirstin (1985) *The Classic Hollywood Cinema: Film Style and Mode of Production to 1960*, London: Routledge.

Crisell, Andrew (1994) *Understanding Radio*, London: Routledge.

Eisenstein, Sergei (1968) *The Film Sense,* London: Faber.

Graef, Roger (1995) 'Flying off the Wall', *Guardian*, 6 October.

Monaco, James (1980) 'American Documentary since 1960' in Richard Roud (ed.) *Cinema: A Critical Dictionary,* vol. 1, London: Martin, Secker & Warburg.

Neale, Steve (1985) *Cinema and Technology: Sound, Image and Colour*, London: BFI/Macmillan.

Nochlin, Linda (1971) *Realism*, London: Penguin.

Overby, David (1978) *Springtime in Italy: A Reader on Neo-Realism,* London: Talisman.

Rotha, Paul (1939) *Documentary Film*, London: Faber & Faber.

Williams, Christopher (ed.) (1980) *Realism and the Cinema*, London: Routledge & Kegan Paul/BFI.

Wolfe, Tom and Johnson, E.W. (eds) (1975) *The New Journalism,* London: Picador.

16 / Case study: Ken Loach and realist codes

Ken Loach and realism

The best-known 'realist film-maker' in contemporary world cinema is probably **Ken Loach**. Loach shares with the early neo-realists a passion for everyday life and its problems. His formative years as a young television director at the BBC, working with Tony Garnett, produced a series of powerful contemporary filmed television dramas about working-class life. *Cathy Come Home* (UK 1966) remains one of the most controversial moments in UK television history – a shocking indictment of the treatment of the homeless which caused a public outcry.

Loach's committed left politics is leavened by a sense of fun and he cites the **Czech New Wave** cinema of the late 1960s as an influence on his work. This cinema of social realism used comedy to deflate the authoritarianism of Soviet communism and its echoes are found in such Loach triumphs as *Kes* (UK 1969). In recent years Loach has found it difficult to get a wide release for his films in the UK, yet elsewhere in Europe they have enjoyed great critical and commercial success.

Many of the characteristics of a Loach film refer back to neo-realism:

- use of actors who are not stars. Some may be members of a stock company (e.g. Ricky Tomlinson, once Bobby Grant of *Brookside*), others may be performers (like Chrissie Rock, the night-club comedian who plays the mother in *Ladybird, Ladybird* (UK 1994)) but not necessarily actors
- naturalistic acting style, built up by emotional involvement in the issues rather than obsession with character or script

- shooting scenes in narrative sequence so that audience involvement develops
- location shooting
- camera style using documentary filming techniques (this is a sophisticated and complex style developed from earlier television work – the films look and 'feel' real, but the visual style is not distinctive).

Although Loach's commitment to realist film-making is clear, he would be the first to point to regular collaborators; in the 1960s and early 1970s, **Tony Garnett** as producer; **Barry Hines** as writer in the middle period; in the early period, and more recently, **Jim Allen** as writer.

ACTIVITY 16.1

Try to look at two or three of Loach's later films (*Riff Raff* (1991), *Raining Stones* (1993), *Ladybird, Ladybird* (1994) are all widely available on videotape).

- Do the films strike you as being about the Britain of the 1990s, which you know?
- If they do, which particular aspects of the films carry the connotations of realism? Is it:
  - the casting?
  - the dialogue?
  - the locations?
  - other aspects?
- Are the references to neo-realism helpful in understanding the films? Or are there other distinctive features which distinguish them from other contemporary films?

Figure 16.1 The press pack photograph for *Land and Freedom* (UK/Spain/Germany 1995)

The 1995 Loach feature *Land of Freedom* had not been released when this chapter was completed, but the discussions about the film at various festivals and the Press Pack which we did obtain suggest that the approach has remained the same. If you look carefully at the image presented in Figure 16.1 you will recognise some of the points we have been making. The image chosen to promote the film is not an 'action' sequence (though the story is about the Spanish Civil War in the 1930s), nor is it a 'star portrait' (the film does not have major stars). Instead, it is a carefully constructed 'realist' snapshot of a fighting group. The group is not properly framed – the four in the centre look at the camera while the two on the outside ignore it. The character in the centre appears glamorous and confident, but he has his arm over the shoulder of a character who might be equally nervous and tense. We have no idea if Loach was involved in staging the shot, but there are certainly plenty of realist conventions being played with in the final image.

Realism and politics

Most realist film-makers are 'left of centre' to some extent – their desire to represent 'the real' very often derives from a wish to expose something and thereby to help to get the situation changed.

Some of the critics who support 'the realist aesthetic' are to the 'right of centre', especially in the UK. They tend to be keen on authentic detail, especially if a film celebrates their view of British history. There have been some very odd controversies over the 'political' films made by Loach and others, where in order to undermine the potential exposure of 'real issues', critics have dismissed the films on the grounds that soldiers are 'wearing the wrong buttons'.

Realist approaches have also been criticised by left critics who object to the **transparency** of the representation of the real world (i.e. that audiences become too easily involved in the story and don't understand the processes of representation). This **anti-realist** position was most evident in the **counter-cinema** movement of the 1970s (see Chapter 27, 'Independents and Alternatives') which in turn referred back to some of the ideas of Soviet Cinema of the 1920s (see Chapter 15, 'Realisms').

Contemporary television drama

We have argued that there are many realisms and a great diversity of realist texts. Many of the innovations of the earlier realist media film-makers (such as the hand-held cinéma vérité camera) have been 'absorbed' into the techniques of the **mainstream** of production. What some critics argue is that realism on television is now a matter of sensational content – the 'real life' crime drama, whether it is the so-called '**tabloid** news' programmes or the **soap opera** that developed from the O.J. Simpson trial. These are all stories that begin with actual crimes, but are highly stylised and 'narrativised' for audiences (a tradition that goes back to *True Crime Magazine* and the other 'pulp' magazines of the 1940s and 1950s). The **realist aesthetic** has become just another style feature, another ingredient in the **postmodern** media environment. We take up this general proposition about postmodernism in the next chapter, but here we will look at one possible example of the divorce between the realist aesthetic and the realist social issue.

The drama series is still a mainstay of American television scheduling and in recent years attempts have been made to develop new visual conventions as well as narrative structures. Perhaps the most successful producer-innovator has been Steve Bochco with the ground-breaking police series *Hill Street Blues* and the more recent *NYPD Blue*. These programmes have typically used multiple lead characters with several different narrative strands running at once, including an interest in the minutiae of characters' lives, and a general feeling of the rush and adrenaline of 'life on the street'. All of the individual elements have been used before and many are taken from realist films or documentaries. The final ingredient, evident in *NYPD* and the most recent manifestations, *Homicide: Life on the Street* and (to a lesser extent) *e.r.*, is the roving camera reminiscent of cinéma vérité.

Modern film-makers have the advantage of the **steadicam** (a stabilising harness allowing the camera to be carried easily without 'wobble') as well as the lightweight hand-held camera which can be used in a confined space. Typically, in these programmes, a conversation between two or three people will not always be shot in the traditional 'shot/reverse shot' (i.e. two **set-ups**) but instead the camera will swing from one character to the next in a swift panning movement (sometimes called a 'whip pan'). This could be accommodated in a relatively smooth movement, but instead the camera operator appears to have been instructed to make it as quick as possible – emphasising the formal device.

The distinctive shot in *e.r.*, as in many hospital dramas, is the rapid tracking shot in which the camera retreats before the Emergency Room team and the stretcher, as they rush down the corridors of the hospital, clattering through doors and eventually arriving in ER. This can be a smooth 'ride' because of the steadicam and the effect is literally to sweep us along in the exciting events of the drama, but again the camerawork is exaggerated and self-conscious. We have a 'folk memory' of both of these shots from the earliest cinéma vérité documentaries and news reports. We know the reporter and camera crew only have the one camera, so by necessity they must record exchanges with pans and they must follow subjects down corridors and through doors.

So, do the modern series use these devices to add a veneer of 'realism' to their fictional stories? If that is the intention, why exaggerate the camera techniques? Why adopt such conventional framings (medium close-ups and close-ups) at other times? Sometimes it appears that these techniques are selected purely for effect – as if there is a knowingness about the visual style which says 'Hey guys, look at these cool camera movements!' The camerawork on *Homicide* in particular seems arbitrary, with glimpses of 'life in the precinct room' or isolated pans or tracks across the rooftops or city streets which seem to have no obvious narrative significance. It's also noticeable that 'realist sound' is not such a priority and we get fewer experiments in the use of overlapping dialogue or the stumbling speech of 'real people' – the characters in these dramas have well-written lines.

The postmodernists would argue that these visual quirks are simply an expression of the breakdown of distinctions between realist and non-realist conventions. TV programme-makers are free to 'play' with visual style without worrying about realism. They merely have to make programmes distinctive enough to gain attention and to give pleasure to audiences media-literate enough to enjoy the play of relatively meaningless signifiers. Some critics have pointed out that this self-consciousness is evident in the script – in *Homicide*, for instance, in one of the many snippets of inconsequential chat, one detective says to another, 'It's television Stan, it's not supposed to be real.'

We'll finish by noting that the two visual devices we have selected in this example were both used by Rossellini in his later works exploring the lives of historical characters. The difference was that he invented a remotely controlled zoom lens which would allow smooth re-framings as the camera panned and tracked.

He relegated the camera code to the service of revealing the action and didn't allow it to draw attention to itself.

ACTIVITY 16.2

Select any modern filmed television series (American ones are currently the most interesting – you might puzzle over the fact that some of the most popular American shows, like *e.r.*, are shown on Channel 4 in the UK). Test out our comments on visual style.

● Can you 'justify' the camera movements and framings – do they help to push the story along or develop the characters – or are they more self-conscious?

Listen carefully to the soundtrack.

● Is it in any way unconventional, does it act as a complement to the visual style?

● Overall, do these realist devices succeed in making you interested in watching – or is your interest taken primarily by the content of the programmes?

● Are they markedly different in visual style to UK series?

● Is the use of realist style features matched by an interest in the social issues covered in the stories?

References and further reading

Christie, Ian (1995) 'Film for a Spanish Republic', *Sight & Sound,* vol. 5, no. 10, October.

O'Reilly, John (1995) 'The Real Macabre', *Guardian*, 3 July.

Movements in the arts and
culture
Postmodernism as a
description of the real

17 / Case study: A note on postmodernism

As soon as you venture into any of the current debates about media theory, you will come across the term 'postmodernism'. Many theorists argue we are living in the postmodern age, recognisable not only in the kinds of media texts we consume, but also in other fields like architecture or fashion. **Postmodernism** extends across all our cultural activity, including the way we shop and eat.

One of the most confusing features of postmodernism is that it seems to refer to two different sets of ideas:

- a *stylistic movement* in the arts and culture generally which comes after, or 'post', modernism and also involves 'the end of realism'
- a *socio-economic sense* of the contemporary world.

Movements in the arts and culture

Historians of arts and culture have attempted to identify particular 'movements' comprising artists (i.e. creative producers of all kinds) whose work over a particular period appears to share recognisable themes, styles and approaches. These movements are seen to represent something consciously new and distinctive and are often viewed as being critical in some way of what went before. Starting with the early nineteenth century, we can distinguish several such movements, the most important being the **romantic**, the **realist** and the **modernist**. The romantic movement which included poets Shelley and Byron and painters Turner and Blake, emphasised passion and imagination and represented an artistic challenge to the newly emerging industrial

society. The realists, as we have seen (in Chapter 15), were concerned to present social issues and the details of daily life in literature, painting and the new medium of photography.

The modernist movement is seen to date from the period around the First World War and the accompanying social and economic changes which prompted new ways of thinking and feeling about the world and new ways of expressing those ideas and sensibilities. The movement was evident in literature, painting, film and photography, music, theatre and architecture.

In literature the work of writers, like James Joyce with *Ulysees* and *Finnegan's Wake* and T.S. Eliot with *The Wasteland*, ruptured existing traditions of 'good' taste, 'proper' rhyme schemes, ways of writing novels, and so on. Such breaks often took the form of a kind of play with the medium of language itself, with its signifiers divorced from their meanings – puns, allusions and fun 'raiding the image bank' of the past. Specific movements like surrealism were part of a broader modernist trend.

Surrealism: Artistic movement spanning painting, film and photography, characterised by distortions of time and space and bizarre juxtapositions, often as in a dream (coinciding with the dream analyses of **Sigmund Freud**). Painter **Salvador Dali** and film-maker **Luis Buñuel** worked together on *Un Chien Andalou* (France 1929) and were part of a distinct Paris community. (See also Chapter 27, 'Independents and Alternatives'.)

The 'modern' period lasted for fifty or sixty years. Throughout this time the texts produced by the modernists tended to be defined as part of **high culture** and to command relatively small and mainly middle-class audiences, which nevertheless included critics and academics, thereby ensuring an influence on other artists. This was in marked contrast to the more clearly 'popular' works of the romantics and the realists (e.g. the novels of Dickens). Modernists saw themselves as part of an **avant garde** (see Chapter 27) developing new media forms. Much modernist work remains difficult for contemporary audiences, but aspects of the modernist style have been slowly absorbed into the **mainstream** of media production.

Throughout the modernist period, the ideas and approaches of the earlier movements are still evident in the **mainstream** culture, as is the persistence of what we might term a **classical** style. This term sometimes refers to artistic forms derived from Greek and Roman culture (e.g. classical architecture with columns and plinths etc.) and sometimes just refers to an established canon of authoritative 'great works' (e.g. 'classical music'). In media production terms, critics have traced the development of a particular form and identified when it established a classic status (e.g. the classic film western). Any critic working in a particular art form up to recent times would expect to be able to approach a text armed with an understanding of what might be classical or 'neo-classical' (a contemporary revival of a classical form), what the romantic and realist traditions in that form have produced, and what the modern style would be. Each of these would be a coherent approach producing recognisable art objects or media texts. It is this neat classification and critical certainty which the postmodernists have attacked.

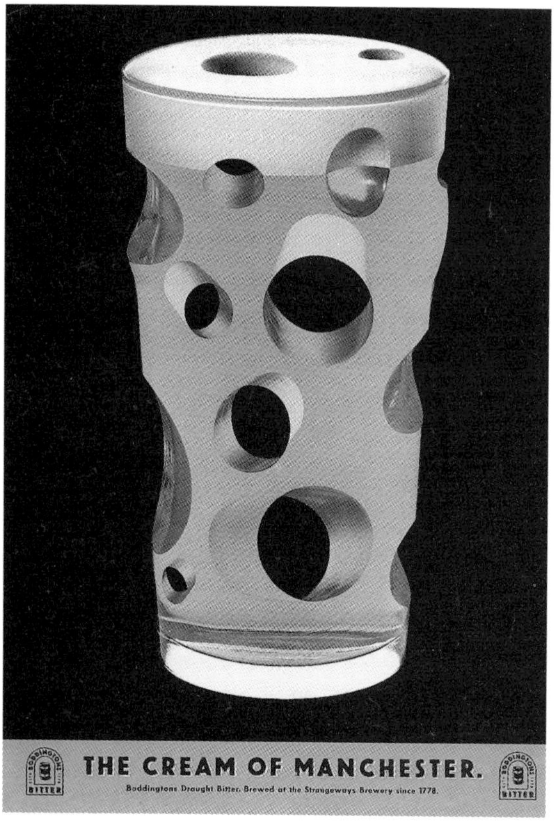

Figure 17.1 A postmodern ad?

THE CREAM OF MANCHESTER.
Boddingtons Draught Bitter. Brewed at the Strangeways Brewery since 1778.

Bricolage

Postmodernism is not a movement as such. It is not represented by a manifesto in which committed artists outline their ideas and beliefs (most 'movements' have some form of statement from practitioners). Instead, postmodernism is said to be a condition in which artists and creative producers feel free to take 'bits and pieces' from earlier styles and to mix and match. One of the terms associated with this new 'non-style' is **bricolage**, a French word which is used by structuralists to refer to the process of adaptation or improvisation whereby aspects of one style are given quite different meanings when they are juxtaposed with stylistic features from somewhere else. The original meaning is changed by the new use – the sign has been resignified. (See Chapter 1 for more on signs and signification.)

Dick Hebdige (1979) in a section entitled 'Style as Bricolage', suggests that youth sub-cultural groups are effectively producing a manifesto when they take clothes associated with different class positions or specific work functions and convert them into fashion statements 'empty' of their original meanings. For Hebdige, the 1950s 'teddy boys' with their Edwardian jackets, the mods in their sharp suits, and the punks in bondage gear were all 'bricoleurs'.

Note that Hebdige is referring to a process of subversion and adaptation through consumption – the clothes and records young people bought. There are, however, plenty of examples of *conscious* attempts by producers to become bricoleurs. Architects, especially when working on largely 'functional' buildings, have tended to work broadly within a contemporary style while serving the needs of their clients. If no firm contemporary style exists, strange things can happen. In the late 1980s, one of the few growth areas in new building was in large supermarkets on the outskirts of town.

> At least one supermarket chain has elected to build stores which resemble, in their upper architecture, nothing more than a country manor house from some indeterminate period in English history, often complete with an antique clock face and a redundant dovecote.
> - What do you make of this? It appears to be an attempt to placate environmentalists.
> - Does it work? Can the bricoleur be this calculating? It is certainly a candidate for a postmodern building.

More obvious candidates for the title 'postmodern' are film directors like David Lynch, and Quentin Tarantino. Lynch with films like *Blue Velvet* (US 1986) and the TV series *Twin Peaks,* and Tarantino, especially with *Pulp Fiction* (US 1994), are seen to revel in playful references to earlier films, genres and characters. They present confusing narratives that break the rules of **continuity editing** and challenge our ideas about what happens in fictional worlds (e.g. Tarantino's now famous discussions about Madonna records, tipping and the French for 'Big Mac'). But unlike earlier directors, who worked within the modernist period and had some form of personal or political agenda, Tarantino and company appear to work for money and to have fun. Critics have described them as having 'nothing to say', but saying it strikingly.

Tarantino is linked to the modernist period by his often quoted reverence for Jean-Luc Godard (see Chapter 27, 'Independents and Alternatives'). However, the references are to Godard's earlier work when his political agenda is less pronounced. Perhaps what attracts Tarantino is the way in which Godard 'played' with Hollywood conventions in these films. Thus in *Pulp Fiction* we have a homage to Godard in the name of the production company, 'A Band Apart': a reference to Godard's 1964 film *Bande à part* (a gangster film, famous for a dance sequence in a cafe in which the characters parody a Hollywood musical). Tarantino then includes a dance sequence in *Pulp Fiction* which is, he claims, inspired by Godard and which at the same time works as an ironic comment on the dancing skills of a paunchy John Travolta, one-time star of *Saturday Night Fever* (US 1977).

Many Hollywood directors make references to earlier films (most of the 1970s generation such as Steven Spielberg, Martin Scorsese, Francis Ford Coppola, etc.), but they have generally done so within a coherent, mainstream Hollywood form (which we might think of as both 'classical' and 'realist'). For Tarantino and Lynch such references do not serve a function within a traditional form but mark a challenge to it. This challenge does not work to alienate the audience, as in many modernist works. Instead it complements the pleasurable playfulness evident in other aspects of the text. It might be argued that Hollywood has effectively swallowed some of the stylistic features of modernism without having gone through the pain of experimentation.

Postmodernism as a description of the real

When we move from postmodernism as 'style' to consider its impact on culture generally, we are faced with a challenge by theorists to the political certainties suggested both by 'realism' and its opposite 'anti-realism' – to the whole discussion on Realisms (Chapter 15) and Independents and alternatives (Chapter 27) in fact.

Our sense of reality is now said to be completely dominated by popular cultural signs and media images. It is no longer possible to argue that art or popular culture should 'hold up the mirror to reality', since reality itself is so full of advertising, film, video games and TV images. This takes to an absolute limit the helpful position that our sense of reality is to an extent formed by the media, and by our perceptions, so a neat separation of the two is impossible. What is now being argued is that we can know *nothing* other than what we get from the media.

Style, spectacle and surface is *all* in such a view: from an emphasis on the costly spectacles in contemporary cinema, to the ways that the simplest purchase at the supermarket is said to be crucially dependent on packaging. However poor we are, this position argues, we have some freedom to choose between products, and thus contribute to the importance of style over content, consumption over production. This has further implications for cultural products like films, where 'authenticity', 'realism', seriousness and so on are downplayed in favour of jokiness and style for their own sake. It's argued that there is a 'blandness' or refusal of serious positions in films like *Pulp Fiction* or TV products like *Twin Peaks* or *The Big Breakfast*. Advertising no longer tries seriously to convince us of its products' real quality but, for example, just shows us an amazing special effects whiz through space towards the bubble in a glass of Guinness.

Such 'blankness' goes along with the suggestion that all distinctions between 'high art' and popular culture have gone, or become blurred. Andy Warhol's multi-prints of Leonardo's Mona Lisa; Talking Heads' eclectic mix of levels of reference; the collage mixes of rap, house and hip hop; or advertising's extensive play with images from all over culture and history – all these contribute to the feeling that there are now no distinctions between the 'high' and the 'popular'.

A heavy emphasis is given to modern technologies' capacity to blur our sense of time and space, as well as to create '**virtual**' reality', which of course has obvious implications for art forms claiming to be realist portrayals of a real, knowable world. Films like *The Terminator* or the *Back to the Future* series or the editing style of music video, especially those for dance music,

undermine conventional relationships between time and space. Think about the speed of travel, or of information flows through modern computers, or the ways that speculation on the fast globally linked computers of stock exchanges can bring down governments' exchange policies. All this is said to link with an emphasis on the unknowability of history (whose knowability, at least to some extent, is crucial for realist media forms). Postmodern theory emphasises that 'history' has always been best understood as 'histories', governed by '**meta-narratives**'. These are large claims to truth, often narratively shaped, such as Marxism's claim that working people uniting together will eventually bring about socialism, or science's claim that it can bring about a good and reasonable conclusion to history by its discoveries and rationality. Much realist art has been inspired by hopes of a future changed in the directions of socialism or of enlightened rationality, and the widespread breakdown of belief in such motors to history has deep implications for its confidence, and way of operating.

The next step is to suggest that the whole of global culture is 'partying at the end of history', in the aftermath of a now triumphant global capitalism.

The limits of these arguments

While the expansion of media images into contemporary life compared to, say, twenty years ago is evident, the argument that the media have taken over reality itself, and left us with nothing against which to test or indeed enjoy media images, seems highly exaggerated. It's also highly reminiscent of many other positions, from the **Frankfurt School** onwards, which deeply distrust popular cultural forms, and the people who enjoy them (see Chapter 29, 'Audiences'). We need not take a simplistic 'window on the world' view of realism to feel that such a position is fundamentally uninterested in empirical research or even simple everyday observation, which suggests that people usually know something of the reality status of the media images with which they have chosen to engage.

When the argument is taken into style and consumption more generally, we need to remember that the ability to consume certain goods is highly dependent on income, education and location – and this is true for media goods too. Not everyone is able to 'shut up and shop' and the issue of production rather than consumption of goods and services, and how that might be transformed, is still key for realist forms. The television sit-com *Absolutely Fabulous* is a good test case of how far you might wish to take the postmodernist approach. Is the sit-com entertaining because it plays with stars, stereotypes and fads, like several other programmes, or does it create a more profound 'disturbance' (about women's lives, consumption, etc.)?

Related to the long distrust of popular forms, many postmodern emphases are uninterested in the extent to which spectacle, special effects, remakes, generic mixing, 'style' as well as 'content' (to make a tricky distinction) have always been a part of Hollywood. The extent to which special effects and spectacle are part of contemporary Hollywood may be relatively new, and the commanding heights of expensive advertising have certainly taken off in this direction. But do these changes render any kind of realist media work impossible?

In some forms (pop music and advertising especially) it's easy to see how the boundaries between 'high' and 'low' cultural reference have been eroded. But important qualifications need considering, such as public funding policies for the arts. In Britain at any rate, these still favour 'high' forms such as opera, Shakespearean drama, and 'serious' music and film – all of which rely on 'classical' forms, even if they may tolerate occasional modernist or postmodernist 'experiments'. For there to be any thrill in transgressing boundaries, like those between 'high' and 'low' forms, those boundaries need still to have some meaning. The scandal in 1995 that large sums of National Lottery money were going to the Royal Opera suggests that the boundaries are still there.

Of course, travel, emigration, and information flows have all accelerated in the last thirty years or so. An Asian-British school student in Cardiff may listen to Madonna on her Walkman while travelling to school, where she will be taught within the Welsh National Curriculum and go home to watch the Australian **soap** *Neighbours* (now owned by a British multinational) or perhaps an Indian film on video. Postmodernism gives a more glamorous, airport-centred impression of such changes, but seems relatively uninterested in trying to understand

- how differences in social class affect such global–local identities;
- how people use and negotiate the global technologies many of us have in our homes. It's much easier to 'read off' effects from such texts, and assert that they are making us all disoriented inhabitants of a virtual, technological reality.

The extent to which you go along with such positions has important effects on your expectations of realisms, and how well they can map the social world.

This spills over into the final point. It may be true that attempts to impose shapes on reality and history are 'meta-narratives' but:

- What else is postmodernism but another such story, a rather melancholy and 'end-of-history' one?
- However conscious we are now of these 'meta-narratives', we cannot easily do without them, and the meaning they give to experience.
- Some of these accounts work far better as ways of understanding and changing the world in particular directions than others.

The same is true for realisms, some forms of which need perhaps to be rethought, without abandoning their ambition of giving an account of the real world.

ACTIVITY 17.1
How postmodern are you?
- List the characteristics of what you understand as postmodernist media products.
- Try to estimate how much of the cinema, TV, computer games or radio that you consume might be termed postmodern.
- And how much of the advertising?

References and further reading

Hebdige, Dick (1979) *Subculture: The Meaning of Style*, London: Methuen.

—— (1988) *Hiding in the Light*, London: Comedia/ Routledge (for a celebration of pomo (jargon abbreviation for 'postmodernism'), and detailed analysis of the Talking Heads' video 'We're on the road to nowhere').

Sarup, Madan (1988) *An Introductory Guide to Post Structuralism and Postmodernism*, London: Harvester Wheatsheaf.

Strinati, Dominic (1995) *An Introduction to Theories of Popular Culture*, London: Routledge, ch. 6. (to which this section is indebted).

18 Technologies

When we brush our teeth or boil an egg we are using technology. We don't give it a second thought and the same is true of the technology we use in school or college or employment. Most of the time we don't notice media technology either, yet its power is such that every now and again we are staggered by the realism of an image or shocked by the emotions that media texts can arouse. We need to develop theoretical ideas to explain how these effects are achieved and what the proper role of technology in the production of meaning might be.

Some of these ideas are being developed in a wider discussion about contemporary society – the fear that the technology is developing too quickly; that it is affecting us (and particularly our children) to an unknown extent; that it is out of control. Other ideas about technology suggest that it might be liberating in allowing us to participate more and learn more, while some ideas refer to artists and producers who must change their methods and patterns of work and perhaps their whole approach to 'creativity'. 'New technology' has also long been viewed as a threat to established employment patterns, on the reasonable assumption that technology usually replaces human labour eventually.

Since the debates about technology are perhaps the least systemised within the Media Studies syllabuses, we need to think carefully about our approach.

Luddites Textile workers in the early nineteenth century who, fearing their jobs would be taken by machines in the new factories, organised themselves and destroyed the new machines wherever possible. The name is said to come from Ned Ludd who began the struggle. Usually a term of abuse (but they were correct in their analysis, of course – the machines were used to replace their skilled labour).

Defining 'media technology'

technology: the practice of any or all of the applied sciences that have practical value; technical methods in a particular field of industry or art; technical nomenclature; technical means and skill characteristic of a particular civilisation, group or period (from the Greek, techne = art)

(*Chambers 20th Century Dictionary*)

'Technology' is derived from the Greek for 'art'. 'Art' has an original meaning which includes the application of practical skills: at one time 'artist' and 'technician' may have had a similar meaning. 'Poetry' comes from the Greek for 'making' (which suggest there has not always been a divide between the 'doers' and 'thinkers').

Technology isn't just about machines or equipment – the **hardware** aspect which puts off those people for whom the insides of a computer or a washing machine represent examples of life's great mysteries. Technology is also about *methods, means and skill* – essentially about how we can make use of our knowledge in order to produce something useful. This forms the **software** in modern systems.

Take a junior reporter attending the local Magistrates Court. He or she uses simple but effective technology – a pencil and a notepad – to record what is said. Of course, these may seem simple, even primitive technologies, but the modern pencil and paper are the result of hundreds of years of technological development in the application of chemical knowledge about graphite and wood pulp and techniques for manufacture and good design, to allow them to be 'operated' effectively.

The technological input does not stop there. A special system of writing, Shorthand, with its own set of characters, was developed to enable the reporter to record material more quickly. Here we have a marriage between hardware (the equipment – pencil and paper) and software (the systemised applications knowledge – Shorthand), which we can recognise in all forms of media production. The reporter works within the **institution** of journalism with its developed techniques for constructing news stories – another example of news technology.

ACTIVITY 18.1
- Can you list the different technologies used in a local radio studio?
- Can you divide them into software and hardware?

Technology: the focus for conflict

The 'methods, means and skill' definition of technology is not always appreciated. This is the result of a mix of factors which tend to obscure the real issues and to promote cruder, more simplistic ideas.

Class undoubtedly plays a role in this – technology and technicians have traditionally had lower status than professionals (even though some professionals, such as architects, are also technologists). The Colleges of Advanced Technology, founded in the 1960s, were quick to rename themselves as 'Universities' when they realised that they were often perceived as inferior. Media representations of technologists offer us white-coated men (and they are usually men) who are either dangerous because of their obsessions or indescribably boring because of their lack of social skills. Media technology is gendered so that in many cases girls will have been put off media production work because of its association with 'boys' toys' and a macho culture of bigger, faster, louder, etc.: some

Scientists In *The Man in the White Suit* (UK 1951), Alec Guinness plays a scientist who invents a cloth that never gets dirty and won't wear out. He is bewildered when laundry workers and textile workers attack him as anti-social. He is saved in this social comedy when the cloth disintegrates after only a few days – but not before his invention has created further social and economic upheavals.

The white lab-coat is the mark of the stereotyped scientist, always on hand to advise the television personality why 'Sudso' washes whiter. This must be the longest surviving stereotype (and advertising script) on UK television.

boys will have suffered from taunts about their excessive interest in
equipment rather than people, 'the trainspotter syndrome' or the 'anorak'.
These gender differences are not all clear-cut. In the film industry, it is
not unusual to find women film editors and there are now a handful of
successful women directors. But you will search long and hard to find a
woman cinematographer (i.e. the person in charge of lighting and
camerawork). There is evidence to suggest that this wasn't always so and
in the early years of cinema, women were very active. Indeed the first
director of a narrative film may well have been a woman, Alice Guy
Blaché, who directed a short feature in 1896. In 1911 she wrote: 'There is
nothing connected with the staging of a motion picture that a woman
cannot do as easily as a man, and there is no reason why she cannot
completely master every technicality of the art' (quoted in Acker 1991).

But these early roles for women were not maintained. Women (the
stereotyped view says) have traditionally 'worked well with people'
(director) or 'at a bench on a production process' (editor) but not in a role
that requires application of both technical knowledge and artistic vision.
The prejudice against women artists and composers has perhaps passed
across to cinema. A more obvious reason is that camera operators have
traditionally needed knowledge of optics and women have suffered from
lack of access to the necessary school physics.

ACTIVITY 18.2
Technical roles for women

Is this criticism of the film industry also applicable to television? Have a look at the
credit lists of a range of TV programmes and films.
- How many women are listed as camera operators/directors of photography?
- Which jobs are most likely to be filled by women?

Another potential difference lies between the 'doers' and the 'thinkers'
in media production and media education. There are many ways in which
these differences manifest themselves. Sometimes it is the commercial
producer versus the creative artist. Sometimes it is the pragmatic
broadcaster versus the academic theorist. Much of the time it boils down
to a difference between those who use the technology on a daily basis and
those who don't.

You will now be getting the picture that technology is a potential
stumbling block in the path of good working relationships. If you know
about technology, you will think it is important and want to consider its

Anorak It is worth considering
what this term of abuse (ironic,
since the word once described an
unusual garment worn by
mountain climbers) says about
general attitudes towards detailed
knowledge of specific
technologies. Is it a recognition
that an obsession about
technology is anti-social and
unhealthy or does it suggest that
those who use it as abuse are
fearful of technology?

Women in Hollywood 'Guy
power dominated the business, as
it still does: to this day it is rare to
have women running studios or
directing films, and unknown – for
here lies the voyeur's magic – to
let them photograph a movie"
(Critic David Thomson on
contemporary Hollywood,
Independent on Sunday, 8 Jan.
1995).

Reel Women by Ally Acker
provides a directory of prominent
women in all sections of the film
industry since the 1890s. There is
plenty of evidence to show that
women were very active in the
early period of cinema. (Even to
the extent of three camerawomen:
in the sound cinema, only one
camerawoman is listed.)

implications. If you don't feel happy with it, you will perhaps try to ignore those implications. This will be a real issue for you when you begin to produce your own media texts. Many media producers and critics would agree that technology in itself is not very interesting, what is important is *what is produced as a media text*. A pamphlet that has changed history, a photograph that will always be remembered, a sound recording that moves a listener to tears may all have been produced on primitive equipment with basic techniques – the lack of sophisticated technology did not stop them communicating. On the other hand, would you choose to ignore the most modern technology if it was available to you (even if it meant tackling something you didn't totally understand)? We won't solve this dilemma, but we should be sensitive to the issue. The best we might hope for is for everyone to agree to select the most appropriate technology for the job, rather than allowing the technology to do the selecting for us.

Technological change

Computer design Early computer graphics showed their origins clearly (suggesting a 'technology-driven' product). The software could not produce 'realistic' colours and textures, but looking 'futuristic' was then fashionable, so the product was acceptable. Now, design philosophies and computer power allow more 'naturalistic' images (i.e. as if painted with an analogue paintbrush).

Technology interests us most when it changes. From the first cave painting to the latest hi-tech feature film, media producers have striven to develop both hardware and software in order to achieve a better product. In media education we want to ask what exactly 'better' means – cheaper/more realistic/more beautiful/more easy to understand/more exciting/more uplifting/more easily available? And who decides the standards against which these are to be judged?

In the 1990s the 'technological imperative' (the general feeling that we are being driven forward by the increasing pace of technological change) is perhaps more evident in relation to the media than in any other area. In past decades, attention centred on the 'Space Race', weapons technology, new cars or medical breakthroughs. Now the biggest industry in the world produces 'information' and more people are employed in it than in any of the traditional industries.

The biggest companies in the media industries are now the manufacturers and distributors of software, rather than the manufacturers of hardware. Companies like **Microsoft**, which makes the world's leading business computer software, and the cable television companies, which are beginning to provide the vast new range of information services, are the rising stars of the media industries. They are at the forefront because they are initiating and exploiting the process of technological change.

Microsoft, founded by Bill Gates, has grown rich by selling the basic PC operating systems, MS-DOS (**M**icrosoft **D**isk **O**perating **S**ystem) and Windows. It has replaced the hardware manufacturer IBM as the world's leading computer company.

In the separate case study, 'Developing widescreen technology' (Chapter 19), we look at a historical example of technological **innovation**, but here we will concentrate on the current period.

Analogue to digital

You won't have failed to notice that **digital** is a key word in all the new technologies. Media producers talk about 'going digital', musicians argue about 'digital sound'. Few stop to think that what we are experiencing is possibly the biggest technological revolution since the introduction of mechanical devices such as the printing press over four centuries ago. In every aspect of media production there has been a shift from analogue to digital; understanding what this shift means will help us to recognise the interrelationship of many of the debates about technology.

> *analogue:* that which is analogous to something else (bearing some correspondence or resemblance) from the Greek *analogia* – according to and *logos* – ratio
>
> *digital:* represented by numbers (digits = fingers)

An analogue device works by recording and storing or displaying information in a suitable form, after first converting measurements from their original form. In this way, what is mediated by the device is an 'analogy' of the real thing in another physical form. The oldest such devices are measuring instruments like the sun dial or the hourglass. The 'chronometer' in all its guises is a good guide to developing technology. The ability to measure time accurately changed the way we live dramatically (timed hours of work was a major feature of the factories built in the Industrial Revolution). Devices developed from reliance on the sun, to mechanical springs of great precision, and finally to the digital accuracy of microchips.

At one time, all media technologies were based on analogue processes. Photography relies on light-sensitive chemicals reacting differentially to the reflected light from a subject captured by the lens. Microphones capture sound by measuring vibrations caused by sound waves and then

Figure 18.1 Analogue and digital watches

converting them, first to electrical impulses and then to magnetic charges which can be stored on tape. In each case, the information stored is a physical representation of the original 'image'.

Digital technology is concerned only with numbers – everything that is captured must be converted to numerical data. The microphone and the camera lens are still used, but a sensing device 'reads' the information and converts it to numerical form. From then on all processing is done by means of computation – the device contains a computer.

The CD Revolution

The first digital media technology to catch the attention of the general public was probably the compact disc. Vinyl records had already started to display the words 'Digital Recording' and now record buyers were being offered a format which promised digital playback and greatly improved sound quality.

A digital recording means that the sound captured by microphones is converted to numerical data and stored on a computer device such as a hard disk or digital tape rather than a conventional audiotape. This recorded information is then mixed and a 'master copy' produced, which is in turn transferred to either an analogue tape or vinyl disc or a consumer digital format such as a **CD** or **DCC** (digital compact cassette) for sale to the public. Gradually the digital formats are taking over for consumer use.

AAD

If you have a CD containing recordings made more than a few years ago, you may find that the disc itself, or the box, is marked AAD (analogue/analogue/digital). This shows that the original recording used analogue instruments and was recorded on to an analogue master tape before being transferred to the digital disc format. If this is the case, you will probably also find an apology about the 'noise' on the disc, which derives from the original analogue recording. If the disc is labelled 'digitally re-mastered' it may well be marked ADD (analogue/digital/digital).

Is CD better?

The manufacturers claim that CDs give a clearer, more 'authentic' sound because nothing is lost or added to the original performance. This claim is worth investigating. If a sound has been produced in a studio, it will have been captured by a microphone and then recorded – in this sense there is no difference between analogue and digital recording. Some musical instruments are digital themselves – a digital keyboard can be programmed to sound like other instruments, because the 'sound' it produces is initially in the form of digital information rather than soundwaves. It comes from the on-board computer's memory rather than, say, a vibrating piano wire, and the digital information can be recorded directly. In this latter case, the recorded data are certainly a replica of what the musician 'played'. Another way to think of this is that you can 'make music' without musical instruments at all – simply by 'playing' the sounds already stored as digital 'samples' in the computer memory. A microphone can, however, only produce a representation of a sound image (just as a camera can only produce a representation of a visual image).

There are some philosophical arguments here – can any natural sound be recorded 'authentically'? Leaving this aside (see Chapter 15, 'Realisms'), the major difference comes during the next two stages of the process. An analogue recording requires a physical transfer of data during the editing and mixing stage and then again during the duplication stage. Every time this physical exchange takes place some data are lost and some extra noise is added. The tape, the recording heads, the cables, the electrical wiring and earthing – all of these can be the source of 'noise' (noise is any unwanted sound). The digital process may use similar media – tape, cables, etc. – but since it is numerical data which are being transferred, the computer can monitor the data exchange, constantly checking that the data 'add up' (computer data have 'check numbers' inserted in the data stream which allow number checking and correction). In this way the digital recording process can guarantee that degradation of data and the presence of noise are kept to an absolute minimum.

This isn't quite the end of the story, however. Digital processes share one feature of analogue processes – the more detail you want in the recorded 'image', the more storage space you need. In analogue terms this means that the area of tape needed to record music is so great that the tape must be passed at high speeds across the recording heads. In digital terms it means that in order to fit all the necessary data on to a suitable disc (or disk), it may be necessary to leave out some of the very high or very low frequencies of a sound recording or to 'compress' the data so that it takes up less space.

Both these actions will alter the original recording and this means that it is still possible that the analogue equipment with the highest specification (and the highest price) can produce a more 'authentic' sound than many digital systems.

Samples are analogue sounds, captured and stored on a computer disk as digital data. They can be manipulated, edited together and turned into new music productions. Use of samples not only provides the means for the 'bedroom recording star' to make music – it also raises interesting questions about the copyright on sounds.

Disc or disk For convenience, we have used the British English spelling 'disc' to refer to conventional vinyl records or music Compact Discs. The American English spelling 'disk' is used to refer to computer disks (floppy, hard, optical, etc.)

Quality

Quality is also a matter of the expertise needed by the user and the technical specifications of equipment. Media technology has for many years been categorised by manufacturers as suitable for 'domestic', 'semi-professional' or 'professional' use. These distinctions are crucial in terms of radio and television with BBC and ITV technical officers decreeing what is suitable for broadcast use. (As more new broadcasters from satellites and 'narrowcasters' on cable begin to consider material for screening, the BBC/ITV regulations will become less important.)

The distinctions are based on a number of factors, the most important being the quality of the audio or video signal that can be recorded and input to an edit suite. In simple terms, the professional technology provides more information from larger **format** media.

The '**domestic**' equipment designed for the home user will often have fixed or automatic controls which limit the possibilities of creating certain types of images (audio or visual). Conversely, the professional equipment, which allows great control over the recording process, also requires considerable skill on the part of the operator. Perhaps the major distinguishing feature, however, is cost – £600 for a **domestic** camcorder, £10,000 or more for a broadcast machine.

Digital technology threatens all these distinctions. The format is no longer relevant because all data are digital, the controls on the equipment are likely to be more flexible, more user-friendly and possibly more 'intelligent' (see next section) and the price differential between domestic and professional is likely to narrow dramatically. Soon an amateur media producer will be able to produce broadcast-quality (in the technical sense at least) material without buying professional equipment. Already there are bedrooms across the country packed with equipment that is more powerful and better specified than similar professional equipment in broadcast studios of ten years earlier. Here is one source of the argument which says that new technology can provide greater **access** to media production and it has been most vigorously championed in relation to music technology with 'bedroom composers' achieving hit records.

But can the professionals 'allow' this gap to be closed? Almost certainly not. The broadcasting industry seeks to maintain its lead in 'quality' sounds and images by developing new delivery systems such as stereo broadcasts and 'high definition' images on widescreen television sets.

Intelligent machines?

If the stored data are digital, they can be accessed and used in many other ways. Digital devices can provide information about what they are doing

Formats Professional analogue formats are usually physically larger to increase definition. The 'large format camera' used by a professional photographer produces a 2.5 inch square negative compared to the 35mm frame of the hobbyist. Digital formats will not have the same requirement of physical recording area.

and can perform automatic operations – in effect they can be programmed to perform, just like any other computer. At the simplest level, a CD player can play the tracks on a disc in any order. At the most complex level, a digital video edit suite can read an edit decision list and put together an entire programme while you go off for a cup of tea (this is called, not very imaginatively, 'auto-conforming'). All of this makes digital technologies potentially more creative in the sense that they can enable new ways of doing things and even possibly suggest new things to do with spin-offs from the extra information they provide. Again, this is most evident with music technology because digital production has been established longer in that field. New forms of video production will doubtless appear over the next few years. (See Stafford (1995) for discussion of **nonlinear editing** and implications for training.)

Nonlinear editing Video and audio material can now be stored on hard disk as digital data and sequenced and manipulated endlessly for viewing before 'printing' to tape or broadcast. Analogue editing was always **linear** – images and sounds would have to be physically 'joined' in a linear sequence to be viewed as such.

Miniaturisation and transmission

Digital storage, via compression, can lead to smaller devices and there is no doubt that consumers prefer CDs to vinyl discs because they are more convenient to handle. Digital processing is handled by microchips which get smaller and more powerful by the day. The process of miniaturisation goes on non-stop. This means new consumer products and especially new portable products will appear. The same advantages also aid the transmission of data which will be generally cheaper, quicker and more

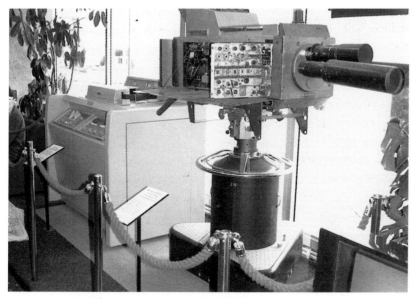

Figure 18.2 Early television equipment was large and bulky. Similar quality is now available from equipment that can be held in one hand

reliable than analogue methods (and can also utilise existing technologies like telephone lines).

Multimedia is the buzzword of the 1990s and **multimedia** texts – texts that combine computer text and graphics, moving images and sounds, and which are controllable by a reader/viewer – have been made possible by digital devices which can use the same hardware to store, manipulate and output sound and images, both still and moving. This is the final stage of the analogue to digital transition. The 'essence' of each separate medium has disappeared and with it many of the institutional aspects of media production in that area.

Sound editing technology now looks the same as video editing or photographic retouching technology: all data appear on a computer screen and are manipulated via mouse and keyboard. To 'write' a multimedia programme, a media producer could simply key in a 'script' and all the component parts of the programme can be activated through this set of instructions.

> 'just as cut-and-splice methods in sound recording suggested an intriguing link with film in the sixties, the exact equivalence of digital "composing" programmes like Cubase and video editing programmes like AVID placed the two disciplines within morphologically similar techno-grids. In both cases the praxis is the same – bunch of folks in an airless city room staring at a screen.'
>
> (Sinker 1995)

Photography is considered to be no longer a useful term by many critics and has been replaced by 'Electronic Imaging or Digital Imaging'. Traditional photography is a medium of photochemistry. In the new 'Digital Darkroom', images from different sources (video, computer, chemical photography) will be combined.

Culture and technology

We have already noted that attitudes towards technology vary enormously. Some of us are 'anti' (technophobes), others are 'pro' (technophiles). Let us look at some of the critiques of technological change which have come from outside the media industries.

Pam Linn, an educationist writing in the mid-1980s, points to several disturbing aspects of the introduction of personal computers and computerised household goods. One is what she terms 'technological immanence' – the way in which technology pervades our lives and changes the way we do things, without our really noticing it. Writers who have changed all their habits to become computer-users are often terrified at the prospect of losing all their work when a hard drive crashes. Technological change has brought 'liberation' and new creative opportunities, but also anxiety and insecurity.

A second issue which she raises is that of 'user-friendliness' and effective 'deskilling'.

- Modern machines have several automatic functions and 'default settings', which allow anyone to use them without having to learn how to operate them fully or to understand how they work.
- Modern computer displays are designed to be 'user-friendly' by presenting the user with a screen which effectively mimics the environment it has replaced. A desktop publishing programme mimics the designer's desk and the software is designed to be 'intuitive' so that the user can move objects about the screen without having to understand what the computer is doing. This feature, especially on Apple Macintosh computers, has been a major factor in the success of the new technologies but Linn argues that it is based on a 'deficiency model' of the user's competence: 'In practice "user friendliness" makes a program easier to use at the cost of understanding how the program actually achieves its effects. Ease of use is related to powerlessness, rather than to control' (Linn 1985).

The issue here is 'skill transfer'. If you learn to use one software package, can you transfer your skill to another package on another machine? And do you know what to do if the computer does not perform as you expect? You cannot transfer your skills if you do not 'own' them and skill ownership is another important issue. Linn might argue that the skills are 'owned' by the software.

Emulation Modern electronics allows most equipment to conform to industry 'standards' through emulation of the dominant system in any specific field of operation. Computers in particular may have different architecture and use different software, but they can be made to 'mimic' each other.

ACTIVITY 18.3
Skill ownership

Think about the media technology you use on your course.
- How much do you know about how it works?
- Can you distinguish between decisions you make about how to use the equipment (altering sound levels, changing camera lens settings) and settings given to you automatically?
- How much do you need to know before you can feel in control of the technology you use?
- Try to think of one production you worked on. Could you describe how you could have achieved a similar result using different technology?

You may have already come to this conclusion if you have learned how to use one computer in lower school and now find that the computers in sixth form or college do not use the same software. Or perhaps you have a machine at home, but find that other computers won't read your disks? The computer manufacturers and software writers could make your life easier, but often it suits them to frustrate you into buying their product and then sticking with it. Your ability to transfer skills is a potential loss to them because you could easily transfer your allegiance. These questions of skill ownership and operator's 'control' over the technology are important in all areas of media production.

We have chosen below two examples which emphasise the wide impact of the 'move to digital' in terms of both 'production' and 'distribution/consumption'. We are conscious that these studies may date quite quickly, but we hope you will be able to grasp the main points and apply them to new developments as they happen.

Example 1: Digital imaging

Coming home from your holiday you take your film of 'snaps' to a shop on the high street. Next day you collect your images, now stored on CD, and rush home to look at them on your television set, using your computer or disk-player. Later, you load the CD into your home computer and edit the best image, cropping it to your satisfaction and perhaps correcting an over-exposure by darkening the image. Then you print it out and send it to your grandparents (or possibly you send it by E-Mail to your best friend).

Photo CD is a new standard for storing photographic images on CD, developed by Kodak. During processing, several versions of each image on a roll of film will be digitised and transferred to disk. CDs can hold up to 100 photographs in different resolutions for use in DTP etc.

A few years ago this would have sounded like a science fiction scenario, but the technology exists (and it is quite easy to use, if set up properly) and when the price drops many of us may take up the opportunity. This is 'electronic imaging' and it is effectively replacing chemical photofinishing. We will continue to use conventional cameras to take photographs (still video cameras cannot yet offer the same high definition, although they are already good enough for news photographs), but from there on the image will be handled as a digital format and the potential for manipulation will be enormous. What are the implications and how should media education take account of this technological innovation?

'Photographic truth': the camera doesn't lie?

The processing and manipulation of news and magazine photographs is already carried out using the new technology. The traditional method was to produce a photographic print which would go to the picture editor. This skilled person would consider how the image should be cropped or retouched. The photograph would then be sent back to the laboratory for processing and reprinting. It would then be 'screened' – rephotographed through a fine mesh screen to produce a pattern of dots. (The printer cannot reproduce the continuous grey or colour tones of the chemical photograph, instead images are made up of many tiny dots of different sizes. The bigger the dots, the closer they are together and the darker the shade. Look at Figure 18.3 and conduct your own test by looking closely at the images in your newspaper.) The resulting screened image was produced at the correct size and pasted on to the page next to the typeset print. The page was then sent to the printer.

This was a complicated process, involving several different processes and several different specialist personnel. In the 'new technology' process, the image arrives on the picture editor's computer screen, already scanned (similar to screening). The editor can crop the image in a matter of seconds, position it on the page and send the page to the printer with hardly a second thought. If all the computers in the building are linked together, digital information can be transmitted to all sections very quickly. The obvious benefit of the system is that pages can be compiled so quickly (and changed again) that they can be held back very close to print deadlines. Soon, it is likely that news reporters will take video pictures 'on the spot' and send the information down the telephone lines straight into the computer. In the Gulf War, we saw a forerunner of this when several newspapers digitised images straight from CNN News, the all-pervasive American cable TV channel, in order to add impact to their up-to-date coverage.

The facility to change the meaning of images with a keystroke or mouse movement strikes a severe blow against the status of photographs as 'evidence'. Of course, it has always been possible to 'doctor' a photograph, but the procedure was quite difficult and the results less than satisfactory. The new technology is easier to use and produces much better results. Even so, it isn't this aspect that is so worrying – rather the challenge to the notion of photography as the 'recorder of reality' and the acceptance of 'image manipulation'. The image that appears on the newspaper page need not have had any origin in reality, even if it gives the appearance of reality. The subject in one image can be 'lifted' and placed in another image, with a new background – one they may never have

Manipulation In July 1995, Russian President Boris Yeltsin returned to public duty after treatment for heart disease. A photograph was released as proof of his recovery. Much discussion followed, in which some observers claimed that they remembered the photograph from an earlier period – only the shirt he was wearing had been changed.

Figure 18.3 Digital images can be 'redrawn' with great accuracy. 'Disappearing' someone from a photograph is straightforward

195

visited. Perhaps we have finally reached the dreadful world of Orwell's *1984* – or perhaps we have been freed from the tyranny of 'real images'?

Certainly, some traditional photographers feel threatened by these developments. Photography is interesting because it is split between a 'commercial' field where photographs serve very specific purposes and an 'artistic' field where photographs are mounted for exhibition in galleries or for sale in large format, expensive books.

Commercial photographers are likely to be ambivalent about digital imaging.

- The new technology will make it possible to produce 'better', i.e. more technically accurate, images.
- On the other hand, the existence of digital images stored on CD and available as 'clip art' means that some of the work of the commercial photographer may disappear altogether. If a client needs a photograph of a product, say a bottle or can, with a new label, why go to the trouble of setting up a studio to create a new image if you can select a bottle clip from a CD and add a label designed on the computer?

The creative or art photographer may have a rather different response – one in which the techniques of digital image manipulation may be seen as too 'industrial', too impersonal. Despite traditional photography's status as a realist or representational medium, some photographers feel themselves to be akin to fine artists in that they can manipulate physical, tangible aspects of the photograph, especially in the printing process. This tactile sense is not there with digital images – something of the romance of creation has gone.

Similar comments are made by some musicians in relation to digital sound – it is too clean, too bright, lacking depth, texture or tone. This isn't true of all photographers or 'artists', of course. David Hockney is a good example of a fine artist who has enthusiastically embraced digital photography and developed new art forms. In the early 1990s, Hockney exhibited large-scale portraits using digital techniques in his home town of Bradford and then 'faxed' a new large-scale image from Los Angeles to the Bradford gallery, sheet by sheet, with a telephone message about how to compile it.

Deskilling

A less obvious consequence of technological innovation is the prospect of 'deskilling' media workers. We have already noted that the new technology means that one or two 'generalists' can now manage the work of several specialists. The traditional crafts of typesetting and picture retouching required highly skilled staff with years of training. These have now been replaced by computer software. With the two 'industry standard' software packages, **Quark Express** and **Adobe Photoshop**, any reasonably computer-literate person can learn the basics of how to lay out a page and how to manipulate an image after only a few days' tuition – the software has effectively given us a concentrated version of all the skills and knowledge which the craft operatives have learned over many years.

But does this make us 'typesetters'? Are we really capable of 'desktop publishing'? Well, sort of. What we don't know is what makes a good page layout, why some typefaces are not appropriate for particular uses – in short, we are not trained designers. The 'best' software will try to do this for us as well, suggesting standard layouts. Unfortunately, most software has very bland standard settings which means that there are now hundreds of badly designed leaflets and posters, immediately recognisable as 'dtp' publications. The same is beginning to happen with images, thousands of which are already available on disk (and even more on CD-ROMs). This use of clip art means that many people without developed drawing skills are able to produce illustrated work (as we have done with a drawing in this chapter). We could see this as increased access to opportunities for a wider range of people to engage in production, but it is also a means of reducing staffing levels and not paying for skill. Introduction of new technology inevitably leads to redundancy and redeployment – investment in capital equipment displaces labour.

The introduction of new technology has led to the disappearance of traditional roles. The clearest example of this was the wholesale war, waged by first Eddie Shah and then Rupert Murdoch, on the Fleet Street print unions. As newspapers moved away from 'hot metal' (blocks of type moulded in molten metal were 'set' on trays for printing and afterwards melted down and re-used), the print unions managed to maintain staffing levels even when the range of job tasks was reduced. Murdoch broke them by computerising the whole process. At the same time, journalists found themselves increasingly responsible for the initial preparation of their copy.

In some local newspapers, the picture editor has gone and the news editor now selects the images. In broadcasting, the television news crew began as a film unit comprising a camera crew of two, a sound operator and a reporter – now with **ENG** there are just two in total and sometimes the reporters might find themselves on their own. What were once 'graded posts', fought for by craft unions, are being replaced by 'multi-skilling'. The ultimate situation is complete automation.

Quark Express This is the software used by nearly all magazine publishers for sophisticated page layout. The only serious rival is **Pagemaker**, which is thought superior for longer texts such as books. Image manipulation is dominated by **Photoshop**. Although the Macintosh is the usual computer for publishing, all three programs are available on the IBM-PC as well.

ENG **E**lectronic **N**ews **G**athering, in which video replaced film, was the first indication of the potential impact of new technologies on broadcast employment patterns. The broadcast companies eventually managed to reduce staffing on news crews after fierce resistance from the union.

VJs or 'Video Jockeys' are the satellite or cable equivalent of the linking presenter on music radio. The term is also now used to describe the roving news reporter/camera/presenter on Channel 1, the local news cable channel in London.

TV-AM, which held the franchise for Breakfast Television on Channel 3 during the 1980s, used to operate a series of remote studios in various provincial cities. These studios had make-up rooms, reception areas for guests and a single set with a lighting rig and a camera controlled from London. *One* full-time employee operated the studio.

'Things don't take less time. Instead you get people doing things in more detail, more accurately and better than they did before. These days most stations are pretty slim, and on air you're using the same number of people' (Paul Fairburn, Programme Controller of Heartland FM interviewed in *Broadcast*, 21 April 1995).

In America some radio stations are completely automatic, broadcasting from banks of tapes with prerecorded continuity announcements and not a DJ in sight. In the better radio stations the computer has not replaced staff, but has instead enabled them to work more quickly and therefore to spend more time 'getting it right'. Technology itself is not a threat to labour – it is always a case of how management attempts to use it.

We can summarise the issues at stake:

- As production processes are computerised, there is an inevitable reduction in the need for specialist skills and a similar increase in the need for generic computer skills. The computer software 'absorbs' the accumulated specialist skills.

- This change in the nature of operating skills can lead to greater access to production (necessary skills and knowledge are learned quickly via the software) for non-specialists.

- The 'deskilling' of traditional roles leads to redundancies of specialist skilled operatives and employees generally have less bargaining power (with less chance of withdrawing 'skilled' labour).

- The status of computer data as evidence is unclear. Many media processes are becoming '**virtual**' rather than '**real**'. Images may give the appearance of realist representation, but not refer to any event which took place in front of a camera.

Virtual and Real. See Chapter 15, 'Realisms', for discussions of 'real'. 'Virtual' is widely used to describe representations on the computer desktop. VR or Virtual Reality describes the tactile experience which can be achieved by immersing oneself in the computer-created environment – typically achieved by wearing a visor and moving a touch-sensitive device.

Example 2: The 'Superhighway'

At the moment, it is almost impossible to avoid references to the Superhighway and the Internet. Everyone seems to be writing about this new means of distributing and accessing information. If we are to believe all the figures, millions of people worldwide are using some form of computer technology to communicate and to gain access to a whole range of media products. In practice, some groups of people have easy access and others very little.

There are a number of different technologies coming together to form the Superhighway. The analogy of the highway (or in UK terms the motorway) is interesting in that it suggests the 'progress' of the new fast road *and* the threat of the destruction of local communities. The communications highway, in physical terms, comprises **broadband fibre optic** cables. These are gradually replacing the old-style telephone cables and their carrying power is so much greater that they will also be able to carry multiple television channels plus radio and other digital signals. In the home there will be a **set-top box** – a computer which will sit on top of the television set and act as an interface with the array of incoming digital material. In the UK, proposals for digital television services were announced in August 1995.

Some analysts relate the **Internet** and the **World Wide Web** to the Superhighway concept. The Internet is a 'network of networks' – based originally on university computer networks – which enables users to send and receive messages and to upload and download computer files to and from electronic addresses anywhere in the world. The World Wide Web is a development of this idea, comprising rather more commercially orientated 'sites' which offer a multimedia experience with graphics, audio and full motion video.

The speed of traffic on the Net is dependent on the number and the carrying capacity of existing telecommunication services. If you want to access the World Wide Web site of the Disney corporation or you want news from the Keanu Reeves fan club, the likelihood is that at certain times of the day you will have difficulty getting a telephone connection in the UK and then you may have to wait while your message is routed around the world. The reality of a system where accessing a computer in California is as easy as phoning your mum a few miles away is still several years in the future (although we should be very careful about making any firm predictions about the pace of technological change).

With analogue products, there are physical problems to overcome in distribution of media products and serious costs to consider. A feature film for the cinema still comes on ten or more reels of film, each in a large metal canister. Newspapers are bulky and litter the house, shelves groan under the weight of reference books. A film on a VHS videocassette is much more portable and on a 5 inch CD even more so. A floppy disk can carry several newspapers in 'text only' form and a CD-ROM can hold hundreds. But these media are just the 'in-between' phase. Digital data can be compressed in order to take up less and less space. Whole films will one day be represented by relatively small amounts of data. Not only will these be easily stored, but with the new transmission and distribution technologies they will all be available via your set-top box. A further development will be 'interactivity' – allowing the viewer to communicate directly with the service provider and request specific programming. Trials of such schemes are already underway. Video On Demand (**VOD**) is one aspect of this, whereby viewers can select what

Broadband refers to bandwidth – the number of channels of data which can be carried by a cable. Traditional cables are made of copper wire. **Fibre optics** refers to glass fibre filaments down which flashes of light can travel at immense speed. Fibre optics can carry multiple channels – multiplex cables.

ISDN or Integrated Services Digital Network connection allows audio and video data to be transmitted at high speed (and high quality), along with traditional 'voice' messages. It is used by printing and recording companies for data exchange. A singer in New York can add a voice track to music playing in Los Angeles.

Digital compression Digital picture and sound files are descriptions stored as numbers. In a film it isn't necessary to describe every frame to be stored, only the difference between each succeeding frame. The international standard for this process is agreed by **MPEG** (Moving Pictures Experts Group).

VOD The current trials are very small scale. Even with compression, storage problems mean that only a relatively small range of programmes is available at any one time (i.e. perhaps 200 – less than what is available at a video rental outlet).

they want to watch from a library of material. The programme is retrieved from the library by the computer and sent down the cable to that specific viewer. In a small community, hundreds of viewers could each be watching a different programme at the same time.

Interactivity could mean direct 'shopping' via television, something already available on Internet, with the set-top box allowing the user to purchase goods and services after seeing them demonstrated. But perhaps most interesting from the Media Studies point of view is the possibility of alternative narratives.

Vidéoway – Interactive Television

Vidéoway has been introduced over five years and is now available to 250,000 households in Quebec and Western Canada as well as a smaller number in London. Frenette and Caron (1995) suggest it has been successful (unlike some other interactive video experiments) because it more closely 'meshes with people's television culture'.

It involves the simultaneous broadcast of different versions of the same programme on four separate channels. The viewer then moves between the four channels using a remote and screen prompts which show the four options. There are also four different ways in which the programme can be varied: content preference, story involvement, knowledge-base and visual composition. The first of these allows the viewer to select what kind of material they would like to see next in the programme (i.e. a film clip or a music performance in a magazine programme) and the second allows control over certain narrative features (what characters wear, locations, character actions). The third asks questions of the viewer (children watching a story might be asked to solve a problem to help a character) – in quiz shows a viewer could compete with on-screen contestants and have the score recorded on screen. Finally, the viewer could alter camera angles by choosing one of the three alternatives.

Interactive TV (or TV-i) is very much like some of the CD-ROM titles which have appeared recently. These offer stories with alternative narratives and sets of questions, different views etc. CD-i is the Philips system which sits somewhere between the standard CD-ROM and interactive video disc and can be displayed on a standard television set. These interactive techniques were first devised for computer games of the 'adventure' type and for training simulations. The difference with TV-i is that it is 'live' in the sense that the viewer is not in complete control of when to play and, the research suggests, it does feel as if you are watching a broadcast channel and not playing a computer game.

ACTIVITY 18.4

All these interactive products (CD-ROM, TV-i, etc.) tend to be marketed in the first instance to children or young people and also to business training providers.

● Why do you think is?

You should be able to think of several different reasons.

A summary of the points raised by this example:

● The distribution and exhibition of media products is being speeded up and expanded (with more products available) by new digital transmission systems.

● Media producers can gain access to materials for production more easily.

● Computer users at work and at home have the potential to access media products more easily.

● There is great potential for 'interactive' consumer media products.

Issues at stake

The pace of change is so rapid that it is difficult to carry out a thorough analysis before the scenario changes yet again. As a consequence, academic research tends to have a lower profile in commentaries on the Superhighway etc. than newspaper and magazine journalism and we need to be wary of some of the wilder arguments being made. Here, we offer you some initial thoughts on a range of questions, which you will need to extend as the arguments unfold.

What kinds of media products?

What will the media providers with access to the new transmission systems use to fill all those hundreds of television channels? Not often original material, that would be far too expensive. Instead they will largely recycle old material (almost inevitably US television, the cheapest form of mass entertainment available). The libraries of old feature films and filmed television series have become very valuable properties, as demonstrated by the frenetic bidding between two major American cable companies to take over the last 'independent' Hollywood studio, Paramount.

If the cable companies do not fill every hour with recycled Hollywood, they will want very cheap programming, produced locally, perhaps even at a community level. The new digital technology will help them here with broadcastable programmes made for very little (you might find

Murdoch and MCI Media industry analysts became very excited when Rupert Murdoch's News Corporation – a software supplier through 20th Century Fox – signed an agreement with the telecommunications service provider MCI in 1995.

yourself producing such programmes, perhaps as part of an education or training course or as a community production). The cable companies will not have the same attitude towards their audiences as the traditional broadcasters. They are regulated, albeit with a 'light touch', and may be required to fulfil certain basic requirements of programming, but generally these are companies whose main aim is to sell services such as telecommunications, rather than to bother about **public service broadcasting**' (see Chapter 24, 'Institutions').

Censorship and regulated content

In the UK, despite protestations to the contrary, we are used to a relatively high level of censorship, or at least regulatory control in our media. (See Chapter 24.) We won't question the rights and wrongs of censorship here, instead we will consider the practical points. Theatrical exhibition of films is easy to censor because cinemas, as public buildings with safety considerations, have to be licensed by local authorities. Cinema managers who go beyond the accepted norms face closure of their screens. UK broadcasters are regulated and accountable through public bodies – if necessary, sanctions can be imposed and franchises withdrawn. Newspapers are published by organisations which are traceable and can be prosecuted.

By contrast, providers of media products on the Superhighway may not be based in the UK at all and the means of providing the service may be a telephone line which anonymously links users to the Internet. Monitoring thousands of these links will be very difficult, at least using current methods. It is possible to develop technological 'defences' of course. The 'freedom' of the Internet has already been curtailed to a certain extent by the creation of so-called 'software nannies' – programs which look for selected strings of characters in a file name (like s-e-x) and effectively lock those files away from certain users. Some cynics have suggested that this will only lead to more efficient young computer hackers who, in many cases, will know more about the computers they use than will their parents who attempt to install and maintain the software.

Perhaps more significant is the decision by certain Internet Service providers (the companies that provide the telephone services and the administration of the systems) to become censors themselves in refusing to carry certain kinds of material on electronic bulletin boards. Access any '**news group**' and you may well come across fierce debates on this issue. These serve as a useful reminder of similar earlier debates. There is a danger in assuming, hoping even, that new technology by its very nature will force changes in society simply because it is 'new'. Technological innovation can have dramatic effects in all kinds of ways, but usually

News groups are like electronic discussion groups. Anyone can suggest a new group and there is a wide variety of topics. Media attention has centred on those discussing sex. This is not unreasonable – according to *Internet* magazine in August 1995, by far the most popular Web Sites on the Internet are 'Adult' orientated.

these changes come about because of prior changes in the general economic, social or political environment.

In the News Corporation case study (Chapter 25), we discuss the enormous impact of new technologies in producing newspapers. The changes in technology did not make printers redundant – Rupert Murdoch did that at Wapping as part of a cost-cutting exercise and as a means of 'clearing the ground' for new work practices. Those printers could have been retrained and they could have been employed producing dozens of different newspaper titles using the new technologies in smaller computerised printing operations. This was not feasible in the marketplace – it may or may not have been welcomed by readers. The self-censoring Internet providers are not much different from the self-censoring studios in Hollywood who adopted the **Hays Code** to protect themselves against charges of corrupting the audience. We could suggest a tentative rule about the development of a new medium:

> As a new medium broadens its appeal beyond the adventurous few looking for new excitements, it is more and more likely that providers of products on the new medium will begin to censor their own products.

Hays Code Production Code named after Will Hays, President of the Hollywood Producers Trade Association. Effective from 1933, it controlled screen sex and violence (e.g. a man in bed with a woman had to keep one foot on the floor). Its power waned with the end of the studio system.

The other aspect of control will be the means to make greater profits from denying free access to Internet services. (See Chapter 20, 'Industries', for developments.)

Rights and royalties

A digital product is easily and accurately copied, indeed the copy is indistinguishable from the original. In practical terms it is difficult to stop piracy. Technology can, however, be used to protect itself, with built-in codes which will corrupt the file if unauthorised copying is attempted. There are also associated legal problems – how do you prove that your version is the original? It is now possible to register your rights as the originator of new software. Computers are also very good at logging digital files as they are used – have you ever thought about how anyone calculates the royalties due to a musician whose recording is played on radio stations and in shops or bars?

ACTIVITY 18.5
Think about the new technologies in photography and music recording and the rights of the originators of a photograph and a music track. They may become available to a wide range of publishers and radio and television producers.

- How would you ensure that the originator was paid an appropriate fee?
- What do you think are the practical advantages and disadvantages for the photographer and musician in this new digital environment? Will they be better off?

The revolution in media technologies is profound and it will throw up new issues which have not yet been documented. You will need to be on the look-out for news stories. Try to use this chapter to develop a starting point for your analysis.

References and further reading

There are very few books that address new media technologies in an accessible form for students; many that do soon become out of date. Articles in newspapers (i.e. the broadsheet dailies and Sundays) and magazines (both 'hobbyist' and professional) are sometimes more useful, but beware of exaggerated claims about the possibilities of change. The following have some historical material and some background on the issues.

Acker, Ally (1991) *Reel Women,* London: Batsford.

'Digital Dialogues' (1991) Special Issue of *Ten 8,* vol. 2, no. 2.

Frenette, Micheline and Caron, André H. (1995) 'Children and Interactive Television: Research and Design Issues', *Convergence,* vol. 1, no. 1.

Hayward, Philip (ed.) (1991) *Culture, Technology and Creativity,* London: John Libbey.

Neale, Steve (1985) *Cinema and Technology: Image, Sound, Colour,* London: BFI/Macmillan.

Linn, Pam (1985) 'Microcomputers in Education: Dead and Living Labour', in T. Solomonides and L. Levidow (eds) *Compulsive Technology: Computers as Culture,* London: Free Association Books.

Sinker, Mark (1995) 'Music as Film', in Jonathan Romney and Adrian Wootton (eds) *Celluloid Jukebox,* London: BFI.

Stafford, Roy (1995) *Nonlinear Editing and Visual Literacy,* London: BFI.

Williams, Raymond (1974) *Television: Technology and Cultural Form,* London: Fontana.

Wollen, Tana and Hayward, Philip (eds) (1993) *Future Visions: New Technologies of the Screen,* London: BFI.

19 / Case study: Developing widescreen technology

The cinema is one hundred years old yet the basic technology of film and projector have remained virtually unchanged. Films today have colour and sound but we can still show the films of the 1890s on the modern equipment. Why have some media technologies developed and others remained unchanged? The history of the shape and size of the cinema screen provides us with a perfect case study into the interaction of technological **innovation** and commercial exploitation.

Early cinema

The original shape of the cinema screen was a squarish rectangle, similar to the standard television screen of today with an **aspect ratio** (the width of the screen compared to its height) of 4:3 (or 1.33:1). To a certain extent this shape resulted from the dimensions of the filmstock used both to capture the images and then to project them on to the screen. Early stock was 35mm wide and derived from the first flexible film produced by Eastman Kodak in 1889. It was produced in rolls 70mm wide and W.K.L. Dickson, the assistant to the early cinema pioneer Thomas Edison, simply cut it in half lengthways. The establishment of a standard was thus partly a matter of *economics* – i.e. to save money. It was also partly an issue of **aesthetics**, of *realism*, in that the 35mm size produced an image of sufficient clarity and sharpness to be acceptable as a 'likeness' of an actual event for a viewer, given the chemical properties of the filmstock – i.e. a smaller film negative would have given too poor an image.

This gives some explanation for the film size, but not the shape of the image. The Kodak still cameras of the period produced circular images and the 'magic lantern' slides, which were a more obvious forerunner of cinema, had no standard size. The largest image that could be projected (or shown in the Kinetoscope, the peepshow device with an eye-piece for the individual viewer on which Edison's early films appeared) would be square. But both the circular and square images were unsatisfactory. They were adequate for portraits, but wasteful of space (i.e. the unused part of the image meant extra film cost with no return in terms of exploitable image) and hopeless for action scenes or landscapes.

ACTIVITY 19.1
You can try this for yourself – use a square mask over a video camera viewfinder and try to compose a simple scene. Try a 'portrait', a landscape wide shot and a two-shot of an interview.
● What do you think of the resulting compositions?

A rectangle was the accepted shape for both portraits and landscapes in nineteenth-century painting and this *aesthetic* consideration was influential. A portrait could be contained within a landscape but not vice versa, so the latter was the most likely model.

The engineering problems of running strips of film through the early cameras meant that the roll of film needed to be placed above the camera and pulled through vertically, using sprocket holes on either side. This left a negative strip about one inch wide and since

Figure 19.1 The 'bioscope' from the 1890s showing the film being pulled down through the projector gate

Dickson was working with units of a quarter inch in designing the camera aperture, a height of either a half-inch or three-quarters of an inch was possible. The former created too small an area to give clarity, so one inch by three-quarters of an inch became the standard negative size, a ratio of 4:3. This *engineering* decision, coupled with the economic and aesthetic factors, helped to establish a standard, but it was the *entrepreneurial* energy of the Edison Company which made it a world standard. It was quickly accepted by Edison's chief competitors in Europe and Edison's move to patent both cameras and filmstock (with George Eastman of Kodak) eventually fought off new competitors in America. Before the First World War, the cinema industry worldwide had accepted a format which is still the standard and a screen size which lasted over sixty years from Dickson's first experiments up to the 1950s.

Edison's success in establishing a standard helped to make cinema an international industry with films circulating widely and was thus arguably 'in the public interest'. But the screen shape of 4:3 was the result of a particular set of factors, as we have demonstrated, and

not a 'natural' occurrence. With the shift from the peepshow to the projected image in the early cinema, several attempts were made in the 1890s to develop different systems, using wider filmstock. That they failed was more to do with the commercial muscle of Edison and the other major players in the market such as the French Lumière Company rather than any intrinsic faults with the new systems. Just as with the rise of the VHS videocassette in the 1980s, which succeeded because the video rental shops supported the format, 35mm films were the only ones that could circulate freely around the film exchanges (the forerunner of today's distribution companies) controlled by Edison and the other **majors**.

VHS and Betamax

The success of the videocassette in the 1980s is an excellent example of a new product succeeding more through **marketing** and availability than proven technological merit. There were three competing **formats**; from Philips, Sony and Matsushita (JVC/Panasonic), all incompatible with one another. The new technology was 'product driven' in that customers wanted to use a VCR to play tapes of feature films which could be rented from a local store. The store operators could not afford to hold three different versions of the same film in stock, so they had to decide on one main format. How would they choose?

The UK was the first market to achieve 'high penetration' of VCRs and this was clearly linked to the then prevailing custom of renting television equipment as distinct from purchasing what was initially expensive hardware. The TV rental companies linked themselves with the manufacturers and it soon became apparent that most rental companies were going with VHS from Matsushita (the major UK VCR manufacturer produced clones of JVC machines). Consequently, most customers in video rental shops asked for VHS tapes and the other two formats were quickly frozen out.

The UK experience then influenced the markets in other countries, where Sony, despite its reputation for high-quality equipment, could not compete with the larger marketing power of Matsushita. In the meantime, the video professionals and home enthusiasts were claiming that the Sony format, Betamax, gave the best picture and had several other distinct advantages. These cries were to no avail – VHS had won and Sony used the experience for what later became the new format for broadcast newsgathering – Betacam. Sony also began to make VHS products. And Philips? Their format found little favour and despite their previous success in setting the standard for the audio 'compact cassette', they had to accept the growing power of Japanese electronics technology.

New technologies in the 1920s

In the 1920s, the novelty of cinema wore off and film projection moved out of the small halls into large new 'picture palaces'. New middle-class patrons were willing to spend more but also wanted more in terms of entertainment. Film producers looked for ways of drawing the audience into 'participation' in the events on the screen – the drive for greater realism in terms of 'just like being there'. One aspect of this was the introduction of sound – another was widescreen.

Involvement with the action on the screen is partly a matter of 'field of vision' – what you can see, not only in front, but also on the periphery of vision, at the sides, on top and bottom. The 4:3 ratio is rather like a painting or a window which you look through. If you could extend the screen so much that you could see the action without being aware of the edges of the screen, then the viewing experience would change dramatically – or so the film producers thought.

An early attempt to do this was *Napoleon*, a film made by Abel Gance and screened in Paris in 1927 using three screens with three interlocking projectors for the battle scenes and reverting to the single central screen during the rest of the film. Similar ideas were tried in America and in 1929 both Fox and Paramount introduced a wider filmstock which allowed a better quality and much wider projected image, but the aptly named Grandeur (Fox) and Magnavision (Paramount) were shortlived experiments. As the Great Depression deepened in America, even the Hollywood studios (also then owners of cinema chains) ran out of money for investment in new equipment in both studio and cinema and the new formats were dropped. However, it was during this period that the French inventor Henri Chrétien patented the device which was to produce CinemaScope twenty-five years later.

At this point in the story it is worth recapping and considering the problems facing the cinema technologist who wanted to improve the screen image in terms of both clarity and size. The quality of the image which we see on the cinema screen depends on a number of different 'technologies':

- *The camera* used to shoot the original footage. The more efficient in terms of utilising light and the more accurately ground the lens on the camera, the clearer and more sharply defined the potential negative image will be.
- *The filmstock* on which the images are recorded. The bigger the area of the film **negative**, the more detail will be recorded. When this is processed as a **positive print**, the size of the image which is magnified and thrown on to the screen is also important – again the bigger the film image, the more detail (less grain) is projected on the screen.
- *The quality of the lens* in the projector – this affects both the brightness and the clarity of the projected image.
- *The brightness of the projector lamp* which must illuminate a screen a hundred feet away or more.
- *The screen* itself. Good quality cinema screens are designed to reflect light from the projector efficiently to produce a brighter, sharper projected image.

With each of these technologies requiring separate funding for research and development and probably replacement, it is not surprising that the Hollywood studios were reluctant to pursue widescreen in the 1930s and 1940s. Any change which was to have a major influence (i.e. beyond the novelty value of a handful of cinemas in major cities) would mean re-equipping thousands of cinemas across North America. For this reason alone, 35mm remained the format and 4:3 the aspect ratio (now with a slightly smaller negative image to accommodate an optical soundtrack) until the early 1950s. You may come across references to this screen shape as **Academy**.

Developments in the technology of filmstock, lenses and lighting were continuous throughout the 1930s and 1940s, without producing a fundamental change to the whole system. The major companies doing the research all had close connections with Hollywood – a factor in preserving Hollywood's leadership of the world industry. Handled carefully, technical research can be a means of 'keeping ahead of the field'. By 1953, however, the Hollywood studios were in a desperate position – audiences at cinemas were dwindling rapidly and something was needed to bring them back. The context for all this is shown in the film *The Last Picture Show* (US 1971), which uses the 1950s closure of the cinema in a small Texas town as the focal point for a melodrama of social change.

In retrospect, it was obvious that the moves towards widescreen in the 1920s had been prompted by competition between the studios – not by any real commercial imperative based on 'consumer demand'. Between 1929 and 1945 cinema audiences increased consistently during the 'Golden Age of the Studio System', despite the lack of any obvious technological innovations. They seemed happy with black and white films on Academy screens (colour also took thirty years to become a standard feature of cinema films). There was no other form of entertainment to draw them away from the cinema.

Post-war pressures

After the war there were new distractions. Americans spent money on cars and houses, and social life changed. Staying at home became more attractive (with the bonus of free television viewing), and for the new 'teenagers', driving out of town was preferable to attending the run-down local cinema (the cinema owners recognised this quite early on and built 'drive-in' cinemas to replace some of the city centre closures).

Apart from a brief flirtation with 3D, the studios' main strategy was to switch production to 'big' pictures to be shown in colour and on a big screen with improved sound (i.e. as unlike television as possible). The first attempt to do this was **Cinerama**, an idea which had been first thought of in the 1930s and had then been developed as a simulator for aircrew gunnery training (in the 1950s and 1960s technological change was often a result of military research). Cinerama used three projectors and a giant curved screen to engulf the audience and seven-track stereo sound to pin them to their seats. The effective aspect ratio was 3:1.

The first Cinerama film in 1952 was an astounding success with critics and audiences alike, but it had little impact on the industry as a whole. The technology was so expensive to install and operate (requiring a major redesign of the cinema), that 50 per cent of the takings for any screening were eaten up in running costs alone. Cinerama was a special format for only a handful of converted cinemas in a few major cities. All the early Cinerama features were travelogues or documentary spectaculars, the first features didn't appear until the 1960s at the end of the format's brief history – and by the end there were only ninety-five Cinerama cinemas worldwide.

CinemaScope

What was needed was something that could be swiftly and inexpensively installed in cinemas across North America. 20th Century Fox came up with CinemaScope. Fox had purchased the rights to Henri Chrétien's 1927 invention, the **anamorphic lens**. This distorting lens 'squeezed' an image as it was captured, allowing a 'wide' image to be recorded on standard 35mm film. A reverse anamorphic lens on the projector then 'unsqueezed' the image and threw it on to a wide screen with a ratio of 2.66:1. The commercial potential of this set-up was obvious. Any

Figure 19.2 This sketch of how the first CinemaScope picture, *The Robe* (US 1953), would appear was used extensively in 20th Century Fox's promotion of the new format

cinema could re-equip with a set of projector lenses and a new screen – an affordable investment.

VistaVision

Paramount hit on a different approach. Instead of running film through the camera vertically, they switched to a horizontal feed (like a still camera). This meant that the negative area was increased greatly and allowed a much wider rectangle. When the image was rotated and printed on to standard 35mm positive stock. it allowed projection of a much sharper, brighter image, although one not much wider than Academy at around 1.66 or 1.85:1. The battle was on for industry domination: which would succeed?

There were many problems with CinemaScope:
- The squeezed image needed a stronger projection lamp to give a sharp definition on screen.
- The CinemaScope camera also needed more lights on set and consequently suffered from shallow depth of focus.
- The lenses were difficult to focus.

By contrast, VistaVision gave a much improved 'big-screen' image (Paramount avoided the 'widescreen' tag) with astounding clarity and good depth of focus. Both formats used colour and both had improved sound. Fox initially offered four-track magnetic stereo; Paramount were less ambitious with a 'mock stereo' effect.

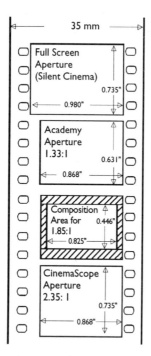

Figure 19.3 The various screen shapes and sizes

If picture quality was what the industry and the public wanted, VistaVision should have triumphed, but, in a forerunner of the VHS versus Betamax battle of the 1980s, the 'less good' system won. Why? Primarily because Fox acted with sound commercial acumen at

Figure 19.4 The same image shown (above) at 2.35 to 1 as CinemaScope and (below) anamorphically squeezed to fit a 1.33 to 1 frame for projection

every stage of the battle. Crucially, they sold CinemaScope as a package to theatre owners at a competitive price with lenses and a screen and a guarantee that all Fox product would be in 'Scope. They also managed to persuade all the other studios (apart from Paramount) to commit to 'Scope for at least part of their production. Assured that there would be product and excited by the response to the first 'Scope release, *The Robe* (US 1953), the cinemas converted – so much so that by the 1960s there were 41,000 'Scope screens worldwide (compare with Cinerama, p. 208). Once again, the distribution/exhibition factor proved most important.

Paramount continued with VistaVision and never accepted 'Scope. In the mid-1960s 'Scope was succeeded by Panavision – a flexible system which has now become the industry standard and can be used to produce aspect ratios of anything from 1.66:1 (the current standard cinema screen ratio) to 2.35:1. This allowed Paramount to come back into the fold (Panavision was at that point an independent company). VistaVision cameras were now obsolete, but they weren't completely finished – a few years later they were to be found in special effects departments providing quality images for sequences in *Star Wars* and the other science fiction films of the 1970s and 1980s.

In the later 1950s, other widescreen processes, using wider filmstock, were introduced but these were all reserved for special 'big' pictures which only played a few theatres in their original form, before being reduced to 35mm for wider distribution. Today you can see 70mm versions of major films at certain big city cinemas or travel to Bradford to see the biggest format of all, IMAX, which uses a horizontal 70mm format.

Widescreen and film criticism

What of the aesthetic impact of widescreen? Did it in fact create the opportunity for greater realism? The influential French critic and theorist of the period André Bazin was in favour on the grounds that the wider screen could encompass several characters doing different things, and that it would lead to longer takes with fewer close-ups –

all, he argued, indicators of a more realist form of representation (see Chapter 15, 'Realisms').

The early fears that deep-focus and rapid-cutting would not work in widescreen were soon proved to be unfounded. The technologists and the cinematographers worked hard to improve picture quality in CinemaScope and within a few years they had managed to reproduce on the widescreen virtually all the visual codings they had managed on the Academy screen. Some directors liked 'Scope and learned to use its opportunities, others despised it.

> The great German director Fritz Lang remarked tetchily that 'Scope was good only for 'snakes and funerals'.

Nevertheless, the high period of 'Scope and the other wide formats, between 1955 and 1975, was the period of many stylish directors such as Nicholas Ray, Akira Kurosawa, Jean-Luc Godard and Sergio Leone, all of whom embraced the widescreen aesthetic.

By the mid-1970s, television was starting to become the major exhibition site for films, and widescreen was becoming increasingly irrelevant. In the 1990s, only a handful of films are released in ratios beyond what is the now the standard 'widescreen' format of 1.85:1 and modern audiences would be quite surprised by the enormous width of the original CinemaScope image.

The future for widescreen

During the 1970s and 1980s, when modern films were made in widescreen, directors were under considerable pressure to ensure that all the action took place in the central part of the screen, so that when it was shown on television, the audience would not notice the missing detail. In order to broadcast widescreen prints (or to put them on videotape), the television and video companies have two options. First, they can **pan and scan**. This is a computer-assisted process which selects a 4:3 ratio 'window' on each scene from the widescreen original. An operator views the film and makes the selections,

panning across the print. A computer remembers all the instructions and transmits the new 'scanned' print.

Alternatively, the whole widescreen image can be broadcast with the top and bottom of the screen left blank – presenting to the viewer the so-called **letterbox** image. This latter technique was previously decried by many broadcasters who claimed that viewers would feel cheated if the image did not fill the screen. In recent years, BBC2 and Channel 4 have both begun to 'letterbox' for their 'minority' audiences and it has become fairly standard practice for programmes like *Film Night* or *Moving Pictures* to use a thin black bar at the top and bottom of the screen to signify that a cinematic image is being shown. The practice is also spreading to advertisements and it is noticeable that European television stations do not have the same fear of letterboxing as that shown by BBC1 and ITV.

If you want to use a video of any film for visual analysis (or indeed any form of film study), you should try to see it in a version as close to the original screening ratio as possible. This is particularly important for films in the high period of 'Scope from 1954–75. In the later 1970s, the television image became so important that even when they were shooting for a film with a 1:1.66 screen ratio, film camera operators were often required to use a mask over the viewfinder which restricted the action to a 4:3 ratio frame.

The kudos of widescreen

One of the reasons for the revival of interest in widescreen in the 1990s is clearly cultural. The advertisements and music videos which 'wear the bars' and the students who produce video narratives in a letterbox form are all attempting to distinguish their images from those of 'television' by associating themselves with 'cinema'. Cinema is fashionable again.

Widescreen television

The major reason why widescreen is returning as a subject of interest is economic – the electronics industry's need to sell widescreen television sets. In the beginning, sets were black and white, then along came colour, then remote controls, teletext, NICAM stereo and now widescreen. Each technological innovation provides a marketing platform from which the consumer can be inveigled into replacing an existing set. Nobody will buy a widescreen set unless there is product available to view. The sets are expensive, so product will be aimed initially at the wealthy minority who watch BBC2 or who can be persuaded to buy videocassettes (or laserdiscs) of widescreen films. (A note of warning here – a film advertised on videocassette as 'widescreen' may still not be as wide as its original cinema release. Widescreen television sets have a ratio of 16:9 or 1:1.77, which is still some way short of the 1:2.35 of CinemaScope.)

The development of widescreen television has been held back by two separate 'failures' of technological innovation. Widescreen was very much linked to High Definition Television (HDTV) – the upgrading of the television picture to twice the current resolution – but the Japanese, American and European manufacturers and broadcasters have failed to come to an agreement and development is languishing. The UK market for widescreen also suffered from the collapse of the satellite broadcaster BSB which promised a superior signal (i.e. one capable of carrying a higher definition image) to that offered by Rupert Murdoch's Sky Channels broadcasting from the Astra satellite.

In summer 1994, Channel 4 and BBC2 began broadcasts of a new widescreen format called PalPlus, which gives true widescreen to owners of the new widescreen television sets, but is also viewable as a letterboxed image by other viewers. A year later it seems that the widescreen moment might have passed again – developments are now appearing in digital television. Interest is shifting to films on CD (at this early stage a relatively low-resolution medium) and to interactive television. There will be widescreen television, but programming sold to viewers simply on the basis that it is 'widescreen' is not very likely. But for a brief moment in the 1950s, it was possible to advertise 'CinemaScope!' above the title and before the stars of a movie and watch the crowds roll in.

Conclusion

- The 'best' technology (i.e. in terms of technical specifications) is not always the one that wins in the marketplace. Economic, political, social and cultural factors are all important and may outweigh technical considerations.
- The timescale for the introduction of new technology can be very short or very long. Acceptance of the new technology is neither automatic nor inevitable.
- The motivation for technical innovation is commercial – the profit motive. Widescreen was introduced because profits from cinemas were falling and largely abandoned when the studios discovered television screenings were more profitable. It may yet return with widescreen television, if its reappearance has a sound commercial basis.
- Despite the pleasure it gave to audiences and the aesthetic arguments in its favour, widescreen didn't change the cinematic experience significantly (i.e. it didn't change the way films are understood or the kinds of films being made). But it is a good illustration of the lengths to which the studios would go to 'differentiate their product'.

This case study provides good evidence for application of a conceptual tool developed by the American cinema historian **Douglas Gomery**. He referred to an economic model that can be used to describe technological change in media industries generally, using the terms 'invention, innovation and diffusion'. Typically, invention takes place in a laboratory, probably in a specialist company, usually with a link to the media industries. Innovation then comes when a media producer adapts the invention to a specific use in one aspect of production or exhibition. The crucial stage is diffusion. Innovation must be successful enough to generate real or potential profits big enough to attract the attention of other producers (usually industry majors) who will make big investments and establish new industry standards. In all three phases, finance and the lure of profits will be important, but at the point of diffusion they become absolutely important. In the widescreen example, the invention and innovation were present in the 1920s, but the potential for commercial exploitation was not fully realised until 1953.

References and further reading

Belton, John (1992) *Widescreen Cinema,* Cambridge, Mass.: Harvard University Press.

Bordwell, David, Staiger, Janet and Thompson, Kirstin (1985) *The Classical Hollywood Cinema,* London: Routledge.

Gomery, Douglas (1976) 'The Coming of the Talkies: Invention, Innovation, and Diffusion' in Tino Balio (ed.) *The American Film Industry,* Madison, Wis.: University of Wisconsin Press.

Maltby, Richard and Craven, I. (1995) *Hollywood Cinema,* Oxford: Blackwell (especially Chapter 4, 'Technology').

Velvet Light Trap, 'American Widescreen', no. 21, summer 1985.

20 Industries

The common view of 'the media' equates their activities with glamour and excitement, creativity and controversy. In practice, media production is an *industrial process* just like many others and in this chapter we explore the activities in the media industries, using the tools of economic analysis and concentrating on the major media corporations and their business practices. In Chapter 27, 'Independents and alternatives', we explore the organisation of media production outside the **mainstream**.

Media production and the manufacturing process

Media production is like many other manufacturing processes – the production of tinned baked beans for instance. Let's take a particular form of media production, a daily newspaper, and compare it with baked beans production. Surprisingly, perhaps, there are several common features:

- initial investment in plant and machinery – fixed assets
- continuous demand for the product, necessitating continuous production and a constant supply of raw materials
- distribution of the product to all parts of the market
- market research to ensure up-to-date information about performance of the product and the satisfaction of customers
- advertising of the product to keep it in the public eye and to attract new buyers.

These common features are important – media industries usually make decisions based on standard business principles. Even so, media industries are different from most other forms of manufacture in a number of ways and it is these differences (or 'specificities') which we want to explore in more detail. Let's stay with the production of print-based news:

- the 'raw material' is not homogeneous – skill and cultural, aesthetic and political judgement are necessary in selection of events that will be marketed as 'news'
- the price of news varies – some is free, some might be very expensive to purchase or access

- the product is not always a necessity and demand could fall dramatically if consumers' tastes change
- production and distribution patterns are not fixed – the product can be transmitted electronically and reproduced locally
- staff costs will generally be greater than in other forms of manufacture because a greater variety of skills is required in the process
- this particular product has a shelf-life of only one day (really, only half a day)
- revenue from sale of the product is only part of the business – a large proportion comes from the sale of advertising space. Advertisers therefore have influence on the fortunes of the product.

These points suggest that managing a media production process is a particularly complex (and risky) business. The two most important considerations for the newspaper producer are the collection and processing of suitable news material and the distribution of the finished product.

The actual production (i.e. page make-up and printing) of the newspaper is perhaps not as crucial as you might think in determining the success of the product. Certainly, the quality of the feature material and the 'look' of the paper will contribute greatly to its long-term reputation, but they won't necessarily boost the circulation dramatically like a sensational story, nor immediately impress the advertisers; furthermore if poor distribution means that the product doesn't get to the customer in time, all the production effort will be wasted. (See Chapter 25, 'News corporation' and Chapter 10, 'Local advertising and newspapers'.)

Long-life media: a different process?

In film or music production, there is a rather different production process, or at least a different emphasis from that of the daily newspaper, or even the daily or weekly television programme. Purchase of these products has to be a more calculated decision. In the case of a visit to the cinema or to a concert, the product is not 'consumed' completely – we may return to experience the same product again at a later date or we may purchase an associated product on tape or CD. With a shelf-life longer than the single day of the newspaper, there is the possibility of building an audience over several weeks and developing a number of associated products.

It is even possible that as a collector's item, the product will increase in value over time. Since the product is also reproducible from a 'master copy', it can be 'relaunched' in the future at minimum cost and attract a new set of buyers. Walt Disney was the first to recognise this phenomenon and in doing so saved his studio. He saw that animated films did not date as quickly as live action features and that since a large part of his audience was made up of young children, he could rerelease classic films such as *Snow White and the Seven Dwarfs* (US 1937) and *Pinocchio* (US 1939) every seven years. This strategy has been altered by the advent of video, but it is still relevant and has been applied to other classic films. A recyclable product is also a recyclable brand-name and the modern Disney company has benefited further from merchandising spin-offs. Like Warner, Disney has recognised the value of its brand names and has opened retail outlets to maximise profits.

The distributors of CDs also recognised that there was an enormous potential market in the rerelease of popular music albums on the new format in the 1980s. Here we are dealing with something very different from other products (although certain design elements of products like cars and furniture can be recycled – the so-called 'retro' look).

To explore these unique features of the film and record business, we need to look more closely at the production process.

> Although newspapers have a brief life as consumer products, they have always had a long-term value as **archive** material. In the past, this tended to be limited by the demands of storage space to one or two titles in major libraries. Now major newspapers are available on CD-ROM and with the advent of global computer networks, almost any material will be available to the researcher (with an automatic debit from a credit card account, of course). What does your library hold on CD-ROM?

The production process: feature films

Every media production process has its specificities. We only have the space to study one in detail – that of the modern Hollywood feature film.

Setting up the project

The idea for a new film could come from many sources, but in the relatively 'conservative' atmosphere of Hollywood it will probably require some evidence of previous success to interest the financial backers (i.e. the major studios). Sources might be:

- a sequel to a recent box office hit
- a remake of a European box office hit (e.g. *Three Men and a Cradle* (France 1985) remade as *Three Men and a Baby* (US 1987))
- an adaptation of a best-selling book (e.g. *The Firm* (US 1993) from the

---

merchandising The marketing of a wide range of consumer goods bearing images from a specific media product has a very long history, but the sheer scale of current merchandising dates from the release of *Star Wars* in 1976.

Retro design is popular in Japan where sports cars have been produced with a 1950s 'look'. Kits of classic cars are sold in the UK. Some critics would see this as part of 'postmodern style' (see Chapter 17).

The 'Hollywood Majors' Studios capable of **distributing** twenty big-budget films every year, in North America and internationally. Half the current list (Warners, Paramount, Universal, Columbia, Disney) have survived seventy years of Hollywood history. Newcomers tend to last a few years before disappearing.

John Grisham novel)
- an original story by a proven scriptwriter
- an original idea from a successful director/star team
- a new twist on a story from a currently popular genre cycle.

The movie business displays a basic contradiction in that a conservative financial sector can take enormous risks in terms of production budget, when the chances of success are actually quite small. (The combined total of *expenditure* on new films by Hollywood studios is often not much less than the total box-office *receipts* in the same period.)

The Player The world of 'the Hollywood deal' is brilliantly satirised in Robert Altman's film (US 1992). One of the best explanations of 'the deal' is in Pirie (1981).

ACTIVITY 20.1

The Pitch

What ideas have you got for a new film – one that would definitely interest a Hollywood studio?

- Look at the list above and develop your idea along the suggested lines. Try to limit your outline to a single page.
- Think carefully about whom you would cast and, most important, try to sum up the idea in a single line.
- Test out your outline on a friend. How well does it stand up?

Each of the major Hollywood studios will finance a **slate** of seven or eight big films every year at a budget of around $30 million or more each, aiming for a smash hit during the two critical periods in North America of early summer and Christmas. With an outlay of over $200 million on the slate, at least one of these must be a big hit (grossing $100 million or more) for the studio to cover its costs. If it is very lucky and has a record-breaking blockbuster (e.g. *Jurassic Park* with over $300 million in 1993), then profits can be substantial. However, many films flop completely (losing $40 or $50 million on a single picture is not unknown – Schwarzenegger in *Last Action Hero* achieved a reputed loss of $120 million in 1993). The most dramatic example of this was the failure of the epic western, *Heaven's Gate* in 1980. So much was lost that the studio, **United Artists**, collapsed completely and is now little more than a name.

Financial pressure has some strange consequences. Investors become nervous about 'low-budget' pictures and often the budget will be artificially forced up towards the average (a form of 'institutional constraint'?) and star names added at large fees, even when the story might not require them. This also means that what might be a 'big budget' production in Europe (say $10 million) is automatically seen as a

United Artists The sorry tale of the decline of United Artists is told in the book *Final Cut* by Steven Bach (1985).

Casting Hollywood has bought several British properties and cast major stars in unlikely roles. Fay Weldon's novel *The Lives and Loves of a She-Devil* became a successful TV 'mini-series' in the UK, but Hollywood adapted it as the film *She-Devil* in 1989, ignoring the British casting and substituting the unlikely pairing of Meryl Streep and Roseanne Barr. It died quickly.

Video and the majors See Gomery (1992) on the growth of the video rental and sell-through in the US and the attitudes of the studios towards it. Jack Valenti of the MPAA once denounced the VCR, claiming it would kill movie-going. By 1986 revenue from video rental and sell-through exceeded the cinema box office, which was itself buoyant. The majors rapidly moved in to control the video market themselves.

Roger Corman began making 'Z' pictures (the cheapest possible exploitation fare) as a producer/director in the 1950s. In the 1960s he made critically acclaimed and commercially successful Edgar Allan Poe adaptations starring Vincent Price for AIP (American International Pictures).

New World Pictures Set up by Roger Corman in 1974 to make exploitation films which would often cheekily steal the audience from the majors' sequels (*Piranha* followed *Jaws* in 1978). Corman's influence on Hollywood is immense and he gave a first start to Francis Ford Coppola, Martin Scorsese and Jonathan Demme as well as many other current front-line directors. Corman is still producing in the 1990s.

'Read the script, rewrite as much as you want, but remember, Marty, that you must have some nudity every fifteen pages ... just to keep the audience interest up.'

(Corman, quoted in Thompson and Christie 1989)

'small foreign film' in Hollywood – another way of keeping out new entrants to the business.

The studios and a handful of independent producers do mostly stay in business. How do they manage it? One important factor is the **pre-sale** of screening rights. Distribution of films is covered later, but here we can note that it is possible to sell rights before the film is completed, so that there will be a guaranteed, if slender, profit. Obviously, if you pre-sell the rights and the film is a box-office smash, you stand to lose a great deal of potential profits. A good example of these kinds of films are those financed by (i.e. 'sold to') 'pay-for-view' channels such as Home Box Office (HBO). Literary adaptations with star names are often solid but unspectacular earners.

The major studios (like Murdoch with 20th Century Fox) can defray the cost of their slate by cross-subsidy from their own television productions, spin-offs to television, merchandising and video sales. **Video** has been a major boost to the studios. Far from damaging revenues as first feared, video has proved to be a lifeline with many films taking more on video release than on theatrical (cinema) release.

There are some small independent producers who succeed because they are very disciplined in their methods and, knowing the business well, they can spot narrow markets in which cheap films can always cover costs if production schedules are kept strictly under control. **Roger Corman**, for example, was famous in the 1960s for making two films back-to-back using the same sets. He stands out as a producer/director whose films always meet their low-budget targets and which manage to be both mildly progressive in social and political terms while offering titillation to drive-in audiences. Corman is an exception, however, and most of the smaller independents survive only a few years before being forced out of business or into some form of dependency on or negotiation with the majors. (See Chapter 27, 'Independents and alternatives'.)

Given these financial considerations, it is not surprising that the setting-up period can be lengthy and scripts might pass through the hands of many producers before they are 'greenlighted'. The gestation period for some films might be ten years or more. During this time a good deal of development money might have been spent by producers on an **option** on the rights to the idea (known as the **property**) without a foot of film ever having been shot. What the owner of the property fears most is it being put into **turn-around** – a limbo-land for script ideas which languish with one studio until another producer comes along who is prepared to pick up the option (i.e. to pay enough to cover the development money paid out by the first studio). It's a wonder films get made at all.

Pre-production

Once the go-ahead has been given, the production company has a great deal
to do before shooting begins. Parts must be cast (the lead players were
probably decided as part of the original deal), locations chosen, costumes
researched, dialogue coaches and wranglers (animal handlers) hired, hotel
rooms booked, etc. All this might take several months, during which time
the script may be reworked and the direction of the project altered. A
starting date will be announced and reported in the trade press (*Hollywood
Reporter, Variety,* etc.) and eventually the cameras will roll (although it is not
unknown for the plug to be pulled on the whole enterprise at this stage).

Production

This stage is often called **principal photography** and it is likely to be
the shortest period of all. Modern films usually **wrap** in around forty
days of shooting – an average of three minutes a day. The low-budget
producer will aim to halve that time by clever use of **set-ups** and tight
scripting. Efficient directors are those who can come in 'on' or even
'under' budget. Keeping a whole crew on location a day longer than the
planned schedule can add considerably to the overall cost, and directors
and crews who can stick to schedules will be rehired.

Special effects which require shooting with actors can be a major
problem and mean some productions coming back to studio lots or
specialist facilities (including those in Britain), where others will go to
locations offering cheaper labour or good deals on **permissions** (using
famous buildings or locations), taxation, etc. In recent years, many
Hollywood films have been shot in the south-eastern United States
(Florida, Georgia, Alabama) or Canada. There are obvious questions here
about 'creativity' and 'industrial efficiency'. (see Chapter 22, 'Case study:
Producing in the studio system'.)

Post-production

The longest stage in the process may well be post-production. Here the
film is edited – some might say this is where the film narrative is actually
created. The relationship between the director and the editor (or 'cutter')
may be relatively distant, or it may be very close (as in the case of Martin
Scorsese and Thelma Schoonmaker, who will work together for many
months to complete a picture).

The increase in importance in film sound during the last ten years has
added to the work in post-production with more time spent on tidying

up dialogue through 'looping' (actors record their lines again while watching themselves on a loop of film, played through until they can lip-synch perfectly for **ADR** (the Additional Dialogue Recording)), and adding sound effects using the **Foley Editor**. Special visual effects will also be added at this stage. The completed film will then go to the laboratories for **colour grading** and other adjustments required to produce suitable screening prints.

Distribution

Every part of the process is important. The success of a film can depend at least as much on how it is handled by the distributor as on the film itself. Distributors promote and market films in particular **territories** and negotiate **release patterns** with exhibitors. The distribution of most big-budget Hollywood films is directly controlled by the majors themselves. In North America each major studio distributes its own pictures. In the UK some of the majors have formed joint distribution companies (e.g. Paramount and Universal are joint owners of UIP, while Columbia/Tri-Star operates as one distributor). In the other important cinema markets around the world they may have an agreement with a local distributor, but as the international market grows they are increasingly opening their own offices in every territory. In 1993, five distributors, representing the seven 'major studios' took 82 per cent of the UK Box Office. In the US and Canada their share was 83 per cent for 1994.

The distribution process begins early. Announcing a project in the trade press is the beginning of a promotional campaign designed to build a 'profile' for the film, first with other potential distributors in different territories or on other formats and later with exhibitors.

Each major film is a separate **marketing** project and the advertising and promotional budget for a single film may now equal the production budget (i.e. $30 million is spent promoting a major film). This terrifying investment places even more burden on the producer to 'get it right' and the consequence is the tradition of Hollywood previews, where selected audiences get to comment on a film before it is released (and before the most expensive part of the advertising campaign gets under way). Depending on audience reactions, producers will change endings, cut sequences, etc., or even decide to shelve the film and not release it at all.

At the preview stage, the producers will have at least some idea of whether or not they have a hit. The next major dilemma is how many prints to make? This is becoming increasingly important as a consequence of the large advertising spend. If a great deal of money is being spent on television advertising and promotional **tie-ins** on review

Foley Foley developed the technology that enables any required sound effect to be produced in post-production and substituted in the final mix for the 'live sounds' recorded on location. Film credits show 'Foley artists' and 'Foley mixers'.

Internet In 1995, Hollywood discovered the Internet. The majors have begun to develop their own **World Wide Web** sites giving previews and information on new releases. If you have Net access this is a good way to get advance news on films you may wish to study.

Shelved films Video has saved many films from total extinction, but it is still an admission of marketing fear when a film with a major star goes 'straight to video'. In 1995, *Blue Sky* (starring Jessica Lange and made in 1991) got a limited release in the US and Lange won the Best Actress Oscar.

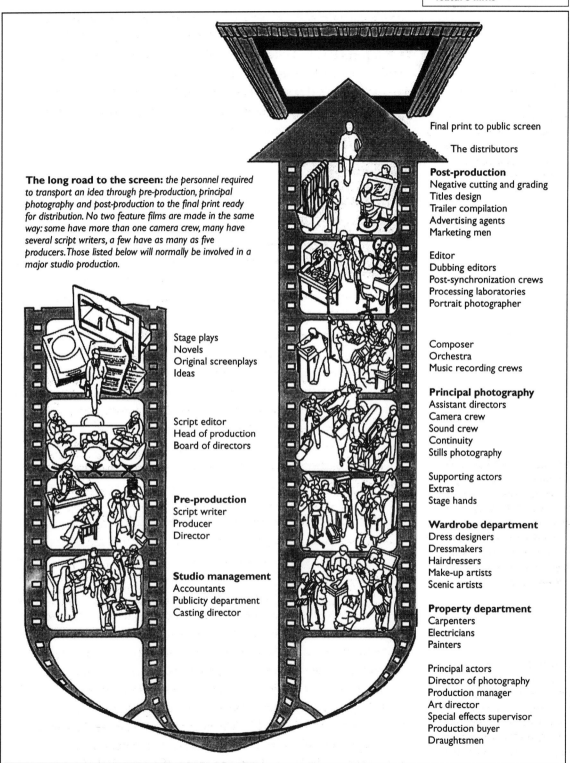

The long road to the screen: *the personnel required to transport an idea through pre-production, principal photography and post-production to the final print ready for distribution. No two feature films are made in the same way: some have more than one camera crew, many have several script writers, a few have as many as five producers. Those listed below will normally be involved in a major studio production.*

Stage plays
Novels
Original screenplays
Ideas

Script editor
Head of production
Board of directors

Pre-production
Script writer
Producer
Director

Studio management
Accountants
Publicity department
Casting director

Final print to public screen

The distributors

Post-production
Negative cutting and grading
Titles design
Trailer compilation
Advertising agents
Marketing men

Editor
Dubbing editors
Post-synchronization crews
Processing laboratories
Portrait photographer

Composer
Orchestra
Music recording crews

Principal photography
Assistant directors
Camera crew
Sound crew
Continuity
Stills photography

Supporting actors
Extras
Stage hands

Wardrobe department
Dress designers
Dressmakers
Hairdressers
Make-up artists
Scenic artists

Property department
Carpenters
Electricians
Painters

Principal actors
Director of photography
Production manager
Art director
Special effects supervisor
Production buyer
Draughtsmen

Figure 20.1 The long road to the screen, from *Anatomy of the Movies* (Pirie 1981)

programmes etc., spreading the message to every part of the country, there is little point urging everyone to go and see the new film if it is only showing in Los Angeles and New York or in London or Paris. What is needed is a print for screening in every major town. In America that means over 2,000 prints (in the UK, 350) and each one costs around $1500 to $2000 to duplicate (70mm prints for the biggest city-centre screens cost more). To gain the benefit from a big advertising campaign, a distributor needs to spend another $2–3 million on prints. Everything then depends on the opening weekend.

Media interest in the US in big new films is intense and to be pronounced a 'hit' a film needs to pull in a screen average of around $3,000 and a three-day total of over $5 million to be certain of rave reviews. A poor opening is very hard to shake off and without the news of 'good box office', advertising will not really take off.

Blitzing every screen in the country is not the only way of course. For an 'art film' or one with a clearly defined audience, a distributor can select a handful of screens, aim advertising locally, and then build on **word-of-mouth** and advertising and promotion in specialist magazines. As an example, on the New Year weekend of 1993/4, the blockbuster was Fox's *Mrs Doubtfire*, which after six weeks was still able to top the box-office takings with $16.3 million over the three days from 2,325 screens with an average of $7,031 per screen. However, Universal released *In the Name of the Father* on just three screens where it took $109,805 or a staggering $27,451 per screen. This was a triumph for Universal and helped propel the film to major success for what was effectively a 'foreign film'.

Film Education Sponsored by the UK film industry, Film Education publishes material for schools on new films, including information on marketing. Your teacher should be able to get on the mailing list.

Table 20.1 Examples of opening returns in the North American market (US$)

Date	Title	Distributor	Screens	3 Day Total	Screen Average
May 1994	*The Crow*	Miramax	1,573	11,774,332	7,485
May 1994	*Crooklyn*	Universal	1,033	4,209,475	4,075
October 1994	*Pulp Fiction*	Miramax	1,338	9,311,882	6,960
October 1994	*The Scout*	20th Century Fox	1,585	1,458,837	920
October 1994	*Jason's Lyric*	Gramercy	804	5,122,600	6,371
July 1995	*Waterworld*	Universal	2,268	21,171,780	9,335
July 1995	*The Net*	Columbia	1,906	10,037,745	5,266
July 1995	*Operation Dumbo Drop*	Buena Vista	2,145	6,392,155	2,980

Source: *Screen International* and *Moving Pictures*

Exhibition

In the US, the major studios were barred from ownership of significant cinema chains (following the **anti-trust legislation** at the end of the 1940s which signalled the decline of the studio system), until very recently. Overseas there were no such restrictions and in the last few years Warner Brothers and UCI (owned by Paramount and Universal) have built multiplexes in many cinema markets, including the UK where other American chains like Showcase are also receptive to Hollywood films.

Ownership or control of every stage of production is known as **vertical integration** and it has obvious advantages for the majors in ensuring that they will have a cinema available to take a film when it is ready for release. This isn't always the case for independent distributors, who are trying to find outlets for their films. Coupled with the cost of advertising and prints, this lack of access to cinemas is one of the main ways in which new entrants to the film business are kept out. In 1994 the five major exhibitors in the UK (MGM, Rank, Showcase, UCI and Warner) had 60 per cent of all cinema screens and sold 74 per cent of the tickets.

The lack of cinema screens on which to release new films became a problem in the UK in the mid-1980s and was a factor in the building boom within British exhibition. The producers and distributors of art films responded to the majors by copying them and becoming integrated distributors themselves (e.g. Artificial Eye and Curzon with three screens each in London available for openings).

The distribution pattern of films and the exhibition practices in the UK have changed significantly since the American exhibitors moved in; they now bear a closer resemblance to what happens elsewhere in Europe and North America. Attendance habits have changed as a result. There are fewer cinemas (older cinemas have continued to close as multiplexes open) and virtually none in suburbs or small towns. Even in larger towns there might be only a single cinema. People will travel further to the cinema; as well as the longstanding MGM and Rank chains, most of us now have a multiplex run by Warners, UCI or Showcase with ten or more screens within half an hour's drive.

Film data Many daily newspapers now carry the Top Ten films in the UK and the US each week. The monthly film magazine *Empire* gives slightly more information, but for the most detailed analysis you must turn to the weekly trade paper *Screen International*. The Annual Handbook produced by the BFI is an excellent source of information on production and distribution of all films in the UK.

ACTIVITY 20.2

How well served is your local area for cinemas? See if you can get a map of your local area. It should include the largest centre of population and a 20-mile radius around it (to account for driving time to the centre?). This is the target area for the multiplex. A ten-screen multiplex needs something like 1 million admissions each year to be profitable. On average the UK population goes to the cinema just over twice per year, so a population of nearly half a million is needed to support a multiplex.

- You will need to calculate the population in your area and then plot the location of the cinemas.
- Do you have a multiplex? Does the population warrant one? Does the exercise suggest you have too few or too many cinemas in the area?

Either way, you might have some interesting material to discuss with cinema managers or local planning officials.

UK cinema audience The class base of the audience has been a factor in the changing nature of film exhibition in the UK since the earliest days. The location of the multiplexes favours cinemagoers with transport and the extra spending power to pay higher admission prices. Research released by CAVIAR (Cinema and Video Industry Audience Research) in 1991 and 1992 clearly shows that even though more people were recognised as belonging to C2DE socio-economic groupings, the cinema audience was skewed in favour of ABC1s (56% of audience in 1992). (See also Chapter 9, 'Advertising, marketing and fashion'.)

The multiplex building programme means that the number of screens has risen to over 1,800 – still only about half the number of screens operating in the 1950s. However, the regular cinema attendance is only 10 per cent of what it was then, so there are more screens per person than ever before – surely that must mean more choice? Unfortunately not. The end of the old Rank/MGM **duopoly** has not meant greater flexibility, in fact the opposite to some extent.

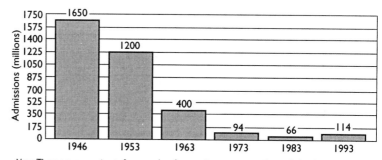

Note: These are approximate figures, taken from various sources and rounded – they should only be taken as indicative of trends

Figure 20.2(a) Annual admissions to UK cinemas, 1946–93

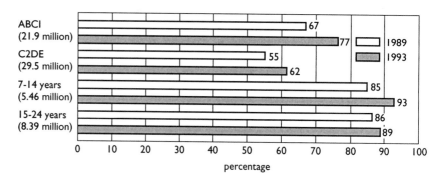

Chart showing the rise in the percentage of the population (aged 7 and over) who 'ever go to the cinema'. The upper part shows the difference between social classes. The lower part shows the two age-groups which are most frequent attenders.

Figure 20.2(b) Trends in UK cinema-going

Films now stay on the same screen, sometimes for several weeks and where there are two multiplexes in the same city (e.g. Derby or Preston), they often show the same films on most of their dozen or so screens. The effect of all this is to increase still further the domination of Hollywood product on British screens and to make it virtually impossible to place an independent film on the screen. Even if an independent does make it, without the massive advertising and promotion spend available to the majors, it is unlikely that a sufficiently large audience will be attracted to justify the venture.

Exhibition duopoly The dominance of UK exhibition by two chains, Odeon and ABC (later Cannon, then MGM and now Virgin), from the 1940s until the 1980s has been criticised as a major factor in the decline of the industry, especially when 'barring' practices stopped independent cinemas getting big films if they might threaten a 'big two' cinema nearby.

Film production services

The film production process depends on access to a wide range of specialist services and it is the provision of these which is another factor in preserving the dominance of Hollywood in the industry. Technology for filming (cameras, lenses, lighting, mounts, etc.) and for post-production (editing and film-processing) is a specialised industry which requires high levels of investment and close co-operation between film-makers and technologists. The major studios have sought to maintain these relationships – even to the extent of buying into the companies involved.

Other services such as financial, legal and promotional are perhaps more mobile and more flexible, but their concentration in Los Angeles remains an important factor in maintaining the 'Hollywood community'.

Film equipment American companies dominate equipment supply, although French and German companies have also been important. UK-produced equipment often copied American designs.

The film production process as a model

Because 'Film Studies' came before 'Media Studies' and because 'film-making' was one of the first media practical activities in schools and colleges, the production process outlined above has been widely applied in media education. We can find equivalents for five production stages in every media industry. (Distribution and exhibition have been merged for general use):

1 negotiating/setting up production
2 pre-production
3 production
4 post-production
5 distribution/exhibition.

ACTIVITY 20.3

To test out your understanding of this five-stage model, jot down some notes on what would happen in each stage of the production process for

● a new magazine for dance enthusiasts

- the first recordings by a new band.

You might have difficulty in deciding into which stage to put a particular activity – don't worry about this. Using the model is not necessarily about getting 'right answers', but more about helping you to study and understand the process. This exercise should help you both produce your own products and study other production processes.

Organisation of production

Once we have been able to develop a model to describe the production process, what kinds of issues do we wish to explore? Here are some of the questions an 'industry study' has traditionally explored:

Structure

How does the production process relate to the ownership and control of different companies or organisations in the industry? How significant is the structure in determining how media products are produced and what kinds of products appear? Two important questions centre on integration and regulation.

Integration refers to the growth of organisations by means of acquisition of other organisations in the same industry. Vertical integration refers to an organisation established in one part of the production chain, gaining control of the other parts of the production process, e.g. the Hollywood studios. A fully integrated media organisation would control every aspect of the production process. In the past, this has meant newspapers being produced by companies who owned the trees from which the paper was made.

Horizontal integration refers to media organisations acquiring control of their competitors within that segment of the production process (it is theoretically possible for an organisation to be both vertically and horizontally integrated, but that would mean that one organisation was effectively the whole industry). Ultimately, one organisation might control nearly all of the market – a **monopoly** position. More usually, there will be at least one other competitor – creating a **duopoly**, as in UK cinema exhibition for many years, or UK television – or a small number of competitors of roughly equal status – an **oligopoly**. Most media industries – indeed most large scale industries of any kind – are oligopolies.

Economists refer to the relationships between organisations in an oligopoly as **imperfect competition**. There are likely to be unwritten agreements between the oligopolists as to standards, pricing policies, labour relations, etc. Because governments are likely to be concerned at the political implications of media monopolies, action is likely to be taken against 'too much' integration. This concern has increased as traditionally separate industries such as publishing, broadcasting and film have moved closer together.

ACTIVITY 20.4

Use the newspaper archives in your library to trace the changes in ownership and control of UK media activities involving any one of these groups: Pearson, Granada, EMAP. This should give you some idea of the complexity of UK media business.

Control of acquisitions in the media industries and subsequent oligopoly practices can be exercised in two ways:

- Public sector media organisations, financed and controlled by the public purse and public accountability, can be set up. Nearly all countries have some form of public broadcasting (radio and television) and many have set up government agencies that play an important role in financing and distributing films and other media products.
- The activities of media organisations can be regulated by government or public sector 'watchdogs'. Regulations often cover not only monopoly ownership or control and financial dealings, but also the range and 'quality' of products (including technical quality) and sometimes the sensitive content of products.

Some media industries (like cinema and popular music) have always been international in outlook, but technological change means that national boundaries are ceasing to be barriers to a wider range of media products. The control of multinational media corporations from a national perspective is becoming increasingly difficult.

Attitudes towards regulation have also changed. The drive towards **privatisation** in the UK, instituted by the Thatcher government in the 1980s, has been mirrored in other countries, and has been fuelled by a belief that the growth of media industries should be encouraged if it will increase employment. **Light touch regulation** is one recent development (e.g. the replacement of the IBA by the ITC in the UK). International regulation is another possibility. Multinational corporations might be required to deal directly with the European Union for instance. The dispute between member states in 1995 (France being in the minority) over how to support indigenous film industries in the face of American imports is indicative of how difficult this may be to put into practice.

Cross-media ownership is a sensitive issue in the UK, which is unique in having a history of a strong national press with large circulations and a public service broadcasting environment. Changes in ownership of the press and deregulation of the broadcasting market led to fears that multinational corporations would gain control across sectors. Government proposals in May 1995 effectively set out to bar media corporations with an already substantial hold in either press or television markets gaining further ground. (See Chapter 25, 'Case study: News Corporation'.) (Government control weakened again with announcements in December 1995. You will need to monitor this situation.)

Quality threshold The UK Broadcasting Act of 1990 set up the much-criticised process of bidding for Channel 3 franchises. In theory, the highest bid would be accepted if the bidding group convinced the ITC that it could pass the 'quality threshold' in terms of promised programming. Assessment of bids in relation to quality was seen by many observers as inconsistent.

Overall, the process of **deregulation** has been the central issue in most media industries during the 1980s and 1990s. On the other hand, more conservative attitudes towards media images have led to an increase in some areas of censorship of the content of media products (see Chapter 24, 'Institutions').

Location and local/global relations

The location of media industries is important for two main reasons:

- As a major employment sector (possibly the largest in some regions), the location of media production facilities is a contentious issue in many countries.
- If the media producers are all located in one area, then their media products are likely to be influenced by the culture of that area, which may or may not align with that of media consumers elsewhere.

The Hollywood studios have always prided themselves on the international appeal of their products. Yet, within the US, studios have traditionally been careful to censor material in order not to offend audiences in more conservative areas. Once, of course, this meant pandering to a form of apartheid in the South. Getting the balance right (between culturally conservative and liberal parts of the country) is difficult. Films and television programmes are usually financed in New York and made in Los Angeles and this twin axis has traditionally controlled the American media. The location of Ted Turner's operation (CNN especially) – a new competitor based in Atlanta – is therefore of some significance. The South is both the area of economic expansion and the home of even more conservative political views. The phenomenon of bigoted talk radio 'shock jocks' (another Southern strength) is also a symptom of a shift in the geography of the American media.

In the UK, the concentration of media production in London and the South East has led to many complaints about metropolitan bias. The growth and spread of a new speech pattern – so-called 'estuary English' – has been blamed on the London base of media commentators and the restructuring of both ITV/Channel 3 and the BBC has been scrutinised for the guarantee of **regional production**.

Perhaps the major concern over location is the fear that media production in one country may be completely controlled from another country. This fear extends to both the news media and those seen to be important agents in building a cultural identity. It can be argued that the spread of 'international news services' like CNN has had a beneficial effect in those parts of the world where repressive governments can muzzle their own media but cannot stop the inflow of satellite images (or

Regional production The sensitivity of the BBC to charges of metropolitan bias has produced some strange practices. In an attempt to be seen to be operating 'in the regions', BBC television transferred departments like Religious Programming to centres like Manchester. When the successful Radio 4 series *The Moral Maze* was tried on television in 1994, it became a Manchester production, even though the presenter and guests had to be flown up from London by shuttle and housed in a hotel overnight, and the programme had to be made in studio space rented from Granada because none was available at BBC North. (As reported in the *Guardian*, 12 June 1995.)

indeed BBC World Service radio broadcasts). On the other hand, most western countries have expressed concern about the ownership of media companies operating within their national boundaries being held by non-nationals (Rupert Murdoch had to take out US citizenship in order to acquire his US television holdings). This fear relates to a general fear over the 'unregulated' international media market outlined in the previous section. (See also Chapter 13, 'Global and local'.)

The economic benefits of attracting media business into an area can be considerable. With a weak sterling/dollar exchange rate, the choice of the UK and Ireland as the base for Hollywood feature film production in the early 1990s has generated a great deal of local business, especially in some of the more remote parts of Wales, Scotland and Ireland (where government policy has been directly to invite production companies in and to offer a range of incentives). Many UK cities, following the lead of Liverpool, have established Film Offices, designed to help production companies find locations and local technicians and support services. Information on a national scale is organised through the British Film Commission and a range of Regional Film Commissions. Film Offices are often run in conjunction with the Economic Development Units of city councils, which try to develop a local infrastructure to attract media business.

ACTIVITY 20.5

Investigate your local authority (at a county or city level) and its attitude to media development. Does it operate a Film Office? Does it have a Media Policy? (If you live in London, which clearly has a large media industry, it is still worth investigating the question of a Film Office since many film producers would rather not use London for locations because it is so difficult to get permission to film.)

Work patterns and employment

Work in the media is often perceived as glamorous and highly paid. In reality, this description fits only a small percentage of the workforce. We can recognise different groups of workers:
- technical (production, transmission, etc.)
- creative (writers, performers, designers, etc.)
- production organisation and management
- professional services (finance, legal, etc.)
- auxiliary support services (clerical, administrative, catering, etc.).

Technical staff represent a problem for employers in terms of both initial training and reskilling and the associated costs. The move to new technologies has produced conflicts in all sectors. Introduction of computerised processes has in some instances lead to 'deskilling' of tasks (see Chapter 18). Elsewhere, it has opened up new production opportunities and led to skills shortages where existing technical staff need retraining (e.g. in broadcast television). Media corporations in some sectors (film especially) have a poor record on training, expecting staff to 'work up from the bottom' or simply recruiting staff trained by somebody else (the BBC used to train the majority of broadcast technicians before deregulation). This 'short-termism' (i.e. not worrying about the future) is now being addressed, but overall it remains a problem.

Lower labour costs for technical staff lead to shifting locations for media work. Much colour printing is now undertaken in the 'Pacific Rim' countries, which have access to both high technology and lower wage costs (and digital material can easily be transmitted from editorial offices in Europe and North America). Hollywood productions are periodically attracted abroad because of lower staff costs. UK studios offer very highly skilled technicians, especially for big-budget productions with special effects (*Judge Dredd* is a recent example). Eastern Europe has become an attractive location with basic studio facilities at very low cost.

Creative personnel have usually been considered by media theorists in terms of how personal expression survives within an industrial system (see the studio system case study, Chapter 22). Other issues relate to the ownership of creative ideas and the rights that ensue. Media corporations attempt to control these as much as possible through contracts. Most of the high-profile cases of disputes over rights have come from the music industry (George Michael's battle with Sony being the most recent).

Production management staff are those who make sure that the project is completed and that it gets distributed. The most significant development in production management, as in the other sectors, has been the move towards freelancing or subcontracting to smaller independent production teams. The trend is perhaps most marked in film and broadcasting (50 per cent or more freelance staff in the UK), but is also common in newspapers and magazines. Media corporations tend to concentrate on ownership of properties and rights rather than direct control over employment. They do, of course, exercise control over freelance staff and

NVQs Like every other industry in the UK, film, video and broadcasting have been required to develop 'standards' and recognised qualifications for various job functions. These National Vocational Qualifications (SNVQs in Scotland) have taken several years to develop and are still being resisted by some sectors of an industry unaccustomed to formal training.

independent production groups through contracts and financial support. Supporters of the system maintain that the arrangement means that production groups are 'lean and mean' and highly competitive, that they are not hampered by institutional inertia. One disadvantage is that training and retraining and other initiatives which require industry-wide action become much more difficult to organise.

The professional services sector in the media industries requires a high degree of specialisation, especially in legal and financial fields and again tends to favour location in metropolitan centres (where specialist agencies will find sufficient work to support a practice). More general support services are not so location-conscious. (Further discussion of employment issues can be found in Chapter 24, 'Institutions'.)

Technological development

Chapters 18 and 19, on 'Technologies' and 'Developing widescreen technology' provide both background and analysis of technological change in the media industries. Technological change affects every part of the production process and not just the 'production' stage. As an example, the development of **broadband cable** and the transmission of digital media products at high speed around the world is primarily about distribution, but there is equal interest in the exhibition of the product in the home or in the presentation theatre (a major battle is developing to develop the 'set-top box' – the computer interface which controls the display of new services on the television set). The 'deal', especially the international deal, will perhaps be aided by video-conferencing and access to Internet sites, enabling dissemination of specialist information and research material. Post-production may also benefit – digital video can be edited 'on location' and beamed back to the studio.

Conclusion

The future of the media industries sector is tied up with the application of new technologies and the collapsing of old sector boundaries. New technologies throw up new companies with only a few staff which grow very quickly and can soon become 'players' – Bill Gates and Microsoft is the classic example. As this book goes into production, the major media corporations are engaged in a frenzied series of takeovers and mergers which may produce a new environment. We explore the issue of 'Who owns the media?' in the next chapter.

References and further reading

Bach, Steven (1985) *Final Cut*, London: Jonathan Cape.

Balio, Tino (ed.) (1976) (revised edn 1985) *The American Film Industry*, London: The University of Wisconsin Press.

Gomery, Douglas (1986) *The Hollywood Studio System*, London: BFI/Macmillan.

—— (1992) *Shared Pleasures*, London: BFI.

Harvey, Sylvia and Robins, Kevin (eds) (1993) *The Regions, the Nations and the BBC*, London: BFI.

Izod, John (1988) *Hollywood and the Box Office 1895–1986*, London: Macmillan.

Maltby, Richard and Craven, Ian (1995) *Hollywood Cinema,* Oxford: Blackwell.

Pirie, David (ed.) (1981) *Anatomy of the Movies*, London: Windward.

Thompson, David and Christie, Ian (eds) *Scorsese on Scorsese*, London: Faber & Faber.

Wasko, Janet (1994) *Hollywood in the Information Age Beyond the Silver Screen*, London: Polity.

Williams, Granville (1994) *Britain's Media – How They Are Related*, London: Campaign For Press and Broadcasting Freedom.

21 / Case study: Who owns the media?

Conglomerates

The ownership and control of media companies is an issue in Media Studies because of a belief that the nature of the product, and in particular the content of news and factual material or the ideology of a whole range of products, may be influenced by business considerations or the 'proprietorial' whims of chief executives. Conversely, the lack of production opportunities for smaller and non-commercial producers creates a lack of balance in the range of media products available.

Recognising the possibility of proprietorial control was relatively straightforward when newspapers were run by 'press barons' and Hollywood studios were ruled by autocratic moguls; or at least that is how the stereotypical view of these entrepreneurs has been presented. (See Chapter 22, 'Case study: Producing in the studio system'.) In the News Corporation case study (Chapter 25) we try to explore one specific example of individual proprietorial power.

Modern media companies are most likely to be part of a **conglomerate** – a division within a much larger company: organised on the principle of multiple profit centres which reinforce each other ... designed not only to generate revenue and profits, but to keep such monies within the corporation.

> (Robert Gustafson on conglomerates, quoted in Izod 1988)

The parent company is likely to be engaged in several different media sectors and probably related sectors such as the manufacture of technology or the provision of telecommunications. We have borne this in mind in constructing the world map of corporate media activity shown in Figure 21.1. We haven't tried to show all the top media corporations, nor have we tried to rank them since it is difficult to agree criteria for ranking (or, indeed, for defining what is a 'media corporation'). The range of activities encompassed by the widest definitions of media is vast and includes some of the fastest-growing industrial sectors. It is inevitable that our representation will need updating by the time you read this, but it should still give you a good grasp of the international market. Note these features:

- The Hollywood **majors** are well represented, even though they are all part of larger groups.
- The major media corporations span North America, Europe and Japan.

Microsoft and TCI, companies which are not primarily media producers, are included because we believe they will have an enormous influence in the next few years.

Financial control

Modern media corporations are effectively owned by shareholders. The 'cross-holding' of shares of one media corporation by another is widespread (especially in Europe). The major shareholders are often institutional – i.e. the shares are owned by insurance companies or pension funds. In other words, the shareholders are often very removed from the production that generates the profit. The future of the corporation lies very much in the hands of accountants and financial advisers who look at the balance sheets rather than the product as an indicator of the health of the company.

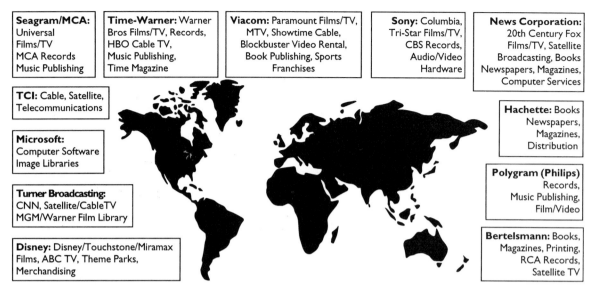

Seagram/MCA: Universal Films/TV MCA Records Music Publishing

Time-Warner: Warner Bros Films/TV, Records, HBO Cable TV, Music Publishing, Time Magazine

Viacom: Paramount Films/TV, MTV, Showtime Cable, Blockbuster Video Rental, Book Publishing, Sports Franchises

Sony: Columbia, Tri-Star Films/TV, CBS Records, Audio/Video Hardware

News Corporation: 20th Century Fox Films/TV, Satellite Broadcasting, Books Newspapers, Magazines, Computer Services

TCI: Cable, Satellite, Telecommunications

Microsoft: Computer Software Image Libraries

Turner Broadcasting: CNN, Satellite/CableTV MGM/Warner Film Library

Disney: Disney/Touchstone/Miramax Films, ABC TV, Theme Parks, Merchandising

Hachette: Books Newspapers, Magazines, Distribution

Polygram (Philips) Records, Music Publishing, Film/Video

Bertelsmann: Books, Magazines, Printing, RCA Records, Satellite TV

Figure 21.1 An indication of some of the media corporations and their interests

This observation, which is relevant for all modern corporations, shouldn't be seen as 'proof' that all industrial media production is devoid of creative work or that because it is industrial it will all be the same. It does, however, suggest the kinds of influences that are present when media corporations make decisions to buy or sell subsidiary companies or to cease production (i.e. close down a newspaper title or shelve a feature film). There are a few media industry figures with a personal fortune big enough to enable them to become significant 'players' in the media market, and there are a handful of executives whose reputation is such that their activity (or even their presence) can dramatically affect the financial status of a company, but even so the accountants set the 'bottom line' on most projects.

Media production takes place in what can sometimes seem a quite contradictory business environment. Financial security matters more than individual creativity, yet in the last few years a financially secure company like Sony has made a mess of operating Columbia, while good creative management has turned round a company in difficulty like Disney. We might argue that some management strategies are more effective in allowing the development of an environment in which creative decisions can be made. We might also note that the attitude of financial markets towards media industries is important. In the US, there is a positive attitude towards investment in the media industries, especially Hollywood, despite the disasters. For good or ill, American investors are attracted by the glamour and risk their money. Contrast this with the UK, where it has proved very difficult to persuade financial institutions to finance British films or new media generally.

Time-Warner: Media conglomerate

The Hollywood majors have been through many ups and downs. After they lost their exhibition chains in the 1950s, they were not large companies by American standards. In the last forty years they have been bought and sold many times – Columbia was once owned by Coca-Cola; Paramount was part of an industrial conglomerate Gulf and Western; United Artists belonged to an insurance group; and MGM, in a sad tale for the one-time industry leader, was bought by a hotel chain.

Our example studio, Warner Brothers, eventually fell into the hands of Kinney National Services in the 1970s. Kinney's main interests were car parks, car rentals, building and funeral services. Warner Communications, as the company eventually came to be known, was a conglomerate offering a range of services, with film product as only a minor factor. New ventures included video games (Warner owned Atari and made big profits before the bubble burst on the arcade games market) and cable television. But it was not until the explosion of video, and in the 1980s the ever-expanding market for filmed entertainment delivered to the home, that the true potential of the Warner 'brand name' was properly developed. Warner Communications then merged with Time Inc., a major publisher and another early entrant to the cable market, to produce the world's then biggest media corporation, Time-Warner. As this book goes into production Time-Warner are attempting to take over Turner Broadcasting – a move that will put them back on top following the Disney acquisition of Capital Cities/ABC.

European media corporations

Table 21.1 identifies a number of UK, French, German and Italian media corporations which have developed into international players.

Table 21.1 **Top Ten European media corporations**

Corporation	Country/Sector	Media turnover ($m)
1 Bertelsmann	Ger/Music, TV, Publishing	8,684
2 ARD	Ger/TV	5,953
3 Havas	Fra/Advertising, Publishing, TV	5,621
4 Fininvest	Italy/TV, Publishing, Sports	5,178
5 Reed Elsevier	UK/Publishing	4,484
6 BBC	UK/Broadcasting	3,416
7 Matra-Hachette	Fra/Publishing, Distribution, TV	3,161
8 RAI	Italy/Broadcasting	3,115
9 Pearson	UK/Publishing/TV/ Theme Parks	2,569
10 Gruner+Jahr AG	Ger/Publishing	2,467

Source: Media Map Weekly Update, CIT Publications, listed in *Wired*, June 1995

Note: News International are not included in this list because the parent company, News Corporation, is American. Philips/Polygram and Thorn-EMI are not included because their activities include non-media and international operations.

Two of these corporations are included on our world map, but generally the European media corporations differ from their American counterparts in the following ways:

- Public sector broadcasters have had a central role in European media. ARD, BBC and RAI up to now have been more secure within their home markets than the private sector American broadcasters CBS, NBC and ABC (ABC and CBS were both taken over in 1995). (The Japanese public sector broadcaster NHK is another major player.)
- Broadcasting and publishing are much more important for European media corporations (i.e. than 'filmed entertainment'). This is partly a matter of 'own language/culture' markets, less easily penetrated by American producers, and also the modern development of long-established companies in industries like printing and publishing. Such national barriers are coming down with digital media processes.
- European corporations (especially German groups) have tended to expand within Europe rather than to look more widely for opportunities. There is a complex web of cross-ownership of shares in different European media corporations. At the time of writing, Silvio Berlusconi has fought off a challenge by News Corporation to buy into his Fininvest operation and has turned to a consortium led by a German media group. UK media groups, sharing a common language with the Americans and with a history of overseas investment, are more international in outlook. Once again, this situation is changing. The Americans are looking towards new European television markets in cable and satellite and the German corporations (especially Bertelsmann) are looking to North America.

Libraries, brands, distribution and synergy

The contemporary media business environment is in a state of turmoil as the conglomerates buy and sell companies in an attempt to keep on board the bandwagon – a wagon which is surely rolling, but no one is sure in exactly which direction. There are extravagant claims about the business potential of new technologies and new media products, but most of these are yet to be realised. We have picked out four trends which do seem to be important and which we think you should study: libraries, brands, distribution and synergy.

Libraries

The major growth in media activity is in distribution systems or 'new media' such as satellite television or CD-ROMs. These are proliferating faster than the output of new product to fill them. Anyone who controls a library or 'back catalogue' of recognisable media products is now in a good position to exploit these resources by recycling them on the new media. Hollywood film libraries, the rights to well-known popular songs, photographic archives – all these are being snapped up by the large media corporations. The computer software company Microsoft has set up a subsidiary specifically to buy important photographic images from around the world. These will then be catalogued and presented on CD-ROM in different collections, generating revenue as immediate product and then again as they are reproduced by their media users.

Brands

As the international media market grows and companies attempt to operate in several different countries, the **marketing** of new products becomes more problematic. If a company wants to build its presence in Poland, Thailand and South Africa, will it need different logos, a different company image to appeal in different cultural contexts? This will be expensive. The power of the international brand, instantly recognisable everywhere, goes some way to explaining the longevity of the Hollywood studios. There cannot be many parts of the world where Warner's shield, Paramount's mountain and MGM's lion are not familiar to a mass audience. The

move to merchandising, utilising the studio logo to the full, is recent evidence of the new importance of the logo. The UK premiere of *Batman Forever* in summer 1995 took place in Leicester where a new Warner cinema opened this Warner picture. The launch was accompanied by Warner Radio broadcasting on a restricted licence from the cinema. Music on Warner record labels, merchandise in the Warner shops, computer games, comics, tie-in deals with McDonalds – the potential is endless.

Selecting a logo will be one of the problems facing a new studio like DreamWorks. Formed by three media producers with excellent individual track records – Steven Spielberg, David Geffen (founder of Geffen Records) and Jeffrey Katzenberg (ex-Disney executive) – the new company has everything going for it. But, to become a 'major', it will have to promote itself very quickly and very widely: developing a logo and an identity will be difficult, it would be easier to buy an existing 'brand'.

Distribution

Chapter 18 on Technologies analyses the move to digital media products, all of which (sounds, pictures and text) will move down **broadband cable**. The companies that control the cable systems will be in a powerful position. Once again, the world market is very much dominated and influenced by the major North American companies which have prospered in the region with the largest telecommunications market. Instead of the Hollywood studios, this story is about Ma Bell and the **Baby Bells**.

The American Trust Laws forced the break-up of the giant Bell telephone company in 1982. This produced AT&T as a separate long-distance service provider and a host of regional telephone companies (the 'baby' Bell companies) which generated spare cash from a lucrative business and wanted somewhere to spend it. In the late 1980s some of the larger Baby Bells were attracted to the new British cable television franchises. The Thatcher government, desperate to force a competitive environment in this new industry, allowed the development of the least regulated cable market in Europe. It was a perfect opportunity for the American telephone and cable companies (and their equally experienced Canadian counterparts) to move in and experiment with their spare cash. Their interest was not in making television programmes, but in developing delivery systems for telecommunications, television and sound broadcasts. The result is a UK market dominated by American interests such as Nynex (the New York Baby Bell), Southwestern Bell and TCI.

TCI is the leading American cable company and it is the prospect of mergers between the cable companies and the telephone companies in the US which is fuelling debates about the 'Superhighway'. Meanwhile, in the international market, News Corporation has formed a link with MCI, the major competitor for AT&T in the long-distance telephone service industry.

The other noticeable feature of the television industry is the takeover of small specialist film and video equipment suppliers by larger companies with more broadly based business telecommunications or information-handling concerns. A good example is the takeover of Lightworks (a supplier of computer editing equipment for broadcasters and Hollywood) by Tektronix (a major video and networking company and a leader in distribution technology).

ACTIVITY 21.1

Investigate the cable market in your area. Unless you live in one of the more remote parts of the country (in which case you may want to look at the telecommunications market), there will have been a franchise offered.

- Has it been bid for? Has a bid been accepted?
- Who has won the franchise?
- Are they connected to the Baby Bells (or to any other supplier of telecommunications or similar services)?
- What kind of services are they offering?

Synergy

Synergy is media industry jargon for integration of different but complementary business interests. It implies that by putting two companies together, the resulting conglomerate will be more valuable than its separate parts, producing new products or creating new markets. The marriage of cable television and telephone supply is one example, but the famous attempt at synergy, which so far has been spectacularly unsuccessful, was the takeover by the Japanese equipment manufacturers, Sony and Matsushita, of the Hollywood studios, Columbia and TriStar (Sony) and MCA-Universal (Matsushita). It seemed like a good idea – guaranteed supply of product for the new technologies in video and computer games being developed by the Japanese parent. But both ventures were disastrous. The pundits have argued that it was the clash of cultures, that the Japanese managers did not understand Hollywood and made poor decisions on appointments. Both companies lost millions of dollars on a string of unsuccessful pictures and Matsushita finally got out, selling well below the buying price in 1995.

In summer 1995 Sony organised the simultaneous release of *Johnny Mnemonic* as a film and as a computer game on CD-ROM, both based on William Gibson's novel. The film cost $30 million, the 'full motion video' sequence for the CD-ROM $3 million. The total US cinema box office for 1994 was $5 billion. The value of the computer games market in the same year was $10 billion (see the *Guardian*, 29 May 1995). The film was a flop in North America.

We began Chapter 20, 'Industries', by observing that media industries are like many other industries – especially when they are buying and selling and distributing products. However, there are 'specificities' to take into account and perhaps Matsushita would have been better advised to buy a cable company first. (See also Chapter 9 for the discussion on synergy through merchandising.)

Independents

'Independent' means several quite different things in the media industries and in Chapter 27, 'Independents and alternatives', we explore the concept in some detail. Here, as a footnote to our study of the majors, we are dealing with companies that are 'independent' only in the sense that they are relatively new in the field or have consciously positioned themselves (or have been positioned) 'outside' the established oligopolies in their sector.

In Hollywood, for instance, the only differences between the majors and the independents are history and market share. The majors have earned a larger market share and maintained it over a long period. There may be no difference at all in terms of the types of films produced. *The Mask* and *Dumb and Dumber* were highly successful 1994 releases which could have come from any of the majors. In fact, they came from the leading independent producer New Line, which in 1994 was more successful than either Columbia or TriStar – both majors – and which has since been acquired by the Ted Turner Organisation, along with another independent, Castle Rock Entertainment. Turner is a major player in the cable and satellite market, but still an independent in Hollywood.

The independents can deal in exactly the same product as the majors (independent production has been a feature of Hollywood since the break-up of the studio system(see Chapter 22)) but being 'outside' means that they are more likely to take risks. They will often pick up quirky projects which the majors turned down and will take the foreign or art house pictures for distribution. When the independents become successful, they are very often absorbed by the majors. Miramax, one of the most successful Hollywood 'indies' of recent years (home to Tarantino with *Pulp Fiction*), is now part of the Disney empire. Since the independent image still has marketing power, which in this case might be damaged by the link to the squeaky clean wholesomeness of Disney, Miramax has kept its identity within a Disney structure which also markets product for older audiences through its Touchstone and Hollywood Pictures brands.

Much the same story is true in the other media, certainly in publishing or music production. Here again most of the large publishing companies or record labels are part of even larger multinational corporations. The independents are smaller and more likely to take a gamble on something new. Unlike in the film industry, however, independent record producers may find they are at the mercy of the major companies who manufacture and distribute CDs and cassettes – and indeed of the major chains which sell music. The **oligopoly** which controls music is even more tightly defined than in other industries. Recorded music across the world is controlled by a handful of companies with familiar names: Time-Warner, Polygram, Sony, MCA, Bertelsmann, EMI. Some of these companies have longstanding operations in Africa, Asia and Latin America which have utilised local language performances. Unlike the film industry, the relatively low cost of record-pressing enabled local music industries to thrive. Thus the spectacle of the majors fighting over the 'Latin' and 'Tropical/Salsa' markets in the US and Latin America. (Warner and Sony dominated respectively in 1994.)

From the perspective of the majors in the various media industries, any new entrant into a market is seen as an 'independent' and therefore a threat. In *Billboard* magazine's round-up of the music business in the US in 1994, great excitement was generated by the success of the combined 'indies' in matching the market share of one of the majors. Indy sales come largely from rap records but the biggest-selling 'independent' album of the year was a soundtrack – 'Lion King' – distributed by that well-known independent, Disney.

References and further reading

The business operations of the media corporations are best followed in the trade publications for each industry. *Screen International*, *Variety* and *Billboard* are particularly useful in that they cover a range of 'entertainment media'. For a more defined UK perspective look at *Broadcast, Media Week, UK Press Gazette,* etc.

Gomery, Douglas (1992) *Shared Pleasures*, London: BFI.

Izod, John (1988) *Hollywood and the Box Office 1895–1986*, London: Macmillan.

Murphy, Brian (1983) *The World Wired Up*, London: Comedia. (For background on Baby Bells.)

Pilati, Antonio (ed.) (1993) *Media Industry in Europe*, London: John Libbey.

Wasko, Janet (1994) *Hollywood in the Information Age Beyond the Silver Screen*, London: Polity.

22 / Case study: Producing in the studio system

The Hollywood studio system offers an example of a fully mature media production system which has been documented in detail. It therefore gives us a useful base against which to measure other forms of production practice.

Defining the system

The terms 'Hollywood' and 'studio system' tend to be used glibly and it is important to try to be more rigorous in definition. The studio system in its full form lasted for no more than twenty years. It had its origins in the 1920s but did not reach maturity until the early 1930s. The full system operated until the beginning of the 1950s and then gradually broke up over the next decade. The 'golden age' of the studio was 1930–50.

During this time 'Hollywood' (a term applied to both the outer suburb of Los Angeles and the **mainstream** American film industry) was dominated by five studios:

- Paramount
- MGM
- 20th Century Fox
- Warners
- RKO.

These were known as the **majors** or the 'big five'. Universal and Columbia were the 'minors'. An eighth 'studio' of note was United Artists, but UA owned no facilities and was effectively a financier and distributor. With Universal and Columbia, UA formed the 'little three'. There were a number of other smaller studios and distributors (Disney, Republic and Monogram are the best known), but the industry recognised the eight majors/minors as dominant because they alone could guarantee access to 'first-run' cinemas (i.e. those that took new films only) for all their product.

The relative market positions of the studios is shown in Table 22.1.

Table 22.1 Gross domestic film rentals from distribution within the United States of ten motion picture companies, 1939.

Studio	$m	%
Loew's (MGM)	43.2	21.5
20th Century Fox	33.2	16.5
Warner Bros	28.9	14.4
Paramount	28.2	14.0
RKO	18.2	9.1
Universal	14.2	7.0
United Artists	13.5	6.7
Columbia	13.2	6.5
Republic	6.2	3.1
Monogram	2.5	1.2
Total	201.3	100.0

Source: Mae D. Huettig, 'The Motion Picture Industry Today', in Balio (1985)

The features of the system

The studio system was a **mature oligopoly** of vertically integrated companies. The majors made their money from exhibiting their own films in their own cinemas. To this extent, the great cinema chains of Loew's and Paramount were as much a part of the system as the studios in

Hollywood. The cinemas demanded a product to show and the job of the studios was to produce it efficiently and punctually. The distributor arms of the majors promoted the films and the stars to the public (see also Chapter 23). We will concentrate on the studio production end.

Division of labour

The system was based on a strict **division of labour** – the dominant mode of capitalist manufacture at the time, often associated with the production line of Henry Ford. The theory was that organising workers so that they concentrated on one or two skilled or semi-skilled tasks would mean that they would contribute more (and more efficiently) to the production process than if they performed a wide range of less specialised tasks. This might mean that their work was more repetitive and that they had less 'control' over their role in production (clearly an important consideration in a 'creative industry').

Unit-based production

The studio owned land on which were based the **sound stages**, administrative offices, preview theatres and writers' accommodation. Directors, crews and stars were all contracted to the studio and production was organised by salaried producers. In some studios there were **units** set up within the system so a producer got to work with the same director and crew over several films. Integration meant that the studio had to provide its distribution arm and its cinema chain with a constant flow of A and B pictures, serials, newsreels and cartoons, fifty-two weeks a year. The distinction between an **A picture** (90 minutes or more run time, a budget of $500,000) and a B (under 90 minutes, budget $200,000) was very clearly defined and offers us a useful guide to the overall approach.

The task of the studio boss was to utilise capital equipment and contracted staff to the full. If work could not be found inside the studio, facilities and stars would be hired out to another studio or to one of the independent producers such as Samuel Goldwyn or David Selznick. During the 1930s, they might also be sent over to England, where several of the studios opened a British operation to make cheap films as part of their quota of 'British' productions (necessary to satisfy UK government regulations).

Specialist product

This constant **production cycle** necessitated the development of particular methods of organisation and specialisation in particular products. The most obvious development was that of genre-based production and a concomitant studio style or 'look'. In modern Hollywood it is not possible to distinguish a film made by an individual studio, there is no consistency. Audiences in the 1940s and film historians in the 1990s would have no difficulty in distinguishing a Warners picture from an MGM feature of the same period during the studio era. Partly it would be the genre – downbeat and gritty for Warners, glamorous and glossy for MGM; partly the style that went with the genre – low-key lighting for Warners, high-key for MGM; and partly the contract stars – Gable and Garbo for MGM, Cagney and Davis for Warners. The directors and other creative personnel would also be recognisable; Michael Curtiz or William Wellman at Warners, George Cukor or King Vidor at MGM.

Unit production at Warner Bros

Warner Brothers operation in the late 1930s is a good example of tightly organised production and it is well documented in two books, Thomas Schatz's *The Genius of the System* (1989) and Nick Roddick's *A New Deal in Entertainment: Warner Brothers in the 1930s* (1983). Schatz places the producer at the centre of the system and identifies a 'production unit' system at Warners. Half the fifty-plus features per year which the studio produced were classed as A features and were divided up between different genre-star production units. One unit concentrated on '**biopics**' of important historical figures such as Louis Pasteur who 'discovered' inoculation, or the controversial nineteenth-century novelist Émile Zola – both characters fighting authority and in many ways in line with heroes from other genres in this 'socially-conscious' studio. Little remembered now, these films were both very popular and critically well received with Paul Muni playing the lead, William Dieterle directing, Tony Gaudio in charge of cinematography and Henry Blanke as producer.

The biopic team had great success with *The Story of Louis Pasteur* in 1936 with Muni winning the Best Actor Oscar. He was then loaned to RKO while the production team made *The White Angel* – another biopic, this time about Florence Nightingale. The team would also be used by other units and in 1936–7, Dieterle directed a total of eight pictures. In the meantime, work began on the script for *The Life of Emile Zola*, which went into production as soon as Muni and the crew were free. Shooting was scheduled for forty-two days but in the event ran over by ten. However, post-production was completed very quickly and the film premiered just three months later.

Now, I could refuse to do it. All Warners directors could refuse three scripts. But here is how it worked:

Figure 22.1 The Warners' biopic unit at work on *The Story of Louis Pasteur* (US 1936)

you get a story you don't like – out it goes; you get one you like even less – so there's your second refusal; then you get one that's even worse, and you begin to think that the first one isn't so bad. That's how it worked. They were so clever at Warners. They knew there were many ways to skin a cat.

(Director William Dieterle, interviewed in *Velvet Light Trap*, no. 15, 1975)

Dieterle went on to make three more biopics with the same unit before leaving Warner Brothers for RKO in 1941.

William Dieterle A look at Dieterle's career tells us a great deal about how the studio system worked in the 1930s. He began as an actor in the Berlin theatre of the 1920s, working with the great theatre director Max Reinhardt before moving into film, first as an actor and later as a director. He did some work for Warners' German operation and in 1930 he was called to Hollywood to produce 'synchronisations' – foreign language versions of new productions designed to maintain Hollywood's position in the world market after the coming of sound.

Learning to reshoot whole features in around ten days, using the same sets and costumes, was good experience and he was contracted to work on English language pictures very quickly. Dieterle's subsequent work is interesting evidence for the industrial production vs. creativity argument. He was popular with the studio bosses because he was efficient and kept to budget and this meant that he was perhaps forced to take on poor material and produce work with little apparent value. But also it meant that he worked consistently; that he brought his theoretical knowledge and his understanding of lighting and set design into a fruitful partnership with director of photography Tony Gaudio and art directors such as Anton Grot. The studio invested in these creative teams over a long period and the end result was arguably a more consistent quality product than is now possible.

Figure 22.2 Kay Francis as Florence Nightingale in the 1936 Warner Bros picture *The White Angel*, Note the detail of the Moorish arches in this scene. The studio resources would enable the art director to benefit from good historical research

A Day in the Studio during the making of *Anthony Adverse*, a prestige costume drama released in 1936. (Taken from material presented by Nick Roddick.)

- Day begins with the arrival on the backlot (eighteenth-century street scene) of the prop men at 7.00am followed by the camera crew and the wardrobe, hair and make-up staff at 7.30. The rest of the crew, including the director, have arrived by 8.15.
- The principal cast members arrive and begin rehearsing at 8.20 and the first shot is completed by 8.35.
- Shooting then carries on until lunch time (12.45) and restarts an hour later (although the crew take only half an hour for lunch) finishing for 'supper' at 3.40pm. The cast do not return for the evening, but the crew go on to complete a number of night street scenes between 6.30 and 11.00pm when the day officially ends.

All of these details were meticulously recorded on the 'Daily Production and Progress Report'. Everyone was timed on and off the set. A note at the foot of the report states that any delays caused by late arrival of artists must be recorded and an explanation given. Sheets like this are still in use on the set today.

Around four minutes of acceptable footage was achieved on a typical day. The 136 minute picture (excessively long for the period) was completed in 72 days.

The continuity system

An important feature of the studio system was the development of particular narrative styles and techniques which Bordwell and Thompson (1994) define as **continuity editing** or the **continuity system**. In the 'Narratives', 'Ideologies' and 'Realisms' chapters (Chs 3, 11, 15), we look at the importance of this system in setting up audience readings of narratives which became 'transparent' in that they disguised the means of their own construction. Techniques were developed for relating **cause and effect** and moving the narrative along economically without drawing attention to themselves. There was also an industrial production line function in laying down **continuity rules** such as 'not **crossing the line**' or **shot/reverse shot** for showing a dialogue exchange (see Chapter 3, 'Narratives', for explanation of these terms).

These rules were first introduced in the 1910s and 1920s but finally developed into a definable system during the 1930s (many had to be recast or introduced for the first time after the coming of sound and the problems with early sound-recording equipment). If ruthlessly enforced, they could speed up the production process. There was no need to agonise over each shot and think about all the various options for camera angles, framings and movement – there was an accepted way to make a Hollywood feature.

There is also some evidence that studios imposed rules in order to emphasise what they believed to be selling points for the picture, such as close-ups. Studio heads were also conscious that some techniques, e.g. using cranes or long tracking shots, were more expensive and more difficult to get right. Consequently they tried to curtail their use.

The best source for material on the continuity system is Bordwell, Staiger and Thompson (1985). What appears to be clear is that there was a general understanding of a system which operated at every studio. There were, however, different interpretations of and attitudes towards it. Some studio bosses demanded that the same scene be shot from several angles so that they could select the most appropriate take at the post-production stage. Others allowed the more respected directors to shoot only one way (i.e. the way the director wanted to see the edited scene). John Ford is perhaps the best known example of a director who 'edited in the camera' in this way. (See Williams 1994, for a sustained critique of the importance attached by Bordwell *et al.* to continuity 'rules.')

Analysing the value of the system

We have identified several common features of production in the studio era and we can add a few more to make a useful summary:

- vertically integrated companies undertook production, distribution and exhibition
- ownership and control of studios rested with companies whose main business was movies (although it is important to note that exhibition contributed more profits than production)
- continuous production of a range of cinema product: 'A' and 'B' features, newsreels, cartoons, etc.
- physical studio assets and equipment in constant use
- a division of salaried/contracted staff into highly specialised departments
- the contracted star system
- a producer-unit system and a definition of genres
- a continuity system governing narrative construction
- a specific studio 'look' or style applied to 'A' features
- an international market for studio product.

The major issue which arises from consideration of the system is the potential conflict of 'industry' vs. 'art'; or the mechanised and organised process of production vs. the creative director and performer. In other chapters we look at this question from different standpoints, but here we concentrate on the value of the studio system as an industrial process.

It is clear that although the system exerted pressure on all those involved to 'maintain production' and that in many ways creative personnel were constrained by budget or genre definition or star vehicle, the discipline so engendered enabled creative teams to produce work of high craftsmanship and powerful narrative appeal. Dore Schary, an executive producer at both RKO and MGM noted that:

Efficiency experts trained in other industries are usually baffled when they try to fit the making of a movie to their standard rules. The fact is, a movie is essentially a hand-craft operation ... but it must be made on a factory-line basis, with production-line economics, if we're to hold the price down within reach of most of the people. The job is to do this without losing the picture's individuality.

One of the lost things you can look back on in that era and say was good was the system of patronage that enabled us to keep together a group of highly talented people and let them function rather freely and profitably.

(Quoted in Bordwell et al. 1985)

The quality of the best pictures produced during the studio era is evident for any viewer of BBC2 or Channel 4. But, it should be remembered that these are perhaps the cream of a very large crop and that the majority may not bear as much scrutiny. (If you have access to the cable channel TNT, you can see a much wider range of features from MGM and Warners.)

The other major question might be 'Who got to choose which pictures were made?' The studios in this period were still run by the men who had set them up, the so-called 'movie moguls', characters like Jack Warner or Louis B. Mayer. The studio bosses had very strong views on what should be made and they exerted their authority. They were effectively producers not directors, but unlike the executives who gained control of the studios in the 1970s, they were creative movie people who wanted to make movies that would fill theatres.

1949, when the federal government attacked the majors as oligopolists and forced them to sell their movie chains, thereby ending the integration which was the basis of the system.

The 1950s saw the rise of independent producers who effectively replaced the in-house production units (there had always been a small number of independents – now they were to become the norm). The studios would still distribute a set number of major films each year, but instead of making them all themselves, they would 'pick up' or finance product from an independent. (See Chapter 20, 'Industries' and Chapter 27, 'Independents and alternatives' for definitions of 'independent'.)

In the 1990s the studio system is in one sense long gone. For a period in the 1960s and 1970s the British television broadcasters tended to organise production on a unit production system with studio complexes turning out dramas, light entertainment, etc. and specialist units for sport and natural history. But this system too has broken up and been replaced by independents and in-house producers using 'facilities' rather than a 'factory production line'. Modern technology and an environment of deregulation and 'free market' competition has seen off the controlled production environment.

The real legacy of the studio system is now revealed to have been the enormous body of work, now growing in value as libraries of material, the extraordinary longevity of copyright images such as the cartoon characters of Disney and Warners, and the trademark of a logo recognised all over the world. Warners, Paramount and Fox, along with Disney, are still on top of the media pile, although now their position is even more dependent on what they distribute and exhibit than on what they actually make.

The legacy of the studio system

The death of the studio system was a prolonged and complex process – too complex to describe here. Many factors led to the break-up, but the major event which precipitated the decline was 'the Paramount case' in

References and further reading

Balio, Tino (1985) *The American Film Industry,* London: University of Wisconsin.

Behlmer, Rudy (ed.) (1986) *Inside Warner Bros,* London: Weidenfeld & Nicholson.

Bordwell, David, Staiger, Janet and Thompson, Kirstin (1985) *The Classical Hollywood Cinema: Film Style and Mode of Production to 1960,* London: Routledge.

Bordwell, David and Thompson, Kirstin (1994) *Film Art – An Introduction,* New York: McGraw-Hill.

Gomery, Douglas (1986) *The Hollywood Studio System,* London: BFI/Macmillan.

—— (1992) *Shared Pleasures,* London: BFI.

Kerr, Paul (ed.) (1986) *The Hollywood Film Industry,* London: RKP.

Maltby, Richard and Craven, I. (1995) *Hollywood Cinema,* Oxford: Blackwell.

Roddick, Nick (1983) *A New Deal in Entertainment: Warner Brothers in the 1930s,* London: BFI.

Schatz, Thomas (1989) *The Genius of the System: Hollywood Filmmaking in the Studio Era,* London: Simon & Schuster.

Williams, Christopher (1994) 'After the Classic, the Classical and Ideology: the Differences of Realism', *Screen,* vol. 35, no. 3, autumn.

23 / Case study: Making stars

One aspect of the Hollywood studio system worth studying in its own right is the phenomenon of the star and the institution of stardom. In this chapter we look specifically at the use of stars within the studio period and then briefly at aspects of the way stardom has developed as an institution in contemporary media.

Richard Dyer (1979), coming out of sociology, was interested in the role of stardom in society generally. He broke with earlier writing, which often celebrated stars as 'magic', and he emphasised the ways that stars were:

- economic factors in the Hollywood studio system (and, we might add, in many other studio systems such as Bombay cinema)
- constructed phenomena, rather than 'gifted' or 'authentic' or 'magical' individuals. This construction of image, or **persona** (originally meaning the mask which players in Roman dramas wore) is significant because it may help to account for the popularity, and therefore economic power of stars. Their images were constructed largely, but not exclusively, by the studios.

This then leads to exploration of why certain stars should be popular at certain times, and to questions of **ideologies**, **dominant discourses** and **representation**.

Stars and the studio system

Although 'stars' as such were a feature of nineteenth-century theatre and music hall, it was not until the popularity of cinema was extended and supported by 'secondary' media, such as radio and illustrated magazines in the 1920s, that the star system was fully formed.

In the early years of cinema, actors' names were not featured in publicity. It was the subject matter or the visual spectacle which was promoted – one argument has been that the producers didn't want to name actors because it might lead them to demand higher fees. It was not until around 1910 that information about the players appeared in trade journals and 'lobby cards' appeared in cinemas. (Cards featuring photographs of the stars were distributed with films and were displayed in the lobby – the foyer in British cinemas – in special holders before and during a run.)

Producers who did name 'featured players' were rewarded with increased rentals of their films – a sure sign that audiences were interested in selecting films to watch on the basis of favourite players. Once this precedent was set, it spread quickly and during the period 1915–20, as films lengthened and became more expensive to produce, the importance of stars was widely recognised. One of the first companies to recognise this called itself 'Famous Players' and went on to form the basis for Paramount – the first of the Hollywood majors. Very quickly it became apparent that this was something more significant as a phenomenon than the fame of 'live' stage performers. A clear indication of this was the formation in 1919 of United Artists, a company founded by three actor 'stars' – Charles Chaplin, Mary Pickford and Douglas Fairbanks – and a 'star director', D.W. Griffith. One of the executives at another studio referred to this as 'the lunatics taking over the asylum' and for the next thirty years the studios would battle to keep control over their contracted stars.

When the studio system ended in the 1950s, the stars emerged in a stronger position and many were able to become their own producer or director and to negotiate a privileged status (and a similarly privileged salary). Kevin Costner is one of the most recent examples, but the disaster of *Wyatt Earp* (1994) and the relative failure of *Waterworld* (1995) casts doubt on his 'bankability' and shows how volatile star status can be. 'You're only as good as your last picture' is a well-known saying in contemporary Hollywood. In the studio system, another star vehicle would be along very quickly to recover the situation, but when you have to raise the money yourself, it gets more difficult.

The 'system' explained

The star was an integral part of the **unit production system** (see Chapter 22 on the studio system). Each studio had a contracted 'roster' of stars, chosen and then groomed to fit the genres and styles of that studio. When first contracted (perhaps from the stage), most young actors would serve an apprenticeship in B features (where they might be leads) or a lower billing in A features. The system operated quite rigidly and weekly salary and the position of a name on the billing (i.e. the 'credits') of a film would be clearly related and renegotiated as status was increased.

Bette Davis

Being a 'star' in the studio systems was hard work. Bette Davis is seen in Figure 23.1 on the set of *Now, Voyager* (US 1942) ready for a scene in which she plays the unglamorous Charlotte Vale (see also Figure 9.2). By 1942, Davis was a veteran of over forty major features and winner of two Best Actress Oscars, all achieved in ten years. She fought hard to gain control over her own image, attempting to have the services of her favourite lighting cameramen built into her contract as well as fighting for stronger roles (see Schatz 1989: 218–20). As a major female star in a predominantly male system, Davis became an icon for women in the industry as well as in the audience.

Contracts usually lasted seven years and were written in the studios' favour. This was a major source of concern to the successful stars and the legal battles of stars like Bette Davis to gain freedom from her contract at Warners were an important feature of the arguments which led to the decline of the system. (You might want to link this to modern football stars contracted to clubs and arguing about 'constraints of trade'.)

In respect of the importance of stars to the economics of cinema, Dyer suggests four ways in which stars could be seen as important economic factors in the studio system:

- Stars were *capital*, just like plant and equipment, to be exploited. The major studios could preserve their position of dominance in the industry by gaining control over the production of stars and keeping control of those already formed. MGM claimed to have 'more stars than there are in the heavens' – and by default everyone else had less.

  > Your studio could trade you around like ball players. I was traded once to Universal for the use of their back lot for three weeks.
  >
  > Jimmy Stewart quoted in Bordwell *et al.* (1985)

- Stars were an *investment*, a security against potential loss. 'Added value' comes in here – a studio which had a cheap story (perhaps a remake) could add stars and offer it for sale as something more special.

- Stars were an *accounting outlay*, an important part of the budget. The hierarchy of stardom enabled the studios to devise ways of costing actors' time and to control payments. It was a way of negating the power of acting unions and of costing elements of the production process which would otherwise be nebulous (i.e. 'talent', 'expertise', etc.).

- Stars represented a way of organising *the market*. The star name offers an alternative to genre recognition as the basis for presenting a film to the public (e.g. 'John Wayne in . . .') and a readily identifiable image. In the most extreme cases this could be an 'iconised' image where only a part of the star's photographic image was necessary to

Figure 23.1 Bette Davis on the set of *Now, Voyager* (US 1942)

summon up the whole: the silhouette of Chaplin as tramp; Marilyn Monroe with skirts billowing over an air vent; Groucho Marx as a pair of spectacles and a cigar.

The star system could be an organising principle for **marketing**, even when a film had no stars. Today you wouldn't see a poster advertising 'a film about ordinary people featuring nobody you have ever heard of', but you may be attracted to a film offering 'a cast of fresh young talent, burning to be tomorrow's stars' or 'destined to become the next Tom Cruise, we present ...' The 'narrative of stardom' was part of the system and used as the basis for **biopics** and musicals especially, as well as in the numerous magazines.

This narrative is neatly summarised in an unattributed gem from *Halliwell's Filmgoers' Book of Quotes*:

(A casting director's five stages in a star's life)

1 Who is Hugh O'Brian?
2 Get me Hugh O'Brian.
3 Get me a Hugh O'Brian type.
4 Get me a young Hugh O'Brian.
5 Who is Hugh O'Brian?

[O'Brian was a 1950s leading man in relatively minor pictures.]

Since stars functioned economically, as commodities, for the studios, the star performance needed to be recognisable and saleable, sometimes via tie-in products such as costumes, make-up, hairstyles. (See Chapter 9, 'Advertising, marketing and fashion'). Stacey (1994) interviewed a sample of British female cinema fans who spoke of their enthusiasm not only for particular 1940s and 1950s female stars as identification figures, but of the pleasures of trying to copy the dress, hairstyles and make-up they wore in films. In wartime Britain, for example, the sight of abundant materials and beautifully made costumes might certainly be argued as one of the Utopian pleasures of Hollywood, as well as the Utopian 'community' pleasures of going to comfortable cinemas with others.

What is a star?

So far we have taken for granted that we share some understanding of what 'a star' was in the studio system (and still is to a large extent today). But it is not as obvious as it seems. Dyer argues that 'stars' are different to their images or personae, which deserve to be considered separately.

> Everyone wanted to be Cary Grant. Even I wanted to be Cary Grant.
>
> (Cary Grant, born Archibald Leach)

Dyer suggests there were four elements which contributed to the star persona:

- *Promotion:* what the studio let be known about a star, especially in the period when he/she was being 'groomed' for possible stardom. (One problem with Dyer's account is that this is often called 'publicity' by both the studios and by other histories.)
- *Publicity:* or public material about the star which was often, though not always, outside studio control, such as newspaper speculation.
- *Films:* including the 'star vehicle', specially built around the star image, involving roles, for example, which allowed Katharine Hepburn's lips to tremble, or Garland to do a wistful solo number.
- *Criticism and commentary:* including that written after the death of the star. In the case of Marilyn Monroe

or James Dean, this already exceeds what was written about them during their lives. (It also helps feed the reputations of modern stars marketed as being 'the second James Dean' and so on.)

John Ellis offers another interesting definition: 'a star is ... a performer in a particular medium whose figure enters into subsidiary forms of circulation, and then feeds back into future performances' (Ellis 1982: 91). This relates to 'subsidiary circulation' in newspapers and magazines in the studio era, and to TV appearances and tabloid publicity today.

The present/absent effect of the star

Ellis, drawing partly on psychoanalytic theory, argues that during the studio period, cinema offered an image which depended on being at once both 'present' and 'absent'. The film we see is obviously a recording of events – we are far removed from the actuality displayed on the screen. Yet the technology of cinema strives to make us feel 'present'. We sit in the dark knowing that what we see on the screen is a recording, but we enjoy becoming wrapped up in the 'now' of the events. This effect (which Ellis argues is much less strong with broadcast television which presents itself as 'live') works with stars in two interconnected ways:

1 The **secondary image** of the star in a magazine was both 'present' and 'absent'. Only part of the full image was available in the posed photograph or the voice on the radio (i.e. in the studio era pre-television) and this acted as an invitation to seek the full **star-image** in the cinema. Ellis defines the magazine image as incoherent, requiring a visit to the cinema to gain completeness. But, at the cinema, audiences still experienced the present/absent tension peculiar to cinema.

2 The major stars all straddled the divide between 'ordinary' and 'extraordinary'. They had to be at once unattainable and god-like on the screen and yet believable as the boy or girl next door, if audiences were to engage in the dream that perhaps they could meet or even *be* a James Dean or an Elizabeth Taylor.

The tension between the screen image and the secondary image in circulation must be there to perpetuate interest in the star – it is the delicious sense of striving for the unattainable which propelled audiences into the cinema.

Stars in circulation

If we take this more sophisticated idea of a star-image on board, it suggests that there was much more to 'stardom' in the studio system than simply the physical qualities of the actor, and we need to consider the role of stars not only in the production and consumption of film texts, but also in 'secondary circulation'. We should look at ideas about performance (which includes acting) and the perceived relationship between the actors themselves, their star-images and the roles they played.

There is a real debate around whether the studio stars could act. They were at the height of one branch of the acting profession, and yet it is often argued, usually of the biggest stars like Wayne or Monroe, that the bigger the star, the worse the acting. Do you think this is true? Might it be a way of devaluing popular cultural forms such as Hollywood? Or indeed of downplaying key qualities for cinema such as physical presence or beauty (an area of huge contemporary debate, especially in terms of dominant discourses around ethnicity)? It is certainly true that some very competent actors, beautiful by conventional standards, have never become stars.

Another way to approach this is to think of the skill with which star-image was used in a film. Richard Dyer refers to the playing of John Wayne and Henry Fonda who starred together in a John Ford cavalry western called *Fort Apache* (US 1948) (Dyer 1979: 165–7). Fonda was generally considered the superior actor and had a star-image which had developed from heroic but 'liberal' and 'democratic' roles. Wayne was a brash cowboy action hero. Ford cast Fonda against type as a martinet – a rigid, disciplinarian, senior officer. The tension in Fonda's role and his ability to 'act' it out contrasted effectively with Wayne's ability to 'look natural' and relaxed. (Think of Wayne's famous swaggering walk,

which served to mark him as a star. How many stars can you think of who are known by distinctive movements?) In fact, this required Wayne to maintain physical control over tiny movements of eyes or limbs, and the judgement about how or when to apply this. It can be argued that a 'reading' of *Fort Apache* depends on an understanding of both Fonda's and Wayne's star-image (and is made all the more intriguing by knowledge about their political views as 'real people'). Dyer points to other critical work which has explored the possible contradictions between roles, star-image and private life. Sergio Leone was clearly aware of the possibilities when he cast Henry Fonda, complete with 'baby-blue' contact lenses, as the sadistic killer in *Once Upon a Time in the West* (US/Italy 1968).

Dyer puts less emphasis on performance than on the way that stars always have a systematic relationship to dominant discourses or ideologies. For example Monroe's star-image, of the 'innocently sexy dumb blonde' formed a focus for audiences in the 1950s partly because of the way it related to an emerging **feminist** emphasis on women's capacity for sexual, as well as other kinds of independence and assertiveness. In such a context Monroe may have functioned as a kind of reassurance to men. (It is said that she never, in films or quoted statements, expressed desire for anyone, but seemed to be innocently the object of others' desire.)

Sometimes, the star-image was so important to the studio that it required suppression of any aspects of the star's 'real life' which might damage the constructed image. The most notorious examples of this concerned the gay actors who had to appear as 'sexually available' to female audiences. Sometimes the star-image crossed over into real life:

Rita Hayworth once turned to her best friend, the screenwriter Virginia Van Upp, when one of her marriages was breaking up and said 'It's your fault!' 'Why?' 'Because you wrote *Gilda*. And every man I've known has fallen in love with Gilda and wakened with me.'

The studio system demanded stars as part of the production system and although many stars received considerable reward for their work, they were on the whole treated like commodities. Modern stars face at least the potential for more control over their lives, both professionally and in private. So what has changed?

Stars in contemporary media

The end of the studio system didn't see the end of stars, but it did see a change in the way they were used. Three factors became important in the 1950s:

- 'Big' films were now promoted much more as single commodities, not as a continuous flow of studio product.
- Stars were breaking free from long contracts – they could select work more widely but they were not guaranteed work on the next 'studio picture'.
- The rise of television and later 'pop' or 'rock' music established competition for cinema as the premier 'star-making' industry.

As a result, we can see a number of consequences for the place of stars within the media industries.

- The 'star-machinery' is now controlled by agents and managers, rather than by studios. Does this give the star more freedom? Or are they still commodities?
- Stars probably make fewer films (or records or television shows) than they would have done under the studio system.
- There are perhaps more minor stars and less major stars – and 'making a star' is perhaps more difficult in the kind of media market which now operates.

Whether or not modern stars have such powerful star-images as those of the studio era is doubtful. You can do your own research by looking at the photo-books and posters available in your local shop or library. There are still an enormous number devoted to long-gone stars such as James Dean and Marilyn Monroe, to name the most obvious.

As cinema (or, more correctly, *film*) audiences increased in the 1980s, movie stars seemed to regain some eminence, but Ellis's present/absent tension does not seem as powerful. Modern stars make fewer films but more 'secondary' appearances, especially on television, where the 'complete image' has less resonance. Does the appearance of Demi Moore in just one or two films each year make each appearance more or less powerful if she is also seen on television talk shows in between? 'Live' appearances now tend to be more powerful, e.g. the attraction of Hollywood stars like Keanu Reeves on stage 'doing Shakespeare' – is this because television is such a mundane medium?

Ellis was writing in the early 1980s, at a time of declining cinema audiences, when it was often argued that the new 'stars' were to be found in pop or rock music rather than cinema. Recently critics have noted that the music industry has not successfully produced a new major star since Madonna or Michael Jackson. Might

Figure 23.2 Sylvester Stallone in *Judge Dredd* (US 1995)

this be because it has been too preoccupied rereleasing old material, and younger audiences are attracted to styles like dance music which don't produce stars in a traditional way? What of sports stars or supermodels, TV soap stars or 'star writers' (Stephen King is a good candidate)? How would you relate these to the writing around Hollywood stars of the studio era?

ACTIVITY 23.1
A modern star-image

How would you go about discussing the casting of Sylvester Stallone in *Judge Dredd*? Here we have a potential clash between a comic-book hero who is an established character (and perhaps relates to the 'star-image' of the artist or writer who creates him?) and one of the major action stars of contemporary cinema.

- What exactly is the current star-image of Stallone and how does it relate to the comic- book character – do they complement or contradict each other?
- Stallone has changed his image in the last few years after the failure of *Rambo III* and appears very aware of the different attractions of the 'masculine' male in 1990s cinema. (See Tasker (1993) and Holmlund (1993)).
- Is *Judge Dredd* part of this change? How does it relate to *Demolition Man*, Stallone's previous SF venture in 1993?

Stars and global appeal

'You're not a star until they can spell your name in Karachi.'

(Humphrey Bogart quoted in Pirie (1981))

The power of movie stars is tied to the worldwide marketing and distribution power of the Hollywood studios. Up until the recent spread of satellite television, cinema was perhaps the only truly international medium. American television series are also seen across the world, but the 'secondary circulation' of television stars is not co-ordinated (series may be five, ten or even twenty years old before they reach some markets) except on rare occasions, like the high point of *Dallas* transmissions.

Every few years, the trade paper the *Hollywood Reporter* surveys the bankability of stars and directors in the international market. Various industry professionals across the world are asked to mark stars out of 100 on whether or not they can carry a film on the star name alone. The latest set of figures (reported in the *Guardian*, 12 June 1995) suggests that the A+ list of stars is headed by five who score 100: Tom Cruise, Harrison Ford, Mel Gibson, Tom Hanks and Arnold Schwarzenegger. Just behind and still A+ are Clint Eastwood, Jim Carrey and Kevin Costner. Michael Douglas, Sylvester Stallone and Jodie Foster top the A list with 96 and are 'no problem if the director and budget are right'.

The A list comprises thirty-one names and is followed by a B+ list (other factors in the production may be more important than the star) with a further twenty-nine names. Remembering that this is an international list, it is interesting that only three stars who don't have English as a first language make the list (top is Jean-Claude Van Damme with 78). There are just sixteen women and five African-Americans, topped by Whoopi Goldberg with 81. Sean Connery is top Brit, with Daniel Day-Lewis, Hugh Grant and Anthony Hopkins also in the A list.

These entries (and omissions) tell us a great deal about the current state of stardom. Apart from confirming somewhat stereotypical assumptions about the film industry and its treatment of all groups apart from white American males, can you think of any other reasons for the outline listings given here?

The *Hollywood Reporter* carries out the same exercise for directors (also treated as star names who can sell a film internationally). The A+ list published in 1993 comprised just three names. James Cameron and Steven Spielberg were obvious choices, but third was Martin Scorsese. It is unlikely that Scorsese would have scored so high in America alone where his box-office record has been patchy. What do you think this suggests about the potential for the international market?

ACTIVITY 23.2
Box Office

Do some research on the top box-office stars during the studio era. You will probably discover that the most successful stars were not those you expected: during the 1940s, for instance, the Top Ten included comedians like Abbott and Costello and 'singing cowboys' like Roy Rogers and Gene Autry. This suggests not only that tastes change but that there are many factors working to produce 'box-office appeal'. Try and match your historical research with contemporary research at the UK box-office.

- Ask as wide a range of people as possible who is their favourite film star and why. Do their replies fit with the view of the *Hollywood Reporter* outlined above?

Action stars are privileged because their star-image loses least when their voices are dubbed into another language. (Non-American action stars benefit as well, e.g. Bruce Lee in the 1970s, Jean-Claude Van Damme recently.) Pop and rock musicians are equally privileged because 'the song remains the same'. Also, the relatively greater success of black performers in music has encouraged the spread of the star phenomenon in parts of the world where cinema and television are less important. (See Chapter 14, Case study: 'Bob Marley Superstar'.) The whole question of the impact of modern black Hollywood stars in the international market has yet to be properly researched. Bogle (1992) provides both a fascinating account of the struggles of black stars in the studio system and a coda on current cinema – but only from an American perspective.

ACTIVITY 23.3
Sports stars

It could be argued that the most universal media activity is that which shows pure action – the coverage of sports on television for instance. Take four sports: football, tennis, boxing and athletics.

- Which of these is most likely to produce a universal star – someone recognised all over the world?

You should think carefully about the popularity of different sports in different countries and with different **target audiences**.

- Has there been or could there be a sports star with as much appeal as the stars of the studio system?

Conclusion

We have concentrated on the mechanics of the star system and the theories about how stardom works as a focus for our interest. What you should note is that stars are both structuring devices in texts (refer to Chapter 3, 'Narratives' and Chapter 7, 'Representations') and a focus for audiences (see Chapter 29) as well as commodities to be marketed.

ACTIVITY 23.4

Test out your understanding of a particular star-image using the **Commutation Test** (Thompson 1978). This involves trying to imagine replacing one star by another in a particular role. It is a good party game and starting point for thinking about stars. Consider Stallone in *Rocky* (any one of the five versions) as the not very bright boxer from the streets of Philadelphia. Now try Eastwood in the role or perhaps Bruce Willis.

- Does the film still work in the same way? If it doesn't, what has changed?

You should be coming up with aspects of the star-image of both stars which don't match and therefore change the meaning. Try the exercise with your own pairings in other film examples. If nothing happens and your 'stars' are interchangeable, then they aren't stars at all. If they have a recognisable, distinct star-image, it will cause a difference.

References and further reading

Bogle, Donald (1992) *Toms, Coons, Mulattoes, Mammies and Bucks: An Interpretive History of Blacks in American Films*, New York: Continuum.

Bordwell, David, Staiger, Janet and Thompson, Kirstin (1985) *The Classical Hollywood Cinema: Film Style and Mode of Production to 1960*, London: Routledge.

Dyer, Richard (1979) *Stars*, London: BFI.

—— (1987) *Heavenly Bodies*, London: Macmillan/BFI.

—— (1990) *Now You See It*, London: Routledge.

Ellis, John (1982) *Visible Fictions*, London: Routledge.

Gledhill, Christine (ed.) (1991) *Stardom: Industry of Desire*, London: Routledge.

Holmlund, Chris (1993) 'Masculinity as Masquerade', in *Screening the Male*, Steve Cohan and Ina Rae Hark (eds) London: Routledge.

Pirie, David (ed.) (1981) *Anatomy of the Movies*, London: Windward.

Schatz, Thomas (1989) *The Genius of the System: Hollywood Filmmaking in the Studio Era*, London: Simon & Schuster.

Stacey, Jackie (1994) *Stargazing*, London: Routledge.

Tasker, Yvonne (1993) 'Dumb Movies for Dumb People', in *Screening the Male*, S. Cohan and I.R. Hark (eds) London: Routledge.

Thompson, John O. (1978) 'Screen Acting and the Commutation Test', *Screen*, vol. 19, no. 2.

24 Institutions

Have you ever visited a television studio and seen a programme being made? Contact with a real production process offers plenty of opportunities to learn about how media products are fashioned and something about the context in which they first begin to develop meaning. But what do you really learn about production? Quite a lot about the different stages of production, something about the technology and the techniques and everything about how the industry likes to present itself to the public. But what's missing?

What might you learn by slipping into the pub round the corner from the studio and eavesdropping on the conversation of the technicians? What might you learn about production from your own attempts to make a video in your school or college? More than likely, you will have discovered that apart from the obvious constraints of time, money and equipment, there are some other factors which you have to take into account. You may discover that all publications carrying the school or college name have to be vetted by a member of the senior management. Some parts of the school buildings may be out of bounds for filming. Equipment may only be available at certain times or may not be allowed off the premises. The other crew members may not turn up on time or may simply refuse to co-operate on the production. You have run into a set of institutional restraints – conditions of the educational environment in which you are trying to work. Every media producer faces something similar.

Defining 'institution'

'Institution' is a slippery term in media theory and it often gets confused with 'industry'. In this book we look at industry in a separate chapter, in terms of the economics of media organisations. We take institution as primarily concerned with **social, cultural and political relations**. (This distinction helps us to undertake an initial exploration of the issues within a clear set of guidelines. Later, you will need to integrate this work with that in other chapters.)

Institutional analysis is derived largely from sociology and is concerned with the social structure of organisation. Tim O'Sullivan defined institutions thus:

> enduring regulatory and organising structures of any society, which constrain and control individuals and individuality . . . the underlying principles and values according to which many social and cultural practices are organised and co-ordinated . . . the major social sources of codes, rules and relations.
>
> (O'Sullivan *et al.* 1994)

O'Sullivan here is referring to institutions generally, and in the lengthy entry from which these extracts are taken (and which you should certainly consult), he demonstrates how every aspect of our lives is in some way governed by institutional factors.

Think about the different kinds of institutions you already find familiar. The great 'institutions of state' such as the monarchy, the church, the law, etc. are recognisable by their outward signs of ritual and trappings of tradition. By contrast, the institutions which might be recognised as part of the Welfare State – education, the health service, the prison service, social security, etc. – are more likely to be characterised by the buildings in which the service is provided and the bureaucracy which administers them (we talk of 'institutional food' and of people being 'institutionalised'). A rather different form of institution is 'marriage' – a social institution, a formalised relationship between two people, recognised by society as serving a particular function. Media institutions are as varied in nature as these very different examples and may share several of their features:

Sit-coms and **soap operas** on television (and radio) are very often based on 'an institution' – think of all the comedies and soaps that have been based on hospitals, schools, prisons, etc. as well as social institutions like 'marriage'.

- Institutions are enduring – they are recognised as having been established for some time. They have a history that informs (and perhaps constrains) the present and the future work undertaken by them. There are no 'overnight' institutions.
- Institutions regulate and structure activities: they make rules and they suggest specific ways of working. In broad terms, institutions provide stability and preserve the status quo (although they can, of course, 'organise change').
- Institutions are, in one sense, collectivist. They constrain individuals and individuality in order to achieve a common goal. (But note that this goal may be that chosen by a small group or even an individual at the top of the hierarchy – institutions are not necessarily democratic.)
- Institutions develop working practices that have an underpinning set of assumptions about the aims of the institution and its ethos.

- All the people associated with the institution – directors, managers, employees – will be expected to share the values associated with the ethos and to behave accordingly in their relations with others, both inside and outside the institution.
- The wider public will be aware of the status of the institution and of their own expected relationship to it.

It might be helpful to think of media institutions in terms of set theory, where one entity might be contained in or overlap with another. So we could begin by taking the media as an institution, perhaps of the same order as 'education'. Then we might see broadcasting as a subset of 'the media', television as a subset of 'broadcasting', and so on. Other institutions might be organised differently. For instance, journalism might be considered as an institution according to the definition. All journalists will share certain ideas about what are proper journalistic practices. They may well share the same training and education and the same facility with certain items of equipment and techniques, even when they work for organisations which might otherwise be distinguished as 'television', radio or the press.

We could refer to **public service broadcasting** as an institution and this would include the BBC and Channel 4 – it wouldn't now include Channel 3 companies or BSkyB or any of the other satellite or cable programme providers which are currently under **light touch regulation**. We could refer to 'the press' as an institution, but it might be more useful to refer to **the quality press**, **the tabloid press** and **the regional press** as separate entities. Again, we could refer to advertising or photography as institutions. A media institution must by definition display the following features:

- It must have a defined code of conduct and a set of values shared by all the practitioners in the institution (and understood generally by audiences).
- It must include all the possible practitioners within its boundaries (there cannot be two separate institutions with identical features).
- It must be staffed by recognised professionals, whose education and training will effectively exclude casual intruders as new staff.
- It will set technical production standards (by default, if not by design) through the technology it uses.
- It will define its own **formal** characteristics – genres, styles, formats, etc.
- It must be recognised by its staff and its audiences as an institution.

Notice that all of these defining features are part of a process of exclusion or, to put it another way, a justification for separate existence. We can test out these ideas by taking an example – professional photography.

Photography and professional practice

Photography has been practised since the middle of the nineteenth century and it is now so widely used that almost every home has a camera or at least a collection of photographs. We can all be 'photographers' and yet we are very much aware that to be a professional photographer demands a command of special skills and in turn justifies a fee for commissions. Is it just a matter of skills? Can anyone develop the skills as part of their hobby and match the professionals? If you obtain the right equipment, can you produce professional results?

A few years ago an ad for an automatic camera played with this idea by reversing it. The comic actor George Cole was shown, armed with a whole array of hi-tech equipment, struggling to grab an image of a celebrity at a public function. Meanwhile, the famous 1960s photographer David Bailey upstaged him with a little automatic camera. The ad made its point very well – this (relatively) cheap little camera would let you take quality photographs in difficult circumstances, and it was so good that the professionals would use it. Like many ads the text works in a slightly contradictory way – we accept the basic premise, but we know very well that David Bailey usually uses a 'proper' professional camera, because he is a 'professional photographer'.

So how do you become a professional and what does it mean? As in most media industries, professional status depends on the right kind of experience and appropriate qualifications and training. These are likely to lead to membership of a professional organisation such as the British Institute of Professional Photographers (BIPP).

Experience relates to working in a commercial context, i.e. you sell your photographs or they are used by your employer in the provision of goods and services. Convince the Inland Revenue that your photographic activities are more than just a hobby and you will be recognised as carrying out a business. All of this suggests that anyone can become a professional, but the likelihood is that you may not be accepted as such by some potential clients (especially the bigger ones) unless you conform to their ideas about what constitutes 'professional'. For these purposes the right experience may mean working with particular equipment in a particular environment and according to a particular code of practice. Not unreasonably they want to know if you can handle the job: do you have the resources – financial and technical; can you meet their standards; can you meet the deadline?

The guarantee that you can do these things is your training and your membership of an association. Your training at a recognised 'education institution' will have assessed your abilities, not just in terms of using equipment, but also in 'professional practices'. Your membership of an association will have been vetted in some way and you will probably receive benefits such as financial and legal advice and discounts on goods and services. You will be a designated member of the institution.

Photography is an institution with clearly defined sectors, which in turn have led to quite distinct photographic forms. Most of these sectors will share some basic ideas about 'professional practice', but if we think of some examples – fashion photography, photo-journalism and medical photography – we can see that they are dealing with very different products and certainly different production environments. They will all demand a high-quality product, but the first will sell on its overall impact as an exciting image creating a particular mood or idea, the second on its immediacy and 'news value', and the third on precision in communicating information.

ACTIVITY 24.1

Take any two contrasting types of photography (e.g. a portrait photographer and a sports photo-journalist). Try and list the differences between them in terms of:

- their responsibility to their client
- the environment in which they work
- the equipment they might use
- a description of a typical working day
- what they might consider as a 'good photograph'.

This should give you some idea of what institution means in this context.

Each of the sectors will be supported by its own professional associations, specialist journals and competitions or award schemes. The leading exponents in each field will know each other's work. They will write about

'Amateur photography' can also feel like an institution, especially if it excludes 'outsiders':

> There is little in amateur or popular photography magazines to help us map our course. There, the concept of photography is limited, being addressed mainly to white heterosexual males. Not much is offered to women and the existence of working-class, black, or lesbian experience is barely acknowledged. It is orientated, primarily, to 'know-how' and assumes an interest in tourism, the landscape and glamour.

> (Spence and Solomon 1995)

the sector in general and review particular exhibitions or books. All this strengthens the sense of an institutional identity which effectively excludes outsiders and is not generally known to the wider public.

Occasionally the ethical issues that develop within the profession become visible to the rest of us. Think of the debates about privacy and the tabloid press. Some of the newspapers have attempted to set up codes of conduct for their staff photographers, which would define when it was acceptable to use a telephoto lens to capture images of the Royal Family. Photographers who saw themselves as professionals in other sectors (such as portraiture) would probably not consider such work as ethical and would not 'enter the market'. At the same time, some newspapers would be quite happy to purchase an image from a freelance, especially a freelance working out of another country, where the institutional constraints may be different (and where the laws governing privacy may be different too). The institutional issues for the newspaper editor are quite different from those of the photographic institution and include consideration of the degree of control surrendered up to the self-censorship of the **Press Complaints Commission**. This leads us into thinking about public accountability and the ways in which different media institutions handle it.

Journalism and partiality

Journalism is a useful institution to study because it straddles different media. The cub reporter at the gardening club show, the columnist on a national paper, and the foreign correspondent reporting for the BBC in Bosnia are all journalists. They share certain values and are subject to similar institutional constraints, but there are also important differences (see also Chapter 12 on selecting news).

Journalism is one of the few media activities with a history of clearly defined training routes for entry and progression through the profession. The NCTJ (National Council for the Training of Journalists) and the large regional newspaper groups have organised training schemes which allow journalists to start 'at the bottom' and learn their trade 'on the job'. To some extent, these schemes are now in competition with degree and postgraduate level courses which produce highly qualified entrants with less experience (an innovation not warmly welcomed in some parts of the industry). Nevertheless, most journalists receive an introduction to acceptable working practices with a strong institutional sense of what it means to be a journalist.

A beginning on a local newspaper is often the first stage on a progression through different media institutions, including local radio, regional television and then national newspapers, radio or television. The maintenance of journalism as a professional practice across the three media has been strengthened by the decision of the BBC to introduce the idea of 'bi-media journalism' (i.e. merging radio and television journalism training). It is also noticeable that Radio Five Live and other talk-based radio and television programmes are making increased use of print journalists as commentators and reporters. This has recently spread to the idea of a 'columnist of the air' during 1994 with television programmes fronted by Andrew Neil, ex-editor of the *Sunday Times* and Richard Littlejohn of the *Sun*.

Journalists in any medium share skills, knowledge and understanding about what makes a good story and how to produce accurate and interesting material to deadlines. However, the different media have different institutional constraints. Broadcast journalism has traditionally operated *impartially*, drawing on a sense of 'balanced reporting' as required by the charter of the BBC or the Independent Television and Radio regulators. (See Chapter 26, 'Case study: BBC and impartiality'.) By contrast, print journalists work in a more politically charged environment where stories clearly have 'angles' and columnists in particular are expected to represent the editorial line. This isn't expressed as partiality of course, but as 'comment'.

Before the changes in the national press which followed Rupert Murdoch's acquisition of the *Sun*, it was possible for popular newspapers to follow a particular editorial line and yet to employ journalists known to hold opposing views.

Lord Beaverbrook, while running an independent right-wing paper, the *Daily Express* from the 1930s to the 1960s, also employed people he admired such as Michael Foot (then a left-wing Labour MP) and the cartoonist Giles, despite their left-wing politics.

ACTIVITY 24.2

Over a couple of weeks try to read all the daily newspapers.
- Can you identify the political position of each paper?
- Can you find examples of reporting or comment which appears to contradict the editorial stance of the paper?

NB: Be careful here – just because a story criticises a Tory cabinet minister, it doesn't mean that it is necessarily an anti-Tory (or pro-Labour) story. You need to consider the ideological position that underpins the story (see Chapter 11, 'Ideologies').

Although it is still possible to find writers with opposing political views on broadsheets (especially in the *Guardian* and the *Independent)*, it is increasingly the case that the press is seen to be 'partisan'. This emphasises the difference between print and broadcast journalism, but also puts pressure on the broadcasters. Newspapers can 'set an **agenda**' on a particular story which is picked up by radio and television. Viewers and listeners then expect **impartiality** from broadcasters, but with the context of the story already set, it is difficult to 're-set' it. And with the increased competition in news presentation, ignoring the story may not be possible. The result is that broadcasters can be sucked in to a coverage they may not be trained or professionally inclined to handle.

We've used three terms for different sectors of 'the press' so far:

- *Broadsheet newspapers* are called that because of their size – the largest size commonly available for print products. In the UK, the national broadsheets (*Times, Telegraph, Guardian*, etc.) are all treated as 'serious news' papers, with a reading age commensurate with further education. This leads to the alternative term, quality press (i.e. the high quality of journalistic writing).

- *Tabloid newspapers* are smaller in size. The term 'tabloid' has generated a second meaning which refers to sensational stories and striking page layouts with large images and headlines which exploit the shape of the page. This second meaning tends to push tabloids 'downmarket' and has also been carried over to television where it again implies sensation and screaming headlines. But beware. In Europe, it is commonplace to find a 'tabloid-sized' paper which is 'serious' and the mid-market papers in the UK like the *Daily Mail* and *Daily Express* clearly decided that the gain from the 'manageability' and lay-out features of the tabloids outweighed the pejorative image when they moved from broadsheet to tabloid in the 1980s. Notice too that the *Independent* has followed the *Guardian* in producing a tabloid second section. 'Tabloid' and 'broadsheet' are also misleading when considering the regional press.

- The *regional press* describes all the newspapers apart from the twenty or so national titles based in London. These may be different sizes and morning or evening dailies or weeklies. In the case of the Scottish morning dailies, they may consider themselves 'national' rather than 'regional', but institutionally they all differ from what used to be called the 'Fleet Street nationals' because of their recognition of a specific 'local' audience and, most importantly, a local advertising market (see Chapter 10, with its 'Local advertising and newspapers' case study).

Talk Radio UK, which went on air in 1995, hoped to generate controversy through deployment of opinionated commentators. It is debatable whether these 'shock jocks' could be seen as 'journalists', but they are competing for audiences with phone-in programmes on BBC and ILR stations, which are on the whole fronted by journalists.

ACTIVITY 24.3

Listen to phone-ins during the same week on Talk Radio UK, a local radio station and either Radio 5 Live or Radio 4.

- Are all three conducted in the same manner?
- How does the presenter approach the issue in question?
- How are the callers treated?

Public service broadcasting

The concept of public service broadcasting has helped to distinguish British broadcasting from that of some other countries (notably the United States) for nearly seventy years. 'PSB', as we will call it for brevity, is a concept which has been developed over a long period of time and which has become deeply embedded in the minds of viewers and listeners. In Chapter 26 we offer a study of one aspect of the role of the BBC as a public broadcaster – as 'impartial' source of news at times of national crisis, when the relationship between broadcaster and state is most severely tested. Here, we look at the challenge to PSB represented by the 'market philosophy' of the Conservative government since 1979 and then at the broadcasters' problems in 'addressing the audience'.

BBC and independent television and radio

The BBC is established under Royal Charter and its funding comes from the compulsory licence fee paid by television and radio users – it is clearly a public sector organisation. The ITV and ILR companies are in the private sector as business organisations, but they have been considered as public service broadcasters because of the requirements of the franchise or 'licence to broadcast' which has required them to operate 'in the public interest' – independent television is a product of legislation rather than Royal Charter. The introduction of 'commercial television' (and later commercial radio), as it was known in 1955, had a galvanising effect on the BBC which became considerably less stuffy and decidedly more 'popular' as a result. Still, however, audiences up until very recently have tended to think of 'Auntie' BBC as opposed to a younger and more vibrant ITV. These ideas may now be changing, but they represent important challenges to both BBC and ITV/ILR managements.

Broadcasting Research Unit was an independent agency, housed in the British Film Institute and funded by both the BBC and IBA and independent research groups. It operated between 1980 and 1991.

PSB is not easily defined, but O'Malley and Treharne (1993) provide a checklist of features put together by the **Broadcasting Research Unit** during the 1980s. PSB should be:

- universally available throughout the country
- cater for all interests and tastes
- cater for minorities
- have a concern for 'national identity' and community
- be detached from vested interests and government
- be one broadcasting body financed directly by the body of users
- promote competition in good programming rather than in numbers
- be run on guidelines which liberate and do not restrict programme makers.

This is more useful for our purposes than the traditional definitions which simply quote the relevant sections of broadcasting legislation or the BBC's Charter. In this list we can identify all the sources of debate about the future of broadcasting which have developed since the mid-1980s when the 'market philosophy' was first brought to bear by the Thatcher government.

If we take the first three points in the list together, we can discuss them in terms of the provision of a **universal service**, which is provided according to need rather than profit. The same argument applies to most of the privatised utilities. A public service provision implies that every consumer is entitled to the same service despite the difference in cost of supply – the low-cost services effectively subsidise the high-cost ones. The easiest analogy is the postal service. We all expect to send and receive letters with the same charge for a stamp and the same guarantees on delivery whether we live in a London suburb or a remote Scottish island. This issue surfaces in media terms in many guises – the 'capture' of popular sporting events by BSkyB is a good example of the 'equal **access**' to a service being replaced by the willingness to pay for an encrypted service.

We look at **national identity** issues in Chapter 26, 'BBC and impartiality', and the next two features are touched on in Chapter 27, 'Independents and alternatives'. What is at issue here is the 'independence' of the broadcaster based on a secure income, which nevertheless makes the broadcaster 'accountable' to viewers. The supporters of PSB would argue that under the regime which existed up to 31 December 1992, the BBC and ITV network operated in this way. The result was a mix of programming which included experimental and minority interest work alongside mainstream material. Financial security also allowed potentially critical material about government policies to be developed without fear of reprisal through financial penalties. In the current environment, the financing of ITV (Channel 3) is now much more uncertain, with competition from cable and satellite and the possibility of takeovers by outside media groups. The BBC faces real cuts in income which we discuss in the next section. This isn't just a question

Hollywood directors Michael Apted and Stephen Frears reminisced about the exciting times and creative freedom they enjoyed at Granada and the BBC respectively in the 1960s and 1970s in *A Personal History of British Cinema* by Stephen Frears BFI/Channel 4, 1995.

of economics, but of the working environment itself – the 'creative' staff in the broadcasting industry are now aware that their ways of working and perhaps their jobs are no longer secure.

Finally we can take the last two points together and consider the impact on the types of programmes being made. There is a great deal more on this issue in Chapter 20, 'Industries' and Chapter 22, 'Producing in the studio system', but here we will concentrate on the importance of **ratings**. The role of ratings in the broadcasting industry is a good signifier of the nature of the system. In the US, ratings are all-important – a drop of a few percentage points is enough to cause a show to be rescheduled or even cancelled. The opponents of the market philosophy fear that this is beginning to happen in the UK as well. Where once a new programme was given one or two series to gather an audience, now if the first series is not an instant hit, there is a danger that there may never be a second series. The consequence of this is a big investment in 'star' names and 'formulas' in the hope of attracting audiences early to a new series. This strategy can backfire alarmingly as the BBC discovered when the much-promoted soap *Eldorado* was cancelled. Is this an example of a PSB beginning to behave like an American broadcaster?

Instruments of institutional change

Changing an institution takes time and the Thatcher government instigated a debate on British broadcasting which began in the early 1980s and is still running. The move to a market philosophy began with the **Peacock Report** of 1986, which suggested a number of ways in which the finances of the BBC could be altered with a view to making the corporation more 'business-like'. The major public issue brought up by Peacock was the possibility of advertising on the BBC. Vociferous opposition led to withdrawal of this suggestion, but the damage to the certainty of future PSB had been done and the discussion of BBC finances moved the debate inexorably towards 'free market' ideas. One subtle move was to tie licence fee increases to the Retail Price Index (RPI) – the annual inflation measure. Since broadcasting costs traditionally rise faster than RPI, this was a 'cut' in funding without anyone noticing (and therefore put pressure on BBC managers to find alternative income). The BBC Charter has to be renewed every so often. It was last achieved in 1980 and the next renewal must take place before December 1996. The debate about the PSB ethos of the BBC has therefore been running for some time and will culminate in a decision, probably before you get to read this book.

One of the major factors that will influence the debate is the selection of the senior personnel at the BBC. In 1986 Margaret Thatcher appointed

The Peacock Report was the result of an enquiry led by the economist Alan Peacock. The context for the enquiry was a continuous attack on the BBC by right-wing policy groups and newspapers. The government was able to play on the image of the BBC as 'extravagant, left-of-centre and managerially incompetent' (see O'Malley and Treharne 1993).

Advertising on the BBC is not obviously in the interests of some of the groups who appeared to be advocating it. The major newspaper groups, for instance, might possibly lose revenue in competition with a 'commercial BBC'. The total advertising spend in the UK is relatively fixed so with more outlets, advertisers would possibly be able to negotiate rates down.

'one of us' (her famous phrase to describe people who agreed with her politically) as chair of the BBC governors in the form of Marmaduke Hussey. He was reappointed in 1991 and was widely seen to be influential in the appointment of John Birt as director-general (the senior executive post) in 1993. Many of the changes in the BBC are seen as 'Birtian' and as representing a new era. Before the 1980s the director-general was assumed to be a strong PSB supporter and was usually free from any suggestion of 'political control' by governors who generally represented a broad spread of political opinion.

The **Broadcasting Act of 1990** introduced a number of changes affecting independent television, including the move to a 'light touch regulation' of what is now called Channel 3. In PSB terms, the major change was to release Channel 3 from the obligation to act as 'a public service' in respect of the range of programming (the charge remains with Channel 4). One of the other changes was the **25 per cent production quota**. This also affected the BBC as it required all terrestrial broadcasters to commission 25 per cent of broadcast material from 'independent producers'. Opening up the broadcast market was welcomed by many small and not-so-small independents (see Chapter 27), but its main consequence for the broadcasters was to bring pressure on production units which would now perhaps not be fully employed. The result was the 'headcount reduction' policy (i.e. making redundant large numbers of staff, who might be invited back on a freelance basis). The BBC then went one step further, as if to meet the free-marketeers head-on, with the introduction of **producer choice**. This allowed producers to use outside production facilities, if these could be shown to be less costly than remaining 'in-house'. This is the idea of 'the internal market' which has also been introduced in the health service and the education service. These two measures have had a number of direct consequences:

- The production base of the BBC and the major Channel 3 companies has shrunk.
- British broadcasters can no longer make some types of programmes without co-production deals, often with overseas broadcasters.
- There are more small independent companies with broadcast production experience.
- Broadcast staff are now more likely to be freelance or employed on fixed-term contracts.

The Broadcasting Act 1990 provides the basis for the broadcasting environment in the UK after its implementation in 1993. It will be remembered primarily for setting up the franchise bidding process which created the new Channel 3 network amid controversy over the inconsistent way bids in different regions were handled.

The broadcasting unions

There are several similarities between the experiences of the print and television unions during the 1980s. Like the print workers, staff in television production were often regarded as craft workers with strict demarcation of graded posts according to job function. The broadcast unions were able to negotiate very tight regulations for what constituted a recognised crew on a broadcast shoot. The result was the development of a workforce with high levels of specialist skill. Broadcast (and film industry) work was virtually a 'closed shop' with all recognised technicians requiring a union card specifying a job grade. The overall effect of this was to create a unique production environment in which work of very high technical quality could be guaranteed and with it a degree of creative freedom for writers and directors who could rely on efficient production practices. In protecting their members' jobs and working conditions, however, the unions (including the actors' union Equity) could also be seen as acting as a brake on any rapid change in the nature of broadcasting production (and programming).

The two main broadcast unions (BETA and ACTT) merged to become BECTU in 1991. This strengthened bargaining power through co-ordination of negotiations, but the environment had changed dramatically with the shift to independent production and the gradual move to 'multi-skilling' within the BBC and ITV companies, which has broken down much of the specialisation. (See comments on ENG (Electronic News Gathering) in Chapter 18, 'Technologies'.) BECTU has become much more concerned about the training of freelances and has slowly come to accept that the changes in work patterns brought about by deregulation and the adaptation of new technologies have to be negotiated.

Broadcasting now looks much more like a competitive industry. Those employed in broadcasting and those with a financial stake in the companies concerned will obviously feel strongly about whether this is a 'good thing' or not, and so will anyone concerned about 'the role of the market'. But what of the viewers and listeners (we should remember that radio has been similarly affected)? Does it make any difference who makes the programmes and under what kind of institutional constraints or ethos?

Broadcasting unions The National Union of Journalists (NUJ) and Equity were joined in 1991 by the Broadcasting, Entertainment, Cinematograph and Theatre Union (BECTU), which replaced the former Association of Cinematograph, Television and Allied Technicians (ACTT) and the Broadcasting Entertainment Trades Alliance (BETA).

The broadcasters and the public

The changes outlined above do cause headaches for the broadcasters. How should they treat the audience – as licence-fee payers, entitled to a public service or as 'customers' in the broadcasting marketplace? (Again, it is the same issue which sees rail travellers complaining of being labelled 'customers' rather than 'passengers'). The Channel 3 chiefs have tried to 'give the customers what they want' while maintaining an idea of quality programming which harks back to the range of programming offered by

ITV before 1993. They recognise that one of the strengths of PSB was the
security it offered to make high-budget and sometimes quite
experimental or controversial programmes. In the face of increased
competition from cable and satellite (i.e. competition for advertising), the
Channel 3 companies can't afford such programmes now, but they hope to
still be able to sell the possibility or the memory of such programming.
(For discussion of 'quality' broadcasting see Brunsdon (1990).)

BBC chiefs face similar problems. They are still officially required to
operate within the PSB framework while becoming more market-
orientated. This has produced some oddly schizophrenic performances
from senior BBC staff in public meetings, as they try to satisfy both
demands. We will explore their problem briefly with reference to BBC
Radio.

BBC Radio: who is the audience?

Radio 1 was, until 1995, the single most popular radio station in the UK
and it still represents one aspect of the BBC's institutional stance – the
provision of 'quality popular programming' to a mass audience.
Providing a service on the basis of 'something for everyone' when there is
little obvious competition is relatively straightforward. From the early
1970s up to the late 1980s, the only effective competition for BBC Radio
was a handful of large local independent radio stations such as Capital in
London and Piccadilly in Manchester. These stations did take some of the
mass audience for popular music in the big cities, but they could not
compete nationally with Radios 1 and 2. However, as more radio
franchises began to be awarded, including specialist music stations and
ethnic community stations and finally national franchises such as those
won by Classic FM and Virgin, the impact on BBC Radio could not be
ignored.

Radio 1 had other problems as well. Much of its audience in the early
1990s had grown up with the station and had been listening since its
inception in 1967. This meant that the audience profile for the station
was growing older and that, in catering to them, Radio 1 might be
alienating younger listeners who would be more likely to defect to the
new stations. The dilemma for Matthew Bannister, the new Radio 1
Controller, was how to keep the broad audience (a 'weekly reach' of 16
million listeners in the first quarter of 1993) and, at the same time,
compete with smaller, but more narrowly focused, independent stations.

Faced with such a problem, most radio stations in the commercial
market would be governed by clear business motives – build the audience
profile which advertisers want to reach. This is not an option for the BBC

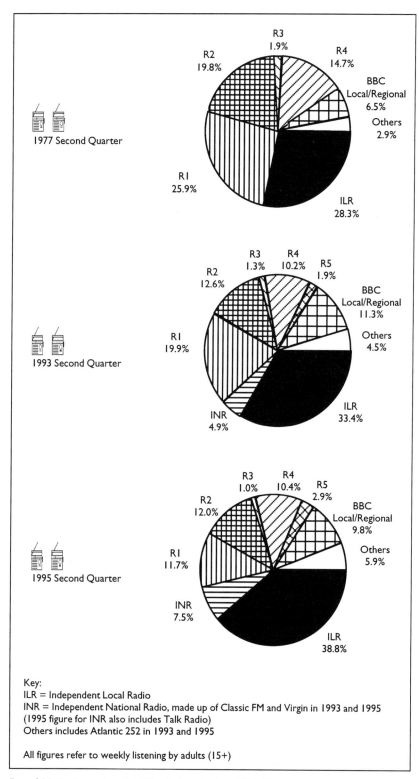

Figure 24.1 Audience shares for UK radio broadcasters, 1977–95

– or at least not in the direct sense. Strategic decisions at Portland Place (HQ of BBC Radio) have become much more linked to concepts of target audience under the Birt regime – so much so that explicit comments have been made about the assumed audiences for the different BBC Radio channels. Radio 2 has been clearly announced as aimed at a '50 plus audience', while Radio 1 is said to be looking for the younger (under 30?) audience. This appears to leave the 30–50 age group in the cold.

Radio 4 represents the most traditional aspect of BBC radio and it is not surprising that many of its programmes have been running for more than twenty-five years (i.e. from the time of the 'Home Service'). Programmes such as *The Archers, Gardeners' Question Time, Desert Island Discs, Woman's Hour, Any Questions?* and the *Today Programme* are almost institutions in themselves – setting broadcasting standards and attracting loyal (and somewhat fanatical) audiences. All of these programmes have been changed in some way and these changes have in turn created an outcry from disgruntled listeners. The causes of complaint and the way in which they have been reported and handled are indicators of a change in the overall approach of the BBC towards its radio service. The BBC has found itself reacting defensively.

In some cases, such as the prospect of 'rolling news' on Radio 4 Long Wave, it has given in to what have often been organised middle-class revolts. In this instance a decision was taken to move the new service to Radio 5 and to lose much of the experimental work, especially in children's radio which that new station was developing in 1993. In audience ratings terms, this decision has been vindicated. Radio 5 Live, combining sport and news, has proved to be very successful. However, the loss of the previous experimental Radio 5 represents a setback for PSB ideals and there is a lingering suspicion that both the Radio 5 models could have been developed. On another occasion, Radio 4 chiefs decided to 'call the bluff' of its stars on *Gardeners' Question Time* who threatened to defect to Classic FM. They left, a new team emerged, and the ratings stayed roughly the same. (In the meantime the Classic FM approach to music clearly caused a rethink at Radio 3.)

ACTIVITY 24.4

Try to listen to three or four broadcasts of *Feedback* on Radio 4 (15 mins broadcast with a repeat). This is the 'open access' or **right of reply** slot for BBC Radio listeners.

● Who are the listeners who write or telephone in to the programme?
● What kinds of issues do they want to raise? How do their concerns differ from those expressed on similar *television* programmes (e.g. *Points of View*)?

- Often, BBC producers or controllers are asked to justify their decisions. How do they approach this?
- The programme is made by an Independent Company. How much do you think this allows a genuine criticism of BBC policy?
- What you should get from this exercise is an insight into how the radio audience views the BBC *as an institution*.

It is clear from past *Feedback* programmes and from the criticism and correspondence in the press that at least one part of the radio audience has strong feelings about what kind of BBC they want (although they don't necessarily all agree on what they want). The situation facing BBC Radio managers is impossible – they can't hope to provide PSB *and* meet **marketing** targets. They must make compromises.

Censorship and respect for the audience

PSB and 'free market' ideas have been presented here so far as polar opposites, but we need to go a little further into the complexities of the free market position. We might want to consider the idea of a 'social market', i.e. a competitive market in which social policies or constraints play a role. In media markets this is quite noticeable in respect of ideas about 'acceptable media products' and the need for 'self-censorship' by media institutions. This goes beyond broadcasting to include print media and cinema.

'I always obey the rules. The BBC rule is that you refer upwards when in doubt. I am seldom in doubt. I don't play games. I simply believe management are much too busy with their enormous problems to be concerned with my small pre-occupations' (Tony Garnett, then a BBC producer. Quoted by Richard Paterson, 'To the limits of Ordinary Address', BFI Summer School material, 1982).

In a 'free market' we might expect to see a thriving trade in pornographic material, as is the case in many European countries, if that is what people wish to buy. However, the very advocates of the free market are often amongst those who wish to control access to the marketplace for certain kinds of products. The result is that in terms of 'sex and violence' we expect to see the development of some form of self-censorship in all media, whereby the distribution companies in that medium agree to set standards for acceptable products. This has happened with film, magazines and more recently video and computer games. It is also largely what happens in broadcasting, where producers are not usually censored as such but attempt to second-guess the regulators in terms of what might be considered acceptable. The Broadcasting Standards Council has been added to this process since 1993. This body, set up by the 1990 Broadcasting Act, has little obvious purpose unless it is to replace the rigour of self-censorship which might have been expected to have been carried out under a PSB remit.

The oddity of the debate about sex and violence in broadcasting (or in print or on film) is that the issue is rarely put to the market test. We don't know what would happen if 'hard' material were freely available – if it is unacceptable to a large number of media consumers, perhaps 'the market' would drop it from general release when it didn't sell? There are many pressure groups arguing for censorship but few actively campaigning against. One argument might be that the current attitude to self-censorship is patronising towards the audience. If someone is capable of making a decision about whether a media product represents 'value for money', why can't they also decide whether or not it is offensive and 'liable to corrupt'? And if they can't decide, what makes a programme-maker better qualified to decide? This is the argument as presented by the libertarian right and is a complete refutation of PSB, without the qualifications of the social market position.

ACTIVITY 24.5

Censorship of offensive material

How do you think censorship of offensive material should be handled in the media? How would you define 'offensive material'? Try to study all the possible arguments:

- What would be the consequences of a media environment without any censorship of offensive material? What do you think would happen in a free market?
- What are the arguments for and against such material only being available through licensed outlets at premium prices (could it be taxed like cigarettes and alcohol)?
- What are the arguments for banning such material altogether?
- Why is self-censorship preferred to an 'official censor' in UK media industries? This topic is a good one to choose if you want to try producing a video or audio 'debate' style programme. You should quite easily find people prepared to adopt specific positions. But first you will have to decide whether it is going to be a 'balanced' programme, or whether as producer you want to slant it in any particular way – in other words, you need to think about the institutional factors.

Censorship in relation to political issues is handled rather differently by UK media institutions. Once again the main burden falls on the PSB sector, which is expected, as part of its role, to uphold access to the media for a range of viewpoints and to present them within a broadly balanced programme schedule (see the 'Selecting and constructing news' case study (Chapter 12)). PSB is always attacked by politicians in power, by either of the main parties. As we have seen, one strategy employed by government to undermine broadcasters is to introduce subtle changes to the funding environment. A second is to conduct a public campaign of criticism in an attempt to move public opinion against broadcasters. In this respect the assistance of newspapers with a similar agenda is useful. In the face of sustained criticism, broadcasting chiefs are made to feel defensive and may be persuaded to act in particular ways.

This 'bad-mouthing' can be accompanied by occasional physical actions which can be very destructive. In 1987 a BBC programme about British spy satellites was not broadcast because the tapes were seized under the Official Secrets Act. Usually, the UK authorities avoid being seen to censor. The stark evidence of censorship – a blank page in a newspaper – is often self-defeating, drawing attention to what can't be said. The best example of this was the ban on the voices but not the image of various people from Northern Ireland before the ceasefire in 1994. This crazy situation ('an actor's voice is reading the words of Gerry Adams') serves as evidence that the workings of media organisations are as much to do with institutional factors (in this case a total misunderstanding of broadcasting by government advisers) as those of technology or economy.

References and further reading

Brunsdon, Charlotte (1990) 'Problems with quality', *Screen,* vol., 31 no.1, spring.

Langham, Josephine (1993) *Lights, Camera, Action!: Careers in Film, Television and Radio,* London: BFI.

O'Malley, Tom and Treharne, Jo (1993) *Selling the Beeb,* London: Campaign for Press and Broadcasting Freedom.

O'Sullivan, T., Hartley, J., Saunders, D., Montgomery, M. and Fisk, J. (1994) *Key Concepts in Cultural and Communication Studies* (2nd edn), London: Routledge.

Rose, John and Hankin, Linda (1989) *Running Your Own Photographic Business,* London: Kogan Page.

Spence, Jo and Solomon, Joan (eds) (1995) *What Can a Woman Do With a Camera?,* London: Routledge.

25 / Case study: News Corporation

Rupert Murdoch
News International
Murdoch 'the demon'
Quality and integrity
Diversity and choice
Oligopoly power

In this chapter we look at the way one media corporation has become the focus for a series of debates about ownership and control in the UK media environment. The major 'player' in the British media environment is News International. Confusingly, this is the UK operation of a global company, **News Corporation**. Unusually, for such a large company, it is the undeniably charismatic founder and 'hands-on' proprietor, Rupert Murdoch, who is the focus for interest. Over the last twenty-five years, Murdoch has become a demonic figure, not only in his native Australia and the UK, but also in the United States and no doubt soon in Europe and Asia as well. We want to ask why this demonisation has occurred and whether it is justified.

Rupert Murdoch

Rupert Murdoch was born in 1931 in Australia. He inherited a stake in News Ltd, publishers of the *Adelaide News* and, in what sounds at times like the narrative of a **biopic;**

> After forty-two years of relentless struggle, in which he has run the gamut of nationality laws, regulators, politicians and bankers and even – for a brief time in 1990 – the threat of bankruptcy, [he] has all but arrived where he always wanted to be: at the top of the global media pile.
>
> (Alex Brummer and Victor Keegan, *Guardian*, 13 May 1995)

In 1985, Murdoch took out American citizenship in order to extend his American interests by meeting federal requirements. In 1995, his activities appeared to be coming to a climax as a series of major media stories appeared in the world's press:

- In the UK, fears grow that News International will bid successfully for the Channel 5 franchise, granting Murdoch a first terrestrial TV channel.
- These fears are expressed in a UK government White Paper on cross-media ownership, widely perceived to be designed to prevent News International gaining a bigger share of the UK media market.
- News Corporation announces an international deal involving the exclusive sponsorship of Rugby League Football in the UK and Australia with plans to broadcast games by satellite over Star TV in Asia.
- Following the Rugby Union World Cup, Murdoch is involved in the 'professionalisation' of Southern Hemisphere Rugby and consequent television deals.
- In the US, News Corporation enters into a joint venture with MCI, No. 2 in long-distance telecommunications. News Corporation's 'software' (Fox films and TV) will travel down MCI's **fibre optic** cables and around the world in conjunction with BT.
- In Italy, Murdoch is 'headed off' in an attempt to buy into the media empire created by Silvio Berlusconi. Rumours also abound that Murdoch is attempting to buy into Ted Turner's operation.
- In Asia, Murdoch is seen to do deals with the Chinese government over news broadcasts and to expel the BBC News service from Star TV which he has acquired the year before.
- Murdoch is invited to make industry speeches in the UK and is widely interviewed and profiled with

attention focused on his increasing domination of UK media production.

- Murdoch invites the British Opposition Leader, Tony Blair, to meet News Corporation Executives in Australia. Controversy surrounds whether a British politician should accept the offer – he goes none the less.

News International

Murdoch began his collection of British media products with the purchase of the *News of the World* and the *Sun* in the 1960s (ironically, the *Sun*, formerly the *Daily Herald*, had been the newspaper owned by the trade union movement). Initially, Murdoch simply copied the best-selling paper of the period, the *Daily Mirror* and then added extra sex and sensation. Expansion came in the 1980s with the purchase of the *Times* and *Sunday Times*, and the launch of Sky Television.

In moving the newspaper offices from Fleet Street to Wapping, Murdoch successfully took on the print unions (with the help of the Thatcher government's anti-trade union legislation). It was the long-established work practices of these unions which had previously prevented a rapid conversion to 'new technology' in newspaper production and the consequent forced redundancies of printing workers.

As part of the war against the unions, Murdoch also ensured his newspaper distribution by making a deal with TNT (in which he bought a 12 per cent share), the road transport carrier company. With his own carrier, he could avoid potential problems with rail unions. At the other end of the process, he could ensure a good supply of 'news' and skilled journalists because of his widespread interests elsewhere. With the purchase of *Today* (founded in the mid-1980s as the first newspaper to be produced using new technology by Eddie Shah – himself a Murdoch figure of lesser stature), Murdoch achieved a 'full house' of **tabloid**, **mid-market** and **broadsheet** daily papers as well as the best-selling tabloid and broadsheet Sunday papers. Add to this his newspaper interests in Australia, the United States and elsewhere, plus his television interests in the UK and the United States (where he owns 20th Century Fox Film and Television Studios plus the fourth network of TV stations) – not to mention the book publishing and specialist magazine titles. It is not too difficult to see that Murdoch can fill his papers with stories derived from his film studio or that he can find the talent he needs within his existing staff or pay to entice it from elsewhere.

This last point, the purchasing power in the marketplace is crucial to the News International operation. The high risk factor in media production can

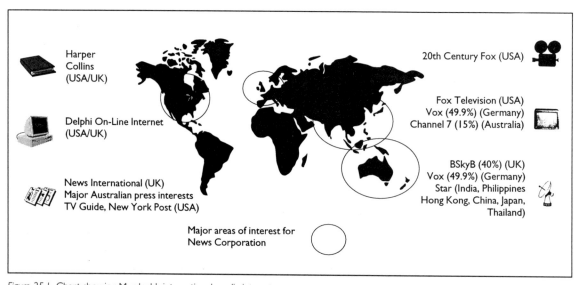

Figure 25.1 Chart showing Murdoch's international media interests

be covered if 'cross-subsidy' is possible. This means that one successful newspaper title can subsidise another which is losing money. In the Murdoch empire, the 'milch cows' – the sources of fat profit – are the *Sun* and the *News of the World*, which make enough money to support the losses on the *Times* (and on some of Murdoch's American papers). In return, the *Times* gives News International status and greater access to AB readers. (One problem for Murdoch in the early days of Sky was that it was seen to be 'downmarket'. Listings for Sky programmes and sympathetic coverage of the output in the *Times/Sunday Times* help to correct this view.) The newspapers originally helped to pay for losses on Sky TV, and now that Sky is becoming profitable (after its merger with BSB), the returns from that can be used to subsidise other areas of operation.

In competitive markets, the major battle is over the entry of new firms or new products into the marketplace. Economists refer to the theoretical 'perfect market' as one in which new sellers are free to enter the market and compete on equal terms with existing sellers for the attention of perfectly rational consumers. In the new market-speak this is known as 'a level playing field' scenario, but in reality, even if the field is flat and open, the biggest players always win the game and they can also manipulate the rules as well.

During 1994 and 1995, Murdoch used his considerable reserves to fight a price war, in both the tabloid and broadsheet markets. The object of the war was simply to destroy one of the current opposition titles and seriously to damage the others, while enhancing the market position of the Murdoch titles. The chosen broadsheet victim was the *Independent*, one of only two new daily newspapers in the last forty years. At the time of writing, the *Independent* is still in business, but looking shaky.

Winning and losing in the Price War

News Corporation accounts for 1994 show a loss of £45 million in the UK newspaper operation, but this was matched by a rise in profits (to over £186 million) at BSkyB in which News International holds a 40 per cent share.

The new strategy for advertising was to increase rates by 15 per cent while guaranteeing to advertisers that the *Times* would not drop below 600,000 circulation or the *Sun* 4 million.

Worldwide, News Corporation saw a general fall in profits from print-based media, but a big rise in film and television profits – further ammunition for Murdoch's well-known belief in the future of television at the expense of print.

(Source: the *Guardian* report on News Corporation Annual Statement, June 1995.)

Murdoch can afford to lose millions on the *Times* in order to lure readers away from the *Independent* and the *Daily Telegraph*. The *Guardian* is relatively safe from Murdoch, not just because of the political stance of its readers, who are the least likely to defect to a right-wing paper, but also because it is supported by the revenue from its successful regional stablemate, the *Manchester Evening News* (and further cross-media interests in GMTV). The Guardian Media Group's purchase of the *Observer*, however, is beginning to look like a very risky venture and more direct competition with a rampant *Sunday Times* may lead to disaster. The *Independent* has been forced to lose its 'independence' in order to fight off the Murdoch attack and now it is part-owned by The Mirror Group and various European newspaper interests.

The other aspect of this 'entry to the market' is the possibility of access to the crucial distribution channels. Most publications that appear on the news-stands are handled at wholesale by two main distributors, W.H. Smith and John Menzies, who also directly own many of the news-stands. If they won't take a publication – and they can be very choosy if they don't like the content or if they have no faith in the appeal to readers – it will be impossible for the new entrant to compete with Murdoch because no one will get to see the product. The power of the distributors is evident when new types of

Football: UK (sold worldwide)
Cricket: UK, West Indies, India, Pakistan, Sri Lanka, Australia, New Zealand, South Africa, Zimbabwe
Rugby League: UK, Australia, New Zealand (sold to Asian satellites)
Rugby Union: UK, Australia, New Zealand, South Africa (sold to Asian satellites)
American Football: Americas and Japan

These are just some of the sports over which News Corporation has acquired rights at various times. They will be screened live in territories where News Corporation's own channels operate and the live rights sold to channels in other territories. Competitors like BBC Sports can purchase recorded highlights.

Figure 25.2 News Corporation and world sports coverage

publication do break through, gain acceptance onto the news-stands and immediately become very successful – the obvious example is *Viz* in the late 1980s and, to a lesser extent, fanzines such as *When Saturday Comes*.

Internationally, News Corporation cannot afford to stand still or one of the other major players will take market share away. In 1995 Murdoch's intervention in the future of Rugby League had an enormous impact in northern England. To many diehard fans who had supported a small-town team for decades it was almost incomprehensible that their game (one of the last to be rooted in local communities) could be taken away from them in order to allow Murdoch to compete with another media corporation in Australia (led by Kerry Packer) and to provide coverage of a top-class sport at low cost for the new Murdoch satellite empire in Eastern Asia. But this is just one example of how the 'national' or 'sectional' interest is swiftly superseded by that of the multinational corporation.

Murdoch 'the demon'

Rupert Murdoch attracts a great deal of media attention and a high level of criticism. He has been called 'the most powerful man in the world' and also the most dangerous.

He is the demon of British media producers and consumers alike – invoked as the cause of most of our

To some Murdoch is 'the dirty digger' (an ironic form of stereotypical abuse in keeping with the style of the *Sun*?), to others 'the Citizen Kane of the global village' (*Guardian*, 13 May 1995) or the 'prince of darkness' (*New Statesman and Society*, 10 September 1993).

troubles. There is evidence to suggest that he has had a considerable effect upon the media environment, but to blame him for everything is a crude response to a complex situation. News Corporation is a major player in the international media market and acts accordingly.

Chapter 20, 'Industries', demonstrates that large media corporations are just like large businesses in other fields. They cannot survive as playthings of rich 'barons'; instead, they will be constantly looking for better ways to increase their wealth-earning potential. Sometimes this will mean buying new companies or even running businesses at a loss in order to win market share. Sometimes it will mean selling businesses in order to raise cash or to move to more profitable markets. Murdoch is skilled in these operations. A few years ago News Corporation was in serious financial difficulty but astute business dealings brought it back into the black (others might note that the accounting methods employed by News Corporation are not widely publicised).

One of Murdoch's strengths in maintaining the position of News Corporation in the marketplace is a conviction about where the industry is going and a resolution to act on that conviction. His success in predicting the future is chilling for critics concerned about his expanding empire. Here is his view of the future:

> we cannot just confine ourselves to being newspaper publishers, or just to television, or terrestrial television, or to pay-television or whatever it is. We are a software company, we believe that what is important and what will always have value are databases, knowledge and books, a copyright if you will – whether it be copyright film, books or news. We have to make sure that we have access to all the different delivery systems that are emerging.
>
> (*Money Programme* Interview on BBC2, reported in the *Guardian,* 22 May 1995)

Rupert Murdoch does not get everything his own way. He is not personally responsible for what happens in his newsrooms or studios. When asked by a BBC interviewer which party his newspapers would support in the next UK General Election, Murdoch replied that the editors of the *Times* and *Sunday Times* would decide for themselves, but that he expected the *Sun*'s editor to 'consult with me and I will have some input into that'.

ACTIVITY 25.1

What do you understand by this different approach by Murdoch to the editorial stance of his UK newspapers? Was he just making a joke perhaps? Which of the following might explain the reason for differentiating between the titles?

- the difference in circulation figures
- the perceived difference in class position and 'normal' voting intention of readers (half the *Sun*'s readers normally vote Labour)
- the space for political comment in a broadsheet as opposed to tabloid newspaper.

Try to look at the *Times* and the *Sun* on the same day.

- Do they both treat 'political' issues in the same way?

When we first wrote this chapter, *Today* was the Murdoch paper most likely to support Labour. In closing *Today*, Murdoch cut a loss-making title, freed up printing capacity and released valuable newsprint so that the *Times* and the *Sun* could compete more effectively with their rivals. Closure did mean, however, that Murdoch was approaching a potential Labour election victory without a Labour-leaning title in his stable.

It is worth noting that despite the criticism of Murdoch as a media mogul and the overall charge that News Corporation has 'lowered standards', the *Sunday Times* and the *Sun* are skilfully produced newspapers which lead their respective markets as much because of professional expertise as sensational stories or low price. In a famous defence of his staff, the then editor of the *Sun*, Kelvin Mackenzie, once claimed that although his staff were quite capable of producing the *Guardian*, he didn't think it was true the other way round. *Guardian* staff were not quick to refute his claim.

What is at stake here (and in similar debates about television and radio) are concepts of 'quality', 'integrity', 'diversity' and 'choice'. These are complicated, ideologically loaded ideas, which you should consider in relation to Chapters 11, 20 and 24 (Ideologies; Industries; Institutions). Let's consider them here in relation to the charges made against Murdoch.

Quality and integrity

Broadsheet newspapers in the UK, at least at national or regional level, are referred to as the '**quality press**'. The debate over the future of the BBC and the franchising of Channel 3 has concentrated on arguments over 'quality television' and the 'quality threshold' which prospective franchise holders must cross. (See Chapter 24, 'Institutions', for definitions of tabloid, quality press, etc.) In a wider context, most UK organisations during the 1980s (including your school or college) have issued 'quality statements'. There are two, possibly opposing, ideas about quality in broadcasting (see also Brunsdon (1990)):

- The **quality document**, now found in most organisations refers to some form of accounting or auditing procedure which looks for evidence that services are meeting preordained targets. To a certain extent, this meaning carries over to broadcasting where targets were initially set for the frequency of news programming, the amount of arts programming, etc. But with the advent of 'light-touch' regulation from the ITC, these targets are less defined.

- For many media producers and consumers, 'quality' is something that distinguishes **public service broadcasting** from more clearly profit-driven operations. Broadcasting quality might then refer to:
  - relatively high-budget programming, designed specifically for broadcasting on that channel
  - coverage of social and cultural issues relevant to the broadcasting context (i.e. the concerns of the specific audience)
  - a wide variety of different kinds of programmes, each with a distinct purpose (to entertain, inform, educate, etc.).

On the newspaper front, 'quality' refers not only to the writing style found in the broadsheets, but also the integrity with which journalists pursue stories and present findings.

The charge against Murdoch is that he has undermined the quality ideal in the UK national press and that he threatens to do so with terrestrial television as well. Dropping the price and introducing up-market bingo in the *Times*, sensational stories in the *Sunday Times* (e.g. the Hitler Diaries fiasco, when large sums were paid for documents which turned out to be fakes), as well as the wholesale corruption of the tabloid market (in the mid-1960s, the *Daily Mirror* was widely seen as a 'quality' tabloid) have all contributed to this view. The battle over the move to Wapping was fought out with journalists as well as printing workers. Many distinguished journalists left News International titles, which were in turn boycotted by readers (e.g. the *Times Educational Supplement*, which also lost advertising to the *Guardian*).

Murdoch's defence against these charges is that without his intervention, the quality press would have succumbed to television. It was hidebound by tradition,

poorly designed, expensively produced and losing readers. The Murdoch 'victory' over the print unions benefited all the papers in that they too could move out of Fleet Street into greenfield sites with new technologies. The shake-up in the market made possible the launch of the first new quality broadsheet daily this century in the *Independent* and prompted major redesigns of the *Guardian* and the *Daily Telegraph*, as well as the *Times*. The broadsheets went on to introduce colour, Saturday supplements and two-part daily papers. They did lose some readers, but not significantly large numbers.

The new sections of the qualities do not necessarily contain quality journalism and the charge that quality newspapers have become more interested in traditionally tabloid material may have some foundation. For a more objective view of the quality press it is worth making a comparison with other national markets. The UK is unique in the number and range of national newspapers available to readers across the country. In the US for instance, the only national newspapers in a British sense are the tabloid *USA Today* and the gossip sheet, the *National Enquirer*. The qualities, like the *New York Times* and the *Washington Post*, are city newspapers which, because they emanate from the financial and political capitals of the country, have some form of national circulation. Newspapers of all types are declining in the US and in most cities there is no competition for readers. In only thirty-six cities can you find more than one newspaper available.

'It is no coincidence that the great American broadsheets all look as if they were laid out in the fifties; no impudent challenger like the *Independent* has ever forced them into a facelift.'

(Ian Katz of the *Guardian*, July 1995)

US newspapers have proportionately fewer readers than in the UK and the qualities are more ghettoised. Their dull style would not attract the broader range of readers expected by UK qualities.

Sky News and Sky Sports have been innovative television channels in the last few years. Sky News provides a rolling news service from a UK base (i.e. in competition with CNN) and carries a full range of news stories. Sky Sports has expanded to two channels and has certainly introduced new ideas into coverage of traditional sports like football and cricket. Even if these are not available to large numbers of viewers, the innovations they bring are diffused through changes in BBC and ITV coverage. Murdoch's main concern as proprietor has been to bulldoze the 'level playing field' which enables News Corporation to operate unilaterally. Since the merger with competitor BSB, Murdoch holds only 40 per cent of the new company. This still makes him a powerful influence in the company, but we should remember that there are other corporations with a stake in BSkyB as well, including Pearson and Granada.

Diversity and choice

The major claim of the free market supporters is that **deregulation** allows competition, which in turn will lead to greater diversity of material available in response to consumer demand. In the debates of the late 1980s, which resulted in the loosening of regulations in radio and television in the UK and elsewhere, Murdoch was a vociferous supporter of 'consumer-led' television programming.

Between 1985 and 1995 there has been an undoubted increase in the number of media products and distribution systems available in the UK. Besides *Today* and the *Independent*, there have been a number of failed national newspaper launches such as *News on Sunday*, the *Sunday Correspondent* and the *Post*. Murdoch's price war will undoubtedly claim more victims eventually, with the *Daily Express* and the *Sunday Express* as two of the weakest titles. The UK tradition will probably help to maintain a selection of titles longer than in other countries, but Murdoch himself has little faith in the future of newspapers in the face of television and electronic media generally.

The big growth has been in cable and satellite television. Although only a minority of viewers has chosen to access the new channels, there has been enough of a take-up to register on the TV ratings:

> In Summer 1995, the total share of the viewing audience claimed by all the new channels (i.e. not BBC1 and 2, ITV or Channel 4) was around 9% (source: *Broadcast*). This is less than either BBC2 or Channel 4, but the figure is rising and is up from around 7% the previous year. If satellite and cable channels are increasing share, where is it coming from? The clear losers are ITV and BBC1 (BBC2 and C4 are also increasing share).

But do more channels mean more diversity and more choice? The standard cable package with an extra subscription to take the full range of BSkyB and other encrypted channels offers viewers over thirty new channels. This is how they break down into rough categories:

News: 5 (Sky, CNN, Euronews, Channel One, NBC Superchannel)
Music video: 4 (MTV, MCM, VH-1, CMT)
Films: 6 (Sky Movies, The Movie Channel, Sky Gold, TNT, HVC, Adult)
Sport: 3 (Sky Sports, Sky Sports2, Eurosport)
Light entertainment: 3 (Sky1, Family, Live TV)
Other language channels: 8 (DSF, Sat-1, RTL, TV5, GalaVision, Asianet, MBC, ZeeTV)
Gold/cult TV: 2 (UK Gold, Bravo)
Lifestyle: 4 (Discovery, UK Living, Travel, Performance)
Children: 3 (The Children's Channel, Nickelodeon, The Cartoon Network)
Shopping: 1 (QVC)

These channels are not available on all cable networks and there may be others available on yours. A 'raft' of new channels including Disney and Paramount is planned and will be in operation when you read this.

If you have the cable package, check out all the channels to get a flavour of what is on offer. If not, get hold of a satellite listings magazine (the newspapers and the normal TV listings guides don't give that much information).

● What is new – not available on the four terrestrial channels?

● What is missing in these channels, which you would find on the terrestrial channels?

● What do you think of the choice on offer? Is there now greater diversity or simply 'more of the same'?

Diversity and choice are subjective matters (which is why you should try the activity above and not rely on what commentators tell you). What is clear though is that the new channels have not offered much so far in the way of new UK-made programmes, unless they are relatively low-budget productions. Much of the new series programming on Sky1 or The Family Channel, for instance, is imported North American or Australian material. Apart from the access to European or Asian language channels, most of the new programming is American (and much of what is shown on the German RTL satellite channel is also American

series programming). Here is where 'quality' meets 'choice'.

Murdoch's critics are going to have a case as long as BSkyB fails to fund new 'quality' programmes (i.e. drama series or documentaries to complement sports coverage). At the time of writing, following a consistent run of profits, BSkyB has announced a £100 million investment on material commissioned from Granada, Thames and independents (*Broadcast*, 8 September 1995). If this means a future commitment to the UK ideal of 'quality programming', Murdoch will have answered his critics, at least in regard to BSkyB.

Oligopoly power

The central charge against is that too much of the UK media market is dominated by News International activities. Whatever side we take in the quality/choice debate, we must always be concerned if one organisation has a very large slice of the market and therefore has the potential to exert some control over how the market operates. The market share chart (Figure 25.3) is derived from figures put out by the British Media Industry Group which comprises the Pearson Group, the Telegraph, Guardian and Associated Newspapers (*Daily Mail* etc.) – not exactly an independent group, representing as it does other players in the market. Perhaps less subjective views are represented by **ABC**, which gives News International 37 per cent of the daily newspaper market and ITC/**BARB**, which sees BSkyB with 4 per cent of the television audience.

The major concern which underpins the cross-media ownership debate is that News International could buy an existing broadcaster or acquire a new terrestrial franchise and build up television interests to match those in the national press. There is now in place a very complex web of rules to prevent any group gaining such control directly. However, there are several other features of media ownership in the UK which the concentration on Murdoch tends to obscure:

● The merger of any two from several other UK media groups could produce a market share to equal that of

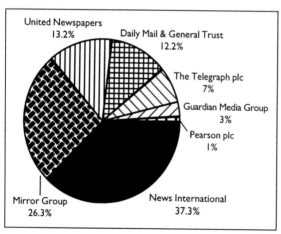

Figure 25.3 Market shares of media corporations in the UK

News International (e.g. Pearson and Associated Newspapers together would control 10.1 per cent of 'national voice').

- Although the major players in the UK market are openly competitive, they also have stakes in each other's businesses (e.g. Pearson has a stake in BSkyB and in Yorkshire Television).
- Other large global corporations are gaining a strong position in UK media markets (e.g. Time-Warner in cinemas, TCI in cable, various groups in publishing, etc.).

What this adds up to is an oligopoly position in which News International is the biggest local player, but not the biggest global player. The UK marketplace is becoming more deregulated and the strength of public service media is declining (look at Chapter 24 for discussion of the public service ethos). An open market will mean domination by the shrinking number of powerful oligopolists. The entry of small independents into the marketplace will become more and more difficult, unless they are sponsored by a major.

References and further reading

Brunsdon, Charlotte (1990) 'The problem of quality', *Screen,* vol. 31, no. 1 spring.

Williams, Granville (1994) *Britain's Media: How They Are Related,* London: Campaign for Press and Broadcasting Freedom.

Most publications in this area date very quickly. The only way to keep abreast of changes in ownership is via the news and financial pages of the quality papers and trade journals such as *Broadcast.*

| Impartiality and the |
| General Strike of 1926 |
| The BBC in the modern |
| era |
| Conclusion |

26 / Case study: The BBC and impartiality

Possibly the most familiar media institution in the UK is the BBC – a large and powerful **public service broadcaster** (PSB), funded by individual viewers through a licence fee. The Royal Charter which set up the BBC, and which will be renewed again in 1996, requires impartiality in the presentation of news and current affairs. The clearest test for the BBC's impartial approach comes when a potential dispute arises between the BBC and the state, i.e. government policies or actions. In this case study we compare the way in which the idea of impartiality was established when the BBC was first set up, and how it figures in the contemporary environment. (You should read this chapter in conjunction with Chapter 24, 'Institutions' and Chapter 12, 'Case study: Selecting and constructing news'.)

> *impartiality*: the presentation of a 'balanced' viewpoint which does not favour either side in a dispute. The BBC is required to maintain impartiality and balance across the range of its programming. This implies an **objectivity** in reporting that many would argue is impossible to achieve – nevertheless the attempt is required.

Impartiality and the General Strike of 1926

The BBC began life in the private sector in 1922 when a government licence, granting a monopoly of radio transmission, was issued to the British Broadcasting Company. The company was private, but it was regulated and the government retained the legal right to take control at any time. In 1926 the United Kingdom came as close as it has ever done to a revolutionary state when the Trades Union Congress (TUC) declared a General Strike to support mineworkers and for nine days the future direction of the country hung in the balance. This was the first major event in which the BBC was to play an important role and the development of the institution as we know it can be traced back to this period.

The tiny band of pioneer radio listeners in 1922 grew rapidly and by early 1926 there were over one and a half million sets in use. Loudspeakers were introduced (the first sets required headphones) and each radio set in a public place could expect a large audience. Both sides in the dispute recognised the potential role of the new medium. Would the company simply assume the government side? Would it be prepared to report the strikers' version of events?

The national newspapers were shut down during the strike but the Conservative government was generally well prepared and was able to put out a newspaper called the *British Gazette*, enthusiastically edited by the chancellor of the exchequer, Winston Churchill, the most hawkish anti-strike minister. The TUC had its own newspaper, the *Daily Herald*, but this too was shut down by the strike and had also had its last pre-strike issue (along with its paper supply) seized by the police under the Emergency Powers Act, on the grounds that it contained an article proposing jamming the BBC signal if it were to be used for government propaganda. Eventually, after lengthy negotiations with the printing unions, who felt they were being asked to break the strike, the TUC Publicity Committee managed to produce the *British Worker* in London and several provincial cities. Even so, Churchill had the resources to distribute three times as many copies of the *British Gazette*.

As the offending *Daily Herald* article suggests, the TUC and most strikers assumed that the BBC would be taken over by the government and, at first, instructions went out to trade unionists to ignore radio bulletins. Churchill was indeed eager to control the BBC, but Prime Minister Baldwin believed that the Managing Director of the BBC, J.C.W. Reith (later **Lord Reith**), could be relied on to: 'reinforce the authority of the government without broadcasting anything which might exacerbate class tensions or appear overtly **biased**' (Morris 1976). Reith, in turn, was keen to retain the independence of the BBC at a crucial time in its early development. Over lunch the 'impartiality' of the BBC was born. Reith agreed to be guided by Baldwin with the threat hanging over him that if he wavered, it would be impossible to stop Churchill seizing the BBC. As a result, the BBC refused to allow any trade unionists or the Labour Party leader to make broadcasts. It still maintained the *possibility* of non-government material being used and the TUC Publicity Committee sent in some news reports which were used in broadcasts.

Organised workers remained sceptical about the BBC and there is evidence to suggest that the TUC's warnings were taken to heart, so that few of the incorrect and false interpretations of the strike's success which were broadcast had any impact on morale. It was the mass of the general public which was caught in the middle of the dispute and for whom the BBC might have offered another voice in a media landscape otherwise occupied only by the *British Gazette* and the *British Worker* (and the provincial papers which did manage to get into print, and which were largely on the government side). In retrospect, Reith's decision to maintain the independence of the BBC was valid. There is little doubt that the Company gave more credence to the government side, but it is not remembered as having done so directly. This is the view of the Labour historian, Margaret Morris:

The virtue of the BBC during the strike was not its impartiality – it was clearly acting to support the government – but its calm tone. It helped to dispel rumours of riots and violence and to undermine the belligerent elements on the government's side ... it took a very down-to-earth approach to the strikers, and attempted to generate a cheerful, stoical spirit among the rest of the population.

(Morris 1976)

Eight months later the BBC was brought into the public sector and incorporated under Royal Charter with Reith as the first director-general, running the service he had hoped to achieve before the strike. The other notable feature of broadcasting during the strike was the flair for 'speaking on the radio' shown by Prime Minister Baldwin – often acknowledged as the first politician to recognise the power of radio to 'sway public opinion' (at a time when there were no opinion polls).

The experience of the BBC during the strike is an important early indicator of what was to follow in the history of the developing relationship between broadcasting and the state, and represents the first stage in the institutionalisation of PSB:

● the establishment of 'impartiality' as the expected position of the broadcaster
● the use of the medium by the prime minister to speak directly to the public
● the broad appeal of broadcast news (by the end of 1926 over 2 million sets were in use with an audience which might be estimated at between 5 and 10 million)
● the development of a concept of 'public opinion' which can be addressed directly by the broadcaster.

The new corporation gained its status very quickly and although it was primarily a middle-class institution, it was able to act as a cohesive force in society. The popular historian, A.J.P. Taylor (who himself would later utilise the power of television to reach a wide audience) was in no doubt about its cultural role:

in no time at all the monopolistic corporation came to be regarded as an essential element in 'the British way of life'... Like all cultural dictatorships, the BBC was more important for what it silenced than for what it achieved. Controllers ranked higher than producers in its hierarchy. Disturbing views were rarely aired. The English people, if judged by the BBC, were uniformly devout and kept always to the middle of the road.

(Taylor 1965)

D.G. Bridson commented, when asked to join the BBC: 'In 1935 I mentally bracketed it [the BBC] with parliament, the Monarch, the Church and the Holy Ghost' (quoted in Curran and Seaton 1991).

The BBC in the modern era

Seventy years after the General Strike, the world is a very different place. The BBC and the media environment in which it operates have also changed, yet in many ways the 'Reithian' ideal of impartiality and attitude to government has remained. One major change in the media environment is the competition in news and current affairs presentation offered by ITN since the mid-1950s and by Sky, CNN and other international services since the 1980s. These organisations also face 'institutional constraints' on their news and current affairs output, but they don't carry quite the same 'baggage' of **national identity** as the BBC. For many viewers and listeners, the BBC is still the authoritative 'voice of the nation' – a status which derives from its long history of PSB and especially for older audiences, its role during the Second World War. This history is kept alive by contemporary dramas and documentaries about wartime. During 1995 these were highlighted by the VE and VJ Day celebrations in which BBC newscasters 're-ran' wartime broadcasts in the style of contemporary television news.

From the late 1960s onwards the impartiality of the BBC began to be tested by political events in new ways. We can identify three different examples of long-running news stories where the BBC found itself in direct conflict with the state:

- the protracted labour disputes of the 1970s and 1980s, culminating in the 1984 miners' strike
- the coverage of the conflict in Northern Ireland (and now the struggle for peace) since 1969
- the Falklands/Malvinas War of 1982.

We don't have the space to explore any of these in detail, but it is worth considering what has changed since 1926 and how the institutional nature of the BBC has developed. British society has gradually moved from a period of high conflict in the 1920s through a long and slow process to the comparative consensus of the 1940s. The process is then reversed and by the 1970s, 'consensus' has broken down. In the same period the BBC, born in the conflict, gradually established itself as an authoritative voice (see the quotes from A.J.P. Taylor and D.G. Bridson above), reaching a high point in the 1940s and gradually declining from that position ever since. We need to be careful not to be too glib in making these very general statements but they are useful in thinking through the relationship between the BBC and the state.

The same question which faced the British Broadcasting Company in 1926 was still around during much of the Thatcher government's time in office. Was there a middle ground in the major disputes? Could, and should, the BBC give equal weight and coverage to those opposing the government? Would 'standing up to the government' threaten the independence of the BBC? The situation was made more complicated when the government labelled its opponents 'enemies of the state', thereby implying that there was no 'middle ground'.

Margaret Thatcher rejoiced at victory over the Argentinians in a war which many in the UK thought should not have been fought. She then termed the miners 'the enemy within', dividing the country. The conflict in Northern Ireland produced not just two opposing sides 'on the ground', but a third position on the mainland – yet all were UK citizens. How can the BBC be impartial in these conditions, when government assumes a 'we' which does not exist?

In Chaper 24, 'Institutions', we looked at how the Thatcher government deliberately tried to undermine the status of the BBC as part of an attack on PSB before deregulation. There is a clear link between the undermining of the BBC's management and finances and its ability to broadcast stories about opposition to government. At the same time, for many commentators outside the BBC, the coverage of such stories as the miners' strike was far too biased in favour of the government side. The BBC response to such claims has typically been that if both sides in a dispute are criticising its broadcasts on the grounds of bias, then it must be 'getting it right'. Do you think this defence makes sense?

> The concept of 'balance' is very slippery and the decisions which broadcasters are forced to make can in hindsight seem very misguided, although at the time they may have appeared at least 'pragmatic'. In one famous incident in the 1970s, a BBC current affairs programme decided to show a documentary film, made secretly in South Africa, which depicted the miseries of apartheid. To provide 'balance', the producers invited the South African Embassy to participate in the programme and they chose to show a 'positive' travelogue about the country which ignored apartheid. This attempt at balance looks pathetic in light of the ending of apartheid, but at the time the simple equation of two 'opposing views' might have been argued to have allowed the issue to be aired and in the anger it caused in audiences may actually have helped the anti-apartheid movement.

There are other factors in the contemporary media environment which also influence the ability of the BBC to adhere to an impartial approach and to maintain its status as an authoritative news source:

- New technology in news gathering has taken many of the decisions about what to broadcast out of the hands of the BBC or the politicians who might wish to suppress particular items. Satellite technology is not bound by borders and the secrecy laws in other countries are not as strict as in the UK. Something banned in Britain may be freely available in the Library of Congress in Washington.
- The BBC has many more competitors for the privilege of speaking to the British public – not just ITV and Channel 4, but also CNN and Sky. Where the BBC may in the past have not accepted an interviewee as 'safe', now that person may turn up on a rival station. The BBC can't assume a position of cultural authority by excluding groups of people (as it could in the 1930s).
- Broadcasting has lost much of its mystique in the last twenty years. People who regularly appear in news and current affairs programmes are increasingly able to manipulate and control their own representation – forcing interviewers to ask specific questions or introducing a new agenda of their own. This applies to 'protestors' such as Greenpeace as well as politicians.
- Public opinion is now something that is constantly sought, analysed and evaluated. It is not controllable by the broadcaster.

All of this means that the BBC is no longer in a 'unique position' to 'speak for' the nation – if it ever did – although there are still viewers and listeners for whom this is a worthwhile aim. The media environment is much more complex and sophisticated than it was seventy years ago when John Reith led the BBC towards a position of authority based on independence from the state (but also aligned to an ideology of social superiority). The writer Stuart Hood, once a BBC employee and aware of the intense political pressures on news and current affairs staff, despite the outward appearance of a smooth-running impartiality, summed up the situation in the 1970s like this:

> In practice it is the expression of a middle-class consensus politics, which continues that tradition of impartiality on the side of the establishment so clearly defined by Reith. Impartiality is impartiality within bounds and is applied to those parties and organisations which occupy the middle ground of politics; where impartiality breaks down is when the

news deals with political activities or industrial action which are seen as being a breach of the conventions of consensus.

(Hood 1972)

Conclusion

The BBC is in a difficult position in the 1990s, especially in terms of its relationship with government. Many of the problems are similar to those of the fledgling company in 1926. The future of the corporation is not secure. A long-running government which has deregulated the market place, but maintained a large element of **public service broadcasting** can still threaten to withdraw licence fee monies or to demand that airtime is sold. This threat hangs over any future attempt by the broadcaster to criticise government in the name of impartiality. However, without the monopoly of cultural authority it enjoyed in the 1920s and faced with a competitive broadcast market and a fragmented audience, how can the corporation maintain the loyalty and the support of its audience in any future struggle with the state? Was opting for the National Lottery broadcast on a Saturday evening a good decision? Should the BBC go for more or less news and current affairs coverage? These questions have far-reaching consequences for the relationship between state, broadcaster and audience.

You can best test your understanding of these complex issues through exploration of a contemporary impartiality issue:

ACTIVITY 26.1

In April 1995, just before the round of local authority elections, the BBC got itself into a damaging crisis involving its claim to impartiality. An interview with the Prime Minister, at a time when his position as Party Leader was being threatened, was scheduled to be broadcast on *Panorama* a few weeks before the local election campaign. The Scottish local elections were earlier than those in England and the broadcast was scheduled for the Monday preceding the Thursday voting day. The Opposition parties asked for the broadcast to be postponed, arguing that it was unfair in giving a platform to the Conservatives on the eve of the election. Eventually, Labour took the case to the High Court who issued an injunction preventing the broadcast in Scotland until after the election. Many commentators pointed to the seriousness of the court case, which called into question the status of the BBC.

- Find out as much as you can about this incident (from newspaper archives), which proved to be a great embarrassment to the BBC management in London.
- Which of the points about the changing media environment mentioned in this case study are particularly relevant here?
- What effect do you think the public reaction to BBC policy in this case is likely to have had on the institutional status of the BBC?

References and further reading

Curran, James and Seaton, Jean (1991) *Power without Responsibility: The Press and Broadcasting in Britain*, London: Routledge.

Hood, Stuart (1972) 'The Politics of Television' in Denis McQuail (ed.) *Sociology of Mass Communications*, London: Penguin.

—— (1980) *On Television*, London: Pluto.

Morris, Margaret (1976) *The General Strike*, London: Penguin.

Taylor, A.J.P. (1965) *English History 1914–45*, London: OUP.

27 Independents and alternatives

Most discussion of media production and consumption involves the **mainstream**: large-scale activity, with a clear commercial purpose, driven primarily by a profit motive. 'Independence' is often presented as an attractive, rebellious place completely outside the commercial compromises of that mainstream. It may seem odd, then, to ask you to think of this 'mainstream' as in some ways a minority part of total media production. All of us produce media texts on a regular basis, even if we don't recognise them as such, and many media producers prefer to work to different priorities and to challenge many of the drives of the 'mainstream'. This chapter looks at some of these **independent** producers, mostly in the area of film and video, although our emphases and approaches apply equally to radio, photography and music.

Non-mainstream media might include educational and training material, parish newsletters, fanzines and the whole range of 'amateur' and hobbyist material which might range from a few 'snaps' to sophisticated film narratives.

Myths of independence and authorship

If you are surprised to learn that the multi-million pound company **Thames Television** is now technically an 'independent' it is partly because the word 'independent' still has strong romantic connotations of being completely 'free', 'creative' and 'outside'. These come in the end from powerful myths of **authorship** and independence which often get in the way of thinking about the actual problems and possibilities of independent production today. So we'll first look briefly at the history of this powerful emphasis.

Thames Television Once an ITV broadcaster and therefore a UK 'major', Thames lost its franchise to Carlton and is now an 'independent producer' for Channel 3, and other broadcasters.

Authorship

The idea that 'the author' is the source of meaning and value in artistic texts has been a persistent one. We talk of **Shakespeare**'s plays or **Austen**'s novels in ways that suggest that William Shakespeare and Jane Austen are uniquely gifted and independent individuals, solely responsible for everything in their work. This view of art credits the author with power through having genius, and/or special experience, and emphasises the individual and 'special' over the social and the shared. This individualism is part of the world view that accompanied the rise of capitalism in Europe in the mid-sixteenth century (Murdock 1986). Until then, the idea of Creation was reserved for God's act of creating the world. Cultural producers such as painters thought of themselves and were treated as merely skilled craftsmen making useful objects. Painters now celebrated as 'geniuses', like Botticelli, were quite happy to design wedding chests and decorate banners – as well as to produce the paintings which later critics have celebrated so differently.

But towards the end of the sixteenth century, culminating in nineteenth-century **romanticism**, artists began to be credited with rather special powers and described via some of the assumptions which had previously been reserved for God:

- No longer just a craftsman, the artist increasingly had 'gifts' which were attributed to divine inspiration.
- Accordingly, artists were seen as 'like God' in so far as they too were now understood as Creating from the Void.
- Flowing from this was an emphasis on the separation of the 'True Artist' from his or her social setting, including the other people they worked with and for. All that was of interest was what 'the creative individual' was able to make from nothing, or against all odds, by means of the 'vision' or 'inner promptings' or 'talent' they had been 'blessed with'.

Figure 27.1 Why do you think this logo is chosen for a prestigious arts programme?

The image in numerous **biopics** (biographical pictures) is of the artist/author working in the garret, wild-eyed with solitary inspiration, and often hollow-cheeked because of concentration on higher things than how to earn enough to eat. Countless tales, films, TV serials of artists such as the Brontës or Van Gogh (favourite suffering examples; see Figure 27.2) have emphasised the virtues of unworldliness, solitude, the pre-industrial nature of paint or quill pen, rather than struggles over contracts, or with publishers and exhibitors, let alone existing and powerful conventions in chosen media.

It's relatively easy to argue for individual inspiration if you're focusing on an apparently lone painter or poet. But once industrial, technological

Figure 27.2 Kirk Douglas as Van Gogh in *Lust for Life* (US 1956): a favourite image of the artist as an outsider, a loner, suffering for art

and mass production of art takes place, such positions become less satisfactory. Typical mass-media products like films, television programmes and CDs are produced by numbers of people often employing complex technology.

The problem of authorship in the mass media has been most substantially confronted in the context of the cinema. In its early history, cinema was dismissed as an art form precisely because films were produced by groups of people (directors, writers, cinematographers, editors, sound recordists, etc.).

A group of French critics writing in the magazine *Cahiers du Cinema* in the 1950s argued that the director was the artist in the film-making process and suggested that a close scrutiny of the films of directors like Alfred Hitchcock or Roberto Rossellini revealed that they expressed a vision of the world in the same way as Shakespeare did in his plays or Jane Austen in her novels. Directors whose work expressed such a vision deserved to be called **auteurs**. The championing of Hollywood directors like Hitchcock was particularly controversial because the Hollywood system was seen as the least sympathetic to possibilities of individual expression.

However, we'd like to take these terms further. Though the contribution of a director like Tarantino or Spielberg may be key to a film, we feel that this longstanding emphasis on the separateness or 'outsideness' of 'authors' and of independent work is not very useful. We want you to look, in whatever kind of media production, for what it is dependent on, at what costs, and with what advantages and disadvantages.

Independents and finance

Our definition of 'independent' in the media industries is very broad, encompassing every production unit which is not an industry major. We must try to categorise production more carefully to make the concept of independent useful.

The highest-profile Hollywood (and other mainstream) output is in the two categories of the global multi-million pound blockbuster and the less expensive, though still star-driven feature film (See Schatz 1993). But there is a third group of films we may get to see at our local multiplexes or Regional Film Theatres which are 'independent' in that they have a less direct dependency on the **majors'** money and corporate assumptions. Film-makers like John Sayles, Allison Anders and Hal Hartley survive partly because the overall market is so big, and the number of niche markets so large that there is always room for a few independents. Sometimes their assumptions are similar to those at work in the majors' films, though often the very fact of the work being small scale brings with it different kinds of recognitions, sometimes more local, more quirky than a huge, predominantly accountant-accountable production can risk.

John Sayles: an American independent

A prominent figure in this independent landscape is **John Sayles**. His first successful film as a director appeared in 1980, *The Return of the Secaucus Seven*. The film is about a reunion of the seven, ten years on from their radical student days. According to one TV guide it had a budget of just $60,000 and yet, somehow, it got a wide distribution on16mm and more than covered costs. Significantly, the same guide refers to it as 'a precursor to *The Big Chill*', the Hollywood film on the same theme which appeared three years later. One effect of independent production might be to introduce new script ideas as well as new formal techniques which are later adopted or absorbed by the majors.

Sayles maintains his independence by writing scripts for more commercial film and television projects, including music videos like 'Born in the USA' for Bruce Springsteen. His career as a scriptwriter was given its first major boost by Roger Corman (see Chapter 20), for whom Sayles transferred the *Seven Samurai* (Japan 1954) into a space adventure in the *Star Trek* mode (*Battle Beyond the Stars,* US 1980) and introduced *Piranha* as a *Jaws* sequel. Sayles realised that to make films, especially the kind of films he wanted to make, would mean making them himself and the budget for *The Return of the Secaucus Seven* came out of the fees he earned: 'I had $40,000 dollars in my pocket.'

Although he doesn't make overt political statements, Sayles is very much on the left in an American context and his own films (i.e. as director) display a concern with social and political issues and a perspective on them rarely, if ever, found in Hollywood features. *Lianna* (US 1983) is a non-sensational story about a lesbian relationship; *Matewan* (US 1987) centres on a miners' strike played out as a western; and *City of Hope* (US 1991) dissects the interrelationships in an urban community beset by corruption in local politics. None of these is a 'difficult' film in formal or narrative terms, and all have the witty dialogue and narrative surety you would expect from a successful writer of genre exploitation films. They are, however, not the films that the majors would make or would support through distribution.

Being labelled as an 'independent' might be seen as a constraint on Sayles' ambitions. His only film for a major so far ('it cost ten times my usual budget') was *Baby It's You* (US 1983), a familiar 'rich girl/poor boy,

John Sayles (b. 1950) Leading American independent film-maker in the fullest possible sense of the word: screenwriter, editor, director, actor and financer, as well as novelist and playwright.

The Big Chill (US 1983) a Hollywood film which tells the same story as *The Return of the Secaucus Seven* using popular music and a young star cast (Glenn Close, Kevin Kline, William Hurt, Jeff Goldblum). Sayles also found his ideas being used as an inspiration by Stephen Spielberg, who commissioned him to write *Night Skies*, an SF film about aliens that was never made – the last page of the script contains the central idea of *ET*.

growing-up' melodrama with a 1960s soundtrack. It sounded like, and indeed proved to be, a mainstream picture of some potential, yet it was initially shelved by its distributors and finally released in the UK on the 'art-house' circuit.

The subject matter and the budget of Sayles' films mark him as an independent and so too do his working practices. His partner, Maggie Renzi, acts in his films and, crucially, as his producer. He has built up a stock company of actors and collaborators and has worked hard to create working-class roles in dramas which grow from his own sense of community. He is independent, but in refusing (or perhaps more correctly, ignoring) the possibility of working inside the framework of Hollywood as a director, he is still supported by an institution – the American independent cinema. This institution has a network of critics and specialist publications, a clutch of small distribution companies and most important a programme of film festivals, the best known of which is now the Sundance Festival in Colorado, financed by Robert Redford's foundation. As long as the films are screened at festivals, they will be written about and booked for other festivals (and eventually BBC2 and Channel 4 in the UK).

'none of my films have played in Jersey city where I live'.

(John Sayles)

Sayles is unusual in surviving as an independent for so long and seemingly wishing to stay within that definition. Even so, he recognises that the cinema market for his kind of film has shrunk. His last two films, *City of Hope* and *Passion Fish* (US 1993), although made expansively for the big screen, have mostly been seen on video and without video pre-sales they would not have been made at all.

Spike Lee: moving towards the mainstream

Spike Lee (b. 1956) The son of a jazz musician and composer. A multi-talented producer-director and actor (including playing lead roles).

Spike Lee is an interesting contrast to John Sayles. Lee produced just one independent film, *She's Gotta Have It* (US 1986), before making deals with the majors in order to get the necessary budgets and distribution for such controversial films as *Do the Right Thing* (US 1988) and *Malcolm X* (US 1992). Lee has embraced the commercialism of Hollywood wholeheartedly, signing up sponsorship deals and publishing through his '40 acres and a mule' production company. (Lee's choice of name for his company is significant – the phrase represents the dream (mostly unfulfilled) of the freed slaves after the Civil War.)

The possibility of an African-American writer-director (or for that matter a Native American or Hispanic American) gaining **access** to the mainstream before the success of Lee's films was slim. Earlier black directors had been largely confined to genre exploitation pictures. Many other African-American film-makers were designated 'independent' whether they wanted to be or not.

Lee was criticised from within the black community for his move into the mainstream, but he could reasonably argue that if he hadn't, such films as *Do the Right Thing* would not have been made or seen by so many people. (See Chapter 7, 'Representations', for further discussion of this issue.) The next generation, led by John Singleton (best known for *Boyz N the Hood* (US 1991)) have not had the same problem in getting mainstream work.

Public funding

Independence for American film-makers is primarily a matter of finance, as this observation in a book on black independent film culture makes plain:

> [W]hat is really an 'independent film'? Anyone who has made even the simplest super 8 film knows that the phrase is a contradiction in terms. No film-maker is independent in the way that, say, a poet is. Film-making, both capital- and labour-intensive is the *most* dependent art form. This is both the blessing and the curse of the form. So the question has never been one of 'independence' or 'dependence', but merely the nature of one's dependence. At least in the US, film-making, more than other art forms, operates under Keynesian, or demand-side, economic constraints. Rather than a film being able to seek out and find an audience once made, many films without well-defined markets may simply not get funding in the first place.
>
> (Snead 1994)

Media production in the US does not generally receive public funding (although some forms of 'art production' such as photography are supported). Snead makes the point that this is in marked contrast to the UK, where 'black independents' have been able to develop projects funded by Channel 4 and the British Film Institute under the umbrella of the 1982 Workshop Declaration.

The 1982 Workshop Declaration was made after discussions between the film technicians' union, ACTT (now BECTU), the Independent Film and Videomakers' Association (IFVA), the Regional Arts Associations and the British Film Institute.

The Declaration enabled 'accreditation' by the union (i.e. professional recognition) for formal production groups who would work together on a non-profit distributing basis. Each group would have a minimum of four full-time members who would be involved in distribution, exhibition and education and training. This was designed to provide continuity of work for independent film-makers and to enable full integration of the production process.

Do the Right Thing A much-discussed film about inner-city racism, based on a true incident and the first mainstream African-American film to generate massive public interest. Lee's background and assumptions about how he should represent issues were at the centre of debate.

Independent Filmmakers Association Founded in 1974 after the BBC2 Controller responded to a group of independent film-makers with the retort 'I'm not having that sort of film on *my* television'. Later to include 'video', the IFVA played an influential if controversial role in developing the independent sector.

As a result of the Declaration, by the beginning of 1985, eighteen workshops had been set up under this 'franchise' arrangement, and the 'workshop sector' had become an established part of the British production scene. Low-cost film and video productions, many with strong local or regional influences and dealing with issues relevant to 'marginalised communities', were produced on a regular basis in the mid-1980s. Many of them with direct Channel 4 funding were screened as part of the 'Eleventh Hour' programming strand – late-night television for 'difficult material'.

'The view of artistic production behind the Workshop Declaration is that it takes time and there has to be a space for failure for worthwhile work to be done. "Talent" is a learnt ability. Paradoxically, Workshops could be seen to be trying to create the kind of environment the Hollywood studios offered.' Alan Lovell from the Birmingham Film and Video Workshop (1990).

Handsworth Songs A controversial film which excavates the history of black British culture through the struggles on the streets of Birmingham. Winner of the prestigious Grierson Award as 'Best British documentary' and acclaimed as well as criticised for its use of sound, archive images and editing.

Co-ops One alternative to capitalist production models is the co-operative. In the UK, the Co-operative Retail Movement in the 1930s recognised the importance of cinema, for both entertainment and education. It opened its own cinemas (often in the same building as its retail outlet) and made films. See Burton (1994).

Workers' Films A wide range of groups was active in the 1930s, making films from within the Labour Movement, often inspired by the works of Soviet Cinema imported by film societies. These were 'political' in content and sometimes 'experimental' in form. See Macpherson (1980) for an investigation of the 1930s practice from a 1970s standpoint.

The higher-profile black workshops such as Black Audio and Film Collective and Sankofa made a series of programmes including *Handsworth Songs* (UK 1986) and *Passions of Remembrance* (UK 1986) which were widely seen and much discussed, both in the UK and internationally. Other franchised workshops with notable productions included Amber in the North-East, Leeds Animation Workshop, Retake (an Asian group in London), and Newsreel Collective and Cinema Action (both based in London). Some workshops were not formally constituted under the Declaration but were still able to get sufficient local funding to develop community-based production and training.

Independent film and video in the UK

The second half of the 1980s in the UK saw a public profile, via Channel 4 in particular, for what might be called the 'independent film and video sector'. The sector developed in the 1970s when the students who had been in further and higher education in the late 1960s and had been politicised by the Vietnam War demonstrations and the events of Paris 1968, began to look for jobs in arts administration, education and media production. They were not prepared to work in the mainstream environment which they had criticised as students and they attempted to set up a new environment. In doing so they were able to take advantage of a relatively well-resourced (by 1990s standards) education system and arts-funding policy and to link up with groups representing a long history of 'independence' in British Cinema.

The independent sector might be seen to be variously concerned with all of the following:
- 'democratic' ways of working – in opposition to the 'division of labour' found in mainstream production (independent film production groups emphasised this aspect of their work by calling themselves **collectives**)
- use of **non-narrative** or distancing techniques in their films so that

audiences would have to work at producing meaning and not be
passive consumers (see Chapter 3, 'Narratives')

- general critique of capitalist ideologies (the groups tended to share a
  political commitment to left ideologies and this was evident in the
  content of many films)
- a resistance to traditional stereotyping (many groups were specifically
  formed to produce work attacking mainstream representations of
  gender, race and class)
- a recruitment policy aimed at creating opportunities for disadvantaged
  people to gain production experience
- support for an **alternative** distribution system, to ensure that the films
  produced were made available to exhibitors
- support for alternative exhibition venues
- an educative role, whereby the ideology of the sector could be
  introduced to larger audiences – groups would often attend screenings
  and talk about their work.

These shared aims were all achieved to a certain extent – sometimes by
indirect means. Because independent film-makers earned very little, if
anything, from their production work, many worked on a part-time basis
in education or training or community work. In this way the movement
became wider and an audience, although small, was developed.
Alternative distribution and exhibition was possible for a time,
particularly as the major funding agencies, the Arts Council and the
British Film Institute, were committed to ensuring that a wide range of
production opportunities and films was available, not only in London,
but also in the regions.

ACTIVITY 27.1

Regional workshops

Most parts of the UK have a regional film and video facility of some kind. Can you find
out about its history? Your Regional Arts Board (or Film Council in Scotland, Wales and
Northern Ireland) should have some details. Otherwise look in the BFI Handbook.

- Was there originally a workshop with a franchise under the Declaration?
- Does the facility/workshop have a policy statement about working practices
  and the kind of productions it supports?
- Is it a membership organisation? If so, what does it offer to members?
- What importance do you attach to the presence of such an organisation in
  your region?

(Most funded workshops still have an education role. Perhaps they would be
prepared to visit your class or invite you to visit them?)

Funding The British Film
Institute's responsibilities are
related to film and television
culture. The Arts Council(s) and
the network of Regional Arts
bodies have some responsibility
for film and television, but also for
radio, music production,
photography and community
publishing. See 'Useful Addresses',
p. 372.

During this period the flagship of the independent distribution and exhibition circuit was The Other Cinema, which was able to maintain a cinema in central London and run a distribution company which handled not only UK independents, but similar work from around the world. Ironically, the cinema was taken over as the first base for Channel 4. Some of the people working for The Other Cinema then set up the Metro in the West End, a more commercially orientated, but still 'independent' cinema. Outside London, the opportunity for audiences to see independent cinema was largely dependent on the existence of a Regional Film Theatre (sometimes associated with a University). These venues, like much else in the independent sector, depended on the support of the British Film Institute.

It isn't possible to understand the development of the independent sector without recognising the role of the BFI. Other countries have similar institutions, usually funded by the state, and charged with promoting and maintaining film culture, but few are as instrumental as the BFI has been in ensuring that an 'independent' film culture survives. Refer back to the list of shared aims above. The BFI has at various times operated a production board, an education service, a distribution service and a regional unit with support for exhibition, publications, etc. BFI funds have gone to small magazines, adult education courses and conferences and a range of other activities, all of which supported the independent sector over a period of a dozen years in the 1970s and 1980s. Funding was so important (few independent films made a profit) that the sector was also known as the 'grant-aided sector'. Funding was both the saviour of the sector and its biggest problem. As the Snead quote above makes clear, if you need money, then you are 'dependent'.

Dependence on funders was a major source of concern and a source of 'institutional conflict'. Even if individual staff members at the BFI might share the ideological viewpoint of the independent film-makers, the BFI as an institution, incorporated by charter and accountable to government for its own funds, could not be expected to act like a workers' collective. Equally, the collectives found it difficult to fulfil some of the funding requirements. The consequence was a sequence of public and private arguments. More seriously, the independent sector was financially dependent on funders who themselves were under pressure, first to cut public expenditure and then to move towards a more market-orientated funding system.

The independent sector in the contemporary environment

The new funding regimes which began to appear towards the end of the 1980s stressed 'performance outcomes' rather than experimentation and diversity. A good example of this might be in relation to training. Previously, groups might have received **revenue funding** on an annual basis, which enabled them to run a course or workshop without constraints, as long as they could show that they were developing access to media production and education in their region. Under the new regime they receive **outcome funding**. This money only comes if they train somebody successfully and they achieve a recognised qualification. The latter method forces a greater conformity on the way the course or workshop is run. Similar changes in funding in relation to other activities also curtail the freedom of independent groups.

Independent production groups have also been persuaded (some might say seduced) into more mainstream production activities by the de-regulation of UK television and the consequent development of an 'independent production sector' based on the definition of independence which we gave at the beginning of this chapter (see also Chapter 20, 'Industries' and Chapter 22, the studio system case study). Instead of producing work that might be screened in the early hours of the morning on Channel 4, the independent groups can now submit proposals for programme commissions in more mainstream slots. Other groups have stayed outside broadcast television, but have moved into 'full-cost', commercial work for clients like charities or trade unions or other public sector organisations. This is more 'mainstream' work, but still with a potentially radical edge. Finally, some groups have turned their attention to production of 'new media' such as CD-ROMs.

The independent film and video sector of the 1970s and 1980s provides an institutional case study, demonstrating the difficulties of what we might call '**oppositional** practice' – trying to set up an **alternative** to mainstream production, distribution and exhibition. It could be argued that, from the funders' point of view, the development of the sector was a success in that it helped to create a pool of freelances with experience gained through 'grant-aided' productions at a time when the mainstream British film industry was collapsing. Without these experienced film and videomakers, the British film and television industry might have been more vulnerable to domination by overseas producers. In the contemporary environment the expansion of more formal education and training courses might now be seen to have filled this particular role.

A second success might be seen in terms of the participation and representation of disadvantaged groups in UK media. Whether or not the numbers of women and ethnic minority entrants to the industry would have been less had there never been an independent sector is something that can't be proven either way. Nevertheless, it was an aim of the sector and there has been some success. (It is also a continuing feature of training programmes, especially those supported by the European Social Fund (ESF).) What is most difficult to determine is the extent to which the independent sector contributed to a change in the formal operation of films and television programmes. We noted above that some (but not all) groups were keen to experiment with non-narrative techniques and an overall aim for those groups working with Channel 4 was to produce new forms of television. To discuss this we need to place the UK independent sector in the context of wider, international, arts movements which have been termed 'avant-garde'.

Avant-garde film

The nearest direct translation of this term in English is 'vanguard' or 'in the front – leading'. Every art form has an avant-garde, a group of artists deliberately intending to break all the rules or conventions and to shock audiences into acceptance of something new. Gradually, aspects of the avant-garde are absorbed into the mainstream or the conditions that encouraged the specific avant-garde change. Later, other avant-garde groups emerge and so the cycle goes on (see Chapter 17, 'A note on postmodernism', for a different view). The cinematic avant-garde is generally recognised as emerging in Berlin and Paris during the 1920s when various modernist groups, including the surrealists, cubists, etc. produced a variety of short features. Many of these artists fled to America in the 1930s to escape fascism and the American avant-garde has its beginning in the early 1940s, becoming a major movement during the 1950s and surviving through to the 1980s.

It is this American movement, especially in the 1950s and 1960s, which brought the idea of avant-garde film to a wider audience as part of a general appreciation of modern art. The American film-makers carried on a tradition from the European pioneers of attacking ideas about conventional narratives. One approach was to explore, through symbolism and disjointed time, the dream-like qualities of film. This approach was heavily influenced by Freud's work on dreams and a good example from the early period is **Maya Deren**'s first feature, *Meshes of the Afternoon* (US 1943), in which the simple actions of a young woman become imbued with violence and violation by the use of specific camera movements and framings and unconventional editing techniques. Deren wrote that the film concerned 'the interior experiences of an individual' and that 'it does not record an event which could be witnessed by another person' (Sitney 1979).

A different approach to film emphasises the physical properties of the medium in relation to the possibilities of narrative – the so-called

Maya Deren (1917–61) made *Meshes of the Afternoon* with her first husband Alexander Hammid (already a documentary film-maker). In subsequent films she drew upon her interest in modern dance and ritualistic behaviour. Her influence spread through writings and lectures on the avant-garde.

'structural film'. **Michael Snow's** *Wavelength* (US 1967) is one of the most famous (or notorious) of these films which severely tested the audience's staying power. In *Wavelength* a fixed camera very slowly zooms in on an object 80 feet away in a New York loft. This takes 45 minutes. Things happen in front of the camera and on the soundtrack (and with the filmstock), but it is the tension created for an audience, used to editing and movement, by the fixed frame which gives the film its power and fascination.

British avant-garde film-makers can be related to the overall history of the avant-garde, with examples of work influenced by both the European and American movements and also by what Peter Wollen in a famous essay (Wollen 1976) described as 'The Two Avant-Gardes'. He argued that there was a second avant-garde tradition which derives from the experimental cinema of the Soviet Union in the 1920s. The difference between these two traditions according to Wollen (1976) and Petley (1978) is that the French, German and, later, American groups were generally 'painterly', interested in film as an artistic medium, allowing opportunities to explore the physical properties of film and light sensitivity, as well as the time and space dimensions of cinema – this is a **formalist** approach. The painterly group included photographers as well as painters (e.g. Man Ray, **Moholy-Nagy** and Dali). It was also a group which presented individual artists with an emphasis on their personal expression. The Russians generally came from experimental theatre (**Eisenstein**) or documentary film (**Vertov**). Although they adopted new approaches to editing and to camerawork, the Russians kept within the confines of a photographic realism and a recognisable, even if revolutionary, narrative structure. In Wollen's terms they were interested in 'contentism' and how to present a political argument.

It is easy to get confused here because you will also come across references in the 1920s to 'Russian formalism'. Film-makers in the Soviet Union in the 1920s were influenced by the modernist movements in Western Europe, but were also charged with producing films that would celebrate and promote socialism in the new revolutionary state. They therefore turned any formalist experiments towards a political purpose.

The Russian tradition was revived by Jean-Luc Godard and Jean-Pierre Gorin in the early 1970s when they called themselves the 'Dziga Vertov Group'. Much of the interest in the work of Jean-Luc Godard can be explained by the way in which he appears to span both avant-garde traditions and the mainstream. In his first feature, *A Bout de Souffle* (France 1959), Godard pays homage to the American B picture in what appears to be a simple genre narrative, but then reveals moments of **surrealism**. During the next decade, Godard's films move increasingly

Michael Snow A Canadian, working out of New York, Snow gained the reputation of the 'dean of structural film' during the 1960s. His work represents one of the most sophisticated attempts to explore film-making as an intellectual activity.

Laszlo Moholy-Nagy 'Theorist, teacher, photographer, designer, painter and film-maker, one of the most important modernist figures' (Petley 1978). Best known for *Lichtspiel* (Germany 1930).

Dziga Vertov (1896–1954) Russian experimental documentarist. Best known for *The Man with the Movie Camera* (USSR 1929), a film about how to construct documentary reality, full of camera tricks and experiments. He produced many short and feature length films between 1918 and the mid-1930s (when the Stalin regime made it difficult to continue experimental work).

Figure 27.3 Using a hand-held camera in a confined space, Godard's cinematographer Raoul Coutard invents a new way of representing the affair between Jean Seberg and Jean-Paul Belmondo in *A Bout de Souffle* (France 1959)

towards a more sustained critique of traditional forms of narrative and Petley (1978) discusses *Une Femme Mariée* (France 1964) under the heading 'The Avant-Garde Feature Film'. By the end of the decade, Godard and his new partner, Gorin, had moved towards a more overtly political kind of film-making ('making films politically, not making political films'). In effect, what was being created, not just by Godard and Gorin, was a new cinematic institution, formulated to be the exact opposite of Hollywood: 'counter-cinema'.

Counter-cinema

As early as 1967, Godard was formulating a manifesto:

> on our own modest level we too should provoke two or three Vietnams in the bosom of the vast Hollywood/Cinecittà/Mosfilm/Pinewood, etc. empire, and, both economically and aesthetically, struggling on two fronts as it were, create cinemas which are national, free, brotherly, comradely and bonded in friendship.

(Quoted in Milne 1972)

The object was to develop a form of film-making practice and a way of watching films which negated the 'hegemony of Hollywood'. After one of the most widely discussed examples of counter-cinema, *Vent d'Est* (France 1972), in which Godard and Gorin examine cultural imperialism via the narrative structure of the western, Peter Wollen formulated a useful checklist of the different ways in which classic Hollywood could be 'countered'.

Classic Hollywood	Counter-cinema
Coherent, linear narrative	Disrupted, non-linear narrative
Identification with characters	Estrangement from characters
Transparency	Foregrounding (making clear the image is being constructed)
Single theme or main story	Multiple themes and stories
Narrative 'closure' or resolution	No resolution
Fiction	Reality
Pleasure	Work (by the audience)
	(Adapted from Wollen 1972)

You will need to look at Chapters 3 and 15 ('Narratives' and 'Realisms') to get a full sense of what these 'oppositions' mean in practice. Let's concentrate on the last pair. Did counter-cinema really mean a denial of pleasure? Many critics would argue that it did. If you take away all the glamour of Hollywood (including 'Technicolor, CinemaScope and Stereophonic Sound') with its stars and easy storylines, what is left? For the politically committed in the 1970s what was left was ideas – difficult ideas in many cases. But there was a pleasure and an interest in political ideas at the time and there were other pleasures; even when Godard was trying not to create visual effects, he still produced arresting and pleasurable images, as well as witty sketches and dramatic moments. If, however, an audience was not already committed to the politics of counter-cinema, there was little chance that it would remain with many of these films all the way through.

The Dziga Vertov Group were not the only practitioners of 'counter-cinema', although they were perhaps the most adventurous in opposing Hollywood. Film-makers around the world were influenced by the politics of the Vietnam War and the protest movements of 1968. **Dusan Makavejev** made *The Diary of a Switchboard Operator* (Yugoslavia 1967) with a primary aim of opposing the hegemony of Soviet Cinema rather than Hollywood. Other examples of counter-cinema can be found in the work of film-makers in Germany, Italy, Latin America, Japan and the United States.

The influence of 'counter-cinema' is also evident in the work of the independent film and video sector in the UK as we discussed above.

Dusan Makavejev (b. 1932) Yugoslav film-maker who acknowledged the influence of Vertov and Godard. His radical approach to sexuality caused controversy in the west after his departure from Yugoslavia and he has been able to make only a few films, usually poorly received.

Many film-makers would have studied both the avant-garde traditions as cinema history and as contemporary practice. Many would also have been involved in the theoretical discussions promoted by *Screen* magazine (which provided translations of international work on counter-cinema). Black British film-makers were particularly influenced by counter-cinema in relation to what came to be known as 'Third Cinema' (and which we look at separately in the case study that follows).

Independence now

The work of all the film-makers we have discussed and of similarly 'independent artists' in photography, music and video, has provided the foundation for contemporary independents. Even film-makers like Quentin Tarantino and David Lynch, seemingly apolitical and intent on commercial success, will admit to influences from the movements we have described. The 1990s might seem a particularly bad time for avant-garde or alternative work. (See Chapter 17, 'A note on postmodernism' for arguments as to why this might be so.) But look more closely, and experimental work is continuing in video and in digital formats associated with **multimedia** and computer graphics. In animation, there is a particularly strong British, Irish and European industry, partly connected to the rebirth of commercial animation under Disney.

In the 1990s, the claymation techniques which have brought acclaim to the Aardman company, with films such as *The Wrong Trousers* (UK 1993), have raised the profile of what was previously a relatively unknown independent sector, financed by work for commercial advertising and public information films. If you are interested in animation, you will find it worthwhile to look back at similarly important British animation teams who worked in the 1930s, in particular **Len Lye** and **Norman McLaren**.

Len Lye (1901–80) British animator (originally from New Zealand) working in the 1930s who used experimental techniques such as painting directly on filmstock on a series of abstract advertisements (e.g. *The Birth of the Robot* (UK 1936) for Shell).

Norman McLaren (1914–87) British animator, influenced by Len Lye, who combined radical politics and experimental animation in the 1930s and went on to achieve international fame on productions for the National Film Board of Canada.

ACTIVITY 27.2

Watching independent film and video

Devising an activity for this chapter is very difficult. Independent films are not widely distributed and therefore we cannot rely on your easy access to them. We have tried to use as examples some of the best-known films in the hope that you might get a chance to see them on your course. If you can find films (perhaps on BBC2 or Channel 4) which seem to fit the categories we have described, try to view them and ask yourself these questions:

- How is the audience being addressed by the film? (Who does the film-maker think is in the audience and how are they expected to behave?)
- What appears to be the main purpose of the film?

- What particular techniques are being used (i.e. in relation to manipulation of the medium itself, to narrative structures or to symbolic objects or characters)?
- Can you summarise what makes the film something 'outside the mainstream'?

It usually helps to have a review or some critical writing about the film to read after you have seen it.

References and further reading

Burton, Alan (1994) *The People's Cinema, Film and the Co-operative Movement,* London: BFI (National Film Theatre).

Georgakas, Dan and Rubenstein, Lenny (1984) *Art, Politics, Cinema: The Cineaste Interviews,* London: Pluto.

Hillier, Jim (1993) *The New Hollywood,* London: Studio Vista.

Johnston, Trevor (1993) 'Sayles Talk: Interview with John Sayles', *Sight & Sound,* vol. 3, no. 9, September.

Lovell, Alan (1990) 'That Was The Workshop, That Was', *Screen,* vol. 31, no. 1, Spring, p. 107.

Macpherson, Don (ed.) (1980) *British Cinema, Traditions of Independence,* London: BFI.

Milne, Tom (1972) *Godard on Godard,* London: Secker & Warburg.

Murdock, G. (1986) 'Authorship and Organisation', *Screen Education,* no. 35.

Petley, Julian (1978) *BFI Distribution Library Catalogue,* London: BFI.

Sayles, John (1987) *Thinking in Pictures: The Making of the Movie, Matewan,* Boston: Houghton Mifflin.

Schatz, Thomas (1993) 'The New Hollywood' in J. Collins, H. Radner and A.P. Collins (eds) *Film Theory Goes to the Movies,* London: Routledge.

Sitney, P. Adams (1979) *Visionary Film, The American Avant-Garde 1943-1978,* New York: Oxford University Press.

Snead, James (1994) *white screens/black images,* ed. Colin MacCabe and Cornel West, New York: Routledge.

Wollen, Peter (1972) 'Counter-cinema: *Vent d'est*', *Afterimage,* no. 4.

—— (1976) 'The Two Avant-Gardes' *Studio International.*

28 / Case study: African Cinema

'Third Cinema'

The counter-cinema of Europe and North America represented an opposition to a cinematic institution founded in a capitalist economy. Film-makers in Africa, Asia and Latin America and black British and American film-makers also needed to oppose what was effectively an imperialist or **colonialist cinema**. The designation '**Third Cinema**' was suggested by two Argentinian documentarists, Fernando Solanas and Octavio Getino. They wanted to promote a cinema that would oppose the dominant-industrial (i.e. Hollywood style) 'First Cinema' and the independent-auteurist (i.e. art cinema) 'Second Cinema'. The term appeared in 1969 but took several years to gain international currency after promotion by Teshome Gabriel (an African film scholar working in America) in 1982. As with most independent or '**oppositional**' groupings, there was no clear agreement as to what constituted Third Cinema, nor did all film-makers in Latin America, Africa and Asia wish to be included under such a banner. It did, however, have an importance in promoting a different theoretical approach to some aspects of World Cinema.

At the heart of the Third Cinema question lies a very important issue, one which forms the basis of the whole independent/**alternative** position. In simple terms, it is whether the medium of film and the development of the institution of cinema have been such that only one way of making films and understanding them is possible. We might consider that counter-cinema, for instance, is only understandable if we know it is the mirror-opposite of Hollywood; or that the **auteurist** art cinema is simply a minor diversion from the Hollywood narrative style. But what if you want to start from the beginning, to invent cinema all over again for a different environment, so that an indigenous culture can produce its own cinema? We are dealing here with an **aesthetics** question (see Chapter 13, 'Global and local', for more about the politics of the issue).

Third Cinema as a term has now lost its currency, but nothing very suitable has replaced it – perhaps because most theorists now accept that such a broad label is inappropriate and each region or 'locality' should be able to speak about its own cinema.

African Cinema

The prospect of making films came late to many parts of Africa (not until the 1960s for sub-Saharan Africa) and the question we have asked faced several film-makers in different countries. Africa is not, of course, one country or one culture, but for political and economic reasons 'pan-African' organisations have been formed to encourage development, and in cinema there are a number of important events and organisations such as FESPACO (the Pan-African Film Festival of Ouagadougou in Burkina-Faso, which screens films from across Africa every two years). These screenings have prompted a vigorous debate about cinematic language and African culture.

The idea of starting afresh or re-invigorating cinema is clearly laid out by John Akomfrah, one of the black British film-makers (co-director of *Handsworth Songs*) who have been profoundly influenced by African Cinema:

Figure 28.1 Religious conversions, slavery and guns are potent symbols of conflict in Ousmane Sembene's influential *Ceddo* (Senegal 1978)

While Europe and North America are almost singing the funeral rites to cinema, people in other parts of the world have still to discover its potential. You really feel this in their film-making – that there is the possibility of rewriting some of the very basic rules of film grammar.

(Akomfrah 1995)

Akomfrah goes on to discuss his first reactions to **Ceddo** (Senegal 1978), directed by **Ousmane Sembene**. We will use Ousmane Sembene and this film as an example because it had a major impact on both film-makers and critics when it arrived in Western Europe and America. *Ceddo* tells the story of the 'outcasts' (the ceddo in the local language, Wolof), the peoples of Western Africa who were displaced by the forced Islamic conversions of the sixteenth century. The film also refers to the slavers and the missionaries who arrived from Western Europe. In the film, we see the strength and leadership of a local princess outwit the Imam at the last, as the slaver slinks off to pastures new. The narrative is not linear, historical time periods are not clear. Compositions and framings are not what we

expect. Seemingly extraneous (but very effective) factors are introduced when American gospel music accompanies the branding of slaves or when one of the characters 'flashes forward' to contemporary Senegal.

> **Ousmane Sembene**: Senegalese novelist and film-maker (b. 1923), often referred to as 'the father of African cinema', who directed the first sub-Saharan African film, *Borom Sarret* (Senegal 1963). His films have maintained a consistent interest in the social issues of Senegal – 'I consider the cinema as a means of political action' (quoted in Martin 1984).

Overall, *Ceddo* is difficult for western audiences, but primarily because of the unfamiliar history it recounts and not because Sembene is adopting devices to produce a distance (i.e. like Godard and counter-cinema) between film and audience – quite the contrary in fact. The ideas explored in the film (a critical view of slavery and organised religions from within the history of one of the regions where they were practised) were so powerful in their 'contemporaneity' that the film was banned in Senegal for a time.

The importance of Sembene's films and those of other film-makers who began to make films in the 1960s and 1970s is that they do offer an 'alternative' to the film-making practices of Europe and North America. They mix African story traditions and the conventions of narrative feature films and then use this new language to tell stories and to explore ideas about their own countries. That a group of film-makers should share a common approach is partly due to the shared experience of growing up in French colonial Africa, receiving training and education with a European perspective but in the context of the *négritude* movement, which fostered a belief in the importance of African culture. The struggles over establishing independent states in the 1960s were a further learning experience and not all the film-makers share the same political stance (see the interview with Sembene in Downing (1987)). But what does unite them is a sense of concern for an African identity.

Younger African film-makers have a slightly different history and what constitutes 'African film' is constantly developing, but as John Akomfrah argues:

> there are enough established precepts about the right way to make an African film, if only because most of these film-makers have been turning up and showing their films to African audiences at such festivals as FESPACO for so long that they have now incorporated a sense of expectation of what an African Cinema should and should not have.
>
> (Akomfrah 1995)

What African Cinema offers is an alternative institution *and* practice, which, although impelled by wanting to be different from the cinemas of Europe and America, is not just a negation, but a new way of conceiving of film drama. In this sense it relates to the idea of a Third Cinema and interests black British film-makers who might otherwise feel themselves trapped between the **mainstream** and the two (European/American) avant-gardes. The next generation of African film-makers will still have a battle to make the films they want (still

'dependent' on funding etc.), but will benefit from the establishment of a body of 'African' films.

Like counter-cinema, the concept of 'local cinema', as we might try to generalise from our African Cinema example, is useful in pointing to alternative cinemas in different parts of the world. In fact from a European or North American perspective, it is possible to create an overview which includes all the film-making practices we have touched upon in this case study and the preceding chapter under the umbrella title of 'Art and Politics'. John Sayles, Ousmane Sembene and Dusan Makavejev are all interviewed in Georgakas and Rubenstein (1984). Some critics have suggested that more recent African films display some of the features of postmodern cinema in Europe and North America. But we can be certain that however these films are discussed, the context of the politics and culture of contemporary Africa will remain important in considering them as in some way 'alternative'.

References and further reading

Akomfrah, John (1995) 'Dream Aloud'. Interview by June Givanni in *Sight & Sound*, vol. 5, Issue 9, September (a special feature on African Cinema supporting 'Africa 95').

Armes, Roy (1987) *Third World Film-making and the West,* London: University of California Press.

Downing, John D.H. (ed.) (1987) *Film and Politics in the Third World,* New York: Autonomedia.

Georgakas, Dan and Rubenstein, Lenny (eds) (1984) *Art, Politics, Cinema: The Cineaste Interviews,* London: Pluto.

Martin, Angela (1982) *African Films: The Context of Production,* BFI Dossier No.6, London: BFI.

—— (1984) *Africa on Africa,* London: Channel 4 (Film Season Notes).

Nicholas, Joe (1994) *Egyptian Cinema,* London: BFI.

Pines, Jim and Willemen, Paul (eds) (1989) *Questions of Third Cinema,* London: BFI.

(*Note:* The BFI celebration of Africa '95 is expected to lead to publications and new releases of African films on video, including examples from both the first- and second-generation directors.)

29 Audiences

Ways of thinking about 'audiences'

This section outlines the main ways in which the relationships of media and audiences have been theorised and discussed. In Media Studies **audience** refers to the groups and individuals addressed and often partly 'constructed' by the media industries: a very different entity to previous uses of the term.

Audiences are unknown but also the subject of much research. It's impossible to think of 'the audience' as a single entity: 'the audience' for the release of Steven Spielberg's latest movie is not one but many 'things', dispersed across an enormous number of different events, throughout the world, in celluloid, TV, CD, cable and video formats, over maybe a year or so.

Research into audiences has been far from straightforward, and the same issues have recurred over and over as each new medium arrives. But there have been two extremes between which assumptions have occurred: the **effects** and the **uses and gratifications** models. Broadly speaking, there has been a shift away from 'direct effects' emphases towards those on the 'active reader'.

The 'effects model'(also called the **hypodermic model**), is the name given to approaches that emphasise what the media do *to* their mass audiences. Power lies with the message here. The media in such work is often called 'the mass media' or 'mass communications' so as to emphasise the size and scale of its operations.

The language used in such writing will often play up the idea that meanings are 'injected' into this mass audience's minds by the powerful syringe-like media. The next step is often to speak of the media as working like a drug, and then to suggest that the audience is drugged, addicted, doped or duped.

On the other hand, the uses and gratifications model emphasises what the audiences for media products do *with* them. Power here is argued to

'There are in fact no "masses" but only ways of seeing people as masses.'

(Williams 1958)

'In 1976, a group of friends from Los Angeles who often gathered together in order to indulge in hour-long sessions of television viewing, decided to call themselves "couch potatoes". With tongue-in-cheek publications such as *The Official Couch Potato Handbook* ... and *The Couch Potato Guide to Life* ... they started a mock-serious grassroots viewers' movement.'

(Ang 1991)

lie with the individual consumer of media, who is imagined as using particular programmes, films or magazines to gratify certain needs and interests. Far from being duped by the media, the audience here is seen as made up of individuals free to reject, use or play with media meanings as they choose. The needs to be gratified, following Maslow (1970), would include those for diversion, information or sexual stimulation.

Models

The term 'model' (in this context at any rate) refers to a way of imagining a complex area. It isn't the same as a theory, but is a description of the 'shape' of the thinking beneath that theory. Often an underlying model is revealed by the use of particular metaphors – such as 'inject', 'bombard', 'manipulate', 'copycat' or 'drug' for the effects model.

The effects model

Let's look in more detail at some specific effects approaches:

The Frankfurt School for Social Research was set up in 1923, mostly composed of left-wing, German, Jewish intellectuals. Key members were **Adorno** (1903–70), **Marcuse** (1898–1978) and **Horkheimer** (1895–1973). After Nazism consolidated its power in 1933, the group worked in exile in the USA.

- **The Frankfurt School** theorised the possible effects of modern media, especially in response to German fascism's use of radio and film for **propaganda** purposes and later to the experience, in exile, of the early power of US media. Its members developed a revolutionary variant of Marxism known as *critical theory* at a time when 'it seemed as though the possibility of radical social change had been smashed between the twin cudgels of concentration camps and television for the masses' (Craib 1984: 184). They emphasised the power of capitalism, owning and controlling new media, to restrict and control cultural life in unprecedented ways, creating what they called a 'mass culture' of stupefying conformity, with no space for innovation or originality.

- A slightly different emphasis on effects was developed by researchers into post-TV USA in the 1950s and 1960s. They were alarmed by a perceived increase in violent acts and their possible relationship to violence represented on TV, though uninterested in linking these to a critical analysis of capitalist society, as the Frankfurt School had attempted. They focused on the power of TV to do things to people – or rather, to *other* people. Self-styled 'moral majority' movements like the contemporary National Viewers' and Listeners' Association (NVLA) in Britain try to have TV and other media more closely censored, on the assumption that they are the most important causes of a society perceived as increasingly violent.

- Yet other researchers within this model, from the 1940s on, were interested in issues such as whether or not TV affected people's political attitudes, as measured in acts like how people vote in elections.

Many researchers, especially those studying the effects of media on children, were influenced by the work of **behavioural scientists** who tried to understand human *social* behaviour by modifying the *laboratory* behaviour of animals. **B.F. Skinner** is one of the most famous **behaviourists**. You have probably also heard of Pavlov's dogs, laboratory animals whose feeding times were accompanied by a bell ringing, until eventually they would salivate whenever the bell rang, with or without the food. Clearly their laboratory behaviour had been violently modified, and scientists working on such experiments were hopeful that such control by reinforcement could be applied to human behaviour – though in different ways. American advertisers were interested and some media researchers felt that there might be similarities in the 'repeated messages' or 'reinforcement' of TV and their effects on audiences.

A now much-criticised piece of research was called the 'Bobo doll experiment' (Bandura and Walters 1963). It showed children some film of adults acting aggressively towards a 'Bobo doll', then recorded children acting in a similar way later when left alone with it. The implication was then extended to violent media content, which was asserted to have similar effects on children.

Here are a few of the problems of trying to transfer findings from (unfortunate) laboratory animals to human beings:

- People (a group which includes the children in the Bobo experiment) are often very willing to please those conducting experiments, and have a shrewd sense of what responses are required to do this – or to entertainingly mess it up.

- A simple, controlled laboratory experiment has very limited application to the complicated conditions under which we interact with the various media in our social lives.

- People, if seen as being like laboratory animals, will be assumed to be empty vessels, passively absorbing simple TV messages. Psychologists gradually replaced such images with the accounts of **cognitive psychology**, which emphasise how children actively construct, rather than passively receive, meanings from the media, and how these interpretations are affected by prior knowledge and experience.

- Entertainment forms, involving fantasy and more complex messages, are hard to fit into the model.

- The 'effect' of watching television may not be shown in our measurable *outward* behaviour, such as voting, or shopping – or violent acts.

Burrhus Frederick Skinner (1904–90) US behaviourist scientist, arguing that all behaviour is explainable solely in terms of genetic dispositions and 'reinforcements' or rewards and punishments, and therefore all that matters is how behaviour is reinforced.

'As she entered a laboratory, one small four year old girl was heard to say "Look, Mummy, there's the doll we have to hit …"'
(Root on the Bobo doll work (1986))

Other problems with the effects model

The effects of the media, especially TV, are usually assumed to be negative, never positive. For example, if you look closely at the kinds of writing (e.g. **tabloid** editorials) that urge censorship, they will often fall into one of two apparently contradictory positions, sometimes called **moral panics**:

- the media produce inactivity, make us into 'couch-potatoes', into students who won't pass their exams or unemployed box-watchers who make no effort to get a job.

- The media produce activity, but of a bad kind, such as violent 'copycat' behaviour, or mindless shopping in response to advertisements.

Geoffrey Pearson (1984) outlined a 200-year cyclical repetition of the fears of 'morally minded people' about the collapse of family, religious and moral decline, youthful insubordination and a looming crisis of civilisation. At each point people thought that just thirty years earlier things had all been much better.

Moral panic First used by Stan Cohen (1972) for a process where 'a condition, episode, person, or group ... emerges to become defined as a threat to societal values and interests'. Used in studies of media scapegoating round issues such as 'video nasties' or youth subcultures. (See O'Sullivan, Hartley *et al.* 1994.)

ACTIVITY 29.1

Take any recent panic over media effects. Make notes on the language of the pro-censorship lobby, including:

- the tell-tale use of 'them' rather than an admission of the researchers' or campaigners' own involvement in media

- implications that 'things were alright' in some earlier age, often thirty years or so ago.

'Let us go into the houses of the poor, and try to discover what is the effect on the maiden mind of the trash the maiden buys ... the higher flown conceits and pretensions of the young girls of the period, their dislike of manual work and love of freedom, spring largely from notions imbibed in the course of a perusal of their penny fictions.'

(Edward Salmon, 1888)

'It is the height of hypocrisy for Senator Dole [Republican Presidential candidate], who wants to repeal the assault weapons ban, to blame Hollywood for the violence in our society.'

(Oliver Stone, June 1995)

'The mass audience' as they/we figure in such discourses is usually assumed to consist of the 'weaker' members of society such as women, especially women of the 'lower orders'. In the nineteenth century, novels were thought to be potentially harmful for such women; in our century there have been similar fears that romantic novels, and then **soaps**, render women passive, helpless, drugged.

Children also feature in such discourses: worried over in the 1950s because of the supposed harm done by American comics, then in the 1980s and 1990s in relation to 'video nasties' and computer games. Such worries are usually strikingly isolated from other factors affecting children's use of media, such as:

- underfunded child care, schools and leisure activities

- children's awareness of the conventions and special effects of horror movies

- children's awareness that the computer skills acquired through playing games are highly job-marketable.

Thinking about these areas in terms of models makes it a little easier to see when the logic of a particular model has led researchers to 'throw out the baby with the bathwater', as has happened with some effects work. More sophisticated versions were able to emphasise the broader capacity of TV to affect our *perceptions* of violence, politics, strikes, etc.:

- Gerbner and Gross (1976) produced work in the USA which suggested that the more TV you watch, the more likely you are to have a fearful attitude to the world outside the home. (These questions have been revived recently around representations of crime on British TV.)

- Lazarsfeld *et al.* (1944) explored, over 6 months, the influence exerted on voters by the media during an American presidential campaign. They concluded that voters were very resistant to media influence. Individual predispositions or political preference influenced which media they consulted. The term *two-step flow* was coined to describe the important influence of opinion leaders, whose views often mediated those offered by the media. Media effect began to be seen as one of reinforcement and *intervening variables* rather than radical change, or brainwashing.

- Greg Philo's (1990) work some years after the British Coal Strike of 1984–5 suggested another form of effect. Over a period of time audiences tended to forget details of news reporting but to remember key themes and even phrases, such as 'picket line violence'. These, through repetition, became part of popular consciousness, and in turn memory, about the strike, even if particular reports at the time have shown them to be mythical or exaggerated.

When the Coal Strike was over, the National Council for Civil Liberties (NCCL) reported that 'contrary to the impression created by the media, most of the picketing during the strike has been orderly and on a modest scale'.

The uses and gratifications model

The **uses and gratifications model** found first expression in the USA in the 1940s and seemed like a breath of fresh air by resisting easy pessimism and crudely behaviourist emphases. It started from very different assumptions, arguing that the media function in an open way, with personality types giving rise 'to certain needs, some of which are directed to the mass media for satisfaction' (Morley 1991). Names associated with this strand include McQuail, Blumler and Katz.

Unlike the Frankfurt School, this was not a position interested in critiquing capitalist mass culture. Instead, some of its extreme adherents came close to denying any influence for the media. Just as metaphors of drugs, addiction, passivity characterise the 'effects' tradition, so 'uses' traditions buzz with words like 'choice', 'consuming', 'users', and 'activity'. Of course, this has one big attraction: we're much more likely to *want* to identify ourselves as active readers, zap-happy operators of the TV remote control than as the passive dupes of some effects theorists.

The term 'consumer'

'**Consumer**' is a word with an interesting history in this context. It was once part of a dismissal of mass-media texts, suggesting their use was like the simple, passive 'consumption' of junk food or alcohol – a 'staple diet' of soaps, or weepies, using the same old 'recipe' for success and so on.

In the last ten to twenty years, however, the word has been used so as to invite us to think of a discerning shopper, carefully and stylishly picking out this or that media product. This is much closer to recent political emphases on our supposed powers as 'customers' in a whole range of settings, from schools and colleges to hospitals and courts. Like the uses and gratifications model itself, the term:

- ignores differences in incomes and in disposable time which limit **access** to the 'level playing field' of 'the market'
- ignores differences in knowledge, confidence and other abilities to discriminate between or to know where to find and feel comfortable with certain kinds of products
- describes consumers as isolated, free floating, rational and empowered individuals. This ignores the fact that we live in very different social contexts and histories, that we are not always rational, and lead lives we have not freely chosen and might want to be able to change. (See Chapter 11, 'Ideologies'.)

ACTIVITY 29.2

Take any advert, from TV or the press, and say what reading might be made of it by (a) an extreme 'effects' critic and (b) an extreme 'uses and gratifications' critic.

- Which kind of reading seems to you more convincing?
- Why? What does each leave out?

'Whereas elitism has patronised the audience by calling it stupid, populism has patronised the audience by calling it subversive.'
(Strinati 1995: 258)

Recent developments in audience research

A few more approaches need to be outlined here:

- content analysis
- **semiotic** approaches
- the broader contexts of **cultural** understandings.

Media texts are still most likely to be approached through **content analysis**. This looks for the frequency with which an element in a media text occurs (such as 'violent acts' or 'images of women in the kitchen'), counts them, and implies or suggests as a result what might be the effect on audiences. (See Chapter 7, 'Representations' for debates and examples.)

'Content analysis stands or falls by its categories ... Since the categories contain the substance of the investigation, a content analysis can be no better than its system of categories.'
(Berelson quoted in Winston 1983)

The violence debate

The **violence debate** is full of such 'countings', which have disastrously narrowed its '**agenda**'. Rightly concerned when horrible murders or other acts of violence take place, campaigners then argue that they might be prevented by censoring 'violence on TV', meaning countable 'acts of violence'. This ignores:

- the problem of defining the violence that is to be counted. It may seem quite a simple thing to decide to count 'violence' or 'violent acts' on TV or in computer games and then to conclude they are affecting audiences. Yet the question of what, in our culture, gets perceived as 'violence' is a huge one. Some kinds of activity are labelled 'violent' and others aren't: the latter are sometimes called 'keeping the peace' or 'war heroism'.
- the differences between the many kinds of representations of violence that get counted. A familiar example: is the 'violence' in a Tom and Jerry cartoon, or a Nintendo game the same as the violence in a news bulletin, or in an action adventure movie? Such differences are rarely taken into account by the 'violence lobby'.

As with any media text, *the counting of elements that can be counted* is a slightly circular process, and ignores the ways codes and resonances of meaning are combined. If researchers talked about 'counting combinations', it might be clearer what a complex business this would

'Since the late 20s an entire research tradition (on violence and media) whose total expenditure must run into hundreds of millions of dollars and pounds, and which has been guaranteed serious political reception and "front page" media coverage on almost every occasion, has dominated the **media research** agenda – and achieved nothing.'
(Martin Barker, letter to *Sight & Sound*, August 1995)

'films and audience responses to films can only be understood culturally and historically … the violence debate itself is part of that cultural history.'
(Martin Barker, letter to *Sight and Sound*, August 1995)

Figure 29.1

be. In the case of film/TV, for instance, it would have to combine the 'act of violence' with

- its place in the narrative
- the stance the audience is invited to take up in relation to it by camera movement, positioning, editing
- costume, lighting and other elements of the **mise en scène**
- casting (is a sympathetic star involved?)
- intertextual reference (is a joke being made about another text?)
- the historical stage of its genre (is it a western at a stage when audiences are likely to be very familiar with special effects of violent death?) as well as the conventions of that genre and so on.

ACTIVITY 29.3

Take a recent film or TV programme which was called violent and go through the above list.

- What would you say is its 'message' about violence?
- How might this strike:
    (a) an audience experienced in its genre?
    (b) an audience inexperienced in its genre?

Finally, it's perhaps worth noting that some representations of violence may have not negative but positive effects in the revulsion they invite us to feel, for example at certain kinds of assault, or military power, or bullying.

ACTIVITY 29.4

Think back to the most horrifying or frightening moment in a media text that you have experienced.

- How does it fit into the discussion above?
- Why was it so horrifying for you?
- Did anyone else share your feeling?
- What kind of text, what kind of genre was it part of? Fairy tale? Video? News?
- Did this make a difference to how you understood it?
- How would you relate this to any current panic about the effects of media texts?

'Screen theory' and audiences

Semiotic and structuralist approaches to meaning (see Chapter 1, 'Images and languages') were applied in Britain from the 1960s onwards, especially in the journal *Screen*. Questions such as:

- How does this programme/advert/movie produce meaning?
- With what codes and conventions is it operating?

promised to understand the making of meaning as a much more mediated, active and social process.

But the theories, along with speculation from psychoanalytic approaches, were often applied in extremely text-isolated ways (notably to films in *Screen* in the 1970s, and later to television by others). One example was an emphasis on the assumed powers of the Hollywood editing system to 'suture' (stitch) or position 'the spectator' in certain ways, making only one reading possible, however unconscious readers were of it. Most influential was the argument, heavily couched in psychoanalytic terms (*fetishism, voyeurism, scopophilia*), that audiences were put into masculine, and therefore inevitably voyeuristic positions by such texts. Despite a rhetoric of Marxist social transformation (using terms such as 'regime','subversion', 'radical'), *Screen* theory was almost totally uninterested in what actual audiences might be doing with these 'texts'.

Voyeurism The pleasure of looking at those who do not know they are being looked at. By extension, a sexual 'perversion'. Similar to **scopophilia**, another key *Screen* term.

The 'Nationwide' work

During the 1970s the Centre for Contemporary Cultural Studies (**CCCS**) at Birmingham, under Stuart Hall, was working with the more sociological approaches of Cultural Studies. David Morley's *The Nationwide Audience* (1980), drawing on a previous (1978) small-scale study of an early evening news magazine programme, argued that audiences worked at **decoding** media texts, in other words, it was using a semiotic model of audience activity. But it tried to understand that semiotic process in relation to:

- power structures *outside* the text which shape audience members: class, gender, ethnicity and so on
- power structures *within* the text and media institutions which mean that such programmes try to promote a 'preferred reading' which is in line with the 'dominant ideology' (see Chapter 11).

This broadly **Gramscian** model of **hegemonic power** in the media, power which was constantly having to win or prove itself, worked with Stuart Hall's 'encoding–decoding' model of three types of audience readings:

- **dominant**, or **dominant hegemonic**, where the reader recognises what a programme's 'preferred' or offered meaning is and broadly agrees with it
- **oppositional**, where the dominant meaning is recognised but rejected for cultural, political or ideological reasons

- **negotiated**, where the reader subjects elements of the programme to acceptance, rejection or refinement in the light of previously held views.

Questions were later raised about this work, not least by David Morley:

- Does it see language and media as merely a conveyor belt for pre-made (especially ideological) meanings or messages?
- Does it blur a number of processes? Are viewers' activities better thought of as 'comprehension/ incomprehension' rather than 'agreement/disagreement' or even 'decoding'?
- How exactly is class defined in this context of 'dominant/oppositional'? Is it equated too easily with occupation? What of age, gender, sexual orientation and education, for example?
- What about *entertainment* forms? This, and much other audience work, had stayed with news and documentary. Where pleasure and play seem central, can we still use the idea of a single preferred meaning?
- Questioning people about videotaped programmes in a college setting is fine. But how likely would they be to watch those kinds of programmes outside that setting? This leads to considerations of **genres**, **discourses** and *domestic contexts for viewing* (see below).

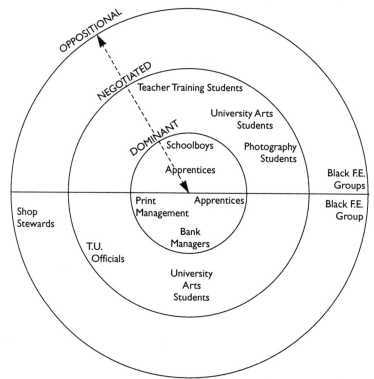

Figure 29.2 The spread of ways in which Morley's groups 'decoded' two current affairs programmes in 1976 and 1977
(Source: Morley 1980)

Overall, however, the *Nationwide* work, though drawing on semiotics, opened up interest in more empirical studies of TV audiences, increasingly in relation to entertainment and fiction forms and to the domestic contexts in which viewing usually takes place. Before we move to this though, one more text-centred approach deserves explanation.

Mode of address

The idea of **mode of address** came out of linguistics. It refers to the ways a text 'speaks to' its audience, just as most of us in ordinary everyday encounters will use slightly different ways of addressing parents, friends, teachers, bank managers. The further implication is that we are likely to assume the identity thus constructed for us, at least temporarily.

> **Q:** How does *The Clothes Show* address its audience? How do you know?
>
> **A:** The mode of address is to an audience which is interested in fashion and in buying clothes, and is quite young (though not exclusively so).
>
> We can argue this because of the kinds of cultural references that are made (for instance to designers); the display of prices, shops (an openly consumerist mode of address); the hi-tech effects, pop music, jokey informal presentation style (addressing a young audience, though not to the exclusion of other groups, who are addressed in, for example, some of the roadshow features).

ACTIVITY 29.5

- Take a current affairs programme and make notes on its mode of address, e.g. *Panorama, Newsnight*.
- Take a tabloid and a **broadsheet** newspaper and compare their modes of address.
- Look at such evidence as: headline and typeface size; kind of language used (is slang or racy abbreviation present?); the proportion of the page taken up by photographs; any use of 'we' or 'you' especially in the editorial slot where the paper 'speaks its mind'; adverts and how they seem to be addressing the audience.

Such textual work suggests that modes of address:
- are linked to assumptions about audiences, and the desire to attract or maximise them or perhaps to target specialised ones.

MALE MODEL COMPETITION INSIDE

MAY 1995 £1.60

clothes SHOW

sizzling lips

MOUTHWATERING SHADES FOR SUMMER

100 sunshine BEAUTY BUYS

boy watch

WHAT SHOULD HE WEAR ON THE BEACH?

NEW LOOK summer skirts

funky fashion

chic CHINESE classics
the season's softest PINKS
cool CASUALS
SEQUIN studded style

9 770953 635079

05>

3 2 PAGE SUMMER FASHION EXTRA

Figure 29.3

- may also reinforce or even help to create these assumed identities, and to define or informally 'teach' them (See Chapter 30, 'Case study: Selling audiences' and Chapter 9, 'Advertising, marketing and fashion'.)

Recent developments

More recently there has been a turn to **audience ethnographies**, or fieldwork research, largely derived from **anthropology** where the researcher attempts to enter into the culture of a particular group and provide an account of meanings and activities 'from the inside'. He or she will often employ *participant observation* methods, participating in the lives of the groups to be studied for an extended period of time, asking questions and observing what goes on. When the research is written up, it often tries to show a respect for the group studied by providing life histories, case studies and verbatim quotes from them.

Problems remain:

- How can the observer ever know the extent to which their questions, presence even, have affected the group 'under observation'?
- Have questions, and what the researcher hears in the answers to them, been selected to fit his/her pre-existing agenda or theory?

Nevertheless, it seems likely that more can be learned from careful ethnographic accounts than from the assertions of theory on its own, or from simple, number-crunched questionnaires alone. The key areas which recent media ethnographic work has investigated include:

- the domestic contexts of reception
- genre and cultural competence
- technologies and consumption.

The domestic contexts of reception

Morley (1986), Gray (1992) and others have explored ways in which the home, or rather, different homes – the domestic context for most of our viewing – affects and structures our viewing.

Firstly, the home, 'the private sphere', the place where we can 'retreat from the world', is as cross-cut by social power as anywhere. In particular, TV viewing is structured by gender and age power relations. A few examples:

- For men, often coming home after work or a day spent outside it, viewing can be a very different experience than it is for women who, whether or not they also work outside the home, are likely to see it as a place of (house)work. It's much easier for men to watch in an uninterrupted way than it is for women, who are often expected to manage the interruptions and disputes that break out among children.
- Because women's (house)work is always there, in the home, many women have spoken of their pleasure in carving out a little time for themselves to refuse their domestic duties for a while and enjoy a video, or a novel.
- The remote control, and who wields it, is a key symbol of power within families (and other groups).

Other work has explored the ways that TV exists as part of a whole flux of domestic happenings and relationships. This has powerful implications for theories such as those of decoding, which imply a very concentrated relationship of viewer/text. TV viewing doesn't feel like that a lot of the

'When talking about children's leisure interests it is all too possible to imagine this as a free space where they can make their own choices ... [but] most of what children do is subject to some form of regulation, if only in terms of the amount of time and money they have at their disposal. Girls are particularly likely to live with constraints on how they spend their time at home ... to be asked to contribute to domestic labour.'

(Gemma Moss in Buckingham (1993: 123))

time, partly because of the **flow** which Williams (1974) and others have suggested is the characteristic experience of TV, especially in commercially funded systems, keen to keep fingers off channel buttons so as to sell more audience attention to advertisers. Instead of being viewed in a concentrated way as separate items, TV and radio programmes are more often experienced as a flow. Within this they can be used as ways of building relationships, signalling truces in disputes and so on.

ACTIVITY 29.6

Interview other students on the following questions :

- How many TVs do you have in your household? Where are they? Are they all colour sets? Who uses which?
- Have you ever successfully waged a struggle for the remote control? How?
- Do you watch any programmes because you know you'll disagree with them, or enjoy ridiculing them?
- Do you have 'special occasion' viewing? If so, what arrangements do you make? Does this make TV viewing more like cinema-going?
- Do you use TV as part of a relationship – to mend it, or help begin one, or even to avoid conversation?

Discuss your findings and the following questions:

- Which of the answers supported a 'uses and gratifications' and which an 'effects' model of the audience?
- If most supported a uses and gratifications model, did you feel there was any case to be made for TV having any effects which are beyond your control?

Pierre Bourdieu (b.1930) French sociologist. After boarding school (which he claims gave him an understanding of factory production lines) and elite education, he was conscripted into the French Army during the Algerian War of 1958 where he began ethnographic work. His book *Distinction: A Social Critique of the Judgement of Taste* (1984) explored how the supposedly natural, universal quality 'taste' is actually formed along class and education lines. Also worked on notions of cultural capital and competences as they affect success in the school system.

Genre, gender and 'cultural competence'

Bourdieu's concept of **cultural competence** is useful in understanding the pleasures which particular audiences take in different media forms and the knowledge they build up of them. The theory suggests that in a capitalist society, just as access to capital (economic power) is differently distributed between different classes and groups, so the media/art forms we feel easy and familiar with will be related to our social class position via cultural competences. Though Bourdieu's work has been largely concerned with class, it was applied to gender and such low-status cultural forms as women's soaps in the early 1980s (before TV companies tried to attract larger male audiences by means of the kinds of 'serious', 'tough' themes as are now found in *EastEnders* or *Brookside*).

Until then, it was assumed that women's soaps were an inferior media form, which anyone could understand, though in which only a rather stupid audience would be interested. Then **feminist** critics pointed out that fans of such genres will sustain such competences in order to engage with the themes of personal, domestic life and intimate, often family relationships which are the ground of soaps, 'women's films', and young women's magazines. For example, they need to know the importance of certain kinds of looks between characters, or the conventions of the cliffhanger. They also need to have an interest in the domestic, personal experiences dealt with in those genres so as to read certain small-scale gestures, silences and so on as having meanings for the narrative. The group most likely to have such knowledge was women, with their informal training for their roles as mothers, or, partly by extension, as carers in such jobs as nurses, secretaries or teachers of young children.

The **TV institutions** will sustain and often create such expectations by their **scheduling practices** (see Chapter 30, 'Case study: Selling audiences') so it becomes easy for women to develop the habit of viewing at convenient times – key for the accumulated pleasure of the soap genre.

We don't want to argue that no male viewers ever come upon, or have the competences to enjoy romances, or women's magazines, nor that some women may not be irritated by them. But we are all in many ways shaped by informal gender training so that certain responses to some genres (like the sad-ending romance) are from very early on made unacceptable for some groups, natural-seeming for others.

From the male side of **gender** dividing, it's been argued that boys are socialised from early on into acting tough in the face of 18-rated videos and horror films which they sometimes find hard to stomach. Our culture still expects men, in the end, to differentiate themselves from women along the lines of 'toughness'. Young men are encouraged not to cry, not to explore feelings, and to try to appear as decisive and hard as the heroes of action adventures.

'When I was 3 or 4 my mother was already teaching me to see dust and other people's feelings.'
(Shere Hite 1988)

ACTIVITY 29.7

Are any of your viewing choices ever ridiculed by other members of your household?

- If so, in what terms, and about what kinds of programmes?
- How insistent is the ridiculing?
- Does it ever prevent you from watching the programme?
- Do you ever describe yourself as an 'addict' of a media form (programme, magazine, novel)?
- Do you think this is a way of apologising for your interest in it?

A **cultural** or **ideological** approach to genres is interested in this area : the intimate relationships between audiences and their pleasure and interest in fitting media forms with the rest of their lives.

- Do young men absorb a sense of how to be a Real Man from action thrillers, or young women learn how to enjoy certain kinds of power over men from romance forms?
- Do the repetitions within certain genres, and the imaginings they exclude as well as the ones they encourage, reinforce dominant and sometimes oppressive sets of values?
- How do the media in such contexts relate to the unequal distribution of power in society generally?

Others (see Geraghty 1991, Ch. 3 for summary) have gone even further and suggested that the very shape of **soaps** is reason for women's enjoyment of them. They cite

- open endedness
- the invitation to identify with many different characters
- the habit of not driving towards a goal (as is argued to occur in genres popular with men, such as police or detective series).

These are said to mirror women's role in the domestic sphere, especially the empathising expected of the ideal mother. Christine Geraghty has also redrawn Dyer's **Utopian** categories (see Chapter 5, 'Genres') to account for other pleasures of soaps (see Figure 29.4). On the other hand it's been argued that men's enjoyment of (even addiction to) news and documentary forms has related to the assumption that their lives, more than women's, will take place within the world of public, rather than domestic, events which they get to 'catch up on' and feel part of through news media.

Ethnicity

Marie Gillespie (1995) has suggested that Asian British young people in Southall watched *Home and Away* and *Neighbours* for the following reasons:

- As popular serials dealing with romance, growing up, etc., they gave some insight into the 'host' British community, which is often unfriendly and even racist, and thus not easily open to exploration.
- The subject matter often deals with rumour and gossip, important in the Punjabi community with its emphasis on *izzat*, or family honour.

The idea that such cultural competences are major determinants on people's choices of media genres tries to challenge emphases on single structures as class. Though cultural resources are class related, they are often determined by education, and by socialisation within family groups.

'It didn't feel sexual as I would now define that. It felt more about wanting freedom. I didn't want to grow up and be a wife and it seemed to me that the Beatles had the kind of freedom I wanted ... I didn't want to sleep with Paul McCartney, I was too young. But I wanted to be like them, something larger than life.'

(Ex-Beatle fan, quoted in Lewis, L. 1992)

'Soap operas invest exquisite pleasure in the central condition of a woman's life: waiting – whether for the phone to ring, for the baby to take its nap, or for the family to be reunited after the day's final soap has left its family still struggling against dissolution.'

(Modleski 1982)

	Energy	Abundance	Intensity	Transparency	Community
British soaps	strong women characters, quick repartee, pace of plot		emotions strongly expressed at key moments, Angie/Den, Sheila/Bobby	sincerity of key characters: Deirdre Barlow, Kathy Beale, Sheila Grant, *True Love*: Deirdre/Ken Chris/Frank	characters offer support, friendship, gossip outside programme
US soaps	strong male characters, business activity, pace of plot	glamorous settings, clothes, luxurious objects, food, etc.	emotions strongly expressed at key moments, Sue Ellen's madness	sincerity of key characters: Bobby, Pamela, Miss Ellie, Krystle *True Love*: Blake/Krystle Bobby/Pamela	asserted within family, rarely achieved, relationship with audience
Romance	strong male character	provided at end by hero	story works towards moment when hero speaks of love	story works towards movement when true love is revealed	community not important
Gothic woman's film	strong male character	wealthy male, luxurious trappings, big house	emotion sought by heroine, withheld by hero	sincerity of heroine, opacity of hero	community presented ambiguously
'Heroine's text' woman's film	strong female character as heroine	heroine works for it, for herself or her children	heroine's expression of love for child, work or man	sincerity of heroine, misunderstood by man	woman initially outside community, may fight her way in

Figure 29.4 Utopian possibilities in women's fiction
(Source: Geraghty 1992)

Technologies and consumption

This brings us to a more recent development: an interest in what has been called the 'double' character of the meaningfulness of the media. This refers to the way the media consist of both

- the programmes, music, etc. brought to us, and
- the significance of media technologies themselves in our daily lives.

These seem to work both in terms of cultural status (the attempts to disguise or conceal the satellite dish, for example, or to show off the mobile phone) and gendered differences in attitudes to technology. Ann Gray (1992) asked the women she interviewed to colour-code technologies and activities on a scale from pink to blue depending on whether they found them intimidating or friendly.

She reports that:

> This produces almost uniformly pink irons and blue electric drills, with many interesting mixtures along the spectrum . . . the VCR [has different colours] . . . The 'record', 'rewind' and 'play' modes are usually lilac, but the timer switch is nearly always blue, with the women having to depend on their male partners or their children to set the timer for them.

Sherry Turkle's (1992) research on the reasons for young women's reluctance to use computers has likewise suggested not that they are incapable of using machines or technology, but that they resist, or feel ill at ease in, the world of the 'computer virtuosos', the 'technoheads'. These are names given to young men who seem to be involved in an intimate relationship with their machines, one which is often strongly competitive and macho – 'mine's bigger and faster than yours' – and centred around very masculine genres such as the action adventure and science-fiction.

Attempts are being made to counter such perceptions, both in TV programmes and in schools, since a very real fear for the next century is that the 'information-rich' and 'information-poor' distinction predicted will work not simply along the lines of class, and the world's North–South divide, but also gender.

ACTIVITY 29.8

Collect some recent images of scientists and computers in advertising and TV programmes such as *The Net* or *Tomorrow's World*.

- How far do they conform to the suggestions above?
- What efforts seem to be being made to change the gender balance of such images?

'Low budget entertainment doesn't come any cheaper. The police traffic videos featured in last September's documentary *Police Stop!* proved to be the highest rating factual programme of 1994.'
(*Observer*, 20 Dec. 1994)

Finally, audiences in the media . . .

A final point is that with the drive to cheaper broadcasting, the expansion of daytime TV and interactive computer technologies, the audience can be thought of as more literally part of the media than has been the case before. Phone-ins, access TV and chat shows, for instance, allow parts of the audience 'into' the media, though on rather special terms.

Access has traditionally meant programme-making where real power, including editorial control, is handed over to a group or individual outside the broadcasting institutions. The BBC's *Open Space* slot, or Channel Four's *Right to Reply* are examples of the genre, based in a critique of **mainstream** broadcasting. This included questioning old ideas of 'balance' between two sides, rather than a plurality of voices needing representation. It also expressed doubts that mainstream TV, full of well-paid professionals often making programmes at least partly for each other, would ever be able to include voices outside its own rather comfortable assumptions and lifestyles.

Chat shows and '**infotainment**' forms, such as *The Oprah Winfrey Show*, are slightly different. Are they simply 'tabloid TV'? Are they saturated with experience but short on expertise? They certainly allow members of the public on to TV or radio, but under what conditions?

ACTIVITY 29.9

Take your favourite radio phone-in or TV chat show and examine on what terms members of the audience manage to get a hearing.

Look at the following:

- What do the titles promise?
- How is the studio set up?
- Where are the microphones and who controls them?
- How does the host organise things?
- How is the show concluded: by interruption?
- What points get taken up, which ones are ignored or curtailed? Why?
- What kinds of ideas and positions can be circulated through such shows?
- What seem to be the criteria for choosing particular experts over others? How are their contributions treated?
- What is the most surprising or unfamiliar position you have ever heard voiced on such shows? How was it treated?

Finally, try to gain access to the show yourself and write an account of what happened, on what terms you feel you were accepted, and how you would like to see (or hear, if it's radio) the show changed.

References and further reading

Ang, I. (1991) *Desperately Seeking the Audience*, London: Routledge.

Bandura, A. and Walters, R. (1963) *Social Learning and Personality Development*, New York: Holt, Rinehart & Winston.

Barker, Martin (1989) *Comics: Ideology, Power and the Critics,* Manchester:
Manchester University Press.

Brunsdon, Charlotte and Morley, David (1978) *Everyday Television:
Nationwide,* BFI Advisory Document.

Buckingham, David (1993) *Reading Audiences: Young People and the Media,*
Manchester: Manchester University Press.

Cohen, S. (1972) *Folk Devils and Moral Panics,* Oxford: Martin Robertson.

Craib, I. (1984) *Modern Social Theory,* London: Harvester Wheatsheaf.

Geraghty, Christine (1991) *Women and Soap Opera: A Study of Prime Time
Soaps,* London: Polity.

Gerbner, G. and Gross, L. (1976) 'Living with Television: The Violence
Profile', *Journal of Communication*, no. 28.

Gillespie, Marie (1995) *Television, Ethnicity and Cultural Change,* London:
Routledge.

Gray, Ann (1992) *Video Playtime: The Gendering of a Leisure Technology,*
London: Routledge .

Hite, Shere (1988) *The Hite Report on Women and Love: A Cultural
Revolution in Progress,* London: Viking.

Lazarsfeld, P., Berelson, B. and Gaudet, H. (1944) *The People's Choice,* New
York: Duell, Sloan and Pearce.

Lewis, J. (1991) *The Ideological Octopus: The Exploration of Television and Its
Audience,* London: Routledge.

Lewis, L. (ed.) (1992) *The Adoring Audience Fan Culture and Popular Media,*
London: Routledge.

McQuail, D., Blumler, J. and Brown, J.R. (1972) 'The Television
Audience: A Revised Perspective', in D. McQuail (ed.) *Sociology of Mass
Communications,* Harmondsworth, Penguin.

Maslow, A. (1970) *Motivation and Personality*, New York: Harper & Row.

Modleski, T. (1982) *Loving with a Vengeance,* New York: Methuen.

Moores, S. (1993) *Interpreting Audiences: The Ethnography of Media
Consumption,* London: Sage.

Morley, David (1980) *The Nationwide Audience*, London: BFI.

—— (1986) *Family Television: Cultural Power and Domestic Leisure,*
London: Comedia.

—— (1991) 'Changing Paradigms in Audience Studies', in E. Seiter, H.
Borchers, G. Kreutzner and E. Warth (eds), *Remote Control Television,
Audiences and Cultural Power,* New York and London: Routledge.

Pearson, Geoffrey (1984) 'Falling Standards: A Short, Sharp History of
Moral Decline', in M. Barker (ed.) *The Video Nasties,* London, Pluto.

Philo, Greg (1990) *Seeing and Believing: The Influence of Television,* London:
Routledge.

O'Sullivan, T., Hartley, J., Saunders, D., Montgomery M. and Fisk, J. (1994) *Key Concepts in Communication and Cultural Studies,* London: Routledge.

Root, Jane (1986) *Open the Box,* London: Comedia.

Strinati, Dominic (1995) *Introduction to Theories of Popular Culture,* London: Routledge.

Turkle, S. (1988) 'Computational Reticence: Why Women Fear the Intimate Machine', in C. Kramarae (ed.) *Technology and Women's Voices,* New York: Simon & Schuster.

Williams, Raymond (1974) *Television: Technology and Cultural Form,* London: Fontana.

—— (1988) 'Culture is Ordinary', in R. Williams, *Resources of Hope: Culture, Democracy, Socialism,* London and New York: Verso.

Winston, Brian (1990) 'On Counting the Wrong Things', in M. Alvarado and J.O. Thompson (eds) *The Media Reader,* London: BFI.

Advertising agencies
TV and advertising
Regions and audience size
Scheduling
Magazine advertising

30 / Case study: Selling audiences

Academic research is a tiny body of work compared to advertising research. The latter is funded by companies who have something to sell, and therefore need to know about and to affect buying habits. Points worth remembering as you study contemporary advertising (See Chapter 9, 'Advertising, marketing and fashion'):

- The much discredited **effects model** of readers' engagement with the media is alive and well in this media sector. Indeed advertising agencies, whatever the playfulness and irony of their products, still need to persuade companies using them that they will have some kind of effect on buying habits.

- Yet oddly enough much contemporary **marketing** rhetoric sounds innocent of any desire to affect people. Terms like 'level playing field', 'the market', 'the discriminating consumer' attribute power to the picking and choosing consumer from the **uses and gratifications model**. This is somewhat surprising given that the biggest change in advertising over the last fifty years has been from working on the product's brand image to researching the audience to be 'targeted'.

- Whatever the arguments about the effects on our immediate buying habits, ads are argued to have other, broader effects. Some of these are outlined in Chapter 9, 'Advertising, marketing and fashion'. Here we'll just mention that the very act of targeting audiences contributes towards their creation and consolidation. One example would be the 'teenager'. This previously unknown concept was by the late 1950s an accepted part of advertising (and political) rhetoric, one that confirmed and actually helped to create a new identity for people in a certain age range.

Advertising agencies

These are businesses that exist to produce and place ads for their customers, the manufacturers of products. They are usually divided into departments specialising in ad design (the 'creative' team) and those who oversee the operation (the account managers).

The JICNARS scale divides audiences into:
Group A: upper middle class, e.g. successful business or professional
Group B: middle class, e.g. senior business or professional, but not at the top of their business etc.
Group C1: white-collar, lower-middle-class consumers, e.g. small tradespeople and non-manual workers
Group C2: blue-collar, skilled working class
Group D: semi or unskilled manual workers
Group E: those at the lowest levels of subsistence, 'casual workers or those who, through sickness or unemployment are dependent on social security schemes'.

Advertisers still use the **JICNARS** (Joint Industry Committee for National Readership Surveys) scales, originally designed to investigate magazine and newspaper sales distribution. But though such class indicators are still important, several objections were made to the JICNARS and other occupation-based surveys of audiences:

- They rely on the occupation of the 'head of the household' and assume that to be a man. In many

households the main wage-earner is a woman, or the income is made up of part-time work by both partners.
- It sees the family as a single, uncontradictory consuming unit, without generational or life-stage distinctions.
- It underestimates the ways in which a 'flexible labour market' has brought about rapid changes of occupation, and kinds of work that no longer smoothly fit the scales used.

'40% of the population no longer has a job that fits the system at all.' This statement is from a *Guardian* report (17 July 1995) on the government's decision to change the way class is measured by the Office of Population Censuses and Surveys.

From the 1970s onwards agencies began to use new categories, aimed at specific audience groups, by means of *demographics* such as used by ACORN

THE MOST IMPORTANT GAP IN YOUR MARKET PLACE

We can target your leaflets one of three ways, making sure that your advertising message is delivered to the heart of your market. Our professional sales team will help you to plan your campaign. You can select by demographical breakdown, geographical area or by postcode areas.

DEMOGRAPHICAL BREAKDOWN

To make sure that your message reaches exactly the right target you can plan your campaign by demographical breakdown ie: distributing to terraced housing only. You can also use this type of targeting in conjunction with either geographical area or postcodes.

Have a look at the demographical breakdown below to see which category would suit your campaign.

CATEGORY DESCRIPTION

A Affluent Suburban Housing
B Modern Housing Higher Income
C Older Housing Intermediate Status
D Terraced Housing
E Better Off Council
F Less Well Off Council
G Poorest Council

GEOGRAPHICAL AREA

Plan your campaign by geographical area, just select the towns or villages you wish to target, i.e. West Cross, Skewen and Trallwn and we can let you know how many leaflets are needed to cover those areas. This can also be used with the demographical breakdown i.e. targeting B type households only within those areas.

POSTCODES

You can plan your campaign by postcode areas and sectors. Just consult the map and select the sectors you wish to reach i.e. SA3 Sector 5 and we can let you know how many leaflets are required to cover your selected area. This can also be used with the demographical breakdown i.e. private housing in SA3 Sector 5.

CONTACT LORNA DAVIES

OR CONTACT NICHOLA LEWIS

Herald Direct Distribution, Cambrian House, Cambrian Place, Swansea SA1 1RH Telephone (0792) 468833 Ext 3540/3600 Fax No: (0792) 472208

Figure 30.1 Herald Direct distribution ad

(A Classification of Residential Neighbourhoods) which divide potential buyers by geographical location (often using postcodes or national census returns).

Psychographic profiles break with such occupational and geographical models. They use questionnaires mailed to members of a panel who are invited to respond to statements like: 'A woman's place is in the home' or 'The use of marijuana should be made legal'. On the basis of the replies, consumers are classified as belonging to a number of *lifestyle categories*. There are various models competing for manufacturers' and agencies' fees, but a typical one would be the American VALS (Values and Lifestyles) system which classifies people into four groups: needs driven, outer directed, inner directed and integrated.

Agencies may also research consumers' feelings about a product using **focus groups** of a few selected consumers presented with an issue to work on, or asked about the image a particular product has for them. For example, 'qualitative research' in 1982 into Levi's jeans before their 'relaunch' is said by one of the big London agencies, BBH (Bartle, Bogle, Hegarty) to have elicited the following:

'They're the sort of thing bank clerks would wear – middle-aged ones, at weekends.'

The availability of remote controls, video and more TV channels and radio stations for advertising also mean audiences' habits have become less easy to predict. **Media buyers** in the agencies are specialists who know the most effective medium, the best vehicle in that medium to carry a specific campaign. Agencies will calculate which audiences can be attracted through *different* media for particular products:

Abbott Mead Vickers (AMV), the agency handling Sainsbury's account, never place an ad for Sainsbury's in a magazine unless it is the first supermarket advertised. If the aim is to sell a bargain, ads are based in newspapers. If sophistication or quality is to be sold, magazines and colour will be used. One in three Sainsbury's

shoppers are housewives with big families who can be tempted into the store by bargains. Day time TV ads can reach them. But if Sainsbury's is being marketed as a quality brand, ads are placed in slots after 8.30 when upmarket AB shoppers are assumed to be watching.

(Summarised from the *Guardian*, 10 December 1990)

They are also hired for their skills in negotiating the best price for their ads. They were active, for example, in pressurising **BARB** (Broadcasters' Audience Research Board) to investigate the effect of video playback on ad consumption.

TV and advertising

Commercial or 'independent' TV is funded by the sale of advertising space by the TV companies, also described as *selling audiences to advertisers*. Actually it is audiences' *attention* which advertisers hope to purchase.

This system of buying and selling produces, and is the result of, the commercial logic for ITV funding, the opposite of the notion of **public service** at work within the early years of the BBC (See Chapter 24, 'Institutions'). It began in the USA during the Depression of the 1930s, when radio proved the perfect medium for advertisers wanting access to audiences who were confined to the home, for a variety of reasons. The huge success of soap-company-funded serials (soaps) soon went along with a construction/selling of housewives' attention during the day and that of men still in employment and some children during the evening. **Scheduling** and the selling of advertising space in programmes likely to attract particular groups, took off. It did not simply *follow* the programmes: it very much helped to *determine* them.

TV and radio programmes are now made with the intention of attracting audiences, so that advertisers can buy time or 'slots' within (and more recently sponsorship deals around) them. Sometimes a *guaranteed audience* will be purchased, spread across a number of slots which will deliver a fixed number of viewers. Interestingly, it has been suggested that advertisers sometimes prefer programmes that are not too involving and so do not detract from attention to the ads (Curran and Seaton 1991: 223). This has important implications for what can be called totally commercial broadcasting ecologies.

ACTIVITY 30.1

If you can, record or take notes on four or five advertising or sponsorship slots from commercial radio and TV across the day, e.g. one from early morning, another from 9.0am or so, through to late night/early morning.

- What does this suggest about the kinds of audiences advertisers expect to be watching/listening?
- How do the surrounding programmes relate to these ads?
- Why do you think these sponsors want these slots?

Repeat the activity for **broadsheet** and **tabloid** newspapers. Look especially at the difference between 'small ads' and whole page ones.

Companies, in paying out these huge sums of money, hope to reach the kind of people who will buy their products. Indeed, they check that broadcasters do in fact put out the ads at the times they contracted to do, and even check the whole range of output and criticise the ITV Network Controller in general terms if audiences slip.

Since the 1990 Broadcasting Act, sponsorship has also become a part of UK TV. (It was deliberately not chosen as the funding mechanism in the Television Act of 1954 which established commercial TV.) The head of sponsorship for the J. Walter Thompson ad agency, which oversees Kellogg's sponsorship of *Gladiators*, is quoted on ways of catching the zapping viewer with a sponsor's credit rather than (or rather, as well as) ads during programmes:

Your brand is closer to the programme and is a message before other advertising cuts in ... It obviously reinforces other brand advertising, but ... allows the advertiser to build a closer relationship with a consumer. By being involved in a programme your consumer watches, it's like saying 'We know what you're into and we support it too.'

(*Observer*, 8 January 1995)

Regions and audience size

One of the arguments for the ITV system of regionally based companies was that they would serve and sustain local identities. In fact the 'Big Five' companies dominate programming; only rarely does a programme from HTV or Border get on to **prime-time** commercial TV. Though it's been argued that Border Television may have strengthened a sense of local identity, the regional companies' main logic is a commercial one. HTV consists of HTV West and HTV Wales, because Wales on its own is not considered advertiser-lucrative enough to sustain major programming.

"'Granada has the skilled workers: surveys prove it!" read an advertisement in a 1959 trade magazine. "Westward where women cook," read another in Campaign in 1962.'

(Curran and Seaton 1991)

Additionally, regional commercial TV means that additional advertising pressure can be applied in any region where sales are slumping.

It is not the case, if it ever was, that advertising simply seeks to reach the largest possible audience. At both national and global level, regional differences are carefully studied. Certain products are test marketed in particular areas. Many magazines produce London supplements to try to catch the attention of a concentrated and relatively affluent, young audience.

TSMS NATIONAL 30" RATES

RATES EFFECTIVE FROM 1ST NOVEMBER 1994

PREMIER RATES

Rate Code	Anglia 30 Sec £	Grampian 30 Sec £	HTV 30 Sec £	Meridian 30 Sec £	Scottish 30 Sec £	S4C 30 Sec £	UTV 30 Sec £	West-country 30 Sec £
P3	24,000	4,800	17,600	33,600	16,320	1,760	4,800	7,200
P2	21,000	4,200	15,400	29,400	14,280	1,540	4,200	6,300
P1	18,000	3,600	13,200	25,200	12,240	1,320	3,600	5,400

STANDARD RATES

Rate Code	30 Sec £	30 Sec £	30 Sec £	30 Sec £	30 Sec £	30 Sec £	30 Sec £	30 Sec £
SR	15,000	3,000	11,000	21,000	10,200	1,100	3,000	4,500
10	13,500	2,700	9,900	18,900	9,180	990	2,700	4,050
20	12,000	2,400	8,800	16,800	8,160	880	2,400	3,600
25	11,250	2,250	8,250	15,750	7,650	825	2,250	3,375
30	10,500	2,100	7,700	14,700	7,140	770	2,100	3,150
40	9,000	1,800	6,600	12,600	6,120	660	1,800	2,700
50	7,500	1,500	5,500	10,500	5,100	550	1,500	2,250
60	6,000	1,200	4,400	8,400	4,080	440	1,200	1,800
65	5,250	1,050	3,850	7,350	3,570	385	1,050	1,575
70	4,500	900	3,300	6,300	3,060	330	900	1,350
75	3,750	750	2,750	5,250	2,550	275	750	1,125
80	3,000	600	2,200	4,200	2,040	220	600	900
85	2,250	450	1,650	3,150	1,530	165	450	675
90	1,500	300	1,100	2,100	1,020	110	300	450
93	1,000	200	733	1,400	680	73	200	300
95	750	150	550	1,050	510	55	150	225
97	500	100	367	700	340	37	100	150
98	300	60	220	420	204	22	60	90
99	150	30	110	210	102	–	30	45

THE FOLLOWING APPLIES TO ALL STATIONS:

The following factors will apply by timelength with rates rounded to the nearest pound:

	10"	20"	30"	40"	50"	60"
DIVIDE BY	2.00	1.20	1.00	0.75	0.60	0.50

Each additional time length above 60 seconds will be pro-rata to the 60 second rate.

Advertisement rates will be slotted into specific breaks and will be pre-emptible by Advertisers paying a higher rate.

Premier rates will be available in selected programmes normally identified ahead of advanced booking deadline. On certain occasions, rates other than Standard or Premier will be made available subject to demand.

Figure 30.2 The economics of selling TV advertising slots

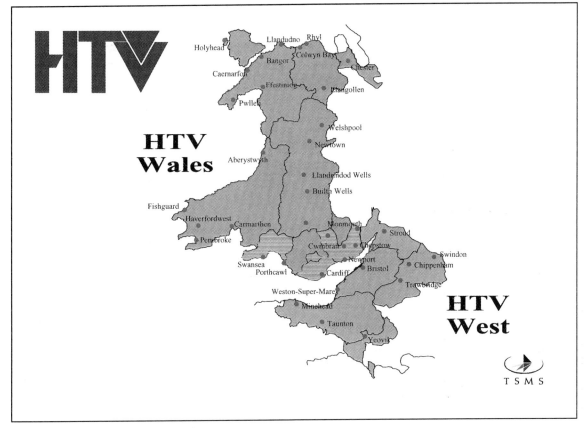

Figure 30.3 Map of HTV area

ACTIVITY 30.2
Next time you watch TV in a different ITV region to your local one, watch the ads to see if any of them is different, and if so, what the differences are.
- Try to think why those products or campaigns have been tried in that region.
- See if you can research the ad rates for the London area and compare them with those for your local area, if you live outside London.

TV and radio **ratings** work within an advertising industry which now **segments** or divides up its **target audiences**, or readerships, whatever the medium. Of course, within these groups ads hope to reach as many people as possible, in fact magazines and TV companies

trying to reach advertisers will talk of CPTs, or 'Costs Per Thousand' (consumers reached).

The Clothes Show Magazine – an essential magazine on your schedule.

Cost Per Thousand Comparison
ABC1 Women 25–44

Rank	Title	000's	Col Pg Rate	CPT
1	Clothes Show	203	3,493	17
2	She	277	4,720	17
3	Cosmo	506	9,900	19
4	Options	205	4,950	24
5	Woman's Journal	132	4,395	33
6	Marie Claire	141	4,730	33
7	New Woman	161	5,600	34

(Source: UK NRS Jan 91–June 91)

Figure 30.4

Another example of ways in which such 'mass media' do not in fact always seek to reach 'the masses' occurred in 1986. British advertising agencies succeeded in persuading BARB, who used to measure social groups D and E together in viewing figures, to separate them out. This was because the 'E's (those 'on the lowest level of subsistence' like retired working-class people and the unemployed) are of little interest to advertisers, yet are heavy consumers of media because they have so much spare time. They were said to be distorting the viewing figures by suggesting programmes had huge audiences of people itching to spend the pounds in their pockets. It's likely that there will be an increasing tendency to ignore such large but unattractive-to-advertisers audiences if cultural activities continue to be funded mostly by commercial advertising. As with the press, what's often sought are more specific viewing and buying audiences.

Relatedly, the ability of advertisers to shape broadcasting by **niche marketing**, encouraging the making of certain TV genres and seeing others as unprofitable or even undesirable (especially in the USA) has been, and should be, cause for concern. Wasko (1994) argues it is even spreading to cinema, in the form of advertiser-preferred projects with 'placement' potential.

Huge amounts of money, time and energy are invested in *audience measurement,* especially in the USA, as competition between the TV networks and the cable companies intensifies. In Britain, where similar trends are visible, research bodies compile 'ratings' of programmes which suggest how many, and what kinds of viewers are watching them. For example, the weekly ratings figures are made up for BARB by recording the viewing habits of a sample of 4,500 viewers. Special machines called *People Meters* attached to these viewers' TV sets, record, every 5 seconds, which channel the set is tuned to and which members of the household are watching. In addition the amount of VCR recording is measured, the playback of broadcast programmes which carry an electronic code, and playback of 'non-coded', bought or hired videos in a desperate attempt to chart audiences

who are now partly freed from the schedules. Interestingly, though, most video recording seems to occur to time-shift at periods of fierce competition, notably the weekend and Tuesdays.

'last week ... the advertising agency Lowe Howard-Spink Lowe ... found that at least one third of the audience "vigorously and continuously" tries to escape TV commercials. And the most zealous practitioners of this "ad avoidance" are that most desirable group, "young and early middle-aged fully employed males".

(Observer, 21 May 1995)

Scheduling

Scheduling is choosing where to put a programme on radio or TV, usually with a competitor's programming in mind. Broadcasters have traditionally worked with ideas such as prime time, the period from around 19.30 to 22.30 hours, when large and relatively affluent audiences are watching. The division of schedules into such viewing periods enables a scale of the commercial value of audiences to be calculated. Because all British broadcasting is partly public-service regulated, though, both ITV and BBC have also worked with the regulated *Family Viewing Policy* which, drawing on effects approaches, has responded to lobbying groups such as the NVLA (National Viewers' and Listeners' Association). The FVP constructs profiles of audience availability and type, and then an image of Family Life from which is prescribed what should be viewable at particular times:

Coffee Time	0925	–	1229
Afternoon	1230	–	1714
Early Peak	1715	–	1924
Late Peak	1925	–	2329
Late Night	2330	–	2629
Moonlight	2630	–	Close
Peak Definition	1715	–	2329

- 16.15–17.15 on weekdays is 'children's hour'.
- 17.15–19.30 is presumed to be family viewing time, but with all material broadcast suitable for children to view alone.
- 19.30–21.00 is when no material unsuitable for children viewing with the family is broadcast.
- 21.00 onwards it is assumed parents are responsible for any children who may still be watching.

(Though we are here exploring the selling of media time, you should consider how far scheduling practices deserve to be considered as part of the spectrum of **censorship** processes, in their ability to make easily available, or unavailable, certain kinds of material.)

Related watersheds also operate, such as the 9pm barrier to certain kinds of language and violent or sexual imagery.

ACTIVITY 30.3

Visit your biggest local magazine/book retailer (such as Menzies or W.H. Smith) and note how similar to scheduling is the arrangement of books into genres and expected audiences.

- What kinds of books get the equivalent of 'prime time'?
- Can you see any other parallels to broadcasting schedules?

Schedulers also use the following terms:

- *pre-scheduling* or starting a programme five minutes before its rival programme on the other channel
- *inheritance factor:* some audiences seem to 'trust' and watch one channel for most of the evening, so programmes of lesser appeal are put on after popular ones, in the hope that the audience will continue watching
- *hammocking:* where a programme of minority appeal is transmitted between two popular ones, again, to try to build up its audience
- *pre-echo:* audiences watch part of the programme before the one they want so they don't miss the beginning. This may be used as a strategy for building up an audience for the less popular programme
- *common junction points:* where two programmes start at the same time on BBC1 and 2, for example, the chance for cross trailing arises: 'And now a choice of viewing on BBC ...'

ACTIVITY 30.4

Watch a few hours of TV with an eye to which scheduling decisions seem to have been made. Make a note on them and explore how they seem to connect to the ads being shown.

You might think that ratings-consciousness only applies to commercial broadcasting, trying to convince advertisers of its desirability, and that the BBC can simply stay aloof from the preferences of commercial TV or radio. But the BBC equally needs to justify the licence fee (as well as to provide a satisfying environment for its programme-makers). An important marker of such success is judged to be how many people are watching or listening to its programmes. Hence ratings and scheduling battles exist even where sales of audiences' attention are not involved.

There is now much emphasis on the difficulty of scheduling. Video, cable and other multi-channel developments as well as the fragmentation of older 'certainties' like family structure, all make it seem a more volatile process than previously. Yet it still seems wrong to argue that viewers are completely unpredictable, too busy 'surfing' the networks, 'grazing' across channels to be hailed by ads, in view of the following facts.

- Programme-makers and advertisers still battle for 'good' slots, i.e. regular ones, and ones within prime time.
- Effective schedulers are highly sought after within TV and radio. Witness the careers and salaries of people like Michael Grade, renowned for his scheduling skills at BBC1, which gained him the job as Channel 4's chief executive.

- Some audiences do graze, at certain times of the day, but most have fixed viewing or listening slots in their routines which schedulers are keen to discover, and to target.

Nevertheless, ratings figures are not transparent in their meanings. High ratings for various programmes may be due to a number of factors, including curiosity, the weather, the fact that there was little on other channels. Ambiguity is built into the process.

A note on the reporting of TV controversies

It is worth remembering in current debates led by the press about deregulation, the selling off of the BBC, its ratings, etc. that the press also lives largely by advertising revenue. The position taken by particular newspapers on TV controversies has to be understood in relation to often contradictory drives, in addition to the ideological positions of those with power and ownership positions in these industries:

- *Deregulation* How far would the extension of TV advertising (for example, if the BBC were to be completely commercialised) undercut newspaper advertising revenues by bringing down costs and widening the pool of media available to advertisers?
- *Ownership* Who owns the paper which is arguing against the BBC? Is it Rupert Murdoch's News International group, which owns 37 per cent of the British press and huge amounts of broadcasting, and has a particular interest in acquiring more?

Magazine advertising

ACTIVITY 30.5

Let's try to apply what you have read to other media such as magazines. Look at the three documents reproduced as Figures 30.5 (a, b, c), circulated by fashion journals.

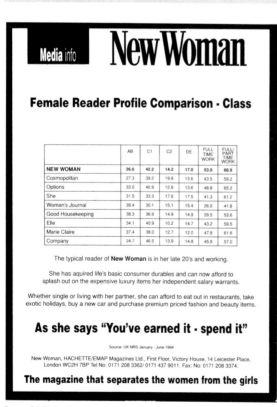

Figure 30.5(a)

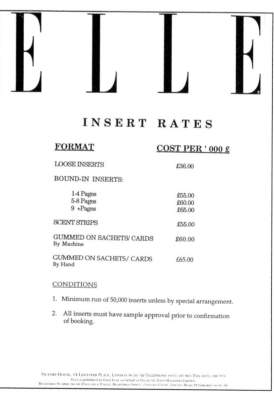

Figure 30.5(b)

- Who do you think they are addressing?
- What is their mode of address (see Chapter 29, 'Audiences')
- If you know the magazines, how does this information cast light on them?
- Which parts of the magazine's style or address to its readers are partly explained by this information?
- How?

References and further reading

Ang, I. (1991) *Desperately Seeking the Audience,* London: Routledge.

Chisnall, P. (1985) *Marketing: A Behavioural Analysis,* London: McGraw-Hill.

Coward, Ros (1984) *Female Desire,* London: Granada.

Curran, James and Seaton, Jean (1991) *Power Without Responsibility: The Press and Broadcasting in Britain,* London: Routledge.

Myers, Kathy (1986) *Understains: The Sense and Seduction of Advertising,* London: Comedia.

Paterson, Richard (1990) 'A Suitable Schedule for the Family', in Andrew Goodwin and Gary Whannel (eds) *Understanding Television,* London: Routledge.

Wasko, Janet (1994) *Hollywood in the Information Age Beyond the Silver Screen,* London: Polity.

Williamson, Judith (1978) *Decoding Advertisements,* London: Marion Boyars.

NOTE: Names of useful journals are located on p. 370. You might also try approaching an ad agency and asking for a back copy of BRAD (British Rates and Data) which will give you the current rate in every UK publication, including broadcasting. You may even find your school or college has a staff member responsible for publicity, who can lend you one.

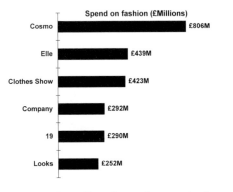

Figure 30.5(c)

Setting out on production
The production process in
    outline
Practical production notes

31 Producing

Production work is an integral part of media education and training. 'Practice' informs 'theory' and vice versa. We assume that you will receive some direct instruction in how to use media technology and that you will seek out appropriate manuals which deal with 'hands-on' issues in specific media. Here we address the important generic or 'common skills and understanding' associated with all types of production.

Setting out on production

Whatever your production task, there are five important questions which you need to ask yourself before you begin work:

'Now that farmers are being paid for *not* growing crops ... might I suggest that this is a policy the Arts Council could adopt ... they could pay writers not to produce books' (adapted from a letter by David M. Bennie to *The Literary Review*). The same view might be applied to a wide range of media products that don't have a clear purpose and a recognised audience.

Purpose Why are you producing a media text? Most likely it will be to 'educate, inform or entertain'. If it isn't one of these, then it is probably intended to persuade. Any other purpose (like the artist's attempt to 'explore the medium') can probably be subsumed under these headings. All production must be entertaining to a certain extent or else readers won't persevere with the text. Your production will be assessed according to the extent to which it 'fits its purpose' and you should bear this in mind throughout each stage of the process.

Target audience The meaning produced by a text depends to a large extent on who is the intended reader and therefore it is futile to try to construct a text if you don't know who that reader is. The audience profile will include the standard age, gender and class information as well as more culturally based distinctions which might include religion, sexual orientation, marital or family status, etc., and environmental factors such as geographical location. (See Chapter 29, 'Audiences', for further discussion of the descriptions used by media industries.)

Style What **style** or **genre** will you use? No matter how 'original' you attempt to be, you will be making references to media conventions – if you don't make these references your readers may have difficulty following the text. You will perhaps be warned not to slavishly imitate professional work, but, at least when you are starting out on your first productions, it is difficult not to draw on work you enjoy or admire. The best advice is to make open your intention to work 'in the style of' an existing producer and to begin by trying to understand all the conventions of a particular genre or style. If you want to go on and break with convention, it is useful to know which 'rules' need to be broken.

If you are clear in the aesthetic or the formal approach which you wish to adopt, you will find it much easier to explain what you want to do, both to the commissioner of the work and to the rest of your production team.

Schedule How long do you have to complete the production process? Planning and preparation are going to be essential for a successful production, but even the best plans will come to nothing if the overall task is impossible. Calculate the time each part of the process will take and ensure that you know everything about the schedule from the outset. For instance, you may be required to show the unfinished work to your commissioner in order to confirm the inclusion of contentious material, but will that person be available when you reach the crucial decision-making stage? Can your **schedule** be adapted to cope with these problems?

Your schedule will distinguish different parts of the process and you will be able to plan when and where each can take place. Be careful, because some aspects of production are more time-dependent than others, e.g. video post-production always takes longer than you imagine. Some parts of the production process are dependent on other parts having been completed first, so, for instance, if you want titles on your video production which overlay the opening sequence, you must prepare them before you start editing – you can't add them afterwards. 'Managing the schedule' is one of the most important aspects of production and perhaps the least appreciated by beginners. You would be well advised to check that you know, at the outset, all the stages which your production will need to go through so that you can map out a schedule which includes sufficient 'recovery time' for each stage in case things go wrong.

Working in a familiar genre can mean greater 'freedom' because the conventions are so well known that audiences can be introduced to new ideas on the back of familiar ones. The film director John Ford famously said 'I make westerns' – a statement of false modesty, referring to a body of work showing great variety.

A schedule for magazine production

Imagine you are setting out to produce a fanzine or a small specialist magazine, say a 16-page, 'single colour' (the cheapest form of printing in which you just choose one ink colour) A4 size magazine. You have a number of friends who are going to contribute articles and you hope to distribute 1,000 copies. All the DTP will be done by you and you will then take hard copy or a computer file to the printer. How do you organise the schedule?

The first decision will be the date of publication. This is the date when you want readers to have the magazine in their hands – you need to set a date before the first date for any events or 'forthcoming attractions' you might list. You can then work backwards to set deadlines for each stage of the production process. This is what you might come up with:

Week 1   Decisions on editorial policy and budget
Week 2   Estimates from printer
Week 3   Contributions commissioned and distribution planned
Week 6   **Copy** deadline and **design grid** decided
Week 8   **Artwork** to the printer
Week 10 Collect copies from the printer for distribution
Week 11 Publication date

This might seem like a very long production schedule for a small magazine and you might well be able to shorten some stages – but even so, it will take you a couple of months to complete the process (in the professional magazine industry, each monthly magazine can take up to three months to produce so that staff are working on two or three magazines at any one time, with issues being planned while one is being copy edited and another is being printed). Notice that you can't run some of the stages simultaneously. You can't be sure about commissioning pieces if you don't know the editorial policy or how much space you will have to fill given the budget (and we haven't considered advertising – you can't sell advertising unless you can give the advertiser a sense of what the publication will look like). Once the artwork (i.e. your designed pages) has gone to the printer, there isn't a lot you can do to affect the timing so 'going to print' day is very important.

If you publish a magazine during your course it will need a schedule like this and you will probably need a whole term to do the job properly.

Constraints Time is one of the constraints, but there are several others. Availability of appropriate technology is an obvious constraint and so is the availability of **talent** (actors or presenters in an audio-visual production) or creative people on the production team. There may be constraints on the availability of inanimate resources as well - locations, props or archive materials. Less obvious, but equally important, are constraints on **permissions** – the rights to use a piece of music, a photograph, a poem, etc. – and restraints created by law – slander, libel, obscenity, official secrets, etc.

Your ability to develop a production in relation to the imposed constraints is a major factor in demonstrating creativity in a vocational context. You will discover that 'problem-solving skills' are an essential part of the producer's portfolio. In fact 'problem-solving' or 'working within constraints' is what defines the effective media producer. Sometimes, working within constraints produces the most interesting work.

Constraints and creativity in film production:

- In the early days of the Soviet Union, when the new state was being blockaded by the west, a shortage of filmstock prompted experiments by Kuleshov in which he spliced together 'offcuts' of exposed film and discovered novel effects of juxtaposing images. This was later developed by Eisenstein, amongst others, into the celebrated Soviet 'montage' style. A modern echo of this 'discovery' was the early 1980s 'scratch video' produced by young and poorly funded video editors who 'stole' clips from broadcast television in order to produce satirical comments on contemporary society (See Chapter 15, 'Realisms', on Eisenstein).

- The American genre of film noir is now seen as a sophisticated visual narrative style, yet when it first developed in the 1940s, crucial aspects of lighting and camerawork were often introduced out of economic necessity in the context of 'B' film production. In 1947, director Edward Dmytryk made a controversial film about anti-semitism called *Crossfire*. It has since become famous for its consistent low-key lighting style:

  > We had to make it very cheaply ... and I wanted to make it very well ... I found that normally at that time 80% of the (shooting) time went on preparation of the set, lighting, etc. and 20% on rehearsal and getting the film. I wanted to reverse that ... I had to get a cameraman who was willing to light very quickly ... It was much quicker to light the people and throw big shadows on the wall ... in the old days every fixture on the wall would have its own three-point lighting set-up.

  > (Edward Dmytryk speaking on *RKO Story*, BBC/RKO Pictures, 1987)

The production process in outline

If you discuss the concept of the production process with professionals who work in different media (i.e. magazine publishing, television, etc.), they will probably stress the differences – the specificities – of their particular work

Important Health and Safety Issues

If you are undertaking a vocational course, Health and Safety will usually be covered as required by the Assessment Scheme. On some 'academic' courses it may not be mentioned directly. You may not think of media production work as being particularly dangerous, but *it can be* in certain circumstances and, like every other 'public' activity, it is covered by a legal obligation on you to protect both yourself and others from injury.

The best way to learn about specific media production hazards is to address them 'on the job'. Your lecturer should always make clear the fire exits from any accommodation you use and should outline the particular safety requirements when dealing with equipment. These include electrical connections, trailing cables, very hot and fragile lights, noxious chemicals in photography, etc. If you aren't told about these things – **ask**. Remember that the legal obligation can fall on you – you have a right to be told. A good source of advice and information is often the appropriate union (e.g. **BECTU** for video), who may well have Health and Safety Advisers. The technicians in your school or college should be well aware of potential hazards.

As a producer, you should be aware of some of the less obvious Health and Safety issues:

- **Stress** is a potential hazard for production personnel who are often under pressure to make decisions or to operate equipment quickly and efficiently. You will notice this in 'live' television or radio productions. Stress can build up and affect performance (which in turn could lead to 'unsafe' decisions).

- **Public liability** requires you to be very careful when out on location, where you might cause an obstruction with cameras, cables, lights, etc. As well as seeking permission, you need to warn passers-by of the hazards.

- **Special effects** and **stunts** can add a great deal to video productions, but there is a danger that in the excitement of creating an effect, you forget about the dangers, especially in driving or attempting falls etc.

- **Lifting and Moving**. In the frenzy of getting equipment to *where* you want it and then *how* you want it arranged, it is all too easy to strain your muscles with heavy or awkward objects (and sometimes to damage expensive equipment). Learn how to handle equipment properly and find the crew and the time to move it safely.

BECTU (Broadcasting Entertainment Cinematograph and Theatre Union). Formed in 1991 by the merger of the film union ACTT with the broadcasting union BETA, BECTU has an interest in media education and training.

practices. In Chapter 20 on Industries, we outline a five-stage production process which, while primarily concerned with film and television, will serve equally well for other types of media production, even if the professionals concerned would not necessarily recognise the terms used:

1 Negotiating/setting-up a production
2 Pre-production
3 Production
4 Post-production
5 Distribution/exhibition

These stages represent the production process for a single, coherent product. A media product which appears daily doesn't involve endless negotiation and pre-production (although the inclusion of some material will still need to be negotiated), but when the product was first devised the production team will have gone through these stages. A television or radio series will be commissioned in blocks and can be treated as a single production.

The production unit and production roles

If we can define a common production process, we can also define a common production unit. The units which you form to undertake production tasks in education or training are not that different from their industrial counterparts. Even in very large media corporations, creative staff work in relatively small teams and in some sectors a production company might be just a couple of people, who hire in freelances to work on specific jobs. In every case, we can identify a close-knit production team, who work together over a period of time and who are augmented at particular stages in production by larger groups of people who perform relatively routine tasks in an industrial process.

Let's take our example of a small specialist magazine and look at its production in more detail. Perhaps this is one of many titles produced by a large international publishing group such as IPC or perhaps it is a private venture. Either way, the 'production team' may comprise only a few full-time people such as the editor and an assistant, a couple of 'staff writers' and perhaps an art editor. Outside this circle will be others, who while committed to the magazine, may also be involved in other 'titles'. The same commitment (i.e. to the individual title) will not be found in the printers and distributors who deal with many different titles over the year.

Each production unit is likely to include the following job roles: producer; director/editor; researcher; creative personnel; technical personnel; administrative personnel.

Producer Somebody must take charge of the production as the 'organiser of scarce resources' and the financial controller. This role will usually also

The production process in outline

'Once I became interested in stories and getting stories told, I realised I had to be a producer to get them told in the right way' (Warren Beatty, quoted in Langham 1993). Beatty is an example of a star turned producer/director. Other well-known film producers such as David Puttnam have remained well away from the director's role.

Time-based media is a term used mainly by practitioners with Art and Design backgrounds to distinguish television and film (and radio) from still photography. Lens-based media is used to bring film/video and still photography together. This latter term is becoming less useful as computer image production expands.

require an overview of the purpose of the production and the 'creative intent'. The term is used in both film and television and radio and sound recording, but there are differences. In film production, the producer is very much the provider of budget and the organiser of resources – in most cases the creative control of the project lies with the director, although there are some very 'hands-on' producers (including well-known directors who retain the producer role themselves – delegating some tasks to assistants). In radio and television, the producer is also usually the creative force behind a series. In sound recording too, the producer might be seen as a creative force. In publishing, the same role is likely to be shared by an editor and a production manager.

Director/Editor This role is about creative control – somebody must make decisions during the course of the production and must maintain a clear idea of the form and style of the product. In **time-based media** such as film, television or radio, the director is the co-ordinator of the creative process, literally directing the crew and the talent. In broadcasting, the creative controller tends to be termed an editor when the programme material is news or current affairs. The editor of a newspaper or magazine tends to oversee creative and production manager roles. The role of the director raises interesting questions about the managerial style of the decision-taker. The director or editor has to take decisions – 'the buck stops here'. This conflicts with ideas about democratic or collectivist production and we will return to this issue below.

Researcher Most types of production require research, although not all will have a named person responsible. Most research is 'background' – the checking of information or the compilation of information and ideas on a specific topic. Some productions rely very heavily on research – so much so that a lengthy period of research is necessary before any planning of the production itself can be undertaken. A good example would be a documentary series using mostly archive material. This kind of research requires special skills and knowledge, firstly in the general academic skills of using archives and checking sources, secondly in relation to a specialist subject (such as military history).

Archives can be very specialised and so film, picture or sound researchers may be seen as specialised roles, perhaps undertaken by freelances or small research companies.

Finding contestants for *Blind Date* or guests for *The Word* would also be seen as 'research', but here the skills are rather different. They may involve developing a 'feel' for what will be televisual; what will be popular; what will be a ratings winner. They may also include the ability to charm or cajole reluctant performers into appearing (for the smallest fee). This aspect of research may be performed by a production assistant – someone much closer to the producer role than the autonomous researcher.

Investigative newspaper reporters might also be seen as researchers. They might also write up their own reports – something denied to most broadcast researchers.

Creative personnel This is a loose term and might include everybody involved in the production, but here we are referring to those members of the team who are charged with making specific contributions based on specialist skills such as writing, camerawork, design, etc. The task for creative personnel is to carry out the wishes of the producer or director in a professional manner, contributing to the overall production as effectively as possible. Conflicts are possible if the individual contributors wish to 'do their own thing'. There are interesting questions about **authorship** here – once a scriptwriter has completed work on a film, does she or he have the right to be consulted if the producer or director then decides to cut from, add to or alter the finished script?

The director or producer will work hard to maintain a good working relationship with all the creative staff, consulting them (which means explaining *and* listening) on particular aspects of their work and perhaps incorporating their suggestions into the overall production. The director's role requires him or her to maintain the coherence of the whole media text, so if a particular contribution is threatening to upset the balance it needs to be corrected, even if, on its own, it represents a very effective and entertaining piece of work. Here are the seeds of conflict, especially in the supercharged atmosphere of most production processes.

The success of a creative team will depend on good working relationships. This doesn't necessarily mean that everyone in the team likes one another, but they must respect one another's work and be prepared to submit to the 'general will' of the team and the ultimate decision of the acknowledged leader. The most successful producers tend to be those who have built up and maintained a creative team that has lasted several years (see the studio system case study, Chapter 22).

Technical personnel They are responsible for the operation of equipment and for its efficient performance (i.e. they must maintain and set up equipment so that it performs to manufacturer's specifications). They ensure that creative ideas can be realised within the constraints which the technology demands. Some technical operations such as maintenance and servicing may be required even when no productions are scheduled.

It is a fine line which separates the 'creative' from the 'technical' and many media practitioners will combine both roles. For example, a **director of photography** (DP) on a feature film is very much part of the creative team, responsible for the overall 'look' of the film and the supervision of camera and lighting operations. Operation of the equipment will be handled by the camera crew, but the DP, who will have begun a career as part of the technical crew, will select lenses and perhaps even override equipment specifications and solve technical problems, based on long experience. Some media practitioners are seen as possessing 'craft' rather than technical skills – implying a more personal, 'creative' skill with technology beyond that of 'operation'.

In an ideal situation, creative staff will have sufficient knowledge of technical operations to be able to communicate effectively with the technical team. In turn, technical staff will be able to recognise the creative opportunities which their equipment makes possible and to advise accordingly. In the production unit, an integrated creative and technical team will generally produce the best results. Often, however, the technical team may be made up of freelances or in-house staff who are allocated to production units on a rota basis. The ability to communicate effectively and to develop working relationships quickly then becomes paramount.

The need for close communication between creative and technical teams raises two issues about media production training which are important for all media students:

- It helps if all production staff know something about each aspect of production – too much specialisation means that effective communication becomes more difficult.
- It isn't necessarily those with the most creative ideas or the best technical prowess who make the best production team members – good working relationships are also important and training should be geared towards development of the appropriate personal and organisational skills.

Administrative personnel Media students are often told about the difficulty of obtaining employment in 'the industry' and the example of starting 'at the bottom'. Making the tea or being a 'runner' are quoted as the lowest entry point. At the other end of the scale, the accountant is sometimes seen as the villain, not only curtailing creativity through budgetary control, but being 'boring' as well. Making tea and doing the books are, of course, essential elements in any enterprise and media production is no exception.

Camera crew in a film production will normally comprise an operator and assistants to look after loading, focus pulling and camera movements (the job of the **grip**) etc. An electrical crew led by a **gaffer** with a **best boy** will set up lighting under the DP's supervision.

A large-scale production like a feature film will involve hundreds of personnel with an enormous variety of skills and qualifications. Even a small production will need an 'office'. For convenience we have termed these personnel 'administrative', in that they are primarily concerned with making sure that production can go ahead with all the needs of the creative and technical teams catered for. Again, we can distinguish between administrative personnel who are integral to the production team – very often in roles as the extra arms and legs of producers – and those who are brought in as needed, either as freelances or from some central, in-house agency.

Some roles may be termed 'organisational' rather than administrative in that they are directly concerned with the operation of the production process. The floor manager in a television studio or the continuity role in feature film production are good examples of such important roles where an understanding of the production process is central. It is also worth pointing out that while the skills necessary for the other administrative roles are generalised rather than specific, the roles do allow new personnel to pick up a great deal of knowledge about the production process.

Production roles in education and training

So what should you take from these role descriptions in terms of your own education and training? First, wide experience of different production contexts will be helpful, not only in helping you to develop your theoretical understanding but also in preparation for 'post-entry' training in any specific production role. Our advice is to try as many roles as possible. You may have thought that being a writer was your dream, only to discover that you have a real flair for sound recording and that the radio studio gives you a buzz.

Practical production notes

The only way to learn about production is to produce, but how do you get started? Too often the production process appears either as 'magical' (the province of romantic artists who appear to produce with nothing more to hand than creative energy) or frighteningly complex with reference to many strange terms. Our task is to try to 'demystify' the process for you. Unfortunately, terms are a problem. Ask a dozen professionals in any given medium and chances are you will hear different terms used to describe the same thing. We will try to take you through all the main issues in production without too much jargon (or at least not without an explanation).

Outline

Your first task is to sell your idea for a production to a commissioner or funder, perhaps in response to a 'pitch document' (as shown in Figure 31.1 for example). To do this effectively you will need to encapsulate the main points of what you want to do into an outline, preferably no more than a couple of sheets of A4 paper.

Proposal

An outline of the product plus an argument as to who the target audience might be and why that audience/readership might be interested in your

```
TENDER DOCUMENT

The documentary department wishes to develop a fresh range of
provocative, polemical programmes for BBC2.

We are looking EITHER for a new strand OR for a variety of
formats capable of being shown in small clusters of, say, four
or five programmes grouped around a theme, yet approaching it
from different points of view.

We don't want genteel, observational essays. We're looking for
the best (i.e. occasionally rough) controversy of the moment.

What really bothers/annoys/terrifies/makes people enthusiastic
at present? 1990s controversy hasn't come packaged in the old
left/right or we/them wrappings. On television at least, the
decade has still to find its focus - we want to find it.

So we're looking not just for heterodox approaches to existing
debates, but also for new objects of controversy. Also, the
programmes should make use of new faces, and not float in the
wake of newspaper comment.

We think that such 'ideas programmes' are most successful at
forty minutes length, though we are prepared to consider the
occasional big blast of sixty minutes.

In addition to such film polemics we'd like to find a number
of provocative ten minute slots - once again about
contemporary objects of fear, irritation or enthusiasm.

All these programmes must address contemporary argument in a
stylish, well-argued way. We are NOT looking for tired-looking
'essay formats, full of people walking and pretending not to
look at the camera. We need a successful, fresh and cheap film
style. And we need to be sure that whoever we commission has
resolved the problem of novice presenter stage fright.

These are highly-produced 'editorial programmes', not DIY
access slots. However, we are interested in all forms of
stylistic innovation, including the (occasional) use of Hi-8.

Please send brief outlines/proposals to:
```

Figure 31.1 An example of a BBC tender document from 'Documentaries'

product constitutes a 'proposal'. Sometimes the proposal will be sent 'on spec' by a freelance or small production company to a major producer. Often, a major producer will invite a 'known' writer to submit a proposal on a given theme.

Recce

Good preparation is essential for effective media production and before any audio or video or photography work takes place on location, a production company will undertake a series of 'recces' (reconnoitres). These will include checks on electrical power sources (often broadcasters' needs are so great they will bring their own generators); on access for people and equipment; and on health and safety generally. Facilities such as changing rooms, refreshments and possibly press and **public relations** spaces are important too. These are the producer's main concerns. The director, camera and sound crews will also want to select locations for aesthetic reasons and to begin to build the constraints created by the **location** into the production schedule.

ACTIVITY 31.1

Take a close look at any film or television series (tape it so you can study it in detail) and carry out an analysis of the locations used.

- How much of it is shot in a studio, how much on location?
- List all the separate locations. Could you find substitute locations in your locality?
- Now consider the task of the producer. Think of your substitute locations: how would you organise the shooting so that you cut down travelling between locations?
- What kind of permissions do you think you would need for the locations you have chosen?

Design

Every media product is 'designed'. Think of a couple of very different products — a magazine and a feature film. In both cases, an important member of the production team will be the art editor or art director. They are responsible for the obvious art and design elements in the products — the dramatic layout of pages and the use of illustrations, especially on the cover of a news-stand magazine, the stupendous sets of a Hollywood musical and the credit sequence of the film. But they also

Location shooting is not just a matter of finding locations which look right. When the BBC chose to shoot the series *Middlemarch* in Stamford, the period houses were 'authentic', but they created enormous problems for the camera crews and extra lighting rigs were required. See the interviews in the 'Middlemarch' Pack produced by BFI Education (1994).

Film commission Modern film and television production often takes place outside the studio and many cities and regions in the UK have established 'film commission' offices which help producers to find appropriate locations and resources and persuade them to come and spend their budgets in the locality.

Saul and Elaine Bass are famous as designers of title sequences for Hollywood, in particular for Alfred Hitchcock (including *Psycho*) and recently for Martin Scorsese. See 'Looking for the simple idea' by Pat Kirkham in *Sight & Sound*, vol. 4, no. 2, February 1994.

Black Narcissus won two Oscars, for colour cinematography and for art direction. Although set in the mountains of India, it was shot entirely at Pinewood Studios and in the Surrey countryside. This gave complete control over the look of the film to the creative team and allowed for some celebrated **mise en scène**. The director, Michael Powell, claimed this allowed for the 'meticulous build-up of atmosphere' (Christie 1978).

contribute to a much broader concept of design – the overall fitness of purpose and coherence of the media product. The opening credit sequence of a film, the choice of typeface in a magazine, are not just attractive and appropriate in themselves. They are designed to announce and complement the other features of the product.

You might want to think about a media product in the same way as one of those exquisitely crafted Japanese lacquered boxes or an Armani suit – whichever way you look at them as you turn them over, they present a beautifully finished surface. And when you use them for their intended purpose, they do the job effortlessly. That's good design and something similar is apparent in a classic film like Powell and Pressburger's *Black Narcissus* (UK 1947) (properly credited to Alfred Junge, 'production designer').

Good design doesn't have to cost a fortune though. A zippo lighter or a box of matches can be designed well and so can the supposedly insignificant media products, such as the continuity announcements and **idents** on television or the local football fanzine. And it isn't just in visual terms that we can detect design features. Radio programmes are designed as well and it will be quite apparent if the sound text is not coherent in its style and 'feel'. Good design means products work well with users, and that must be the first priority for media production.

Research

There are two main types of research: primary and secondary. **Primary research** implies that the researcher is the first agent to collect and collate material. An interview is the clearest possible example of primary research – asking questions and obtaining responses which are 'original'. Interviews may be used to form the background material from which a script or an article could be written. Alternatively, the interviews may appear in the finished text as in the traditional Sunday magazine profile of a prominent figure. A new genre of film documentary based on 'witness testimony' has also developed where eye-witnesses describe what happened at the time. Such interviews are usually rerecorded for the production itself.

Other primary sources might be government records such as the register of births and deaths, or the correspondence and personal papers of individuals or organisations. These are sometimes formally organised into 'archives' (see below).

'Deep' research, rather like the ethnographic studies carried out by academics, might begin by the researcher living in a community for some time and simply recording daily life. This is the kind of research novelists might undertake to 'get the feel' of a location.

Secondary research implies that someone other than the researcher has collected and organised material and made it available for research. Secondary research takes place in a library or archive and/or uses compiled records such as reference books. Media production relies heavily on specialist archives, not just as a source of information, but also as a resource, material to be used directly in a media product.

Picture libraries Many newspapers and magazines as well as television companies will have an in-house picture library where they keep carefully filed copies of images they own (or where they have acquired reproduction rights), covering topics like famous personalities, important buildings, locations, etc. These are then instantaneously available if a news story breaks. All photographs taken by staff reporters on a newspaper will be automatically filed for possible future use. These libraries represent important assets for the media corporations and can be sold or leased for considerable sums. In some cases such libraries have survived the deaths of the publications that created them and have become profit-earners in their own right.

Hulton-Deutsch Picture Library One of the biggest photographic archives in the world, this grows daily by receiving all the photographs taken by the Reuters International News Service. It reached its current size by acquiring other libraries such as those of the celebrated *Picture Post* magazine of the 1930s to 1950s and also the *Daily Herald* library of the same period.

The market for images is such that photographers have built up their own archives of standard shots (sunsets, cute babies, etc.) which they offer as commercial library pictures. With the growth of CD technology and on-line services via the **Internet**, there are now many ways in which media producers can acquire high-quality images for advertising or promotion at a relatively low cost. At the moment the competition in the marketplace is still fairly cut-throat, but it is worth noticing that the 'international image market' is such that companies like Microsoft are carefully buying up the rights to an enormous range of images, all of which will eventually be available on CD – as long as your credit card can stand the debit of course.

In all these cases, users of images will pay for different services. An access fee will usually produce an image for study (this may mean producing a new print from a negative). If you then wish to use the image in a media product, a reproduction fee will be required. This will vary according to the type of publication, the size of the image, the intended audience, etc.

Sound libraries 'Library sounds' – collections of mood music and sound effects at relatively low cost, are available on CD or cartridge to be used by corporate producers via various licence agreements. Other audio recordings are owned by the broadcasters or the large recording companies. There is also a National Sound Archive which holds a collection of historic and representative recordings.

Film and video libraries Again, the major film and video archives have been developed by the production companies themselves. After many years of recklessly throwing their products away, they have now recognised the value of their products and have begun to archive them carefully. In the early days of both cinema and television, product was destroyed after an initial screening. Even during the Hollywood Studio period, previous versions of a film would be destroyed if the story was remade. Now, it is apparent how much archives are worth.

Film archives have the advantage over video in that the basic technology has not changed over 100 years and, provided that the film has survived physically, it is usually possible to make a viewing copy of any footage. Video formats change frequently and it is already proving difficult to replay some of the older formats because the players are no longer in working order.

The National Film and Television Archive provides a service for film students and researchers and other national and regional organisations have now begun to market their materials for educational and commercial use. Film research is a highly specialised business and the British Universities Film and Video Council publishes a guide for researchers.

Regional Film Archives Your region may have established a film archive, possibly associated with a university or a library. Films made in the region by professionals and amateurs may be held, along with stills and production materials. Some material is being issued by archives (e.g. Scottish and North West Film Archives).

ACTIVITY 31.2

Set yourself a research project aimed at collecting material for a magazine article. Choose something general like 'National Lottery winners' or 'medical stories'.

- Compile a cuttings library over a couple of weeks (get yourself a folder or a box).
- Look through the papers for text and photographs (look at a good spread of papers).
- Tape TV or radio programmes or use a notebook to jot down programme details. Make sure you always record your source reference, including the names of photographers or the rights holders for images.
- At the end of your allotted time, review your material. Do you have enough material to help you generate ideas for an article?
- Have you found good images or quotes?
- Have you got all the references?
- This is a good practice exercise for all media students – at some stage in your course you will probably have to do this as an assignment.

Drafting and rewriting

It's very unlikely that you will get your production right first time. Sections in this book have gone through several versions – sometimes altering radically, sometimes just a tweak. During your academic career you have probably suffered from constant pressure from teachers to check your work and even when you think you've finished, to go back and rewrite parts or even the whole of your work. If you took that advice and got into good habits, you are now going to reap your reward.

Rewriting shouldn't be seen as simply a process of spotting mistakes and correcting them. It should also be a creative process – material is 'shaped' during production. Both the original writer and the editor will be involved in trying to work on the script/text. It is worth reminding yourself here that editing is a constructive process, not just a 'cutting out' of the bad bits. It is also time-consuming and a sensible schedule will take rewrites into account. Do be careful about labelling each version of your text, especially when working on a computer means that you could create several versions of the same picture or text extract in a few minutes – there is nothing more frustrating than finding that when you want to go back to a previous version, you can't easily distinguish which is which.

Budget/funding

Media production requires money – large amounts in many cases. In Chapter 20, ' Industries', and in the case studies we have referred to examples of the economic decisions which producers take. Here we want to think in general terms about the sources of funding available to media producers, including those with few resources of their own.

Direct sales Not many producers can be self-funding, i.e. generating enough income from sales to fund the next production. In most cases, the preparation costs and the delay in receiving income mean that the outlay is too big for a small company to cover. There are then a limited number of options available. Borrowing the money from a bank will mean high interest payments, putting more pressure on the 'need to succeed'. Selling an interest in your production to a backer is perhaps a less risky venture, but of course it means that if you do well, a share of the profits goes to your backers.

Pre-sales Continuing production can be guaranteed if you can pre-sell your products at a fixed price. This way you might cover the whole of your budget with a guaranteed sale. The disadvantage is that if your product is very successful you will have forgone your profits.

Selling rights Another short-term solution is to sell the rights to your product. This saves you the trouble and the risk of selling your product in territories (or to other media) which you don't know much about. A distributor pays you a fixed sum. Once again, you lose profits if the product is successful.

Selling ideas If you can sell your production idea, you can save yourself the bother of producing at all. You can also negotiate to make your product as a commission for a major producer, leaving someone else to worry about budgets while you just take a fee.

Sponsorship Finally, you can get someone else to pay for the production (or part of it) as part of a sponsorship deal. Companies may be interested in being associated with a quality product, or they may wish to own the product and use it in some way. A specialised form of sponsorship involves '**product placement**'.

Product placement This refers to the prominent position of consumer items in the decor of films and television programmes and crucially the use of such products by stars – Coca-Cola and Pepsi are reputed to have spent millions getting their products used by stars in Hollywood features (see Chapter 9, 'Advertising, marketing and fashion').

Grant-aid If you have no money and little experience, you may actually be better placed to get started on a project than if you have a track record. Many arts agencies offer grants to new producers. These may be quite small – a few hundred pounds up to a few thousand – but enough to get started. Look in the reference section for details of the British Film Institute, Arts Council and Regional Arts Boards, etc. Be warned: grant applications have strict schedules tied to annual budgets and quite detailed application forms. Make sure you have enough time to get advice and fill in the forms properly. You will also need to evaluate your work – you will probably find that your Media Studies work is useful in explaining what you want to do. Many grants are aimed at giving help to particular groups of new producers or new forms of production.

Whatever decisions you do take about funding, you will consider that for many producers, 'independence' from control or 'interference' from funders is a major factor. On the other hand, some funders can be helpful in budgeting for you (and also giving you 'backing' which will allow you entry into other negotiations with potential buyers etc.).

Grant aid has enabled many currently successful film-makers to make a start. (See Chapter 27, 'Independents and alternatives'.)

Freelances

The freelance (derived from the term for the medieval knights who roamed Europe looking for work after the Crusades) is a longstanding figure in many parts of the media industries. At one time, it referred to relatively well-known figures such as high-profile writers or journalists who were in such demand that they could afford to offer their services to whoever would pay, rather than relying on the security of permanent employment. This usage continues and now includes television personalities as well as film directors. However, the big growth is in the number of rather less well-known media workers who would probably prefer to be 'employed' as they were in the past by broadcast television companies or daily newspapers, but who now find themselves made redundant and perhaps offered work on a short-term contract basis, often for a series of articles or work on a television series. Whether this should be called 'freelance work' in the strict sense is debatable (they may in some cases be little better off than the notoriously badly treated 'homeworkers'), but in the film, video and broadcast industry, freelances now constitute more than half the total workforce.

Freelances pose problems for the continuity of the production team and they are less likely to be followers of a 'house style'. On the other hand, they may bring new ideas and ways of working to a team. In practice, freelances might end up working for a particular production unit on a fairly regular basis so this might not be a great change. What is likely, however, is a gradual breakdown of the 'institutional' ethos of some of the large media corporations like the BBC and a reliance on more generic output (i.e. an industry 'standard') from the host of smaller independent companies (see Chapter 27, 'Independents and alternatives').

As a media student, you should note that in your own productions, it is often possible to 'buy in' some freelance help from students on another course who may have specific expertise (especially in areas like design). Also, if you are looking for employment in the media industries, you should prepare yourself for possible freelance status. A good start is to begin preparing your portfolio of completed production work as soon as possible, keeping a CV up to date and looking for opportunities to gain experience and to acquire a wide range of skills. Freelances have to manage their own financial affairs and actively seek work – it is a very different life from that of a paid employee who only has to worry about doing what he or she is told and then waiting for the salary cheque to appear in a bank account. Many higher education courses now include units on business studies, personal finance, portfolio management and CV writing, which are designed to help the potential freelance to survive.

Copyright/permissions

Media products are often referential or intertextual, making use of previously recorded material. In a highly commercial industry, almost anything that has any kind of commercial potential – i.e. it could be used in another publication – will be 'owned' in terms of the rights for reproduction.

If the reproduction rights on a work have lapsed (which according to new European legislation is now seventy years after the author's death) and have not been renewed, the work passes into the **public domain** and anyone can reproduce it without charge. There is a difference, however, between the work of art and the physical media product. For instance, most nineteenth-century novels are now in the public domain and this means that any publisher can sell a new edition of Dickens etc. But the 'Penguin edition' will remain in copyright as a printed text – you cannot simply photocopy it.

If you want to use an image in a magazine article, you will need to do three things: get a copy of the original photograph (you may need to pay a fee for a 10×8 print, the preferred size); obtain permission from the rights holder; and probably pay a further reproduction fee based on the nature of your publication, the size of the image on the page, and the position of that page in the publication (you pay most for the front cover).

Audio-visual recordings can involve you in several different sets of 'permissions' and rights issues. Say you want to use a recording of a popular song in a video programme. There are three potential rights holders here. First, the person who wrote the song will want a 'reproduction fee'. Next the singer needs payment for reproduction of the performance, and finally the record label wants a fee for reproduction of their specific recording. In practice two of these may be dealt with by the same agency.

The industry has developed specific paperwork for media producers to use to request permissions – usually producers don't buy a whole song but only a few seconds. One solution for small producers is to use 'library music'. This is music specifically written and recorded for audio-visual productions and catalogued on CDs according to themes. A producer buys the CD and then pays a set fee for a track. This is usually cheaper and less administratively complex than using well-known pieces. Use it carefully though as overfamiliar library music can sound bland.

Test marketing/previewing

If you are unsure about your product in some way (perhaps the design features are not quite right or you simply panic about your great idea), it may be possible to test the product on a small selected group of readers and see what kind of a response you get. This isn't fool-proof and you could select the wrong test group. Some might argue as well that you shouldn't be frightened of making mistakes and that the previewing policy leads to very bland products.

Public Domain and digital technology. Computers can copy files in a twinkling. This has led to a new set of concepts. **Public Domain** (PD) software can be distributed free of charge as long as the distributor does not attempt to profit by distribution. **'Shareware'** allows products to be used free, but expects a small fee if they are used consistently or for business.

Music rights Performers' rights are handled by the Performing Rights Society. Recordings are handled by the Mechanical-Copyright Protection Society (MCPS). PPL handles Phonographic Performance Licences for use of recordings by broadcasters etc.

Author's rights are negotiated by the Society of Authors and the Publishers' Association.

Sunset Boulevard (US 1950) is narrated in flashback by a corpse floating in a swimming pool. Director Billy Wilder originally opened with two corpses discussing the story in a morgue, but the Illinois preview audience thought that was too much (according to Otto Friedrich in 'City of Nets').

Proofing

When you get very wrapped up in a production project, it is sometimes difficult to be objective about your own work. Sometimes it is even difficult to see what is there at all and this is where a proof reader comes in. Ideally someone who proofs not only has a sharp eye (or ear) but knows something about the subject as well.

Elsewhere we refer to a 1940s film *Now, Voyager*. In a recent Hollywood magazine, advertising soundtracks, the film had miraculously split in two and become 'Now' and 'Voyager'.

Presenting

One aspect of production work which many of us fear is presenting – speaking on radio or television (especially direct to camera), or introducing events at screenings or exhibitions. No matter how embarrassed you feel, you should try it a couple of times for the experience and so that you have some idea about what presenters feel in the situations which you might create for them as writer or director. If you are going to become a presenter, then you will need to seek out specialist advice on how to train your voice, how to breathe and how to use a microphone and how to read a script. You will also want to study a range of professionals (not just one, or you might end up a mimic).

If you are a writer, the most important thing to remember is to provide the presenter with 'spoken language'. A speech may look great on

Figure 31.2 Students in a radio studio

Broadcast News (US 1987) is a melodrama about television newscasters which explores the skills and temperament needed to be a presenter. William Hurt is the photogenic presenter who reads well but knows little about the news. Albert Brooks is a good reporter but no presenter.

paper, but it may sound laboured when read out. If you can't find a presenter amongst the other media students, look elsewhere, just as you would for actors. Studying the media doesn't necessarily mean you want to appear as the 'talent'.

Finishing

The most successful media products offer the audience a special pleasure which derives from a quality 'finish'. This means that presentation is as good as it can be within the constraints of the format and the medium. Good finish means that your video begins from black with music and titles fading up smoothly in synch. Titles are accurate and carefully designed to complement the visuals. If you have a great set of photographic prints, it does matter how you present them. A good display with thought given to lighting and carefully printed captions or catalogue will enhance the experience for your audience.

Distribution

If you don't present your product to your audience directly, you will be dependent on some form of distribution. We have seen in other chapters that in the media industries this can be the most important part of the production process. You don't want to produce a magazine only to discover that no one gets to read it or to broadcast a radio programme which nobody hears. Student productions can get a wide audience if distribution is organised in good time. Check back on our magazine schedule at the start of the chapter where we suggest organising the distribution at an early stage – perhaps finding shops, pubs, cinemas, etc. who would be willing to distribute copies (you can afford this if you sell advertising to cover your costs). Several schools and colleges have taken the opportunity under the radio broadcasting legislation to apply for a Restricted Service Licence (RSL), allowing them to broadcast for a couple of days in a local area. Video productions can be timed to be ready for the various festivals of student work. If you have any ambitions to become a media producer, here is your starting point to get your work recognised.

Audience feedback

At the beginning of this chapter we made the point that media production is only meaningful if you know the audience to whom you hope to present your work. It follows that your production isn't finished until it has reached the intended audience and you have gained some feedback. Only then will you be able to evaluate the production decisions you have made. You will also be able to use the feedback material to inform your next production – audience feedback supplies the link which helps to make production a cyclical process, not just a linear process with a distinct beginning, middle and end.

There are numerous ways in which you can gauge audience reactions to your work. Sitting in with an audience can be very useful – when do they go quiet and concentrate? When do they fidget and yawn? What kind of comments do they make to each other? You can formalise this by organising some form of discussion after a screening, or when everyone has read through your magazine. Get someone else to chair the session and be prepared to be open with your audience about what you were trying to do. If all of this sounds a little daunting, you can always devise a simple audience feedback questionnaire which can be given to everyone when they first come into contact with the product. Audiences can be happy to fill in questionnaires if the questions are appropriate and if the spaces for answers are inviting. If you are lucky, the questionnaire will produce a greater number of responses and perhaps a wider range of respondents than the face-to-face discussion.

What will you expect from your audience feedback? We all like praise and to know that what we have produced has given people pleasure, but more important we want confirmation of what has worked and what has caused confusion or even misunderstanding. You should not be dismayed if audiences have read your work in very different ways (in Chapter 3, 'Narratives', we have emphasised that this is a function of the reading process). Every response is useful and will make you more aware of the range of possibilities.

After studying the audience feedback on your work the final task is to undertake your own evaluation of your production experience. In order to help you do this, your tutor will probably want to organise a formal 'debriefing'.

Debriefing

Most media production courses operate a procedure whereby you are briefed before an activity on what you are required to do and what constraints you face. You are then debriefed at the end of the activity. This is an important part of the process – perhaps the most important part, because it is here that you work out what you have learned and identify your strengths and weaknesses. Most debriefings are group discussions – either everyone has worked individually on the same activity or work has been organised in groups.

Debriefings work best when everyone is committed to the activity and is supportive of each other. This means accepting criticism from the other group members and in turn making positive, constructive comments about their performance. This isn't easy. If the production has not gone well you might be sorely tempted to 'get your blame in first' or to defend your own actions. If it has gone well you might be tempted to simply tell each other 'you were great'. Neither of these approaches is particularly helpful. If it worked well, why was that? If it didn't, can you work out why, without apportioning blame? The likelihood is that you will have to follow-up the debriefing with an evaluation, so you need answers to these questions.

Learning from production

We hope these notes will be helpful, but there is no substitute for production work itself. Get involved as much as you can. Make things with a view to finding out about the production process as well as reaching an audience. Listen and learn from other producers. Above all, reflect on what you have done and try to do better next time. And have fun.

References and further reading

One of the few books written for students at this level is:
Dimbleby, Nick, Dimbleby, Richard and Whittington, Ken (1994)
    Practical Media, London: Hodder & Stoughton.

Similarly, for teachers:
Stafford, Roy (1993) *Hands On: A Teacher's Guide to Media Technology,*
    London: BFI.

Job roles in film and television are well covered in:
Langham, Josephine (1993) *Lights, Camera, Action!,* London: BFI.

Useful reference sources, published annually:
BFI Film and Television Handbook
The Guardian *Media Guide*
The Writers' and Artists' Year Book, London: A.C. Black.
The Writer's Handbook, London: Macmillan.

Technical manuals, dealing with different aspects of production and different technologies are published by:
- **BBC Enterprises** The full range of material can be seen in the BBC shop opposite Broadcasting House on Portland Place, London, W1.

Publications include guides to scriptwriting and training manuals which are listed in a catalogue obtainable from BBC Television Training, BBC Elstree Centre, Clarendon Road, Borehamwood, Herts WD6 1TF.

● **Focal Press** This imprint specialises in media technical handbooks and manuals, in particular the Media Manuals series. A catalogue can be obtained from: Focal Press, Linacre House, Jordan Hill, Oxford OX2 8DP.

(Most of these manuals are written for professional or semi-professional media users.)

Useful addresses

BECTU, 111 Wardour Street, London W1V 4AY

Community Radio Association, 5 Paternoster Square, Sheffield S1 2BX

Co-op Young People's Film and Video Festival, c/o CRS Ltd., 29 Dantzic Street, Manchester M4 4BA – annual festival including events supporting student film-makers

Mechanical Copyright Protection Service, Elgar House, 41 Streatham High Road, London SW16 1ER – information and advice available on request

Performing Rights Society, 29-33 Berners Street, London W1P 4AA – information available from the Public Affairs Department

32 / Case study: Writing this book

We thought you might find it interesting to read a short account of how this book was produced. How does it work in relation to those big concepts we have been using, as well as to some of the funny and infuriating happenings that are always part of production, even the production of theories?

The institutional setting of production

Routledge is a large academic publisher, selling books mainly to students and teachers, and to librarians. The commissioning editors talk to lecturers about books needed for particular subject areas. One such gap was thought to exist in Media Studies, and the writers of this book were approached over two years ago, to write an introductory textbook. A proposal was prepared, some sample chapters written and sent to teachers and students for comment, and when terms were agreed, the writing began in earnest, taking the comments into account.

Several of Routledge's staff and some freelances were involved in the long publishing process. When we say long, this section is being written last of all, in December 1995, prior to publication next summer.

The Routledge budget worked as an *institutional determinant*: enabling some things (a much wider audience than either of us could command outside the book; the expertise of a big publisher) but ruled others out. Like early snooker commentators on black and white television, we've only been able to *assure* you that certain ads or stills are working with golden tones or

bright reds, rather than show those colours. An early idea to use AIDS awareness red ribbons as a case study was partly scuppered on the oddity of doing that in black and white. Nor can we show you clips of video or play you radio extracts to illustrate some ideas, though most of them are readily available.

The process of book production is remarkably like the process of making, distributing and exhibiting a film, despite the absolute difference which some would argue between 'high' status forms like books and 'low' status forms such as popular films.

- The 'package' was agreed: what we would produce; how it fits into a particular market which allows us to be paid an advance on royalties and Routledge to cover costs and to make a profit.
- Writing and editing with all its delays, accidents (one serious car crash and two major operations spread equally between the two authors and editor); negotiations over our slightly different attitudes to some of the big, changing concepts in the field, and so on.[1]
- Then, after the writing, will come publicity, distribution to a number of bookshops, and as the equivalence-with-difference to the exhibition of a film: purchase and reading. One of the major differences is that you

---

[1] **Negotiation** A key term in Media Studies. Draws on the sense of 'negotiate' as used by trade unions or diplomats: the give and take of arriving at compromises. Also draws on 'negotiating' a tight bend when driving, emphasising that progress is made through twists and turns, braking and accelerating.

can read bits of the book over again at your own speed, in fact you can do what you like with it: the book remains your property (except that you can't resell it or any extract from it again, except as a second-hand book). With a movie you purchase only the right to see one screening.

Both of us have thought more about the absurdities and inequities of copyright than we ever wanted to in a lifetime. Some snatches of (almost verbatim) telephone conversations and other encounters:

- 'I want to use a still from *Thelma and Louise* for a Media Studies textbook. Phone New York? Probably £100 each? Thanks. Bye. Hello. I'd like to use some stills from *Psycho* for a Media Studies educational textbook. $180 each? $100 because I want to use eleven of them? Thanks. Bye. Hello. I'm trying to get permission to use a few stills from the *Creek* ad for Levi's jeans … $5,000 each for the last educational publisher in the US? We need to ask everyone involved in the ad? Does that include the horse? He has an agent?' (This last bit is a joke – but only just.)

- July 18, the week of the UK release of *Judge Dredd*, we hear that the distributors have refused us permission to use stills from the publicity pack for the film! We can understand now why media books like one study of *Batman* come out without a single still in them.[2]

- On the other hand, the *Sun* newspaper, owned by Rupert Murdoch and the object of some criticism in this book, faxed back immediately to say that we could use one of their front pages free. And some of the biggest ad agencies (BBH, Saatchi and Saatchi) were extremely helpful.

---

[2]**Permissions** Why do you think that somebody would refuse 'permission' to use an image, or would price it so high as to deter most publishers? Clearly, it isn't a financial consideration – refusal brings in no revenue at all. Presumably, they are concerned that it might damage the image of a 'property' to be published elsewhere – but such damage could be averted by making conditions on use. Anyone who wanted to damage the property would go ahead anyway and risk being sued. So why the refusal?

Authorship and the creative team

Two authors or two creative 'voices' working on a media text is not unusual, but it does require some thought about work practices. We don't always agree with each other about how something should be presented or what the priorities should be – what can be left out, what must stay in? We have had to learn to compromise as part of a professional working relationship and sometimes, as in the examples outlined above, we have had to accept restraints. You might be surprised that two teachers could disagree about a subject discipline, but this shows that the subject is dynamic and that we all engage with it differently – we hope that some 'creative tension' will enliven the book.

In the text, we have warned you away from the romantic idea of the single author and we want to stress that the team that produced this book included editors and designers as well as a range of other staff who contributed at various times.

Audience research

Know your audience! That's the advice we give in the 'Producing' chapter and we have tried to follow it. We do know you through our teaching, but sometimes it is difficult to distance yourself from your experiences and it is certainly true that you can get too close to your subject. So we produced a couple of sample chapters and sent them out to a range of student readers. The response we got was helpful in confirming some approaches and casting doubts on others. We can't guarantee you'll like the book, but we can be sure that we've tried to reach our target audience.

Genre, discourse and this book

We wanted to produce something in between an academic textbook discourse and an enjoyable piece like an interactive video. One of the main differences between academic discourse and ordinary or common sense discourse is that it tries to be responsible for what it argues. We've tried to make the book clear with plenty of examples, so that you can apply the concepts and at the same time check up on us through the references to sources for quotes, facts and figures and theoretical work. We've also tried to maintain an air of user-friendliness which is not perhaps as austere as some academic texts. Can you categorise this book according to your knowledge of similar texts? Can you determine its discourse and recognise how you are being addressed? We'll finish with one final activity, concerning the way you use the book:

ACTIVITY 32.1

Finding your way round a book like this, and in particular using the index, is an important skill in academic study.

Think of a topic in Media Studies that you know something about, but would like to know more.

- Now jot down the key words or ideas associated with your topic and any names of theorists, media producers or example texts.
- Use your lists to go through the indices and bibliography at the end of the book.
- How well do they work in pointing you towards full definitions or explanations? Are all the terms on your list indexed? If some are left out, which are they?
- How accurate a picture of this book do you get from the contents page and the indices? Can you think of any other ways to find your way round the book?
- Do you feel that you can make full use of all the media reference sources available to you? Now is the time to find out – it's a useful skill you will need in higher education.

Select bibliography

For a detailed list of sources and ideas for further reading on specific topics, see individual chapters. The titles below provide general introductions to the major debates in the book. You can use them as starting points for background reading and consult *their* bibliographies for further ideas.

Abercrombie N., Hill, S., and Turner, B.S. (1980) *The Dominant Ideology Thesis,* London: Allen & Unwin.

Allen, R.C.(ed.) (1987) *Channels of Discourse,* Chapel Hill and London: University of North Carolina Press.

Alvarado, Manuel and Thompson, John O. (eds) (1990) *The Media Reader,* London: BFI.

Ang, Ian (1991) *Desperately Seeking the Audience*, London: Routledge.

Armes, Roy (1987) *Third World Film Making and the West,* London: University of California Press.

—— (1988) *On Video,* London: Routledge.

Bach, Steven (1985) *Final Cut,* London: Jonathan Cape.

Baehr, Helen and Dyer, Gillian (eds) (1987) *Boxed in: Women and Television,* London: Pandora.

Barker, Martin (1989) *Comics: Ideology, Power and the Critics,* Manchester: Manchester University Press.

Barthes, Roland (1972) [1957] *Mythologies,* London: Paladin.

—— (1977) *Image-Music-Text,* (trans. Stephen Heath) London: Fontana/Collins.

Berger, Arthur Asa (1995) *Essentials of Mass Communication Theory,* London: Sage.

Bogle, Donald (1992) *Toms, Coons, Mulattoes, Mammies and Bucks,* New York: Continuum.

Bordwell, David and Thompson, Kirstin (1994) *Film Art – An Introduction,* International edition: McGraw-Hill.

Brunsdon, Charlotte and Morley, David (1978) *Everyday Television: Nationwide,* London: BFI Advisory Document.

Buscombe, Ed (ed.) (1988) *The BFI Companion to the Western,* London: BFI/Andre Deutsch.

Christie, Ian (ed.) (1978) *Powell, Pressburger and Others*, London: BFI.

Cohen, Stan (1972) *Folk Devils and Moral Panics,* Oxford: Martin Robertson.

Crisell, Andrew (1994) *Understanding Radio,* London: Routledge.

Curran, James and Seaton, Jean (1991) *Power without Responsibility: The Press and Broadcasting in Britain,* London: Routledge.

Curran, J. and Gurevitch, M. (eds) (1991) *Mass Media and Society,* London: Edward Arnold.

Dimbleby, Nick, Dimbleby Richard and Whittington, Ken (1994) *Practical Media,* London: Hodder & Stoughton

Dyer, Gillian (1983) *Advertising as Communication,* London: Methuen.

Dyer, Richard (1973) 'Entertainment and Utopia', in *Only Entertainment,* (1992) London: Routledge.

—— (1979) *Stars,* London: BFI.

Eagleton, Terry (1983) *Literary Theory: An Introduction,* Oxford: Blackwell.

Ellis, John (1982, 1992) *Visible Fictions,* London: Routledge.

Evans, Harold (1978) *Pictures on a Page: Photojournalism, Graphics and Picture Editing,* London: Heinemann.

Geraghty, Christine (1991) *Women and Soap Opera: A Study of Prime Time Soaps,* London: Polity Press.

Glasgow University Media Group (1976) *Bad News,* London: Routledge & Kegan Paul.

—— (1993) *Getting the Message: News, Truth and Power,* London: Routledge.

Gledhill, Christine (ed.) (1987) *Home Is Where the Heart Is,* London: BFI.

Goffman, Erving (1976) *Gender Advertisements,* London: Macmillan.

Golding, Peter and Elliot, P. (1979) *Making the News,* London: Longman.

Gomery, Douglas (1992) *Shared Pleasures,* London: BFI.

Goodwin, Andrew and Whannel, Gary (1990) *Understanding Television,* London: Routledge.

Harrison, Martin (1985) *TV News, Whose Bias?,* Policy Journals.

Hartley, John (1982) *Understanding News,* London: Routledge.

Hawkes, Terence (1977) *Structuralism and Semiotics,* London: Methuen.

Hillier, Jim (1993) *The New Hollywood,* London: Studio Vista.

Hood, Stuart (1980) *On Television,* London: Pluto.

Keeble, Richard (1994) *The Newspapers Handbook,* London: Routledge.

Langham, Josephine (1993) *Lights, Camera, Action!: Careers in Film, Television and Radio,* London: BFI.

Leiss, Klein, Jhally (1986) *Social Communication in Advertising,* London: Marion Boyars.

Lusted, David (ed.) (1991) *The Media Studies Book,* London: Routledge.

McGuigan, Jim (1992) *Cultural Populism,* London: Routledge.

Maltby, Richard and Craven, Ian (1995) *Hollywood Cinema,* Oxford: Blackwell.

Moores, Sean (1993) *Interpreting Audiences: The Ethnography of Media Consumption,* London: Sage.

Morley, David (1991) 'Changing Paradigms in Audience Studies' in E. Seiter, H. Borchers, G. Kreutzner and E.-M. Warth, (1989) *Remote Control,* London: Routledge.

Myers, Kathy (1986) *Understains: The Sense and Seduction of Advertising,* London: Comedia.

Neale, Steve (1985) *Cinema and Technology: Image, Sound, Colour,* London: BFI/Macmillan.

—— (1990) 'Questions of Genre', *Screen,* vol. 31, no.1.

O'Malley, Tom and Treharne, Jo (1993) *Selling the Beeb,* London: Campaign for Press and Broadcasting Freedom.

O'Sullivan, T., Hartley, J., Saunders, D., Montgomery, M. and Fisk, J. (1994) *Key Concepts in Cultural and Communication Studies* (2nd edn), London: Routledge.

O'Sullivan, Tim, Dutton, Brian and Rayner, Philip (1994) *Studying the Media,* London: Edward Arnold.

Philo, Greg (1990) *Seeing and Believing: The Influence of Television,* London: Routledge.

Pines, Jim (ed.) (1992) *Black and White in Colour: Black People in British Television since 1936,* London: BFI.

Pirie, David (ed.) (1981) *Anatomy of the Movies,* London: Windward.

Pumphrey, Martin 'The Flapper, the Housewife and Modernity', *Cultural Studies,* vol. I, no. 2, May 1987.

Root, Jane (1986) *Open the Box,* London: Comedia.

Sarup, Madan (1988) *An Introductory Guide to Post Structuralism and Postmodernism,* London: Harvester Wheatsheaf.

Schlesinger, Philip (1987) *Putting 'Reality' Together,* London: Methuen.

Selby, Keith and Cowdrey, Ron (1995) *How to Study Television,* London: Macmillan.

Shohat, Ella and Stam, Robert (1994) *Unthinking Eurocentrism,* London: Routledge.

Stacey, Jackie (1993) *Star Gazing: Hollywood Cinema and Female Spectatorship,* London: Routledge.

Strinati, Dominic (1995) *An Introduction to Theories of Popular Culture,* London: Routledge.

Turner, Graeme (1993) *Film As Social Practice,* London: Routledge.

Wasko, Janet (1994) *Hollywood in the Information Age beyond the Silver Screen,* London: Polity.

Wilby, Peter and Conroy, Andy (1994) *The Radio Handbook,* London: Routledge.

Williams, Christopher (ed.) (1980) *Realism and the Cinema*, London: Routledge & Kegan Paul/BFI.

Williams, Granville (1994) *Britain's Media – How They Are Related*, London: Campaign For Press and Broadcasting Freedom.

Williams, Raymond (1976) *Keywords: A Vocabulary of Culture and Society,* London: Fontana/Croom Helm.

Wollen, Tana and Hayward, Philip (eds) (1993) *Future Visions: New Technologies of the Screen,* London: BFI.

Magazines

The following magazines are very useful sources of specialist material on the industries concerned. The American magazines are all available in the UK, although outside major city centres they would need to be ordered. Trade magazines are expensive, but access to only one or two copies can give you a valuable insight into industry concerns, unavailable elsewhere.

Billboard, American music and related entertainment industry trade paper.

Broadcast, the trade magazine for the broadcasting industry.

Campaign, the trade magazine for the advertising industry.

Free Press, magazine of the Campaign for Press and Broadcasting Freedom (CPBF) available from 8, Cynthia St, London N1 9JF.

Hollywood Reporter, American film industry paper.

The Journalist, magazine of the National Union of Journalists.

Marketing Week, the trade magazine for marketing.

Media Week, the trade magazine for media buyers.

Music Week, trade paper of the UK music industry.

Screen, academic journal for film and television studies in higher education.

Screen Digest, monthly international television industry news magazine.

Screen Finance, fortnightly news and financial analysis of UK and European film and television.

Screen International, the trade magazine for film production, distribution and exhibition (includes video and television films).

Sight & Sound, monthly magazine from the British Film Institute, giving details of film and video releases plus critical writing and features.

Stage, Screen and Radio, journal of the media union BECTU.

UK Press Gazette, trade paper of the UK Press.

Variety, the American trade paper for the entertainment industry generally.

Yearbooks

BFI Film and Television Handbook
Guardian Media Guide
Writer's Handbook, London: Macmillan
The Writers' and Artists' Year Book, London: A.C. Black

Useful addresses

The following organisations all offer advice and information which may be useful for media students.

Advertising Standards Authority (ASA)
2 Torrington Place
London WCIE 7HW   ☎ 0171 580 5555

Arts Council of England
14 Great Peter Street
London SWIP 3NQ   ☎ 0171 973 6443
(Contact the Arts Council for details of your own Regional Arts Board.)

Arts Council of Northern Ireland
185 Stranmillis Road
Belfast BT9 5DU   ☎ 01232 381591

Arts Council of Wales
9 Museum Place
Cardiff CFI 3NX   ☎ 01222 394711

BBC
Television Centre
Wood Lane
London W12 7RJ   ☎ 0181 743 8000

Broadcasting House
Portland Place
London WIA IAA   ☎ 0171 580 4468

Bartle Bogle Hegarty
24 Great Pulteney Street
London WIR 4LB   ☎ 0171 734 1677

British Board of Film Classification (BBFC)
3 Soho Square
London WIV 5DE   ☎ 0171 439 7961

British Film Institute (BFI)
21 Stephen Street
London WIP IPL   ☎ 0171 255 1444

Broadcasting Complaints Commission
35-37 Grosvenor Gardens
London SWIW 0BS   ☎ 0171 630 1966

Broadcasting, Entertainment, Cinematograph and Theatre Union (BECTU)
111 Wardour Street
London WIV 4AY   ☎ 0171 437 8506

Broadcasting Standards Council (BSC)
7 The Sanctuary
London SWIP 3JS   ☎ 0171 233 0544

Channel 4 Television
124 Horseferry Road
London SWIP 2TX   ☎ 0171 396 4444

CIC Video
4th Floor
Glenthorne House
5–7 Hammersmith Grove
London W6 0ND   ☎ 0181 741 9773

Community Radio Association
5 Paternoster Square
Sheffield S1 2BX ☎ 0114 279 5219

Film Education
41-42 Berners Street
London W1P 3AA ☎ 0171 637 9932

Independent Television Commission (ITC)
33 Foley Street
London W1P 7LB ☎ 0171 255 3000

Media Education Wales
Cardiff Institute of Higher Education
Cyncoed Road
Cardiff CF2 6XD ☎ 01222 689101/2

Northern Ireland Film Council
7 Lower Crescent
Belfast BT7 1NR ☎ 01232 324140

Press Complaints Commission
1 Salisbury Square
London EC4Y 8AE ☎ 0171 353 1248

Radio Authority
Holbrook House
Great Queen Street
London WC2B 5DG ☎ 0171 430 2724

Scottish Arts Council
12 Manor Place
Edinburgh EH3 7DD ☎ 0131 226 6051

Scottish Film Council
Dowanhill
74 Victoria Crescent Road
Glasgow G12 9JN ☎ 0141 334 4445

Wales Film Council
Screen Centre
Ty Oldfield
Llantrisant Road
Llandaff
Cardiff CF5 2PU ☎ 01222 578633

Glossary of key terms and index

Key terms as used in this book

This is a form of combined Index and Glossary. Listed below are some of the key terms we have used, and which you will need to know, with short 'thumbnail' definitions. The page references will take you to the first use of the term in a chapter, where it will usually be shown in **bold**. It could be in the main text or the margins. Some common words are only referenced when they have special meanings in Media Studies and for the major concepts which run throughout the book we have given only the main chapter reference. This isn't a full index so you should use it in conjunction with the contents page and chapter 'menus' to find the material you want.

Advertising Standards Authority 105, 372
regulator of advertising in newspapers and
magazines

aesthetics 149, 151, 155, 205, 306
originally concerned with 'beauty', in media
studies referring to an interest in the formal
characteristics of a text and how they are
used to address a reader

age profile 115
the audience for a particular media text,
classified according to age group

agenda 134, 263, 287, 315
prioritised list of items dealt with by a
media text – powerful media producers are
'agenda setters'

alternative 119, 133, 200, 297, 306
alternative to **mainstream** (q.v.)

analogue 187
any device which represents a quality or value
by a physical change in a measuring agent, e.g.
the silver nitrate on photographic film which
changes colour according in response to light

anamorphic lens 208
distorting lens which 'squeezes' an image –
used in widescreen film projection

anchoring 10
as used in semiotics – written text used to
pin down a specific reading of a visual image

anthropology 18, 320
study of the human species – applied in
audience studies

anti-realism 171, 179
an aesthetic based on denying any attempt to
represent surface reality

anti-trust 223
American government action against
perceived monopolies in an industry

arbitrary signifiers 11
term used in semiotics; see **iconic**, **indexical**
and **symbolic**

archive 216, 346, 352–4
any collection of similar material which can
be used in future media productions, e.g. a
film archive

artwork 342
term used in printing to describe any
material which will be used to make a
printing plate – could be text or illustrations

aspect ratio 205
the ratio of height to breadth of a cinema
screen or lens aperture

audience 309
complex area of Media Studies which
emphasises the importance of how socially
formed readers engage with the media

audience ethnographies 320
research using ethnographic approaches;
joining a specific audience group and
working from the inside

auteur/auteurist 292, 306
French term for author, used in *la politique
des auteurs* (see **authorship**)

authorship 74, 289, 347, 365
approach to film studies which places
emphasis on an individual author (usually
the director); see **auteur**

avant garde 178, 300
an artistic movement which is 'ahead of the
mainstream'

'B' picture 241
in the studio era, the second feature in a
cinematic double bill

BARB 282, 332
Broadcasters' Audience Research Board

disk 189

American spelling used here to refer to digital (computer) devices

display advertising 112

advertising using a substantial area of a newspaper page (including graphics)

dissolves 43

film term for the transition between two images in which one dissolves into the other

division of labour 241

work organised in specialist roles – traditional in the Hollywood Studio System

documentary 156

media text dealing with 'real world' events; see also **actuality**

docudrama 161

fiction narrative using documentary techniques

domestic 190

term used for 'personal' or 'hobby' media equipment

dominant 119

referring to the most powerful ideas in society at any time – expressed in **discourse** and **ideology**

dominant discourses see **discourse**

dominant ideology see **ideology**

drafting 355

first stage in preparing a media text

drama-documentary 67, 161

documentary which uses techniques from fiction drama (also 'dramadoc')

dumb blonde 91

stereotype, used in different ways, in media texts

duopoly 224, 226

an industry in which two companies control the market

Dziga Vertov Group 301

counter-cinema (q.v.) group named after Soviet filmmaker

economic determinist 119

theory in political economy which looks for economic conditions as the basis for explanations of the social, cultural, etc.

editing (see **continuity editing**) sequencing of text, images and sounds

editorial 108

either a statement in a publication by the editor or any feature material (i.e. not advertising)

effects model 309

model concerned with how the media 'does things to' audiences

empirical 20

referring to the collection of 'real life' data or 'observed experience'

ENG 197

Electronic News Gathering – term used to describe the shift from film to video in news gathering

equilibrium 26

the status quo which is 'disrupted' in a narrative

escapist 56

term pejoratively applied to genre entertainments; compare with **realist**

establishing shot 166

the opening shot of a conventional visual narrative sequence showing the geography of the narrative space

ident 23, 352

a logo or sound image used on television or radio to identify the station

ideology, ideological 117

complex term relating to ideas and understanding about the social world and how these ideas are related to the distribution of power in society; also about how ideas and values are posed as 'natural'

Ideological State Apparatus (ISA) 123

term from Althusser to describe education, judicial system, church, etc.

image 5, 21,

a 'representation' of something expressed in visual or aural terms

impartiality 140, 263, 284

not showing favour to any side in an argument, a condition for public service broadcasting

imperfect competition 226

in economics, any 'market' in which a group of buyers or sellers are able to influence market forces; the basic condition for oligopoly – competition is always 'imperfect' in the real world

independent 238, 289

any media producer outside the **mainstream** (q.v.) in a specific media industry

indexical 11, 160

of signs which refer to concepts via specific relationships (e.g. heat signified by the reading on a thermometer)

infotainment 1, 67, 327

new genre of media texts which combine information programmes and light entertainment

innovation 67, 186, 205

the development of a new form of media text

or the phase of exploration which follows the invention of new media technology

institution 256

complex term, used in Media Studies to refer to the social, cultural and political structures within which media production and consumption is constrained

institutional documentary 165

common genre type, a documentary about school, hospital life, etc.

Internet 2, 141, 199, 220, 353

the global 'network of networks' offering information to anyone who has a computer modem and appropriate software

intertextuality 69

aspects of a media text, which can only be understood by reference to another text

ISDN 199

Integrated Services Digital Network – a high-speed digital version of the familiar telephone system

Italian neo-realism 166

national film movement of 1940s and 1950s

jargon 127

terms with strict definitions within a subject discipline (i.e. Media Studies in this case)

language register 23

category of language use (from discourse theory)

leader 109

another name for the main editorial statement in a newspaper

light touch regulation 227, 258

a loosening of regulatory controls associated with Free Market policies in the 1980s and 1990s

completed, giving some security to the production

Press Complaints Commission 261
newspaper industry body set up to monitor the publication of unethical material

primary research 352
research into the original source of a media story – an interview, personal letters or government records

prime time 333
that part of a radio or television schedule expected to attract the biggest audience, e.g. 19.30 to 22.30 hours

principal photography 219
the production phase on a film shoot

privatisation 227
process by which public services or utilities are transferred to private ownership

producer choice 267
BBC policy encouraging producers to consider less expensive non-BBC facilities

product placement 100, 356
an unofficial form of advertising in which branded products feature prominently in films, etc.

production cycle 241
in the Hollywood Studio System, the constant film production process involving strict division of labour

progressive aesthetic, representations 84, 149, 166, 218
an approach to presentation of images which seeks to promote change in society

propaganda 58, 94, 98, 117, 310
any media text which seeks to openly persuade an audience of the validity of particular beliefs

property 218
any original story, the rights to which have been acquired by a production company

public relations 101, 141, 351
professional services in promoting products by arranging opportunities for exposure in the media

public service broadcasting (PSB) 128, 202, 258, 280, 288
regulated broadcasting which has providing a public service as a primary aim

quality document 280
an audit document showing how an organisation maintains the integrity of its administration systems

quality press 258, 279
the 'serious' newspapers – in the UK synonymous with **broadsheet** (but not in Europe)

Quark Express 197
industry standard computer software used in page layout

ratings 266
viewing and listening figures presented as a league table of successful programmes

reader panels 114
groups of readers who can be questioned about their responses to a media product

reader research 109
research into who 'reads' a media product

real, realist 155
of media texts, that they refer to events and conditions in the 'real world' and/or to the social issues in contemporary society

real time 49
time taken for an event in an audio-visual

secondary research 353

research using reference books or previously annotated or published sources (compare with **primary research**)

secondary image 250

the image of a film star used in another, 'secondary' medium such as television or magazine publishing

segment 335

(verb) the practice of dividing up a target audience into even more specialised groups which can be addressed by advertisers

semiology/semiotics 5

the study of sign systems

serif 112

a typeface which has a bar (or 'serif') across the end of each stroke of a printed character (e.g. the face used for the text in the chapters of this book)

set-top box 199

computer which sits on top of a television set and controls the variety of possible incoming signals

set-ups 175, 219

term for the separate camera, lighting and sound positions necessary for shooting a feature film

shot 38

the smallest element in any film sequence, a single 'take' during shooting which may be further shortened during editing

shot/reverse shot 42, 244

term for the conventional way of shooting an exchange between two characters in a film or television programme

sign/sign systems 5

see **semiotics**

signified/signifier 6

the components of a sign

slate 217

film industry term for the list of major features to be produced during a production period

soap, soap opera 44, 60, 91, 147, 175, 181, 312–25

the radio and television multi-strand continuous serial narrative form originally designed as a vehicle for sponsorship by soap powder manufacturers

social psychology 98

the study of human behaviour

socialist realism 170

the prescribed realist form forced on Soviet filmmakers by the Stalin regime in the 1930s – featuring romanticised heroic workers

sociobiology 118

theory that social behaviour can be explained by recourse to explanations from genetics or natural history

software 184

the programs written for computers or the films, music, etc. which could be played on them

sound effect 159

frequently used to refer to artificially created 'sounds' produced for audio-visual texts; also could be extended to refer to all aural material in a production apart from dialogue and music

sound image 21

compare with 'visual image'

sound libraries 353

used in research

sound stages 241

term describing the individual buildings

text 8
> any system of signs which can be 'read' –
> book, poster, photograph, etc.

tie-ins 99, 220
> products which accompany a major film or
> television release

transparency 175, 303
> the way in which media texts present
> themselves as 'natural'; their construction is
> invisible to casual readers

turn-around 218
> film industry term for a script, dropped by
> one studio and waiting for another to pick it
> up

type/typical 90
> classification of characters in a narrative
> according to selected common features; see
> **stereotype**

unit production system, unit-based
> production 241
> way of organising production under the
> Hollywood Studio System

universal service 265
> (in relation to public service broadcasting) a
> service available to everyone at the same
> price

uses and gratifications model 309
> 'active' model of audience behaviour

Utopian 58–9
> referring to Richard Dyer's ideas about the
> pleasures of genre texts

verisimilitude 68
> quality of seeming like the real world

vertical integration 223
> business activity involving one company
> acquiring others elsewhere in the production
> process

violence debate 315
> focus for debates over audience behaviour
> and the possible 'effects' of representations of
> violence

virtual 180, 198
> something which is a representation rather
> than the 'real' thing, thus 'virtual reality'

VistaVision 74, 209
> trade name for a film shooting and
> projection aspect ratio – introduced by
> Paramount as a response to CinemaScope

word-of-mouth 222
> informal way in which media products
> become known about by audiences

Workshop Declaration 295
> an agreement by independent video
> production groups to work according to a set
> of guidelines – allowing union members to
> work at lower rates of pay on 'non-broadcast'
> jobs

World Wide Web 199, 220
> the network of 'pages' accessible on the
> Internet

wrap 219
> industry jargon for the completion of a film
> shoot

Name index

This is a selective Index for some of the major theorists and media producers covered in the text

Television programme index

Film index